PARADOXICAL STRATEGIES
IN PSYCHOTHERAPY

The Role of the Father in Child Development *edited by Michael E. Lamb*

Handbook of Behavioral Assessment *edited by Anthony R. Ciminero, Karen S. Calhoun, and Henry E. Adams*

Counseling and Psychotherapy: A Behavioral Approach *by E. Lakin Phillips*

Dimensions of Personality *edited by Harvey London and John E. Exner, Jr.*

The Mental Health Industry: A Cultural Phenomenon *by Peter A. Magaro, Robert Gripp, David McDowell, and Ivan W. Miller III*

Nonverbal Communication: The State of the Art *by Robert G. Harper, Arthur N. Wiens, and Joseph D. Matarazzo*

Alcoholism and Treatment *by David J. Armor, J. Michael Polich, and Harriet B. Stambul*

A Biodevelopmental Approach to Clinical Child Psychology: Cognitive Controls and Cognitive Control Theory *by Sebastiano Santostefano*

Handbook of Infant Development *edited by Joy D. Osofsky*

Understanding the Rape Victim: A Synthesis of Research Findings *by Sedelle Katz and Mary Ann Mazur*

Childhood Pathology and Later Adjustment: The Question of Prediction *by Loretta K. Cass and Carolyn B. Thomas*

Intelligent Testing with the WISC-R *by Alan S. Kaufman*

Adaptation in Schizophrenia: The Theory of Segmental Set *by David Shakow*

Psychotherapy: An Eclectic Approach *by Sol L. Garfield*

Handbook of Minimal Brain Dysfunctions *edited by Herbert E. Rie and Ellen D. Rie*

Handbook of Behavioral Interventions: A Clinical Guide *edited by Alan Goldstein and Edna B. Foa*

Art Psychotherapy *by Harriet Wadeson*

Handbook of Adolescent Psychology *edited by Joseph Adelson*

Psychotherapy Supervision: Theory, Research and Practice *edited by Allen K. Hess*

Psychology and Psychiatry in Courts and Corrections: Controversy and Change *by Ellsworth A. Fersch, Jr.*

Restricted Environmental Stimulation: Research and Clinical Applications *by Peter Suedfeld*

Personal Construct Psychology: Psychotherapy and Personality *edited by Alvin W. Landfield and Larry M. Leitner*

Mothers, Grandmothers, and Daughters: Personality and Child Care in Three-Generation Families *by Bertram J. Cohler and Henry U. Grunebaum*

Further Explorations in Personality *edited by A.I. Rabin, Joel Aronoff, Andrew M. Barclay, and Robert A. Zucker*

Hypnosis and Relaxation: Modern Verification of an Old Equation *by William E. Edmonston, Jr.*

Handbook of Clinical Behavior Therapy *edited by Samuel M. Turner, Karen S. Calhoun, and Henry E. Adams*

Handbook of Clinical Neuropsychology *edited by Susan B. Filskov and Thomas J. Boll*

The Course of Alcoholism: Four Years After Treatment *by J. Michael Polich, David J. Armor, and Harriet B. Braiker*

Handbook of Innovative Psychotherapies *edited by Raymond J. Corsini*

The Role of the Father in Child Development (Second Edition) *edited by Michael E. Lamb*

Behavioral Medicine: Clinical Applications *by Susan S. Pinkerton, Howard Hughes, and W.W. Wenrich*

Handbook for the Practice of Pediatric Psychology *edited by June M. Tuma*

Change Through Interaction: Social Psychological Processes of Counseling and Psychotherapy *by Stanley R. Strong and Charles D. Claiborn*

Drugs and Behavior (Second Edition) *by Fred Leavitt*

(*continued on back*)

Paradoxical Strategies in Psychotherapy

A COMPREHENSIVE OVERVIEW AND GUIDEBOOK

LEON F. SELTZER

A WILEY-INTERSCIENCE PUBLICATION

JOHN WILEY & SONS

New York • Chichester • Brisbane • Toronto • Singapore

Library of Congress Cataloging-in-Publication Data:

Seltzer, Leon F., 1940–
    Paradoxical strategies in psychotherapy.

    "A Wiley-Interscience publication."
    Bibliography: p.
    1. Psychotherapy. I. Title. [DNLM:
1. Psychotherapy—methods. WM 420 S468p]

RC480.S343 1985   616.89'14   85–12226
ISBN 0-471-82661-8

Printed in the United States of America

10 9 8 7 6 5 4 3 2 1

To
my Wife,
my Father,
and
the memory of my Mother

Series Preface

This series of books is addressed to behavioral scientists interested in the nature of human personality. Its scope should prove pertinent to personality theorists and researchers as well as to clinicians concerned with applying an understanding of personality processes to the amelioration of emotional difficulties in living. To this end, the series provides a scholarly integration of theoretical formulations, empirical data, and practical recommendations.

Six major aspects of studying and learning about human personality can be designated: personality theory, personality structure and dynamics, personality development, personality assessment, personality change, and personality adjustment. In exploring these aspects of personality, the books in the series discuss a number of distinct but related subject areas: the nature and implications of various theories of personality; personality characteristics that account for consistencies and variations in human behavior; the emergence of personality processes in children and adolescents; the use of interviewing and testing procedures to evaluate individual differences in personality; efforts to modify personality styles through psychotherapy, counseling, behavior therapy, and other methods of influence; and patterns of abnormal personality functioning that impair individual competence.

IRVING B. WEINER

University of Denver

Acknowledgments

I would like to thank Bren Reddy, Dave Kniskern, and Tony Grasha for reviewing and constructively commenting on an earlier draft of this manuscript. To my editor at John Wiley & Sons, Herb Reich, I am grateful for several judicious suggestions which enabled me to enhance both the clarity and utility of this undertaking. Finally, I would like to express my love and appreciation to my dear wife, "Maxx," whose tireless and unstinting patience, encouragement, and support during all phases of this project are frankly beyond my ability to requite.

The chapter on paradoxical strategies in gestalt therapy appeared, though in somewhat abridged form, in *The Gestalt Journal* (Fall 1984). It is reprinted with the permission of the editor.

L. F. S.

Preface

The subject of this book, considered formally at least, is comparatively new in the field of psychotherapy. Explicit references to therapist strategies as "paradoxical" have become popular only since the early seventies, and even now many tactics warranting the designation are not actually cited as such. Yet this method of inducing change essentially by discouraging it has, particularly in the form of "negative" or "reverse" psychology, been with us for centuries. The increasing *professional* interest in the subject, therefore, is probably best appreciated in terms of therapists' becoming more aware of the advantages of indirection in constructively altering behavior. Paradoxical tactics—seemingly irrational and sharply opposed to the kinds of expectations clients bring to therapy—would in fact appear to owe much of their effectiveness to the very unorthodoxy that has so often rendered their use controversial. Contrariwise, most practitioners have come to realize that straightforward counseling techniques, however sensible, intelligent, or well-meaning, may have surprisingly little impact on their clinical recipients.

Explanations as to just why "useful advice" is so often of little use in modifying problematic behaviors vary. Writers have talked about the magnitude of human negativism and the consequent need to maneuver around or, indeed, *utilize* this deep-seated oppositionalism if substantive change is to be produced. More specific explanations, mostly revolving around notions of client resistance, also abound. Neutralizing or even exploiting this resistance by using paradoxical interventions is apprehended as enabling such defensiveness to become therapeutically transformed. Although the concept of resistance is undoubtedly the one most frequently advanced in justifying the employment of paradoxical tactics, a great many other explanations have been offered—as is abundantly illustrated in this book. Perhaps the one thing that most therapists do agree on is pragmatic: namely, that such "if you can't beat 'em, join 'em" tactics generally do not represent the first treatment of choice. Typically they are chosen only after more conventional procedures have failed; and writers have repeatedly described their value in helping clinicians break through difficult treatment barriers and stalemates. Literally hundreds of published case studies bear enthusiastic testimony to how a paradoxical treatment plan can enable therapists to help individuals, couples, and families confront and overcome resistances, fears, or self-defeating perceptions of reality.

Such case descriptions not only involve a broad array of patients and clients treated in a multitude of clinical settings, but also encompass an extremely wide-ranging variety of dysfunctional behaviors and interactions. Moreover, the literature is remarkable in cutting across theoretical boundaries traditionally held to be distinct. The very fact that paradoxical procedures have been implemented by every major school of therapy—that they transcend theoretical differences rather than mechanically follow them—strongly suggests that they may reflect something seminal in the therapeutic enterprise. Beyond the specific vantage points of psychoanalysis, behavior therapy, gestalt therapy, and interpersonal communication and systems theory, the widespread adoption of paradoxical techniques points to commonalities among these disciplines too often overlooked.

Virtually all paradoxical strategies are designed to counteract stubbornly maladaptive responses by not actively contesting their existence. By so doing, by not feeding into the symptom through inadvertently setting up a power struggle, they subtly contrive to redefine or "reframe" the symptom in a way that renders its alteration or removal newly feasible. By ironically joining forces with nonchange, they may effect a fundamental shift in client attitude that clears the path for productive—and *self-initiated*—change. Regarded in this way, the use of paradoxical tactics suggests that all therapies strive to weaken or "undo" problematic behavior by fatally undermining its perceived meaning. Oppositionalism may therefore be forestalled or circumvented because its very terms are inverted. The pronounced pragmatism in the literature on therapeutic paradox intimates an essential compatibility among divergent theoretical approaches grounded on their implicit agreement as to the therapist's primary task in therapy. Reduced to its essentials, this task would seem to hinge either on the neutralization of client resistance to others (the therapist included) or, indeed, to oneself.

This book is the first work to examine therapeutic paradox extensively from each of the major theoretical perspectives. Given the geometrically expanding literature on the subject and its concomitant unwieldiness (during the preparation of this study some 47 different terms for paradoxical procedures were encountered), the timeliness and practicality of such an integrative effort should be apparent. It might be pointed out, for instance, that the comprehensive bibliography that concludes this book contains more than

500 items. Over two-thirds of these studies have been published since the mid-1970s, and about half have appeared only since 1979. In fact, in 1980 alone some 60 books and articles dealt significantly with the subject. Certainly these figures indicate how richly blossoming an area of clinical investigation therapeutic paradox has become. And the far-reaching clinical interest demonstrated toward it—as indicated by the circumstance that each of the currently dominant schools of therapy has shown an increased interest in this subfield—again suggests the scholarly and professional need which this book is designed to address.*

By now several writers have complained about the tendency for paradoxical procedures to be oversimplified, misunderstood, or—worse—misemployed. For in actual practice, these tactics can be as intricate as they are intriguing, and as tantalizing as they are tempting. Although potentially they offer the therapist an extremely efficient detour around the client's self-erected obstacles to change, there is no ready-made shortcut for mastering their correct use. To adequately conceptualize and carry out these often deceptively simple techniques requires not only much clinical patience but also a sound knowledge of their dynamics and a considerable awareness of how and when they are most fittingly employed.

In the effort to assist the interested clinician in gaining such proficiency, this book represents the first attempt to systematically clarify the nature and application of therapeutic paradox both from within and across the major theoretical orientations. As the title indicates, it endeavors to provide both a comprehensive overview of, and convenient guidebook to, the prodigious assortment of paradoxical strategies that have been employed in therapy. So that these techniques will not be administered in a potentially hazardous theoretical void, it also presents a coherent conceptual framework for understanding them. As such, the book may be viewed as a consummation of the hundreds of studies attempting in various ways to shed light on their increasingly pervasive use. This exhaustive sorting out and elucidation of all the many different methods of intervening paradoxically is without precedent in the literature. For until now the key writings in this area have focused on their use in family therapy, the treatment context in which they have been most elaborately employed. The present investigation, while indeed having much to say about their implementation with couples and families, also deals at length with their use in individual treatment.

*It should be noted, however, that it has not been possible to take into account many of the studies published subsequent to 1982. Although several computer searches enabled me to "track down" most of these works in time for inclusion in the book's comprehensive bibliography (and Appendix B), they were discovered too late for discussion in the text itself. This is particularly true for empirical studies in the behaviorist realm, many of which had not yet appeared when this section was written.

Intended primarily as a comprehensive though concise introduction to paradoxical strategies as they have been adopted and explained by different schools of therapy, this book nonetheless seeks to go substantially beyond such straightforward exposition. Its concerns also include the empirical and the theoretical. By way of examining the evidence for the effectuality of these tactics, it reviews and evaluates the clinical research undertaken on them. And, by way of bringing some order and cohesiveness to a topic most distinguished perhaps by its disorganized multiplicity, it evolves a theory of the rationale and function of therapeutic paradox that is more unified and encompassing than any now available. Exploring the theoretical underpinnings of each of the considerable miscellany of paradoxical techniques, it eventually moves toward an integrative *metatheory* of their existence, designed to help all "students" of paradox develop a more holistic and coherent perspective on them.

To recapitulate, this book is designed to be a broadly useful reference work in its thorough delineation of the many varieties of paradoxical techniques, in its critical examination of the empirical research on them, and in its concluding theoretical discussion, intended to help resolve discrepancies which from the beginning have suffused these techniques with a certain cloudiness and confusion. However, as the very extensiveness of Appendix A should suggest, this project embraces yet another important dimension. That is, in the effort to make this study a complete professional tool, some of the best—and most *pragmatic*—contributions on the administration of paradoxical strategies have been included. These basically "utilitarian" writings should aid interested professionals of virtually all persuasions in expanding their knowledge of how and when to intervene paradoxically, especially in difficult cases. It is hoped that as a unit they will enable practitioners to develop their expertise in this area, so that they may begin to deal more confidently, and creatively, with frustrating treatment impasses. For it may be precisely during those periods in which therapists are ready to throw up their hands in defeat that a radically revised treatment plan— that is, a "noncommonsensical" or paradoxical one—may most fruitfully be implemented.

Given the voluminousness of writings on paradoxical techniques, it is surprising how little discussion exists on their actual planning and execution. This conspicuous lack in the therapy literature may well relate to their occasionally being employed more out of a beginning therapist's frustration with a particular clinical situation than from any carefully formulated conception of just how they may apply to it. Paradoxical strategies, it bears repeating, do not warrant being seen as handy therapeutic contrivances, as tactics convenient to use when the intricacies of a case are not well understood. Although they are sometimes implemented as "tactics of last resort," this hardly suggests that they can be effectively adopted without time-consuming preparation—or without a clear diagnostic grasp of the specific person, couple, or family to whom they are directed. Indeed, *any* clinical procedure having the kind of power so frequently ascribed to paradoxical techniques may be expected to carry its own limitations and dangers. To minimize such risks, it is essential that therapists develop their skills and judgment in this area. Paradoxical strategies do not—almost by definition *cannot*—follow any simple formula. Resisting ready-made standardization, their very nature must remain somewhat experimental.

These reservations having been stated, it can still be asserted that a number of recent writings do succeed in establishing useful guidelines for helping therapists acquire the confidence needed to implement paradoxical strategies effectively. By including a generous selection of these efforts in Appendix A, this book should assist the clinician in gaining proficiency both in the planning and administration of these strategies. For these highly practical papers offer a multitude of suggestions about how therapists can determine when such methods are indicated, as well as which particular method may be indicated in a given situation. Conversely, another crucial consideration involves when paradoxical techniques probably should *not* be employed, and several of the essays reprinted here are expressly concerned with delineating contraindications for their use.

Immediately following Appendix A is "A Checklist of Symptoms and Problems Treated Paradoxically." Given the rather forbidding massiveness of the book's final comprehensive bibliography, it was thought that such a checklist—seeking to relate many of the items in this bibliography to the clinical problems they principally deal with—was very much in order. Supplementing Appendix A (itself developed to the point where, practically, it may be seen as stretching the very concept of a "supplement"), Appendix B should add a still further dimension to the utility of this undertaking.

Not including the appendixes, this book consists of three major divisions, or "Parts." Part 1 presents a broad survey of paradox in therapy. It provides a much-needed working definition of therapeutic paradox by scrutinizing it in the light of three perceptual vantage points: the relativistic, the interactional, and the dialectical. Next it locates the philosophical origins and analogues of therapeutic paradox in Eastern thought generally and in several Oriental disciplines specifically. It then traces the growth of paradoxical strategies in the West: from their earliest recorded beginnings in the eighteenth century to present-day developments. Finally, it attempts an exhaustive listing of the many varieties of these techniques, as they have been categorized by four of the most dominant schools of therapy.

Part 2 is designed to aid the reader in better understanding the contributions made by each of these schools of therapy to paradoxical theory and technique. Its four chapters, arranged by theoretical orientation, explore paradoxical procedures as they have been employed and explained from a psychodynamic, behaviorist, gestalt, and communication-systems perspective. In addition to providing definitions and descriptions for all of the large variety of paradoxical techniques, this part reviews—again, from within each theoretical viewpoint—the empirical evidence supporting their use.

Whereas the central purpose of Part 2 is analytic, the intent of Part 3 is at once synthetic, speculative, and theoretical. Its key point, as has been already suggested, is that paradoxical strategies, in crisscrossing (or "violating") conventional theoretical boundaries, may be viewed as reconciling certain seemingly disparate ideas of human motivation and change held by these major orientations to psychotherapy. Topics covered in this final section include the challenge for research in validating paradoxical procedures; the therapist's control of symptomatology (through normalizing, legitimizing, or otherwise "sanctioning" symptoms); the extensive use of paradox in hypnotherapy; the form and format of psychotherapy as inevitably imbued in paradox; and—what may be the final paradox of all—the ways in which all accomplished therapists take responsibility for the *clients'* taking responsibility for their problems.

The structure of this book is also, in a sense, grounded in paradox. Despite its final contention that the major schools of therapy are profoundly related through their use of kindred paradoxical strategies, its chapter arrangement nonetheless conforms to traditional treatment boundaries. This organizational principle is meant to highlight the fact that paradoxical methods figure significantly in each of the major divisions of therapy. Additionally, the exposition of these methods according to such divisions helps clarify a great number of tactics in many ways so *theoretically* heterogeneous as to make the whole subject seem hopelessly complex or chaotic without such familiar dividing lines.

Nonetheless, it should be noted that using conventional theoretical boundaries to comprehensively examine paradoxical procedures ultimately functions to demonstrate how these procedures serve to "qualify," or "transcend," such boundaries. In so doing, in being similarly employed (though divergently explained) by different theoretical approaches, they also provide convincing evidence for what emerges, inductively, as the book's final thesis: that certain assumptions about human nature made by opposing schools of therapy may in the end be much less contrasting than complementary. The theoretically integrative nature of Part 3 suggests that at the highest levels of abstraction the four major approaches to therapy begin to converge and share commonalities far more crucial than any of their well-enunciated differences. Indeed, the design of this book would seem especially well-suited for revealing the underlying kinship that binds the systems theorist to the analyst, or the humanist to the behaviorist. Although it is undoubtedly practicable for students to study these major theoretical viewpoints separately, it may finally be equally instructive to understand them as each comprising a set of variations on a single theme. That theme is the therapeutic enterprise—an enterprise that *across* motifs, *across* obvious melodic differences, remains quite decipherably the same for all practitioners.

In many ways, the audience for this book should be at least as diverse as the theoretical orientations it presents. That is, regardless of theoretical persuasion, virtually all mental health professionals should have an interest in this volume if they are interested in increasing their knowledge of paradoxical strategies and how best to apply them. This undertaking also stands as a basic "text" for clinical professors and therapy instructors interested in having at their fingertips accurate descriptions of all of the considerable array of paradoxical methods, as well as a clear synopsis of the history, theory, and research related to them. In brief, this book should address the practical and professional needs not only of the user (and potential user) of these strategies but to the concerned teacher of them as well.

LEON F. SELTZER

San Diego, California
September 1985

Contents

PART 1   INTRODUCTION   1

   1. Background, Definition, and Historical
      Considerations, 3

      The Increasing Popularity of Paradox in Therapy, 3
      The Range of Problems Treated Paradoxically, 4
      Evolving a Working Definition of Paradox, 5
        A Relativistic View of Paradox, 6
        An Interactional View of Paradox, 7
        A Dialectical View of Paradox, 8
      Paradox and Eastern Thought, 10
        Zen and Tibetan Buddhism, 12
        Morita Therapy, 12
        "Tantric Therapy," 13
        Judo, 14
        Aikido, 15
      Paradoxical Techniques in the West: A Brief
      History, 15
      An Encapsulation of Paradoxical Techniques, 19

PART 2   SPECIFIC PARADOXICAL STRATEGIES IN
        THEIR THEORETICAL CONTEXT   23

   2. Psychoanalysis and Paradigmatic Psychotherapy, 25

      Freud, 25
      Adler, 27

John Rosen,   30

Robert Lindner,   31

Paradigmatic Psychotherapy,   33

Empirical Research on Paradox in Psychoanalytic
Therapy,   40

3.   Behavior Therapy,   42

Behavioral versus Nonbehavioral Paradoxical
Techniques,   42

Specific Paradoxical Techniques,   46

Negative Practice,   46

Massed Practice,   48

Stimulus Satiation,   50

Implosion and Flooding,   51

Paradoxical Intention,   55

Anticipatory Anxiety and Its Therapeutic
Antidote,   57

Other Theoretical Explanations of Paradoxical
Intention,   60

Research on Paradoxical Intention,   61

*"Instructed Helplessness": A Postscript on Behavioral
Paradox,   69*

4.   Gestalt Therapy,   72

Affinities between the Gestalt and Psychodynamic
Approach,   72

Affinities between the Gestalt and Behaviorist
Approach,   73

Gestalt Therapy and the Dialectical Theory of
Change,   75

Gestalt Therapy and Eastern Thought,   76

Paradox in Gestalt Procedure: Change through Being
More of the Same,   77

*Identifying with, or "Becoming," Dissociated Parts of
the Self,   78*

*Accepting, or "Staying with," the Symptom or
Unwanted Experience,   79*

*Accentuating or Exaggerating Submerged Elements of
the Self,*   82

Empirical Research on Paradox in Gestalt
Therapy,   83

5.   The Systems Approach—Theory and Therapy,   84

Systems Theory as Applied to Therapy,   84

*Systems Theory versus Psychodynamic, Behavioral,
and Gestalt Theories,*   84

*The Bateson Project, Family Systems Theory, and the
Double-Bind Concept of Schizophrenia,*   88

The Therapeutic Double Bind,   90

First- and Second-Order Change,   93

The Mental Research Institute,   94

The Milan Center for Family Studies,   97

The Role of Symptoms in Systems,   98

Erickson and Systemic Paradox,   99

*Some Theoretical Undercurrents of Strategic
Therapy,*   101

Techniques and Tactics of Strategic Therapy,   103

Introduction,   103

Reframing, Relabeling, and Redefinition,   105

Positive Connotation,   109

Prescription,   110

*Some Extensions and Variants of Symptom
Prescription,*   117

Symptom Modification,   118

Symptom Exaggeration,   119

System Prescription,   120

Paradoxical Family Rituals,   121

Paradoxical Written Messages,   122

Restraining Change,   123

Relapse Prediction,   125

Relapse Prescription,   125

Declaring Helplessness,   126

"The Confusion Technique,"   128

Empirical Research, 129

  Introduction, 129

  Clinical and Quasiclinical Studies, 132

  Academic Counseling Experiments, 138

PART 3 CONCLUSION   149

  6. Toward a Theory of Paradox in Psychotherapy, 151

  Therapeutic Paradox as Bringing Together Diverse
  Theoretical Outlooks, 151

  Transcending Theoretical Boundaries to Evolve a
  "Metatheory" of Therapeutic Paradox, 156

  From Theoretical Speculation to Empirical Examination: The Challenge for Research, 165

  Symptom Acceptance and Encouragement: How the
  Therapist Gains Control of the Therapeutic
  Relationship, 171

  Paradox in Hypnotherapy: The Connecting Link? 173

  The Utilization of Symptoms, 173

  The Utilization and Reframing of Resistance, 174

  *Directing Patients "Spontaneously" to Change Their
  Behavior, 177*

  The Essence of Therapy as Paradoxical, 177

  The Paradoxical Nature of Symptoms, 177

  The Paradoxical Nature of the Therapist's Role, 178

  *The Paradoxical Nature of the Therapeutic
  Process, 181*

  The Therapist's Taking Responsibility for Clients' Taking
  Responsibility for Their Problems, 183

  *The Therapist's "Benevolent Refusal" to Help
  Clients, 183*

  *The Therapist's Helping Clients to Recognize the
  Voluntariness of Their Behavior, 186*

APPENDIX A   SELECTED WRITINGS ON THE
PLANNING AND EXECUTION OF PARADOXICAL
STRATEGIES   189

Introduction,   189

Selections

Joseph R. Newton, "Considerations for the Psychotherapeutic
    Technique of Symptom Scheduling"   192

Jay Haley, "Giving Directives"   205

Carlos E. Sluzki, "Marital Therapy from a Systems Therapy
    Perspective"   209

Peggy Papp, "Paradoxical Strategies and Countertransference"   220

Steve de Shazer, "Brief Family Therapy: A Metaphorical Task"   223

Jeffrey K. Zeig, "Symptom Prescription Techniques: Clinical
    Applications Using Elements of Communication"   229

Lawrence Fisher, Ann Anderson, and James E. Jones, "Types of
    Paradoxical Intervention and Indications/Contraindications
    for Use in Clinical Practice"   237

Michael Rohrbaugh, Howard Tennen, Samuel Press, and Larry
    White, "Compliance, Defiance, and Therapeutic Paradox:
    Guidelines for Strategic Use of Paradoxical Interventions"   249

Gerald R. Weeks and Luciano L'Abate, "Paradoxical Letters"   262

D. Sean O'Connell, "Symptom Prescription in Psychotherapy"   269

APPENDIX B   A CHECKLIST OF SYMPTOMS AND
PROBLEMS TREATED PARADOXICALLY   274

A COMPREHENSIVE BIBLIOGRAPHY ON PARADOXICAL
THERAPEUTIC STRATEGIES   282

AUTHOR INDEX   313

SUBJECT INDEX   317

PARADOXICAL STRATEGIES
IN PSYCHOTHERAPY

PART ONE

Introduction

CHAPTER 1

Background, Definition, and Historical Considerations

THE INCREASING POPULARITY OF PARADOX IN THERAPY

Since 1950, several hundred articles and books have in some way testified to the value of utilizing seemingly irrational—or paradoxical—strategies in psychotherapy. From the vantage point of psychoanalysis, behavior therapy, humanistic psychotherapy, and interpersonal communications and systems theory, paradoxical interventions have been described as capable of effecting dramatic change in even the most difficult clients. The popularity and acceptance of these unorthodox methods seem to increase almost yearly, and approximately two-thirds of the burgeoning literature on therapeutic paradox has appeared since the mid-1970s.

Specifically, the flourishing of interest in paradoxical interventions is suggested not only by the impressive number of writings dealing with the topic but by the fact that seminars, workshops, and conferences on the therapeutic employment of paradox have also proliferated (Weeks & L'Abate, 1982). It has been only a few years since the first bibliography on such techniques, focusing exclusively on their use in family systems, made its appearance (L'Abate & Weeks, 1978). Yet one cannot but be struck by how arbitrarily restrictive, and even outdated, this checklist now seems. Doubtless the formal introduction of paradox into psychotherapy is most accurately associated with systems-oriented therapists working primarily within a family context. And the actual use of such methods, if not necessarily more prevalent among practitioners of couples and family therapy, is certainly most frequently recounted by them in the literature. Nevertheless, any introduction to therapeutic paradox aspiring to suggest something of the variety and complexity of these noncommonsensical techniques must take into account the circumstance that they have been

3

employed by every major school of therapy—even though, generally, they have not been explicitly labeled "paradoxical."

THE RANGE OF PROBLEMS
TREATED PARADOXICALLY

If such methods have been used across therapeutic schools, they have also been used "across symptoms." It is in fact almost easier to compile a list of symptomatic behaviors *not* reported as yielding to paradoxical treatment than it is to enumerate the broad range of psychological problems that have been so reported. Stanton (1981b), writing on the strategic approach to family therapy—an orientation distinguished by the paradoxical nature of so many of its interventions—suggests the almost unlimited applicability of therapeutic paradox by cataloging the disorders successfully treated from a strategic viewpoint. His admittedly partial listing, which he himself calls "a sampler," includes no less than 42 diagnostic categories and 181 citations. Not so briefly, his headings include adolescent problems, aging, alcoholism, anorexia and eating disorders, anxiety, asthma, behavior problems and delinquency, childhood "emotional" problems, crying, depression, dizziness, drug abuse and addiction, encopresis, enuresis, firesetting, homosexuality, hysterical blindness, identity crises, insomnia, leaving home, marital problems, obesity, obsessive-compulsive behavior, obsessive thoughts, chronic pain, paranoia, phobias, postpartum depression and psychosis, premature ejaculation, public speaking anxiety, schizophrenia, school problems and truancy, sexual problems, sleep disturbances, stammering, suicidal gestures, excessive sweating, temper tantrums, thumb-sucking, tinnitus, vomiting and stomach aches, and work problems (pp. 368–369). Stanton also notes that the cases involving these dysfunctions and behavioral problems have varied widely in "age, ethnicity, socioeconomic status, and chronicity" (p. 368), offering still further testimony to the utility of paradoxical strategies.

Although at this point the plethora of personal and interpersonal problems treatable through such strategies should be obvious, Stanton's ambitious listing might be extended even further by bringing in two other authors who explore the different applications of paradoxical methods. Newton (1968b), adopting the term "symptom scheduling" for a number of related paradoxical techniques, cites its reported effectiveness with tics, hysterical aphonia, and specific compulsive disorders involving gambling, swearing, and masturbation. And Fay (1978)—whose book *Making Things Better by Making Them Worse* is addressed more to the layperson than to the therapist—writes of the usefulness of paradox in dealing with such problems as self-derogation, complaining, jealousy, perfectionism, and antisocial behaviors.

EVOLVING A WORKING DEFINITION OF PARADOX

Given the number and variety of studies on paradoxical therapeutic approaches, curiously little has been written about what makes a treatment method paradoxical in the first place. This lack of concern with definitional matters is understandable given the highly pragmatic nature of most of the literature on the topic. But overly inclusive usage of the term has contributed to a certain carelessness of explanation that has only increased the theoretical confusion surrounding a concept inherently difficult. As one critic of this unfortunate development, observing the broad range of interactional and therapeutic phenomena now commonly designated "paradoxical," has observed: "The meaning of the term has been blurred and corrupted almost beyond usefulness" (Dell, 1981b). Although this attack seems finally exaggerated, there is little denying that the present tendency to employ the term "paradox" gratuitously has interfered with the full understanding and acceptance of this mode of intervention.

Discarding as only marginally relevant to this study many of the fascinatingly complex issues relating to *types* of paradox (i.e., logico-mathematical, semantic, and pragmatic, as differentiated, e.g., by Watzlawick, Beavin, & Jackson, 1967), we may confine ourselves to fundamental explanations of the concept in order to evolve a working definition facilitative to discussing it specifically in a therapeutic context.

What, then, *is* a paradox? What constitutes its essence, its inmost "core"? The dictionary is probably the best place to turn for a preliminary sketch of the logical or linguistic circumstances necessary for calling an utterance or event "paradoxical." One basic definition regards paradox as "a statement or proposition seemingly self-contradictory or absurd, and yet explicable as expressing the truth" (*The American College Dictionary*). As an especially pointed illustration of this definition, it might be useful to consider a passage from a book by a Western psychologist attempting to elucidate the paradoxical quality of his experience with Zen meditative discipline:

> The great simplicity of the tasks—observing my breathing and observing my walking—made them difficult to do. . . . I have since learned that some masters prescribe a gradual progression from a complex task to a more simple one to the simplest and most difficult of all—observation only of breathing. The effect of this procedure . . . was to allow the student to

move forward in increasingly difficult steps—from complex counting to simpler counting to the most difficult task of all, the simple observation of breathing with no counting. I believe one could say, the more complex the task, the easier to do; the simpler the task, the more difficult to do. The more there is to do, the less the distraction; the less to do, the greater the distraction. (Huber, 1968, pp. 83–84)

Such a description demonstrates the strangely two-faced nature of paradox, the final sensibleness of that which, at first sight, must seem irrational or absurd. Perhaps more than anything else, paradox relates to the defeat of one's "commonsensical" expectations. Surely, a difficult task should not be simple, nor a simple task difficult. But in the psychologically complex world of reality—versus the worlds of abstract logic or semantics, or even of the mind—the nature of "difficult" and "easy" can reverse themselves at any moment. And thus are the reactions of confusion and surprise often intimately associated with paradox; in fact, they are virtually a *prerequisite* for perceiving a thing as paradoxical.

A second definition, more involved logically, is also much more problematic. It defines paradox as "an argument that apparently derives self-contradictory conclusions by valid deduction from acceptable premises" (*Webster's New Collegiate Dictionary*). This definition bears close comparison with that of Watzlawick et al. (1967), whose even pithier explanation of the term has been cited so regularly in the literature on therapeutic paradox it has become almost standard. To them, paradox may be understood as "a contradiction that follows correct deduction from consistent premises." The ultimate puzzlement of ascertaining the necessary and sufficient conditions for paradox soon becomes evident, however, as these writers begin to qualify their encapsulated summary:

> This definition allows us to exclude immediately all those forms of "false" paradoxes that are based on a concealed error in reasoning or some fallacy deliberately built into the argument. However, already at this point the definition becomes fuzzy, for the division of paradoxes into real and false ones is relative. Today's consistent premises are not at all unlikely to be tomorrow's errors or fallacies. For instance, Zeno's paradox of Achilles and the turtle he could not overtake was undoubtedly a "true" paradox until it was demonstrated that infinite, converging series (in this case the constantly diminishing distance between Achilles and the turtle) have a finite limit. (p. 188)

A Relativistic View of Paradox

Finally, the relativity of paradox is not merely temporal or historical but, far more significant to the present undertaking, psychological. For paradox is essentially a subjective phenomenon. It derives not from the accumulation of facts but from human perception. As Dell (1981a) soberly remarks, "All 'paradox' exists only in the mind of the beholder" (p. 127), so that efforts to define paradox restrictively as a "thing" or intervention are misguided. Supporting his position with two dictionary definitions more closely related to the layperson's use of the term than those already cited, Dell concludes that paradox—dependent on premises, opinions, beliefs, and common sense—is consequently "an epistemological phenomenon." In a second article on paradoxical issues in therapy, somewhat cantankerously entitled "Some Irreverent Thoughts on Paradox" (1981b), Dell reiterates his viewpoint that the occurrence of paradox hinges on an individual's belief system. That which is alien to one's common sense (i.e., one's assumptions about reality) is correctly identified as "paradoxical."

Jessee and L'Abate (1981), commenting directly on some of Dell's provocative ideas, note that the only *real* way of determining the paradoxicalness of an intervention is through estimating the "existential reality," or "phenomenological world view," of the client (p. 43). The therapist's own conception of the intervention is irrelevant. In fact, most interventions commonly accepted as paradoxical because of their flagrantly violating client assumptions about therapy do *not* seem paradoxical to the therapists administering them.

To conclude, then, in the world of pragmatic reality paradox "exists" only to the extent that it characterizes a sharp divergence from individual expectation. Given the definitional relativity of paradox, its only *enduring* antonym is "common sense," which of course is itself a concept of considerable historical—and personal—relativity. The circumstance that it is not particularly uncommon for parents, in the last-ditch attempt to overwhelm the recalcitrance of their children, to use "negative" or "reverse" psychology on them, indicates that laypeople as well as therapists are able to appreciate the ultimate practicality of that which, initially, may appear hopelessly inimical to sound judgment.

An Interactional View of Paradox

So far the phenomenon of paradox has been defined largely in terms of individual perception. It remains to examine briefly the interactional ramifications of the concept: that is, how paradox may be located in certain peculiarities of the therapeutic relationship. Definitions of paradox in therapy, even the best of them, typically focus on technique, even though the effectiveness of such techniques is finally inseparable from their purveyor. In other words, the interpersonal context crucial to paradoxical interventions (and perhaps to *all* therapeutic interventions) is often ignored or left implicit. Newton (1968b) defines the essence of paradoxical techniques in their encouraging clients to continue with symptomatic behaviors, a basic description frequently alluded to in the literature. Rohrbaugh, Tennen, Press, and White (1981) succinctly characterize paradoxical interventions as "strategies and tactics in apparent opposition to the acknowledged goals of therapy, but actually designed to achieve them" (p. 454). And Jacobson and Margolin (1979) similarly describe such interventions as "instructing clients to engage in the very behavior that has been identified as a target for elimination in therapy" (p. 150)—citing as two common examples the recommendation of a relapse and the encouragement of more frequent arguing for a couple whose presenting complaint is uncontrollable verbal abuse.

What should be apparent in all these definitions, however, is that the therapist's role as devil's advocate is the one indispensable condition for therapeutic paradox. Without the therapist's calculated defiance of client assumptions and expectations—ironically, in behalf of *fulfilling* those very suppositions—no paradox would exist. It is essential, therefore, to recognize that any adequate introduction to paradox in therapy must acknowledge that paradox may be detected not only in the unorthodox method of treatment but in the special intricacies of the therapeutic relationship. Jay Haley, whose extremely influential *Strategies of Psychotherapy* (1963) expounds at length on the communicational view of paradox, was one of the first writers to emphasize its relational prerequisites. Discussing Viktor Frankl's "paradoxical intention" technique in relation to phobias, Haley notes that it would be inaccurate to designate as paradoxical per se a client's deliberately performing that which he fears. What makes the client's act appear paradoxical derives from incongruities in therapeutic procedure. To Haley, when a therapist offers to help a client overcome a problem and within that framework proceeds to encourage the problem, a formal paradox is proposed. The message at one level of communication directly conflicts with the message it qualifies. Or (as it would be expressed in more semantic terms), the two messages exist on different levels of abstraction, with the statement on the lower level opposing the statement on the higher.

A Dialectical View of Paradox

Another way of approaching paradox in therapy, by now well suggested, is through dialectics. The philosophical principle that ideas and events inevitably generate their opposites, demanding some sort of resolution, would appear to describe accurately the "thesis–antithesis–synthesis" nature of therapeutic paradox. The manifold relationships between dialectics, psychological behavior, and psychotherapy have not gone unnoticed, and the literature on paradox in therapy offers rich testimony to the viability of a dialectical conceptual framework. As Mozdzierz, Macchitelli, and Lisiecki (1976) observed: "The paradox is dialectics as applied to psychotherapy. It consists of seemingly self-contradictory and sometimes even absurd therapeutic interventions which are always constructively rationalizable, although sometimes very challenging, and which join rather than oppose symptomatic behavior" (p. 169). These authors, adopting an Adlerian perspective toward paradox in therapy, note the importance of developing a dialectical understanding of behavior—of realizing that, with humans, things are often not what they seem. In partial support of this theoretical stance, they also cite Jung's statement in *Symbols of Transformation* (New York, 1952) that "every psychological extremity secretly contains its own opposite or stands in some sort of intimate and essential relationship to it" (p. 375).

In a sense, then, what a client responds to as paradoxical in therapy is the counterpart of what is apprehended dialectically by the therapist. And a dialectical understanding of psychodynamics, involving as it does the therapist's awareness of the various ways a single behavior may be interpreted, can become very complicated indeed. As L'Abate (1976) pointed out, because interpretations of behavior depend on attribution they contain a certain arbitrariness. This appreciation of arbitrariness leads unavoidably to the espousal of a dialectical position—which may, for instance, come to regard family members paradoxically as at once persecutors, victims, and rescuers, and recognize that sometimes winning in a family may take the form of losing and losing the form of winning.

L'Abate's dialectical orientation is developed at considerable length in *Paradoxical Psychotherapy* (Weeks & L'Abate, 1982), the first full-scale attempt to elaborate on the principles and methods of the paradoxical approach to therapy. Given its strong, though justifiable, theoretical bias toward the systems approach (particularly as it relates to family treatment), this book fails to acknowledge the fairly obvious fact that the dialectical viewpoint toward psychotherapy has been articulated by proponents of virtually every therapeutic school. Whether or not the actual term "dialectics" is employed, the profound and at times multileveled relationship between opposites has been pointed out regularly since the early writings of Freud. And, practically, perceiving human behavior within a dialectical framework is indistinguishable from apprehending such behavior paradoxically.

At this point, it may be advisable to combine what has been said about the relativistic, interactional, and dialectical components of therapeutic paradox. Any adequately integrative definition of this concept must take into account the circumstance that such paradox is not an objective entity so much as a subjective perspective based on a client's belief system, or general assumptions about reality. Moreover, it must indicate an awareness that these assumptions do not pertain simply to the symptom or presenting complaint but to the therapeutic relationship as well. Given this conceptual situation, the following "working" definition is proposed: *A paradoxical strategy refers to a therapist directive or attitude that is perceived by the client, at least initially, as contrary to therapeutic goals, but which is yet rationally understandable and specifically devised by the therapist to achieve these goals.* Inasmuch as this definition implies that paradoxical strategies purposefully defeat client expectations about therapy, a "corollary" should be appended to it: namely, that such tactics regularly elicit—and in fact are to be associated with—reactions of surprise, confusion, and/or disbelief.

In the end, however, a therapist's approaching client problems paradoxically is, as Shore (1981) has remarked, "not something one does but something one feels" (p. 13). It is not simply a shrewd but mechanical contrivance to trick the unaware client into behaving asymptomatically but a general philosophical orientation toward problems and solutions that guides the therapist toward empathic realizations which themselves facilitate beneficial change. Perhaps one of the best statements on paradox as a philosophical—rather than a strictly psychological—position comes from Goldberg (1980), who reflects:

> From the philosophical perspective, I assume that truth is paradoxical, that each article of wisdom contains within it its own contradictions, that *truths stand side by side*. In Western thought logical sequences rule our reason and by so doing dominate our psychology. We need to realize that our attitudes, feelings, and behaviors rest upon assumptions which we rarely question. The core assumption in many instances is of a logical, sequential universe in which if *A* is true and *B* is logically the converse, then *B* cannot be valid. In the paradoxical mode each may be simultaneously *meaningful*. Contradictory truths do not necessarily cancel each other out or dominate each other, but stand side by side, inviting participation and experimentation. (pp. 295–296)

PARADOX AND EASTERN THOUGHT

The "paradoxical mode" of thought, so unorthodox in traditional Western logic, has a long history in the East. Here fixed distinctions between things apparently opposite are not rigidly observed, and reality is appreciated dialectically rather than dichotomously. As D. T. Suzuki (Suzuki, Fromm, & DeMartino, 1970), the most famous exponent of Eastern philosophy in the West, has commented in an essay on Zen Buddhism:

> In the West, "yes" is "yes" and "no" is "no"; "yes" can never be "no" or vice versa. The East makes "yes" slide over to "no" and "no" to "yes"; there is no hard and fast division between "yes" and "no." It is in the nature of life that it is so. It is only in logic that the division is ineradicable. Logic is human-made to assist in utilitarianistic activities. (p. 10)

The possibility of "negative affirmations"—or "affirmative negations"—is recognizable only when reality is viewed as fluid and variable, and conventional (though pragmatic) distinctions between things are acknowledged as illusory. In his paradoxically titled *If You Meet the Buddha on the Road, Kill Him!* Kopp (1976)—an American therapist advocating an Eastern viewpoint—argues against the not uncommon Western assumption that truth is teachable, by reiterating the *ultimate* paradox, one already suggested by Goldberg: the opposite of each truth is perceivable as equally true.

Allusions to Eastern thought can be found in a wide variety of theoretical and applied studies on therapy. In a collection of essays called *The Meeting of the Ways: Explorations in East/West Psychology* (Welwood, ed., 1979), it is noted that in recent years Western therapists have been exploring a multitude of potential therapeutic techniques, most of which are in fact many centuries old and originated in the East (Deatherage, p. 208). And, referring specifically to the increasing interest of psychoanalysts in Zen Buddhism, Fromm (Suzuki et al., 1970) cites Jung, Benoit, and Horney as especially sensitive to the psychological wisdom of Eastern writings. Such an interest in what, literally, can hardly be seen as anything other than culturally distinct thought is easily understood when it is realized that such thought focuses sharply on that which is well-nigh universal in human nature. It needs to be understood, as Deatherage (1979) has emphasized, that "Buddhism, far from being a 'religion' concerned with higher beings external to the individual human, is more accurately an exquisitely introspective but highly systematic psychology and philosophy which obtains its data from the very bases of human experience, namely, sensations, perceptions, emotions, thoughts, and consciousness itself, all of which taken together are frequently termed 'mind'" (p. 208).

Not much literature has yet emerged that seeks to relate in depth certain Eastern practices to the adoption of paradoxical procedures in Western therapy. The comparatively few writings that do bear on this subject, however, are suggestive and warrant a brief review.

Zen and Tibetan Buddhism

One of the first serious attempts to examine the theoretical-therapeutic links between cultures is that of Watts, whose *Psychotherapy East and West* (1961) constitutes a natural starting point for this discussion. Watts' book, which makes explicit use of several of Haley's ideas, describes the principles and methods of Zen Buddhist teaching in ways that make evident its relationship to therapeutic paradox. Basically, the position of the Zen master is not to resist the position (cf. symptom) of the naive or unenlightened student (cf. patient or client) but to accept this position and indeed encourage it to the point that it loses its tenability and must, spontaneously, be abandoned. Paradoxically, the student's position might be described as extinguished through its very fulfillment. As Watts explains it, the guru endeavors to induce the student to carry out his delusional ideas, since he is aware that the student will always oppose that which threatens his props of security. Ironically, the teacher of liberation instructs not by rational explanation but by indicating new behaviors grounded on the student's false assumptions until the student finally comes to recognize their falsity. Similarly, writing about Tibetan Buddhism, Welwood (1979) identifies neurosis as a path to enlightenment in the sense that a genuine awakening ensues from the developing awareness of how one's thoughts and feelings are self-imprisoning. Liberation is not facilitated by efforts, however strenuous, to escape one's pain or sense of confinement but by facing it squarely, making friends with it, and then working through it.

Morita Therapy

Zen philosophy, a centuries-old tradition in Japan that conceptualizes change paradoxically, was translated into a systematic psychotherapy by Dr. Shoma Morita in approximately 1920, and is now known as "Morita Therapy" (Mozdzierz et al., 1976). This method of treatment is fairly comprehensive and includes hospitalization, prescribed tasks, and the fostering of intellectual awareness. But its key element is in the therapist's assisting the patient to drastically alter his orientation toward the symptom. The underlying principle of Morita therapy is to help the patient overcome the conflict besetting him by inducing him to affirm his situation and become one with it. For example, if the problem is insomnia, the doctor's prescription is to keep awake until sleep comes. As Sato (1958) explains it:

> Obsessions [come] from the conflict between some primary disturbance and the struggle to get rid of that disturbance directly. This struggle does not make the situation better, but it causes much more conflict and the trouble. When

one leaves oneself to the dynamics of the situation—this is a sort of "egolessness" and samadhi (identification and concentration)—then the urge for health arises and the disturbance cures itself. (p. 215)   •

This explanation looks ahead to Watzlawick, Weakland, and Fisch's (1974) interpersonal, systems-oriented viewpoint of psychopathology, which postulates that the "solution" is in fact the problem: that is, the *real* problem is centered in what the human system has attempted to do to solve the supposed problem, so that any effective therapeutic intervention must confront directly the "problem-engendering pseudosolution" (Watzlawick, 1978, p. 159). And, as Noonan (1969) has noted, Frankl's technique of "paradoxical intention" also seems reminiscent of Morita therapy in that both approaches advise the patient not to evade worries or problems but, on the contrary, to allow them to be.

Additionally, Frankl's (1960, 1967a, 1975) conceptualization of symptomatic behaviors as becoming firmly entrenched through the vicious-circle mechanism of anticipatory anxiety echoes Morita's interpretation of the self-perpetuating nature of symptoms. As expounded by Kondo (1975), Morita perceived that the more one pays attention to symptoms, the greater one's sensitivity is to them, and the greater one's sensitivity to them, the stronger the attention to them becomes, resulting in a vicious circle of psychological interaction. In such a situation, the antidote for one's inauspicious condition is, paradoxically, to embrace it. Unlike Freudian psychoanalysis, the aim in therapy is not to gain insight into the symptom as such but to befriend it and unreservedly accept its reality. Such assent is what leads to cure, or the restoration of full functioning, *regardless* of whether the symptom is still present. It is one's misguided will that is seen as creating and aggravating the problem, and so the patient is persuaded not to seek to obliterate his symptoms through force of volition ("Four Walls Treatment," 1972).

"Tantric Therapy"

In his article "Tantric Therapy," Kopp (1978) discusses the internal conflict of clients between awareness and avoidance. If the therapist applies pressure for increased awareness, the client's anxiety may mount, thus strengthening defenses against this awareness. The unfortunate consequence of the therapist's push toward health is that what began as a personal problem may take the form of an interpersonal deadlock between therapist and client. In the practice of Yoga, Kopp observes, this sort of impasse may be transcended through *Tantra*, which works by transforming distractions into new methods of achieving spiritual awareness. In Tantric rites, previously disallowed acts of eating, drinking, and sexual indulgence become sacramental elements, with the guru's actually guiding the student's participation. Because the student performs these acts in a state of controlled consciousness, they become true acts of devotion and serve the original purpose of spiritual illumination. Kopp views Tantra as paralleling the modern therapeutic technique of paradox, which "transforms 'resistances' into the very consciousness from which they previously served to distract" (p. 132). For here too the therapist accepts, and even promotes, the patient's avoidant behavior. By so doing, the therapist regains command of the situation, since if the patient follows the therapist's instructions the therapeutic alliance is reestablished and, if the patient chooses to resist these instructions, the countertherapeutic behavior must be abandoned. In either case, like *Tantra*, the meaning of the behavior has been redefined so that the patient's avoidances now become acts of healthy participation.

Judo

Judo, a form of jujitsu that is both a sport and a weaponless means of self-defense, represents another Eastern antecedent for present-day paradoxical techniques. In a judo contest the expert waits patiently for the opponent's attack, and when it comes he does not counter it but moves with it in such a manner as to precipitate his opponent's downfall. Watzlawick et al. (1974) compare their therapeutically disarming technique of reframing the patient's symptoms to induce him to relinquish them with this judo practice of accepting an attacker's thrust and actually amplifying that thrust through yielding to it. Such a reception catches the opponent off guard so that his advantage is lost: his very resistance is utilized as a vehicle to alter his behavior. Contrariwise, *resisting* his resistance is viewed as leading not to change but to persistence.

In an article entitled "Reaching Emotionally Disturbed Children: 'Judo' Principles in Remedial Education," Mandel et al. (1975) discuss the benefits of employing judo tenets in treating children with problematic behaviors. Their approach involves reconceptualizing the destructive behavior as representing a strength that is potentially constructive and not merely a weakness or pathology requiring direct alteration. The authors term their approach "judo," since it concentrates on supporting the child's strength in such a way as to disincline him from continued combat. The child's symptom/strength, used against him and in spite of himself, must now be expressed in a healthier, more adaptive, manner.

Aikido

An exploratory study by Saposnek, "Aikido: A Model for Brief Strategic Therapy" (1980), attempts a systematic comparison of these two modes of interaction largely on the basis of their paradoxical elements. Aikido is a more modern form of Japanese self-defense, founded in the late 1920s and employing the principle of nonresistance to turn the antagonist's momentum against himself. In Saposnek's essay, the Aikidoist is pictured as never actually opposing or clashing with his challenger. Rather, "he accepts, joins, and moves with the challenger's energy flow in the direction in which it [is] going" (p. 229). Because of such "blending," resistance no longer exists since nothing is offered for the challenger to confront. Moreover, when the challenger prepares to attack, the Aikidoist responds "with open arms and open palms"—another accepting, even "welcoming," maneuver that surprises and serves to disarm the challenger through its unexpected lack of opposition. Saposnek also perceives close similarities between Aikido and brief strategic therapy (practically, synonymous with the communication–systems orientation) in such matters as (1) their "one-down therapeutic stance," (2) their "philosophical and attitudinal positions," and (3) their "eclectic flexibility," by which is meant the ideal of accepting "*any* attack or challenge coming from *any* direction, in *any* form and [being] able to neutralize the negative energy or redirect it as positive energy into more constructive, humanistic directions" (p. 233).

PARADOXICAL TECHNIQUES IN THE WEST: A BRIEF HISTORY

In this section an attempt is made to outline the different forms that paradoxical therapeutic strategies have assumed in the Western world, as well as to suggest some of the more prominent figures working within this mode. It should be emphasized at the outset that although modern schools of therapy have adopted closely related paradoxical techniques, the *rationale* proposed for such techniques has been explained variously, in accordance with the doctrine of each orientation. Moreover, the actual term "paradox" frequently does not appear at all in descriptions of these highly complementary, and at times even synonymous, methods.

The earliest forerunner of present-day paradoxical strategies that I have been able to locate is in Foucault's *Madness and Civilization* (1965), which discusses the treatment of insanity in the eighteenth century, the so-called

Age of Reason. In this book the highly unorthodox cure of "theatrical representation" is delineated. Although this technique does not really involve formal paradox, it is broadly paradoxical in the sense that it seeks to cure through joining—and then *enjoining*—the patient's delusional system. As the author very rhetorically but suggestively conceptualizes it:

> Here, the therapeutic operation functions entirely in the space of the imagination; we are dealing with a complicity of the unreal with itself; the imagination must play its own game, voluntarily propose new images, espouse delirium for delirium's sake, and without opposition or confrontation, without even a visible dialectic, must, paradoxically, cure. Health must lay siege to madness and conquer it in the very nothingness in which the disease is imprisoned. . . . Illusion can cure the illusory—while reason alone can free from the unreasonable. . . . If illusion can appear as true as perception, perception in its turn can become the visible, unchallengeable truth of illusion. Such is the first step of the cure by "theatrical representation". . . . [Besides] *representation* within the *image* . . . it is also necessary to *continue* the delirious *discourse*. . . . The same language [of the patient] must continue to make itself understood [in the contrived dramatization of the delusion], merely bringing a new deductive element to the rigor of its discourse. . . . The delirium . . . must be led to a state of paroxysm and crisis in which, without any addition of a foreign element, it is confronted by itself and forced to argue against the demands of its own truth. (pp. 187, 188)

This literary–philosophical description is almost uncanny in the way it manages to intimate the theoretical explanations not only of Rosen's "direct analysis" and modern "paradigmatic therapists," but also the double-binding tenets and tactics of Bateson and his followers. One of the examples that Foucault cites of this "delusional" treatment involves a melancholic who, believing himself dead, refuses to eat and is therefore actually dying. The cure devised for him consists of a group of people, made pale and dressed as though dead, entering his room and proceeding to feast before his bed. When the starving man's attention becomes aroused by this banquet, the group expresses astonishment that he does not join them, since the dead eat at least as much as the living. Persuaded by their images and arguments (not really incompatible with his own), he is induced to eat. Taking nourishment restores and quiets him, and his delusional ideas quickly disappear. Ironically, the calculated representation of unreal death serves to save him from the real death that would inevitably have resulted from his imagined one.

Early in the present century several instances are on record of the therapist's being professionally advised to align himself with patient symptomatology. Barrack (1978) observes that Dubois, in his *Psychic Treatment of Nervous Disorders* (1908), clearly evidences an appreciation of anticipatory anxiety and the corresponding value of having a patient approach his symptoms with humor. Oppenheim's *Textbook of Nervous Disorders* (1911) is also recognized as looking ahead to the modern notions of paradoxical intention and symptom prescription in its suggesting exercises to make patients more comfortable with their phobias. Finally, Buda (1972) cites a book published in Vienna by Stekel (1920), which describes a method of treating impotence through simultaneously prescribing intimate physical contact and prohibiting intercourse. Such a procedure harbingers a variety of sex therapy practices currently in use.

The earliest systematic use of a paradoxical technique in America is typically associated with Knight Dunlap (1928, 1930, 1932, 1942, 1946), who advocated a procedure he called "negative practice" to help patients break undesirable habits. As the term implies, patients were encouraged to repeatedly rehearse their adverse behaviors (e.g., tics, stammering, and nail biting) in the effort to eliminate them. Also classified as a behavioral technique is Frankl's "paradoxical intention" (1955, 1960, 1963, 1967a, 1975), which the author (1975) claims to have employed as far back as 1929, although his literature on this method begins in 1946, in the original German editions of *The Doctor and the Soul* and *Man's Search for Meaning*. Used mostly with obsessives and phobics, and similar to negative practice—though theorized within an existential framework—this method involves encouraging patients intentionally to bring on their symptoms, as well as persuading them to adopt a humorous (and therefore more detached and liberating) attitude toward them. Historically, Frankl is particularly notable in being the first therapist explicitly to identify his technique as "paradoxical."

Although Alfred Adler (1956) did not label as "paradoxical" his particular methods of prescribing and predicting symptomatic behavior, his strategy called "anti-suggestion" looks ahead generally to "joining" devices used by therapists who work deviously in their efforts to foster more prosocial attitudes in their clients. John Rosen's *Direct Analysis* (1953) dramatically applied paradox to schizophrenics by instructing them to "re-enact an aspect of their psychosis" (p. 27), especially when a relapse was feared or appeared imminent. Paradigmatic psychotherapy—an offshoot of psychoanalysis which includes such practitioners as M. L. Coleman, B. and M. C. Nelson, R. J. Marshall, M. H. Sherman, and H. S. Strean, and which was formally introduced mostly in writings of the sixties—has received little attention in recent literature on paradoxical strategies. Yet the frequently ingenious methods utilized by this school in helping patients work through resistances by ironically supporting or reflecting them through various forms of exaggerated imitation is worthy of mention. Paradigmatic therapists operate from the premise that straight "Freudian" interpretation of patient resistances may at times be countertherapeutic. Similar to other paradoxical practitioners, they therefore choose to join or otherwise side with these resistances so as either to reduce the patient's defensiveness or turn it against itself. Such tactics as "using the patient as a consultant" (Strean, 1959) and "outcrazying the patient" (Spotnitz, 1969) should suggest something of the "if-you-can't-beat-'em-join-'em" flavor of this approach. And, paradoxically, joining the patient's arsenal of defenses is precisely what makes possible the ultimate defeat of this chronically *self*-defeating system.

Although not a therapist at all but an anthropologist, Gregory Bateson (1956, 1963) is generally viewed as the grandfather of the systems approach to family therapy. The pioneering research project (1952–1962) he spearheaded on communication in Palo Alto led to the now well-known double-bind theory of schizophrenia, a formulation emphasizing the interpersonal and reciprocal dynamics underlying schizophrenic development. Also involved in this project investigating the behavioral repercussions of paradoxically demanding (and therefore double-binding) communication—and introducing the seminal term "prescribing the symptom"—were Don D. Jackson, Jay Haley, and John Weakland. Members of the so-called Palo Alto group—which, confusingly, has come to include workers both in the Bateson Project and the theoretically aligned Mental Research Institute—have gone on to elaborate not only the nature of a pathological double bind but what is seen as the mirror-opposite cure for it: the "therapeutic double bind." Paul Watzlawick (1967, 1974, 1978), perhaps the key figure in evolving this communicational theory of paradox, has written or co-written a series of intellectually stimulating books that elucidate both the psychological pitfalls and potentials of a paradoxical language. A paradoxical paradigm of family therapy emerging from the conception of double-binding interactions among family members has taken root in Milan, Italy, in the work of Mara Selvini Palazzoli and her associates. Their principal contribution, a book entitled *Paradox and Counterparadox* (Selvini Palazzoli, Boscolo, Cecchin, & Prata, 1975/1978), has already gained considerable influence in the understanding and treatment of seriously disturbed family transaction.

To complete this brief historical introduction to paradox in therapy, the brilliantly conceived techniques of master hypnotherapist Milton H. Erickson, legendary even before his death in 1980, need to be cited. Along with Bateson, Erickson can be viewed as having a powerful effect on the thought and practice of therapists with a communication–systems perspective. Much of his work has been promulgated by Haley (1967, 1973), who first established his fruitful contact with him early in the Bateson Project. Although Erickson himself did not explicitly categorize his methods as "paradoxical," Haley accurately discerned the paradoxical essence of Erickson's most original and individualistic work. In what Erickson designates as "naturalistic" and "utilization" techniques (1958, 1959), or double binding generally (Erickson & Rossi, 1975; Erickson, Rossi, & Rossi, 1976), Haley perceives the complementary paradoxical devices of "symptom prescription" and "relabeling"—of at once accepting and positively interpreting the patient's symptoms and, by so doing, achieving therapeutic control over them. Fundamental behavioral and attitudinal alterations are brought about indirectly, as the patient's resistances are systematically, though subtly, overcome.

The ultimate heterogeneity of paradox in therapy should by now be clear, given this preliminary discussion of its employment across theoretical orientations. Specifically, the multisource origins of contemporary paradoxical practices is best suggested by scanning the life and work of Viktor Frankl. Having early ties with Freud and Adler, he nonetheless established himself as an existential psychotherapist. Yet his extremely influential technique of "paradoxical intention" is commonly regarded as behaviorist (or cognitive–behaviorist) and theorized in accordance with basic learning principles. Adding to these problems in classification (and suggesting something of the capriciousness of such classification), key elements in Frankl's method are intimately associable with communication and systems theory, particularly as regards the use of reframing and certain interpersonal aspects of the therapeutic relationship. In short, although it is useful to explore paradox as it has been employed and explained by different theoretical schools, paradoxical maneuvers are most reasonably seen as *linking* these schools and hinting at the final arbitrariness of some of the descriptions typically used to distinguish supposedly incompatible perspectives toward personality and clinical practice.

AN ENCAPSULATION OF PARADOXICAL TECHNIQUES

Despite the circumstance that paradoxical stratagems transcend clear-cut theoretical orientations, the reader may acquire a fuller sense of such procedures if they are classified by school. Ultimately similar, and at times synonymous, paradoxical methods go by an almost astounding variety of names. And since, as a large number of the appelations below should indicate, many if not most of these techniques may be viewed as ramifications of a *single* technique—or better, therapeutic perspective—the highly varied titles may indeed suggest more about their namers' theoretical bias than about the individuality of the method. Moreover, given the many crossovers, overlaps, and even "borrowings" among schools in their employment of paradox, it should be admitted that the identifications of terms with specific schools is in some instances debatable.

From the psychoanalytic perspective, which includes the work of paradigmatic psychotherapists, we have inherited the descriptors "antisuggestion," "going with the resistance," "joining the resistance," "reflecting (or "mirroring") the resistance," "siding with the resistance," "paradigmatic exaggeration," "supporting the defenses," "reductio ad absurdum," "re-enacting an aspect of the psychosis," "mirroring the patient's distortions," "participating in the patient's fantasies," "outcrazying the patient," and "the use of the patient as consultant." From the vantage point of behavior therapy, we may appreciate paradoxical elements in such procedures as "blow-up," "implosion," "flooding," "instructed helplessness," "massed practice" "negative practice," "paradoxical intention," "stimulus satiation," and "symptom scheduling." In gestalt therapy, an approach where the actual term "paradox" is rarely employed, the attempt to foster change paradoxically may be recognized in the therapist's cruel-to-be-kind suggestions to "stay with the [negative] experience," or to "exaggerate the feeling" (sensation, experience, speech, movement, etc.). Lastly, in the communication–systems school of therapy—by far the most vocal in endorsing and elucidating paradoxical strategies—we have the following miscellany of terms and titles: "the confusion technique," "declaring hopelessness," "exaggerating the position," "paradoxical injunction," "paradoxical instructions," "paradoxical rituals and tasks," "paradoxical written messages," "restraining (or "inhibiting") change," "predicting a relapse," "prescribing a relapse," "positive connotation" (or "interpretation"), "reframing," "redefinition," and "relabeling," "symptom prescription" (or "prescribing the resistance, symptom, or system"), "therapeutic paradox," and the "therapeutic double bind." R. P. Greenberg, in an article intriguingly subtitled "The Power of Negative Thinking" (1973), refers generally to several of the above methods as "anti-expectation techniques," which should serve as a reminder of the point made earlier that the paradoxical essence of all these methods is in their apparent irrationality *from the perspective of the client*.

Two additional procedures that have a flagrantly irrational flavor—and which somehow bypass the theoretical categories so far delineated—deserve mention. The first is aptly designated "psychotherapy of the absurd," a term coined by well-known family therapist Carl Whitaker (1975). This form of "nonrational therapy" enhances or escalates the unreasonableness of the patient's problematic symptom or circumstance to the point of absurdity so as, finally, to resolve it. To Whitaker, "the therapeutic problem is to increase the complexity of the situation . . . to induce chaos and craziness rather than to restore order" (p. 12). Such an absurdist orientation to helping families is complemented by the secondary paradoxical technique of "acting-in" (Keith & Whitaker, 1978). This method, contrasting sharply with acting-out, is aimed at intensifying anxiety rather than alleviating it. As it is existentially described, the technique represents the therapist's effort "to increase the level of interpersonal stress, to bring about an experiential breakthrough into a new way of living, a new way of being in the here and now" (p. 76).

One last technique that eludes categorization goes by the somewhat forbidding name of "provocative therapy" and has been depicted at length in a book of the same name by Farrelly and Brandsma (1974). Provocative therapy is viewed as "a travesty of traditional approaches" in that it "*over*-focuses on what is wrong with the patient in an effort to provoke the patient's affirming what is right with him" (p. 43). As do so many paradoxical techniques, this mode of therapy accepts the patient's negativity or resistance and strives to exploit it for therapeutic purposes. And here, once again, we come full circle as we encounter the profound *psychological* rationality of procedures ostensibly designed to unravel reason itself into ambiguity and confusion.

PART TWO

Specific Paradoxical Strategies in Their Theoretical Context

CHAPTER 2

Psychoanalysis and Paradigmatic Psychotherapy

FREUD

By no stretch of the imagination might Freud be seen as a paradoxical psychotherapist—unless the definition of paradox is itself stretched to the breaking point. Yet the seeds for approaching human problems paradoxically can be viewed as planted by this first great analytic theorist in his increasingly strong recognition of patient resistance to change.

Sander (1974) has sought to demonstrate the ways in which Freud's earliest published case study of an effective hypnotic treatment (Freud, 1958) bears serious comparison, in the "strategic" nature of his intervention, to family systems theory of the past twenty years. Neither Sander nor Freud is inclined to conceptualize this prepsychoanalytic case in terms of resistance, but some such explanation would seem essential to fully appreciate its unusual dynamics. Briefly, Freud was requested to attend the home of a young woman unable, because of vomiting and agitation, to feed her newborn child. After attempting through hypnosis to suggest away her symptoms (a cure that lasted only a day), Freud on his return visit took a far more devious approach. During the woman's second hypnosis Freud told her that almost immediately after his departure she would complain bitterly to her family that they were withholding her dinner, and would actually confront them as to whether they intended for her to starve—adding that she could hardly feed the baby when she herself had nothing to eat. When Freud returned the following day, the young woman assured him the problem had been satisfactorily resolved. Her husband, agreeing that she was now cured, remarked that she had been "quite unlike herself" after the doctor's last visit, vehemently demanding her food and remonstrating with her mother.

The paradoxical essence of Freud's posthypnotic suggestion should be apparent: if a patient is vomiting all the food she consumes, instructing her to demand *more* food would seem tantamount to telling her to increase her vomiting (i.e., augment, or aggravate, the symptomatic behavior). However, having the young woman angrily clamor for food from her mother would appear in this case to have enabled her to express with impunity her longstanding hostility toward her mother and (on a symbolic level) freely voice her own early sense of maternal deprivation. Formulating Freud's curiously roundabout treatment in terms of resistance, it might be said that his directive—supporting or even "joining" the young woman in her passive-aggressive resistance toward her mother—provided her with the opportunity to express (and thereby move beyond) the negative side of her filial ambivalence, which had become so ascendant as to be out of conscious control. Freud's noncommonsensical intervention, devised we may assume as a convenient detour around his patient's anxiety-based resistance toward overt maternal confrontation, would seem to have nullified this defensiveness, allowing the young woman to deliver the antagonistic message necessitated by her temporary fixation in such a way as to render no longer necessary her covert (or dissociated) acting-out of hostility. Empowered through Freud's posthypnotic suggestion to express her unresolved anger *verbally*, her regressive compulsion to behave symptomatically disappeared.

If, indeed, this woman's cure resulted from Freud's helping her to articulate—and abreact—repressed anger, Freud was still many years away from conceptualizing his ingenious solution as facilitating the patient's active confrontation with unconscious resistances. As Musliner (1980) notes, it was not until 1913 (thirty years after this fascinating vignette was published) that Freud was ready to abandon his belief in the sufficiency of exposing the roots of a patient's neurosis to effect a cure and acknowledge the key role which resistances played in sustaining dysfunctional behavior even *after* its subterranean determinants were brought to the surface. "Conscious knowledge," Freud was obliged to conclude, proves "powerless against those resistances, [so that] there was no choice but to cease attributing to the fact of knowing, in itself, the importance that had previously been given to it and to place the emphasis on the resistances" (from Freud, 1958, Vol. 12, p. 142). Musliner perceives Freud's movement from hypnotic to psychoanalytic treatment as a redirection of attention from helping the patient uncover the origins of symptoms to helping him give up the elaborate defense mechanisms perpetuating them. The patient's pathological defenses thus became the primary focus of therapy.

Typically, these defenses—or the patient's maladaptive solution to his problems—are characterized by avoidance. Many writers have by now observed that Freud eventually came to realize that unless the patient's irrational fears were dealt with through some kind of action no final cure was obtainable. Raskin and Klein (1976), for example, cite Freud's paper on phobias (Freud, 1958) in which he indicated that the physician needed to convince the patient to reexperience the phobic situation, without which no amount of insight would produce symptom remission. With agoraphobics, Freud maintained that successful treatment depended on the patient's being induced to go outdoors by himself and struggle with the ensuing anxiety. As Raskin and Klein observe, although Freud stopped short of actually prescribing the symptom, he did point out that the reexperienced anxiety served to promote the patient's therapy, and was thus "good" for him.

As Freud's therapeutic emphasis shifted from examining with the patient the roots of neurosis to persuading the patient to confront the resistances comprising it (i.e., the characteristic defenses against primal fears), so did his increasing stress on the therapist's facilitation of transference intimate his disillusionment with the curative potential of insight alone. B. Nelson (1965) calls attention to the main thrust of Freud's theoretical evolution by noting:

> He came to perceive . . . that in the course of treatment, the patient's presenting neurosis emptied into the "transference neurosis." In the absence of a "transference neurosis," no cure was possible; yet it was precisely the transference neurosis which was to prove the foremost resistance to cure. Psychoanalysis was now identified as analysis of the resistance to cure, centered in the transference neurosis. (p. 379)

Wynne (1980) sees this development in Freud's thinking as a shift in the direction of paradoxical intervention and as in many ways precursory to conceptualizing change within a systems framework. For promoting a regressive transference, which represents a state of increased psychological instability or disequilibrium, is capable of generating, homeostatically, a new stability or reduced disequilibrium. Or—to describe the process in more succinctly paradoxical terms—the therapist's engineering a stumbling backwards (i.e., regressive) movement in a patient may finally be the most effective way to prompt this patient to readjust his faltering balance and move steadily forward.

ADLER

Freud's eventual belief that treatment needed to center on patient resistances is reformulated by Adler, who saw such resistances as testimony to an underlying "depreciation tendency" characterizing neurotics (Adler,

1913/1956). To Adler, it was self-deceiving to assume that patients revealed this tendency only in the later, transference phase of therapy, for patients *entered* treatment with the strong inclination to belittle the therapist. As Adler compellingly puts it: "I expect from the patient again and again the same [deprecatory] attitude which he has shown in accordance with his life-plan. . . . At the moment of his introduction to the physician and often even earlier, the patient has the same feelings toward him as toward important persons in general" (p. 336).

The therapeutic relationship is implicitly regarded by Adler as paradoxical in that the patient, although on one level wishing to be freed from his symptoms, aspires on another level to sabotage the goals of treatment so as (neurotically) to assert superiority over the therapist. *Every* patient, to Adler, attempts in some way to depreciate the therapist, undermine his influence, and jeopardize his own treatment—even to the point of missing sessions during periods of increased improvement. Given the perverse mental operations of the neurotic personality, successful treatment spells defeat for the interpersonal advantages gained, though at great psychological expense, through failure. So from first to last the neurotic responds to the therapeutic endeavor with ambivalence; and the therapist must regularly anticipate the neurotic's counterproductive strivings if he is effectively to neutralize them. What Freud terms "resistance" Adler appreciates as essentially the neurotic's defense against treatment, grounded in his unwillingness to undertake useful social activities because of a pervasive fear of failure. The decidedly paradoxical flavor of several of Adler's interventions follows naturally from his conviction that given the patient's deep-seated reluctance to relinquish his face-saving symptoms, it is imperative that therapy avoid any semblance of coercion. In Adler, the "gentle" approach and the paradoxical approach are almost synonymous.

Adler has been described as the first psychotherapist in Western civilization to advocate paradoxical strategies to effect behavioral change (Mozdzierz, Macchitelli, & Lisiecki, 1976). Whether or not this statement is literally correct, Adler's methodical articulation of techniques designed to "disarm" the neurotic's tendency to defend himself through attacking another does appear without precedent. To Adler, employing such tactics helped the therapist avoid the danger of being "treated" by the patient. One prerequisite for successful treatment was for the therapist to relinquish the role of superiority and place himself, as a friendly "coworker," at the patient's disposal. Thus abandoning his one-up position, he minimized the patient's chronic impulse to disparage persons associated with authority and control. Understanding how the neurotic's life revolved around self-defeating power struggles, Adler recommended that the therapist offer very little of a target to attack. Defining neurosis as largely a deficiency in meeting the normal demands of life—manifested through a noncooperative or disinterested social attitude—Adler used paradoxical strategies to re-engage the patient socially and secure his cooperation. And generally these techniques seek to support—or at least not to resist—the patient's defensive negativism. Mozdzierz et al. (1976) distinguish between Adler's *nonspecific* (or relational) paradoxical tactics and his *specific* paradoxical tactics; and surely the latter set of strategies may be appreciated as deriving from (and perhaps even secondary to) the former, which serve to alleviate the patient's feelings of vulnerability and consequent need to thwart treatment. Summing up his dialectical interactional style, contrived to put in check the patient's socially destructive tendencies, Adler states that:

> a basic principle for the therapist is never to allow the patient to force upon him a superior role such as that of teacher, father, or savior, without contradicting and enlightening the patient. Such attempts represent the beginning of a movement [by] the patient to pull down, in a manner to which he has been previously accustomed, all persons standing above him, and by thus administering a defeat, to disavow them. (p. 339)

Consciously renouncing the one-up position that, ironically, would reduce his potential authority, the therapist may employ a whole host of techniques, several of which may be designated paradoxical. Consider Adler's deferential advice to depressives motivated by feelings of revenge to consider suicide. "Never do anything you don't like," he proposes to them as the cardinal rule in treatment (Adler, 1931/1956, p. 346). His reasoning is simple: "If a depressed person is able to do anything he wants, whom can he accuse? What has he got to revenge himself for?" More complicated is the circumstance that this advice, while appeasing the patient's craving for a godlike superiority over others, frustrates his customary style of interaction, characterized by controlling and blaming others. With the therapist's agreement—essentially analogous to what later, "paradigmatic" analysts came to call "supporting the resistances"— the *patient's* cardinal rule, based on interpersonal domination, is put to the test and used therapeutically against him. When the patient seeks to nullify the therapist's agreement by claiming that there isn't anything he likes doing, Adler calculatingly replies, "Then refrain from doing anything you dislike." His whole approach is to react to the patient's various protests and provocations through acceptance and agreement, so that the patient's habitually counterproductive mode of interaction will not be able to obstruct treatment.

Adler's thoughtful exploitation of patient resistances is apparent in his other, defiance-based paradoxical interventions as well. He predicts the likelihood of the exacerbation of a disorder—such as fainting spells or agoraphobia—in order to minimize the possibility of its occurrence. And convinced of "the marked negativism of neurotics" (Adler, 1913/1956), he scrupulously avoids showing pleasure in or boasting about a partial success derived from treatment, for fear of prompting a relapse. Calling attention to the cautions that must be taken in persuading the patient toward prosocial ventures, he remarks that the therapist must remain neutral in such matters, merely commenting that "while convinced of the success, he could not quite judge whether the patient was really ready for the venture" (1933/1956, p. 339). If we assume the patient's reluctance to follow authoritative directives, we can appreciate the therapeutic double bind created by Adler's ambiguous recommendation. For the choice given is either for the patient to express his resistance toward more prosocial behavior by cooperating with the therapist and "going slow"; or to express his resistance toward the therapist by proceeding with the socially cooperative undertaking. In either case the patient's symptomatically resistant attitude is subtly enervated as his choices are redefined in the therapeutic context as between two types of cooperation.

Adler's therapeutic objective of increasing the patient's social cooperation or interest is fostered by a double-binding orientation that recasts one type of rebellion into another type of cooperation. Options are set up such that defying or depreciating the therapist is tantamount to cooperating with society, and vice versa. In either case what the patient, however unwittingly, is obliged to sacrifice is his overriding symptom of asocial, noncooperative behavior. In slightly different terms, Fisher, Anderson, and Jones (1981) view the patient's ultimate improvement with this approach as attributable to increased self-esteem following a successful power move against the therapist supporting the symptom. The patient's need to control the therapeutic relationship can be achieved, finally, only at the expense of his ambivalently held symptom. And so the strategic advantage of the therapist's scrupulously *renouncing* his advantage should be fairly easy to comprehend.

JOHN ROSEN

Preempting—or taking charge of—a patient's dysfunctional behavior through supporting it is a theme with many variations. John Rosen, in his *Direct Analysis* (1953), describes a technique he calls "re-enacting an aspect of the psychosis," which involves the therapist's insisting that the patient act out precisely the psychotic behavior that his irrational manner suggests may be imminent. Rosen offers two speculations as to the effectiveness of this seemingly perverse method. First, he considers that the boldness of the directive reassures the patient fearful of losing control that the therapist no longer regards him at serious risk for such decompensation. Second, he conjectures that ordering the patient to do something foolish and reminding him that this is how he used to act arouses in him a healthy sense of shame. By demanding that he repeat his symptom, the therapist motivates him to summon up sufficient ego strength to renounce it.

A second paradoxical technique in Rosen's arsenal is appropriately designated "reductio ad absurdum," or "the trick against the trick" (Rosen, 1953, p. 148 ff.). To Rosen, a patient's delusion can be understood as a "trick" contrived by his "unconscious censorship faculties" to conceal from consciousness something even more threatening than the delusion. The therapist's *countertrick* consists of challenging this delusion with a still greater unreality, such that the patient will be compelled to make certain all-important distinctions between metaphorical and literal levels of communication. By dramatically *increasing* the confusion of the situation, the therapist may indirectly help the patient discern the outlines of that situation more accurately. And by enhancing the falsity or ("fakery") of the patient's delusional system to the point of patent absurdity, the patient may be prompted to use that small portion of his ego still in touch with reality to begin to free himself from the rigid perceptual binds of his psychosis. As one recovered patient suggestively remarked to Rosen: "You did not introduce reality. Nothing can do that. You introduced a bigger unreality, and then I got totally confused and went to pieces. I suspected that it was a fake" (p. 149). It is as though Rosen's forcing the obdurately jammed pendulum of the patient's psyche to the farthest possible extreme facilitates this pendulum's at last swinging freely and reestablishing a flexible balance in the center.

Rosen's other, closely complementary paradoxical strategies revolve around his aligning himself with a patient's psychosis in such a manner as to loosen the patient from its incapacitating grip. "With the paranoid patient," he comments for example, "you have to confirm the delusional system and then try to find a way to undermine it in order to promote anxiety" (p. 142). Temporarily sanctioning the patient's symptomatic behavior, Rosen maneuvers himself into this conceptually distorted world in the circuitous effort to lead the patient out of it. Thus the patient's stubborn resistance is gradually worn away by the therapist's eliminating its felt necessity.

ROBERT LINDNER

The curious idea of a therapist's prodding the patient out of his psychotic world by entering into it himself is hardly new. Lindner—whose famous case of "The Jet-Propelled Couch" (in *The Fifty-Minute Hour*, 1955) perhaps illustrates this drastic stratagem most eloquently—himself acknowledges Rosen and others for establishing the therapeutic precedent of "joining" a patient's fantasy so as to pry him loose from it. Such participation, besides having a fascination of its own, is also of great theoretical suggestiveness.

Lindner's much-cited case involves a young research physicist whose psychosis was grounded in an exceptionally elaborate fantasy life, including time/space travel, adamantly proclaimed as fact. Given what Lindner describes as the "life-sustaining necessity" of this patient's highly wrought delusional system, as well as his unswerving conviction of his sanity (treatment was not elective), Lindner experienced intense feelings of futility until he sensed that the only way he could help his patient was to become a willing participant in his psychosis. The result of Lindner's "sharing" the patient's delusion—not, incidentally, without some risk to his own mental equilibrium—is the patient's gradual abandonment of his psychosis. In the author's words, the patient's hitherto private fantasy life:

> somehow lost its potency . . . [and] excitement. With this reduction in the appeal of the fantasy, moreover, the insights gained but not employed during the long months of our dynamic exploration of the past at last came into their own. Kirk's former ability to enter the fantasy, to achieve that abnormal state of sensitivity to his needs that had catapulted him into his mythical universe, began to diminish. It was not long before the whole amazing defense—for such Kirk now recognized his obsession to be—collapsed or, better, decayed, to be replaced, item for item, by reality. (p. 291)

Lindner offers some interesting explanations as to why the full acceptance of his patient's delusion, and even active collusion in it, was able to bring about its ultimate disintegration. Considering his unorthodox cure in nonpsychological terms, he alludes to the principle that no two things can occupy the same place at the same time. The patient's narrowly circumscribed delusional structure is viewed as having room for only a single occupant; with the invasion of a second person into this previously private psychic space, the original tenant is forced to step aside. If Lindner's patient began to question the reality of his fantasy world, his skepticism would appear to have originated in the circumstance that the very existence of this world depended on its utter seclusiveness.

Explicitly recalling the hypotheses of Rosen (as well as anticipating one of the central ideas of the paradigmatic psychotherapists soon to follow), Lindner reflects that when the therapist acts similarly to the patient, expressing the same notions and in the same language, the patient's image is projected outside himself. Irresistibly pushed to the side of his own reality, he is obliged to judge critically the behavior before him. As Lindner—who at times even *ordered* his patient to travel to his mythical universe to secure certain necessary "facts"—conceptualizes the therapeutic process: "My direct involvement in the fantasy that had, until then, been his private preserve, constricted his '*lebensraum*' [life space], confronted him with his mirror image, and maneuvered him into the critical reality position" (p. 276).

PARADIGMATIC PSYCHOTHERAPY

Many of the unorthodox tactics of Rosen, Lindner, and other innovative analysts became formalized in the late 1950s under the label "paradigmatic psychotherapy." Such a term was intended to call attention to modern analysts prepared to take on the role of model, mirror, or "paradigm" of the patient's resistances in order to lead him toward a better understanding of the crucial intrapsychic and interpersonal circumstances of his life (see, especially, Coleman & Nelson, 1957). Focusing on the present as well as the past, these analysts present the patient with dramatic paradigms in order to promote insight not attainable through a classical interpretive mode. The techniques employed to achieve this awareness of pathological defenses most often come under the heading of "joining" or "siding with" the resistance, and involve not simply the therapist's passively agreeing with the patient's utterances but actively *exemplifying* (nonvocally as well as verbally) these irrational viewpoints. In paradigmatic psychotherapy the analyst's role is shaped by his assumptions about the patient's neurotic, or psychotic, pattern of self-protection. The interventions deriving from such role-playing are at once less intellectual, and more primitive and emotionally direct, than those typifying traditional analytic procedures.

All the same, even though paradigmatic techniques represent a broad expansion of classical psychoanalytic *process*, they do not depict any major defection from basic psychoanalytic tenets. Moreover, the sharp recognition of these later-day analysts that mere interpretation of resistances is not always sufficient to produce change was hinted at much earlier by Freud himself, as has already been mentioned. Even the "joining" devices of these modern analysts would appear to have been anticipated by Freud. As Ormont (1974) notes, the advisability of maneuvers similar to joining was intimated by Freud in his preface to Aichhorn's *Wayward Youth* (1925/ 1965) when he suggested that with such recalcitrant cases as juvenile delinquents "something other than analysis must be employed, though something which will be at one with analysis in purpose" (cited by Ormont, p. 430). Certainly Aichhorn's book presents an approach to dealing with delinquent aggression that bears comparison to later joining methods. And one of Anna Freud's works (1928/1946)—also alluded to in Ormont's essay—describes her efforts to mirror systematically the affect and mood of disturbed children she treated.

The key distinction between classical analysis and paradigmatic therapy is in the handling of resistances: Whereas the former seeks to interpret them intellectually, the latter endeavors to act them out in such an unparalleled, "irrational" way as to challenge the patient's fundamentally negative attitude toward therapy and increase the chances of his achieving, spontaneously, some sort of cathartic self-discovery. But although the techniques of paradigmatic therapy represent a clear departure from orthodox analytic procedure, their aim is indistinguishable from classical analysis. That is, the noninterpretive joining of resistances is designed to foster the development of the same transference relationship conceived as the basis of cure by Freud. Additionally, it has been suggested (Davis, 1965) that if we can understand these interventions as at bottom interpretive—though on a preverbal level—then the compatibility of these methods to a traditional analytic approach, and even their essential identity with it, is easily appreciated.

In brief, paradigmatic psychotherapy is best viewed as an adjunct to, or extension of, psychoanalysis. It is not really an autonomous entity, and its practitioners see themselves as working within a broad analytic framework. As Coleman and Nelson (1957) and Strean (1964) have observed, the paradigmatic approach may be viewed as reflecting the modern convergence of psychoanalysis and social science in its central assumption that social–psychological factors determine both the etiology and treatment of psychological disorders. Building on the theoretical base established by Freud and his immediate followers, these later-day analysts show the influence not only of psychoanalytic ego psychology but also of contemporary trends in American sociology and psychology (particularly in the realms of role theory, small-group dynamics, and learning theory). Their tactics, selectively employed, are designed to enhance their resourcefulness with patients whose defenses make them poor candidates for more classical kinds of interpretation. That is, the main prerequisite—or indication—for the use of these methods relates closely to a variety of client resistances that render futile more straightforward, "cerebral" interventions.

Coleman and Nelson (1957), considering the usefulness of paradigmatic techniques with juvenile and borderline patients, emphasize the mature, intellectual appeal of interpretation versus the more primitive allure of demonstration, which appeals to such early learning processes as introjection, identification, and imitation. Since children and borderlines are seen as lacking an ego capable of translating intellectual awareness into emotional understanding until late in treatment, rudimentary communication procedures that dramatically set forth examples and patterns are viewed as invaluable in making these patients accessible to the final stages of analysis. In an article entitled "Externalization of the Toxic Introject," Coleman (1956) illustrates the momentous impact such strategic "setting forth" may have:

> Under the guise of understanding herself, a young woman was in the habit of castigating herself severely during her analytic sessions. Classical interpretations failed to modify the masochistic pattern; she simply felt I was being tolerant of her shortcomings.
>
> Finally one day, in a tone of full conviction, I agreed: "You are quite right. You are no good, a failure. At last you recognize that everything is hopeless. You will never change. Give up."
>
> She lay in stunned silence for a few moments [a reaction that helps define the intervention as "paradoxical"—ed.]. Then she leaped off the couch and sailed out of the office, slamming the door violently.
>
> Tremendous movement developed in the analysis. A few months later she said, "Do you remember the time you agreed with me that I was a failure? It was a turning point in my analysis. . . . From then on everything changed. . . . It's as if everything that went before was black and everything that followed was white. Before that I provoked and tortured myself endlessly."
>
> I asked why she had needed me to attack her. "Because it was the only way I could see what I was doing to myself," she replied. "*You* had to do it to me before I could stop doing it or even feel how I was hurting myself." (p. 241)

This example should suggest how paradigmatic interventions are calculated "to educate the irrational ego" (M. Coleman Nelson, 1962, p. 120). Patients whose egos are predominantly rational do not, on the whole, require these techniques, for they are able to benefit from standard analytic interpretations. But when such interpretations are responded to as intrusive or attacking, the therapeutic advantage of paradigmatic tactics— covert yet carefully aimed at the target of the patient's resistance—should be obvious. The patient who reacts negatively to any interpretation of his resistance typically feels compelled to respond otherwise when this resistance is mirrored by the analyst.

The special utility of paradigmatic techniques with children and adolescents has, not surprisingly, received considerable emphasis in the literature (e.g., Evans, 1980; Kesten, 1955; Marshall, 1972, 1974, 1976, 1982; Spotnitz, Nagelberg, & Feldman, 1956; Strean, 1959, 1961). Given the young person's frequent reluctance to talk about his life, his tendency toward acting-out behaviors, and the insecurity of his defense system, the therapist's temporarily abandoning all interpretation and finding instead an appropriate way of supporting the youth's shaky defenses is at times strongly indicated in order to promote a therapeutic alliance. Paradigmatic tactics, with their primitive appeal to the regressed as well as the mentally and emotionally immature, have also been recommended for treating hospitalized schizophrenics within a short-term analytic context (Davis, 1965) and for establishing with this population a facilitative "narcissistic transference" (Spotnitz, 1969).

The dynamics (or process) involved in a successful paradigmatic intervention can be inferred from the brief example already cited. As delineated by M. C. Nelson (1962), the analyst's supportive joining of the patient's conscious or unconscious projections and resistances usually prompts the patient to respond in the following sequence. First, the patient observes—through the analyst's paradigm—his own defense mechanisms, but perceives them as existing outside himself. (His usual *reaction* to the joining intervention is one of surprise.) Second, he ventilates thoughts, feelings, and even fantasies which have been evoked by the paradigm, and through such release strengthens the healthy part of his ego, renouncing "the toxic introjects, the pathological projections, and the self-destructive resistances" (p. 121). As Davis (1965) somewhat differently hypothesizes the patient's experience: "It is as though a powerful new ally has intervened in the life of the patient, taking over some of the more onerous of his tasks (his defenses), thus forcing him to experiment with new attitudes or heretofore repressed feelings" (pp. 441–442). Finally, through this self-empowering process, the patient is able, nondefensively, to recognize in the analyst's contrived representations important elements of his own psyche. When this stage of awareness is reached, paradigmatic techniques become superfluous and the remainder of analysis resorts to classical interpretation, with the patient's coming, spontaneously, to apprehend that which has gone before.

As is characteristic in the literature on paradoxical procedures, paradigmatic tactics go by a large variety of names and phrases. Terms such as "joining the patient's resistances," "supporting the patient's defenses," "participating in the patient's fantasies," and even "using the patient as consultant" are commonly encountered. More fanciful titles—such as "outcrazying the patient" (Spotnitz, 1969)—bespeak the verbal ingenuity of their creator more than they indicate a significantly different approach to handling a patient's resistance to orthodox analysis. Marshall (1974) conveniently divides the many joining techniques he employs with children and adolescents into such categories as ordering, hypervaluing, tutoring, mirroring, and consulting. But perhaps the most comprehensive schema suggesting the ways that a patient may be analyzed *implicitly* through the creation of paradigms until he is ready to respond to classical interpretation is offered by M. C. Nelson (1962):

Analysis of Resistances
(a)   By actively mirroring (either imitative or exaggerated joining of resistance).
(b)   By duplicating reported interpersonal experience.

Analysis of Introjects and Imagos
(a)   By assuming role of self-image (patient's idealized, hated, or unconscious self).
(b)   By assuming role of introject (patient's idealized, hated—toxic—or unconscious introject).
(c)   By assuming role of 'stranger' (alien, uncomprehending, distant).

Analysis of Fantasies and Transference
(a)   By entering into ongoing fantasy.
(b)   By following patient's self-dosing recommendations.
(c)   By adopting any of methods listed under resistances and introjects. (pp. 121–122)

In all the above techniques the analyst's "covert externalization" of patient defenses may be seen as gently and supportively prodding the patient toward overt admissions not previously possible. With the analyst's strangely collusive accommodation of therapy-hindering defenses, the patient's pathological burden is lightened, thus greatly facilitating the spontaneous release of thoughts and feelings.

Although this discussion of paradigmatic psychotherapy has so far concentrated on matters of definition and background—as well as the indications for, and process and tactics of this therapy—inevitably it has also suggested something of the rationale behind these circuitous stratagems. As might be expected, the literature on paradigmatic techniques is replete with theoretical accounts for their usefulness. Some attempt to present these different explanations is therefore in order.

The utility of paradigmatic tactics in making the patient more amenable to treatment—that is, their value in helping the analyst create an interpersonal context without which *no* therapy may be feasible—is frequently noted as the primary rationale for their employment. By joining or mirroring the patient's resistance, the therapist is seen as inducing (perhaps even "seducing") the patient to cooperate. His irrational, self-protective barriers to open communication begin to give way as the therapist, bypassing his conscious resistance, signals that such barriers are no longer needed. By receiving the message that his defense system will not be attacked by the therapist—who in fact totally accepts it and is apparently desirous of helping him preserve it intact—the patient is encouraged to participate actively in his analysis.

Because the patient feels adequately defended when the analyst supports rather than confronts his resistances, such joining not only strengthens the therapeutic alliance but also enables the patient to experience anxiety reduction, with a consequent lessening of defensive behavior. Marshall (1976) attempts to provide a learning theory rationale for the diminution of anxiety associated with paradigmatic techniques, citing Neal Miller's conflict model of drive gradients (in *Comprehensive Psychiatry*, 1966, *1*, p. 7). Demonstrating graphically that with drive held constant an increase in defense/resistance lowers anxiety levels, Marshall argues that although joining techniques may have the immediate effect of moving the patient farther from the therapeutic goal, the patient's decreased anxiety (as well as the *analyst's* reduced negative feelings toward him—whether of anger, frustration, or guilt) may well expedite the therapeutic process. In short, temporarily lowering the avoidance gradient would appear a more effective way of doing therapy with difficult (because more anxiety-laden) patients than raising the approach gradient. Marshall's employment of behavioral postulates to elucidate techniques otherwise portrayed in an analytic framework is, incidentally, anticipated in an earlier paper (1972), in which he alludes to the learning theory phenomenon of extinction to explain the success of joining techniques in lessening patient resistance.

As much of the literature suggests, reducing resistance is a direct result of reducing anxiety—and in the end these two obstacles to therapy may be so entangled as to be practically inseparable. What needs to be emphasized is that through the anxiety reduction fostered by the inherent supportiveness of paradigmatic techniques the patient is enabled to begin the difficult process of surmounting personal barriers to change. The consequently enhanced ego strength, frequently hypothesized as an outcome of the patient's lowered anxiety level, is perceived as increasing his willingness to tolerate the strains and stresses involved in moving toward therapeutic goals.

One of the first benefits of the patient's feeling adequately defended through the therapist's joining his resistances is the healthy ventilation of buried emotions. The desperate paradigmatic tactic of siding with the patient's self-negativity, for instance (as in the vignette quoted from Coleman, 1956), may incite the patient to turn this negativity against the therapist, thus overcoming his chronic resistance to feeling and expressing aggressive components in his personality (see also Sternbach & Nagelberg, 1957). As Strean (1964) conceptualizes the self-destructive patient's encounter with his mirror image:

> When instead of meeting an expected version of his idealized self, an omnipotent parental figure, the patient encounters a therapist who *can* refuse help, the patient may then project his own destructive wishes on this therapist. His defense of infantile helplessness can be rendered inoperative when he is given the opportunity to verbalize his destructiveness [through] the therapist['s] portray[ing] an unhelpful attitude. (p. 377)

Thus we can appreciate how the therapist's surprisingly helpless stance in the face of the patient's protestations of powerlessness can free the patient to release pent-up feelings against another, and at last begin to recognize something of what he has long felt beneath his habitual self-denigrations. The *why* of his feelings, of course, comes later, as paradigmatic devices gradually yield to more orthodox analytic procedures.

Ironically, endorsing the patient's irrational feelings or attitudes may lead him to diverge from formerly fixed behaviors. Fay (1978), whose theoretical orientation is eclectic, speaks of therapist "mirroring" techniques (particularly as they involve some sort of exaggeration) as helping inflexible patients recognize the irrationality of the imitator and take a stand against him—while at the same time they develop consciousness of *their own* irrationality and begin to readapt accordingly. Siding with the patient's rigid defense system is viewed as particularly valuable in dealing with paranoid patients, where direct assaults on the pathological viewpoint are useless and even dangerous. As Sherman (1961) has indicated, such cases require the therapist not only to identify with the paranoid system but also to endorse the patient's negative transference. Done appropriately, the patient comes to feel that the therapist is the only one in the world who understands him. And when this positive transference progresses, the patient comes to question his paranoid ideas, developing *by himself* the self-critical faculty till then so conspicuously absent from his thought processes. Maneuvering the patient toward a position of self-insight—or rather, using his resistance against him so that he will feel obliged to adopt a more rational orientation toward himself and others—is theoretically justified by Sherman's belief that "whichever side the therapist aligns himself with, the patient will usually feel impelled to leave" (p. 55). Echoing the position of Lindner (1955), Sherman goes on to reflect that it may be impossible for two people to coexist in the same psychic space, perhaps because the key prerequisite for the evolution of a sense of self is a certain amount of opposition and negativity.

Such an inner necessity toward rebellion—or, we might even say, irresistible impulse toward resistance—obviously plays into the hands of a therapist employing joining techniques. Confronted with nothing at all to oppose, the patient is somehow incited to oppose *himself* and experiment with attitudes and feelings that previously he could not allow himself to—or had not the courage to—explore. As the therapist designedly "takes over" his pathology, his inmost urge is to abandon it. And as his drive toward resistance continues to "boomerang," deep feelings and repressed memories may emerge, such that he may be viewed as spontaneously taking charge of the therapeutic process. Kesten (1955), in a paper discussing mirroring techniques specifically with children, observes that reflecting the unconscious negativistic portion of the child's ego permits the child to deal more effectively with unconscious resentments and repressed negative attitudes. The underlying thrust of Kesten's essay (as in most of the work of paradigmatic therapists) is that the *structure* of the therapeutic relationship must accommodate the special needs and resistances of the patient to succeed.

All the same, while paradigmatic therapists stress the interpersonal context of their interventions, the benefits of establishing this context are generally understood intrapsychically. Therapeutic progress seen as deriving from their employment is commonly described in terms of self-confrontation, self-understanding, self-insight, self-responsibility, ego growth, and mental synthesis. In short, the conceptualizers of paradigmatic tactics never really forget their theoretical origins. However innovative in technique, they nonetheless keep to the psychoanalytic faith, so that they manage at once to look back to their founding father and forward to other schools of therapy similarly experimenting with the uses of paradox to facilitate the often arduous process of therapy.

EMPIRICAL RESEARCH ON PARADOX IN PSYCHOANALYTIC THERAPY

There is little denying the therapeutic suggestiveness of the many case studies published on the analytic employment of paradox. But all the testimonials to its effectiveness cannot undo the fact that not a single empirical examination of significance on these techniques can be found in the literature. Davis (1965) makes an effort to assess the utility of joining the resistance in an investigation focusing on six hospitalized schizophrenics. But his case descriptions are lacking in the sort of data that would make possible an objective evaluation of the "encouraging" results he reports. Obviously, essential variables relating to therapist, patient, and interpersonal process resist exact measurement; and it is understandable that no study has yet appeared that would serve empirically to justify the analytic paradoxical techniques here discussed. Still, regardless of the difficulty in unraveling and quantifying the variables involved in such procedures, without the presence of such data it must be conceded that hard evidence for the special efficacy of these devices remains lacking.

CHAPTER 3

Behavior Therapy

BEHAVIORAL VERSUS NONBEHAVIORAL PARADOXICAL TECHNIQUES

It should be stressed at the outset of this section that behavior therapy has many facets. There are, in fact, *several* behavior therapies: from the classical conditioning approach of Wolpe and Eysenck (emphasizing mediational variables, such as fear, in the clinical treatment of problems); to the operant conditioning model of Skinner (focusing on observable behaviors and environmental control); to the cognitive–behavioral model of Ellis and Beck (centering on an individual's perceptions and attributions, and the negative self-talk underlying dysfunctional behavior); and, finally, to the more intricate paradigm of social learning theory advanced by Bandura (endeavoring to integrate all the above outlooks and stressing symbolic modeling and observational learning—as well as the reciprocal interaction of behavioral, cognitive, and environmental factors in determining one's psychological functioning). Additionally, in contrast to earlier conditioning models and similar to most other therapeutic orientations, recent revisions and refinements of behavior therapy have revealed considerable awareness of the importance of the therapeutic relationship in effecting change.

This said, it should be noted that the particular variety of behavior therapy described in these pages—because theoretically aligned with most of the paradoxical procedures presented here—is typically *not* representative of current cognitive or social learning developments in the field. Rather, this approach tends to mirror that mode of behavioral intervention sometimes designated "behavior modification," predominant in the 1950s and 1960s. This version of behavior therapy, although embodying many traditional behaviorist tenets, needs to be clearly distinguished from more recent behaviorist conceptualizations of motivation and change.

Of all therapeutic approaches, behavior therapy is at once the least mentalistic and (or so it is frequently alleged) the most scientific. Its no-nonsense orientation would seem to furnish rather hostile surroundings for the devious practice of therapeutic paradox. Yet several behavioral procedures are commonly regarded in the literature as including paradoxical elements, though such recognition rarely appears in specifically behaviorist writings. Behavior therapists do acknowledge the legitimacy of the title as it is employed in Viktor Frankl's existential (or, to use his own term, "logotherapeutic") technique of "paradoxical intention"—a procedure that they have put to their own clinical use. But an examination of how Frankl's technique has been incorporated into a behavioral framework reveals how its humanistic emphasis has largely been eliminated, as behaviorists have conscientiously striven to account for its utility in terms of learning theory. Other, more "home-grown," behavioral methods involving paradox—such as negative practice, massed practice, stimulus satiation, implosion, and flooding—are almost never characterized by behaviorists as paradoxical.

Despite the many practical similarities between behavioral and nonbehavioral paradoxical procedures, certain broad distinctions may be noted. For example, the *relationship* between client and clinician, an important and deliberately manipulated "tool" in the employment of therapeutic paradox and generally regarded as crucial to its effectiveness, is frequently minimized by behavior therapists. Such practitioners, focusing sharply on methodology, generally perceive the association between themselves and clients as irrelevant to the final success of their change-inducing techniques. If one of these techniques should fail, such therapists investigate this failure in terms of misdiagnosis of symptomatology, or misapplication of technique, rarely as a consequence of a "failed" relationship. Conversely, successfully removing a symptom is frequently seen—in contrast, for instance, to psychodynamic theory—as tantamount to removing the root of a client's problem rather than as simply eliminating its overt manifestation. One behavior therapist, for example, considers the dysfunctional response of stuttering and reflects that this behavior may not be merely a symptom of social maladaptation but one of its prime causes, so that curing a socially maladjusted stutterer may itself enable him to make adequate social adjustments (Lehner, 1954).

Paradoxical behavioral techniques may also be differentiated from kindred, nonbehavioral methods in their not being confined strictly to clinical applications or to human subjects. Besides helping obsessives give up their obsessing and ticquers their ticquing, Dunlap's device of "negative practice," for example, has been used to help typists overcome habitual errors and actors gain control of stage fright. And the similar learning-based method of eradicating certain behaviors through the "massed practice" of them has been employed more with animals in laboratories than with clients in therapy. Moreover, the behaviorist *presentation* of therapeutic paradox to clients is typically simple, straightforward, and determinedly *nonparadoxical* in its carefully emphasizing the cause–effect rationale of procedures that might otherwise seem to defy reason. The very word "paradox" seems implicitly judged by most behaviorists to be synonymous with confusion and deception (as in "paradoxing the patient"); and such practitioners strive, in preparing clients for paradoxical procedures, to make their finally commonsensical basis transparent.

In brief, paradox is not understood as an orientation, or "place to come from," but as one of only many techniques in the behaviorist repertoire for facilitating change. Indeed paradoxical therapeutic devices are frequently combined with one or more nonparadoxical methods, so that the overall flavor of therapy hardly impresses most clients as imbued with irony or contradiction. As distinguished from most nonbehavioral applications of paradox, the symptomatic behavior is not supported or "sided with" (i.e., *relabeled*), but rather confronted, at times even assaulted, and worked through directly—as will later be illustrated in the discussion of such procedures as implosion and flooding. The direct reality testing involved in these techniques, through the repeated exposure of the client to aversive stimuli, little resembles the therapist's consciously ironic encouragement of symptoms typical in most nonbehavioral counterparts to these techniques.

So far this discussion has centered on the technical differences between behavioral and nonbehavioral applications of paradox. The essential differences, however, are not in the actual employment of paradox at all but in the theories proposed to elucidate their utility. This is not the place to describe such theoretical discrepancies at length, but some of the most obvious dissimilarities might at least be suggested. Rarely outside the context of behavior therapy, for example, are paradoxical strategies hypothesized in the language of conditioning or learning theory. And almost nowhere in the nonbehavioral literature is the concept of experimental extinction invoked to account for their effectiveness. Yet behaviorist literature is rife with theoretical references to extinction in explaining how such techniques operate. One encyclopedic text in the field, *Behavior Therapy: Techniques and Empirical Findings* (Rimm & Masters, 1979), considers the related therapeutic methods of negative practice, massed practice, stimulus satiation, implosion, and flooding all in a single chapter designated "Response Elimination and Extinction Procedures." As is usually the case in behaviorist literature, the actual term "paradox" is nowhere to be found in the review of these "symptom-inviting" strategies. The decidedly atheoretical—or operational—focus of behavior theory is suggested by such other terms as "habituation" and "conditioned inhibition" (or "reactive inhibition") to explain these techniques. And such titles seem much better designed to account for the specific What of behavior than to illuminate any ultimate Why of it.

Despite the technical and theoretical differences between behavior therapy's utilization of paradox and its employment by other schools of therapy—as well as the reluctance of many behaviorists to employ paradox deliberately—the acceptance of such devices is definitely on the increase. This acceptance (often rather begrudging) relates more to the willingness to adapt certain strategies from the communication–systems approach toward couples and families than to any willingness to reconceptualize behavioral techniques in explicitly paradoxical terms.

A quote from one recent article on behavioral marital therapy should serve to suggest the typical behaviorist's position on therapeutic paradox, and also the subtle shift in this position:

> Until the last few years, behavioral marital therapists tended to discount the necessity, value and effectiveness of paradoxical techniques. This view was determined by several factors. First, a reading of the family systems literature indicates that paradoxical techniques are specifically employed to counter the "almost inevitable" resistance of partners to changing their relationship. However, *resistance* itself has been seen by behaviorists as essentially resulting from ineffective case management. . . . Accordingly, behaviorists are generally taught to remediate poor therapeutic progress through the more effective use of *overt*, skill-oriented techniques, rather than having to resort to *covertly* manipulative strategic techniques, such as paradox. In addition . . . many behaviorists view covert manipulations as inconsistent with an above-board social learning approach. . . .
>
> However . . . during the past two or three years especially, behaviorally oriented researchers . . . have increasingly concerned themselves with that phenomenon called *resistance*. Moreover, these investigators have described treatment approaches designed to combine certain strategic and behavioral interventions. The addition of the "strategic" technique is, in part, a recognition of the inadequacy of the current behavioral model to effectively facilitate change in a high enough proportion of distressed couples and families. (Birchler, 1981, p. 92)

Birchler goes on to add—somewhat defensively—that "when applied sparingly and judiciously" the use of paradox is "quite compatible" with a behaviorist orientation. This sentiment is also expressed in a book on behavior marital therapy, which devotes a section to the employment of paradox and justifies this inclusion by arguing that such interventions may at times conform to a model stressing "the environmental control of behavior" (Jacobson & Margolin, 1979, p. 153). Theorizing on the dramatic efficacy of a paradoxical procedure used with a contentious couple, for example, these authors refer to the therapist's value "as a discriminative stimulus for polite, rational behavior." And again, it may well be that the only *crucial* difference between applying paradox in a behavioral and nonbehavioral clinical setting is in the rationale offered to explain its use. For, practically, almost all paradoxical strategies involve the encouragement of problematic behavior (whether of an intra- or interpersonal nature) so as, finally, to empower clients to gain control over it.

The intention of the following sections is to provide a brief introduction to each of the behavioral methods commonly regarded in the general therapeutic literature as paradoxical. Such an introduction will include a definition and description of the technique as typically implemented, its theoretical underpinnings, and a statement on the empirical evidence supporting its clinical use. The technique of paradoxical intention is, as should be almost self-evident, by far the behavioral technique most frequently acknowledged as paradoxical. Because of this circumstance, and also because its employment has been restricted to therapeutic contexts and in recent years attracted a number of experimenters seeking to validate its clinical use, it will be given the most emphasis—especially in the realm of empirical research.

SPECIFIC PARADOXICAL TECHNIQUES

Negative Practice

Knight Dunlap, who coined the term "negative practice" back in the 1920s to describe his corrective learning procedure, has defined this technique as "the practice of a response for the purpose of breaking the habit of making the response" (Dunlap, 1946, p. 191). The logical paradox of removing a response through repeating it should be apparent, although neither Dunlap nor his followers were inclined to conceptualize this method in any terms other than human learning. From Dunlap's viewpoint, in negative practice what a person repeats is not the *total response* involved in the habitual behavior but a new response that repeats only the behavior itself, while introducing significantly different affective and cognitive elements (Dunlap, 1942). Such new behavioral components are seen as enabling the person to terminate the unwanted behavior. Problematic responses treated through this curiously inverted learning process include habitual spelling and typing mistakes, muscular tensions, stage fright, obsessions, hypochondria, social anxieties, chronic "worrying," protracted thumbsucking, enuresis, compulsive masturbation, homosexuality, tics, nailbiting, and stammering (Dunlap, 1928, 1946).

To Dunlap, the dislike associated with the performance of the unwanted habit gives way during negative practice to feelings of satisfaction. Individuals, after they are informed of the rationale behind the procedure, begin to practice the habit actively and without conflict. Rather than continuing with futile attempts at avoidance, the attempt is now made consciously to perform the previously unwelcome behavior. These efforts are made only at prescribed periods and in conjunction with prescribed thought processes. The assumption underlying the method is, again in Dunlap's words, that "undesirable traits, like desirable traits, are habits, the results of learning processes which can be unlearned by appropriate procedures, in which the normal learning process is reversed and into which factors that are destructive to positive learning are introduced" (1946, pp. 193–194). The fundamental principle behind this "unlearning technique" relates to bringing the involuntary response or behavior pattern under voluntary control. For once the habit becomes voluntary its involuntary occurrence is eliminated (Dunlap, 1942, 1946). However, as Dunlap himself acknowledges, this "principle" is really not an explanation of negative practice so much as a description of its results.

Several writers have sought to elucidate the therapeutic mechanism involved in negative practice, and some of their theoretical speculations might be cited here. One frequent explanation has to do with sensitizing clients to relevant stimuli. To Lehner (1954), for example, as clients begin to perceive the cues for correctly performing their newly "voluntary" behaviors, they also come to recognize the relationship between such voluntary performance and its previously involuntary counterpart—with the eventual disappearance of the latter as the new response is perfected. In this sense, negative practice is hypothesized as a way of replacing old cues with new, more fitting, ones. Unlike most other therapeutic methods, this technique does not depend primarily on client verbalizations to effect change but other, more direct, motor responses. In developing his viewpoint, Lehner alludes to Guthrie's (1935) interpretation of negative practice as making explicit the cues precipitating an act. Since the individual may not be aware of these stimuli—which through conditioning lead to uncontrollable behavior—negative practice may prove useful in reconditioning to these stimuli, ultimately enabling the individual to gain voluntary control over heretofore involuntary behavior. Similarly, McGeoch and Irion (1952) emphasize the importance of repeating the unwanted act in increasing the individual's *attention* to it and thus making clearer the choice between the desired and undesired behavior.

Experimental evidence in support of negative practice is undeniably inconclusive. In practice, Dunlap supplemented the technique with many secondary ones, so that isolating and assessing the role of negative practice in treatment became impossible. Other empirical investigations of negative practice have likewise been contaminated by employing this procedure in conjunction with other devices; for example, systematic desensitization or a variety of self-control techniques. In a number of studies specifically comparing negative practice to other behavioral methods in eliminating such habits as stammering, smoking, and tics, results have been somewhat mixed. In brief, while many experiments have shown definite promise in validating the technique, the superiority of negative practice over other methods has not yet been demonstrated and, additionally, the frequent use of negative practice as only one of several treatment devices (especially in case studies) has precluded any clear estimation of its effectiveness. As Rimm and Masters (1979) conclude after their review of the experimentation on this method: "Overall, negative practice does appear to have merit, and it is hoped that sufficient research will be conducted within the next few years to allow more extensive evaluation of [it]" (p. 296).

Massed Practice

Distinguishing negative practice from massed practice is difficult. In fact, these two closely related techniques have at times been discussed under a single heading (e.g., Raskin & Klein, 1976), or dealt with as though synonymous (e.g., Hersen & Eisler, 1973; Rabkin, 1977; Yates, 1958). Although the technique of massed practice stresses almost unremitting diligence in the repeated performance of unwanted behaviors, negative practice also involves an important element of repetition, so that frequency of execution alone cannot separate the two procedures. One more viable distinction is intimated by Rimm and Masters (1979), who reflect: "The concept of negative practice is usually reserved to describe the treatment of problem motor behaviors (e.g., tics) by forced repetition (massed practice)" (p. 292). This observation suggests that perhaps the most meaningful way of discriminating these two kindred terms is to regard negative practice as the informing principle behind the actual procedure of massed practice; that is, massed practice might best refer to the *manner* in which the undesired behavior is executed and negative practice to the very *fact* of such ostensibly perverse execution.

Be that as it may, experimenters and practitioners employing the name "negative practice" to describe their mode of treatment have tended to adopt or extend Dunlap's explanatory rationale, whereas those using the term "massed practice" have resorted to somewhat different learning principles in explicating their viewpoint. There appears to be a general preference in the modern behavioral literature for the term "massed practice," and this may well have to do with the fact that such a title carries no evaluative connotations and is more concrete and "operational"—thus better conforming to mainstream tenets of learning theory derived from laboratory experiments with animals. Among the *human* behavior (or symptoms) treated by massed practice are tics, examination anxiety, compulsive gambling, agoraphobia, head-banging, and Gilles de la Tourette (varied tics and compulsive swearing) syndrome.

When symptoms do disappear through this seemingly perverse act of repeating problematic behaviors in rapid succession, what is it that actually occurs? By now several interpretations of the procedure have been offered. Unquestionably the most commonly proposed explanation reiterates Clark Hull's (1943) construct of "reactive inhibition." According to this theoretical formulation, based on Hull's two factor inhibition–interference theory, the "massed practice" of a response causes the development of a negative drive state incompatible with the response and therefore acts as a motivator for *not* responding. Repeatedly executing a response is seen as leading to the simultaneously aversive effects of fatigue and boredom, inclining the organism to inhibit future practice of the behavior (i.e., "reactive inhibition"). Additionally, the rest period following such massed practice is experienced by the organism as positive—or negatively reinforcing to the response performed—thereby further contributing to the behavior's eventual elimination.

Raskin and Klein (1976) suggest that invoking an operant learning paradigm also raises the possibility that massed practice may be effective because extensively performing the behavior involves practicing it "in a whole variety of stimulus settings and under conditions different from those in which [it] was first reinforced or learned." Citing Ullmann and Krasner (1969), these writers argue that "the change in 'stimulus props' makes it thereby unlikely that the response would be spontaneously emitted in the original setting" (p. 549). Still another possible explanation proposed by Raskin and Klein (and one that has been advanced for negative practice as well) is that the procedure forces the individual to attend to the kinesthetic cues preceding the response. Insofar as volition relates to the deliberate processing of external cues, the intensive reexposure to such signals—especially with a set toward attending to them—must almost necessarily foster symptom control.

While it is generally agreed that the clinical application of massed practice still lacks sufficient empirical validation, a number of experiments do exist to support the validity of the reactive inhibition theory of its effectiveness, at least as regards its employment with such motor habits as tics (see Jones, 1960; Lazarus, 1964; Rafi, 1962; Walton, 1964; Yates, 1958). The circumstance that so much of the experimental attention paid to this procedure continues to focus on infrahuman subjects, however, has obviously not helped to facilitate any sound judgment on its therapeutic usefulness.

Stimulus Satiation

"Stimulus satiation" refers to the repeated presentation of a positive stimulus to the point of satiety, in order to lessen or eliminate its abnormally high positive valence. As a method of *response removal*—since the extreme attractiveness of the stimulus motivates a variety of inappropriate behaviors—it is nowhere as common as negative or massed practice. In fact, even though it has been cited many times as a behaviorally oriented paradoxical technique, discussion of its clinical utility with human adults has generally been confined to a single case study published by Ayllon in 1963 (but see also Carroll et al., 1978). This study involved a psychotic patient whose disturbing habit of hoarding towels had characterized her entire nine-year hospitalization. The program instituted to remove this behavior consisted of permitting the patient to keep the towels she had collected *and* handing her additional towels. Although the patient expressed less and less interest in the towels as the number distributed to her rapidly increased (eventually even requesting that the towels brought to her be taken away), the satiation procedure continued until, by the sixth week of the program, her room contained no less than 625 towels (!). At this point the patient, having futilely implored the nurses to "get these dirty towels out of here" (p. 57), began removing them herself. Commenting on the effectiveness of this towel-inundation procedure, Ayllon notes (in line with Hullian drive theory) that a reinforcer loses its positive valence and becomes aversive when an excessive amount of it is administered. Consequently, the response caused by the reinforcer is undermined.

As Rimm and Masters (1979) have observed, stimulus satiation is frequently confounded with negative practice (and, indeed, with massed practice as well), for a particular response on the part of a client may be required to furnish the treatment stimulus. In dealing with difficult smoking behaviors, for instance, clients may need to chain smoke for extended periods of time in order, finally, to break their habit. As has already been suggested, no assured verdict on the value of treating dysfunctional behavior through stimulus satiation is yet possible. Besides the well-known Ayllon experiment, only a modicum of such experimentation (typically involving either children or animals) has been reported, so that additional empirical evidence is needed to adequately assess the technique's usefulness.

Implosion and Flooding

The behavioral techniques of implosion and flooding are not only extremely similar to each other, but closely related also to negative and massed practice and to stimulus satiation. All these strategies, at least when employed therapeutically, focus on the repeated presentation of stimuli to eradicate the problematic responses connected to them. Implosion and flooding differ, however, from the techniques already delineated in repeatedly and systematically evoking anxiety responses—in "frontally assaulting" them so as, eventually, to extinguish them altogether. Both techniques involve exposing individuals to increasingly intense phobic stimuli while preventing their habitual, and ultimately costly, response of avoidance. Such aversively prolonged exposure to the point of spontaneous reduction in the amount of anxiety experienced may be understood summarily in terms of *forced reality testing*. And, as has been pointed out (Baum, 1971), this designation has been used interchangeably with the name "flooding"—which, it might be added, is frequently used as synonymous with the phrase "response prevention." Such redundancies in nomenclature suggest how similar or even identical procedures may, because of certain discrepancies in conceptual emphasis, carry different identifying labels.

Although the terms "implosion" and "flooding" are themselves often employed interchangeably and involve similar procedures and theoretical rationales, they are nonetheless distinguishable. Implosive therapy, as initially conceptualized by Stampfl and Levis (1967, 1968, 1973), involves a set of assumptions derived from psychoanalytic theory; as such it represents a composite of Freudian and behaviorist tenets. To these authors, the individual's preoccupations at various psychosexual stages provide the material for treatment. Since childhood trauma is postulated as the origin of most avoidant responses, therapy is viewed as appropriately focusing on the presentation of visual imagery associated with such typical conflict areas as (to use Hogan's, 1968, description) "fears, rejections, prior humiliations or deprivations, or conflicts related to expression of, or fear of, aggression, sexual problems of various types, and guilt related behavior" (p. 423). The therapeutic device of flooding, on the other hand, does not include these hypotheses, or the Freudian interpretations sometimes utilized in (though hardly essential to) implosive therapy. Also, it is less elaborate and extreme in its imaginary depictions of anxiety-generating stimuli, preferring in fact to use real-life presentations whenever feasible (e.g., exposing snake-phobic individuals to a harmless reptile directly rather than having them picture poisonous snakes crawling around in their stomachs and biting them).

Despite the above differences between implosion and flooding, in actual practice there is frequently very little that differentiates them. Both concentrate on the presentation of dramatically powerful, anxiety-provoking scenes (generally arranged hierarchically) and confront clients with these situations (whether imagined or in vivo) without relaxation or pause, so as to elicit the maximum sustained emotional response possible and thus "exhaust" this response. The two therapeutic devices have been applied to a broad range of phobic behaviors, as well as to such diverse problems as poor impulse control, stress, insomnia, fear of rejection and unassertive behavior, depression, morbid grief, guilt, sexual abnormalities, and aggression.

The paradoxical component in implosion and flooding is generally more difficult to grasp than in the other behavioral methods so far described. Certainly the therapist here cannot be viewed as allowing, siding with, or otherwise encouraging the symptomatic behavior. Regardless of whether the symptom is seen as the client's persistent anxiety or the likewise self-defeating avoidance behavior adopted to keep this anxiety at bay, both the immediate and ultimate work of therapy is to overwhelm, exhaust, and finally obliterate the client's distressing responses to aversive stimuli. In short, the technique actively challenges or *resists* symptoms by obliging clients to work through them directly. What makes this procedure paradoxical, therefore, has to do with its insistence that clients "choose" their involuntary behavior (i.e., anxiety) and, indeed, "practice" it until it becomes, almost literally, worn out. Such overexposure to highly charged stimuli leads, at least theoretically, to an ever-decreasing emotional response, so that self-control is regained through the very process of the individual's agreeing to allow himself to be put *out of* control. It might be noted that Raskin and Klein (1976) distinguish implosion (which they deem paradoxical) from systematic desensitization (which they do not) in that the latter technique involves the client's attending to the situational cues for anxiety but does not permit the client fully to experience this anxiety. To these authors, what makes implosion paradoxical is that rather than helping the client (through relaxation) to avoid being overcome by any heightened anxiety response, it dramatically evokes—or "prescribes"— the most forceful expression of this response.

Lastly, as was emphasized in the Introduction, the question of whether the related techniques of implosion and flooding appear paradoxical *to the client* needs to be addressed. Unfortunately, published reports on these procedures have very little to say about this subject. It is reasonable to assume, however, that clients' expectations for assistance are initially dealt a disconcerting blow when they are informed that the solution to their problem is in being deluged with precisely the dreaded anxiety from which their avoidant behaviors have at least partially protected them. In other words, although the behavior therapist routinely takes pains to explain the rationale for the specific treatment program selected, before such clarification is completed clients can hardly help but experience befuddlement as to whether the proposed cure may not be considerably more painful than the problem itself.

Almost nowhere in behaviorist literature is implosion or flooding explicitly identified as paradoxical, and given the well-established learning principles on which these procedures are based, such a circumstance is not surprising. Because of the psychodynamic assumptions informing the practice of implosion, its theoretical rationale differs slightly from that of flooding. Yet even though it postulates that the avoidance of situations inducing anxiety is typically learned as a child, it accounts for the acquisition of this anxiety by resorting to learning tenets derived from animal experimentation. As Rimm and Masters (1979) have pointed out: "Following the two-factor theory of learning from aversive consequences [implosive theorists propose] that (1) various behaviors, feared situations, or phobic objects are persistently avoided, and that (2) such avoidance behaviors are consistently covertly reinforced by the termination of anxiety each time these behaviors, situations, and objects or people are avoided" (p. 298). To extinguish these reinforced avoidance behaviors, therapeutic procedure must recreate the stimuli or cues to which the anxiety response has become conditioned and stop clients from practicing their habitual avoidance behaviors (if only in imagination)—thereby obliging them to reexperience their original intense anxiety without the recurrence of negative consequences. When this corrective learning condition takes place, such aversive repercussions will no longer be anticipated and the anxiety will disappear. Such is the process of extinction (see, e.g., Stampfl & Levis, 1967) on which both implosion and flooding are theoretically grounded. And it should be clear that what is being extinguished is the conditioned avoidance response that has become symptomatic.

Closely complementary accounts of what occurs during this relearning (or reconditioning) procedure have been suggested by Malleson (1959), who describes the method of maximizing nonreinforced exposure to anxiety-generating stimuli as a "reactive inhibition" technique; and by

Wilson and Davison (1971), who view the process as eradicating the phobic response-sustaining "safety signals" connected with escape or avoidance behaviors. Smith, Dickson, and Sheppard (1973), however, in an exhaustive attempt (75 references) to review flooding/implosion procedures in both animals and humans, express the notion that the explanatory principle of extinction has been used excessively and seriously question its role as the primary agent of change. Considering the possible contributing roles of habituation, toleration, modeling, discrimination, and cognitive rehearsal in the stimulus-flooding process, they finally offer as the most "appealing" explanation (citing Helson, 1964; Hodgson & Rachman, 1970; Smith, 1970) "a contrast effect brought about by a shift in adaptation level" (p. 370). The representation of catastrophic flooding scenes involving a snake, for instance, is seen as producing an upward shift in one's adaptation level, since formerly frightening stimuli relating to snakes become, by contrast, much less frightening. All the same, these authors concede that further experimental justification for this theoretical rationale is needed.

While being similarly tentative about the effectiveness of flooding/implosion procedures in therapy, Smith et al. (1973) conclude that the experimentation in this area warrants the verdict that such devices are capable of significantly reducing both individual reports of fear and avoidant behavior—providing the conditions of stimulus exposure during treatment are appropriate. Other reviewers of this anxiety-inducing process have been more guarded. D'Zurilla, Wilson, and Nelson (1973), for example, deem the evidence for the efficacy of prolonged exposure to irrational fear as overall "inconsistent and inconclusive" (p. 673). Likewise, Morganstern (1973) and Rimm and Masters (1979), after reviewing the empirical studies on implosive therapy, characterize the results of this research as mixed, at times contradictory, and regard the experiments themselves as in general so methodologically inadequate as to be far less than convincing. These authors view studies on flooding procedures as tending to be sounder in design and execution, but point out that much of the experimentation here has involved animals rather than human patients, so that the effectiveness of the technique requires careful interpretation.

In the past few years, however, a substantial number of well-controlled studies have led to a much less reserved evaluation of the therapeutic efficacy of flooding. Moreover, critical reviews of the use of flooding with clinically distressed subjects have generally found it more effective and widely applicable than systematic desensitization (Leitenberg, 1976; Levis & Hare, 1977; Marks, 1978; Marshall, Gauthier, & Gordon, 1979; Rachman & Hodgson, 1980). In their admirably comprehensive handbook, *Flooding and Implosive Therapy* (1983), Boudewyns and Shipley articulate the position that the direct, or "ungraded," therapeutic exposure of flooding and implosive treatments is in most cases "more efficient and effective" than "graded" methods (p. 3). Moreover, citing a report by Barlow and Wolfe (1981), these authors add that at a recent professional conference several prominent behavior therapists and researchers concluded that direct therapeutic exposure was indeed the treatment of choice for phobic and obsessive–compulsive disorders.

In summary, although earlier reviewers of flooding and implosion have tended toward skepticism, more up-to-date evaluations have been predominantly favorable. As Boudewyns and Shipley have observed, this discrepancy probably relates to the circumstance that early reviews were limited largely to animal and human analogue studies of the late 1960s and early 1970s, whereas more recent reviews have been able to take into account outcome studies on actual patient populations. Because analogue studies are heavily influenced by uncontrolled expectancy factors and demand characteristics, later-day reviewers have recognized that such studies cannot legitimately be given much weight in gauging the clinical effectiveness of flooding procedures.

Paradoxical Intention

Viktor Frankl's existentially derived technique of paradoxical intention has attracted an increasing number of behavior, and cognitive-behavior, therapists. It has been reported as successfully employed mostly in cases involving phobias, obsessive–compulsive disorders, and anxiety states— especially those related to insomnia and sexual dysfunction. Defined briefly, paradoxical intention advises clients to experience their symptoms freely, frequently, and to an extreme (ultimately laughable or absurd) degree. In requesting that clients attempt to precipitate the feared event by deliberately practicing behaviors they have assiduously avoided, or *tried* to avoid, the process exposes or "opens them up to" their anxiety directly. As such, the affinities between paradoxical intention and implosion/flooding procedures should be apparent. Ascher (1980), one of several writers making this association, also regards negative practice—involving as it does the repeated practice of an undesired response—as largely a translation of Frankl's device into behaviorist, or learning theory, terms.

Frankl himself (1975) has explicitly related his technique to no less than eight later behavioral variants, which he lists as "flooding," "prolonged exposure," "modeling," "anxiety-provoking," "exposure in vivo," "implosion," "induced anxiety," and "modification of expectations" (p. 232). And elsewhere, Frankl (1960) intimates another tie between his technique and behavioral methods in stating that paradoxical intention is "intrinsically nonspecific" (p. 527), by which is meant that it can be used with a variety of neurotic and psychotic conditions regardless of etiology. In fact, Frankl suggests that symptoms may at times be ameliorated or removed without having to deal with their underlying origins—as would, of course, be necessitated in psychoanalysis or other insight-oriented therapies.

Having outlined some broad similarities between paradoxical intention and other, more orthodox, behavioral change methods, it should be stated that although Frankl appears proud that his technique anticipated the devices of many later behavior therapists, he does feel the need to distinguish his "logotherapeutic" technique from nonexistential procedures growing directly out of learning theory. In one essay (1960) he emphasizes that the crucial element in therapy is less the method employed than the special *relationship* between therapist and client. And later in this same essay he notes that although paradoxical intention treats symptoms directly, its primary concern is not with the symptom but the client's *attitude* toward his condition and its pathological manifestations. Logotherapy, as a general therapeutic orientation rather than a specific method of symptom removal, is based on the universal need to experience life as meaningful. Within this framework, the procedure of paradoxical intention is designed to put individuals in touch with their freedom to choose a course of action and take ethical and spiritual responsibility for it. For the most part, therefore, clients are asked to take the initiative in applying this technique during therapy. Frankl's uneasiness about having his existential procedure adopted by behavioral "conditioning therapists" decidedly *nonexistential* in their thinking and who generally cast the client in a much more passive role is even more apparent in a later essay (1967a), in which he states that "in contrast to behavior therapy . . . logotherapy is not satisfied with reconditioning" (p. 153).

Perhaps Frankl's emphasis on clients' taking command of their symptoms and, by so doing, coming to regard them in a radically different light is best suggested by his often quoted definition of paradoxical intention as a process in which "the patient is encouraged to do, or wish to happen, the very things he fears" (1967a, p. 146). Emboldened to bring on the feared symptom, the patient's typically demoralizing avoidance response is replaced by "intended" behavior affirmative of individual volition. Considering that this treatment plan more or less "prescribes" the presenting complaint, thereby obliging the patient to respond symptomatically—or at least in a manner seemingly at odds with therapeutic goals—the paradoxical nature of Frankl's technique should be easy to grasp. Certainly, evoking, exaggerating, and even accepting one's symptoms would hardly appear the most efficient way of eradicating them. But Frankl and his

followers have frequently claimed dramatically speedy results from employing this ostensibly symptom-supporting procedure. It is a procedure
usually calculated to decrease the frequency of a response through its
immediate increase—and, in this sense, the kinship between paradoxical
intention and the methods of negative and massed practice should be
evident.

Obviously, there are many clients who come to therapy wishing to
enlarge or *augment* a particular behavior. In these cases Frankl resorted to
his second logotherapeutic technique: "dereflection." Here clients complaining of the *infrequency* of a response are ironically counselled to
further inhibit it. Dereflection and paradoxical intention are sometimes
confounded since, in moving toward therapeutic objectives, they both
operate "in reverse." Indeed, though the direction of frequency change is
directly opposite in these two procedures, both techniques are governed by
the same principles of theory and application, and warrant discussion
(given the emphasis in the literature) under the common heading
"paradoxical intention." Ascher's (1980) behavioral review of paradoxical
intention has already taken this position and, for the sake of simplicity, it
seems one worth following here.

Anticipatory Anxiety and Its Therapeutic Antidote

As first enunciated by Frankl and many times reiterated by later proponents of the technique, paradoxical intention is based primarily on the
phenomenon of anticipatory anxiety. As Frankl (1975) explains this
mechanism:

> A given symptom evokes, on the part of the patient, a response in terms of the
> fearful expectation that it might recur; fear, however, always tends to make
> true precisely that which one is afraid of, and by the same token, anticipatory
> anxiety is liable to trigger off what the patient so fearfully expects to happen.
> Thus, a self-sustaining vicious circle is established: A symptom evokes a
> phobia; the phobia provokes the symptom; and the recurrence of the symp-
> tom reinforces the phobia. (p. 226)

The "flight from fear" that typically results from this "fear of fear" is, of
course, what underlies the individual's increasingly frantic avoidance behaviors. And this running away from one's fear represents the beginning of
what Frankl calls the individual's "anxiety neurosis" (p. 227), since phobias are related precisely to this endeavor to avoid or escape the situation
from which anxiety arises.

Designating the neurotic habit of avoidance—or "phobic pattern"—as
the first of three pathogenic types distinguished by logotherapy, Frankl
goes on to describe the second, or "obsessive-compulsive pattern." In these

cases individuals are fearful not of their fear (as, for instance, phobics might be frightened of an anxiety attack's leading to fainting or a stroke), but of *themselves* (since they are afraid, for instance, that their uncontrollable thoughts about death might drive them to suicide, or bring on a psychosis). Whereas these latter individuals futilely battle against their obsessions and compulsions (as compared to phobics, who vainly strive to flee from their fears), the third pathogenic pattern—which Frankl calls the "sexual neurotic" (p. 233)—fights *for* something: namely, sexual fulfillment. But here once again, all the efforts and struggles to solve the problem succeed only in maintaining, or even exacerbating, it.

The viciously circular feedback mechanism that is anticipatory anxiety and which in one way or another informs all three of these dysfunctional behavioral patterns is, as it were, "derailed" by a technique supportively advising clients either to directly confront or surrender to their problematic behavior. By voluntarily "intending" the symptom, pathogenic fear can be circumvented by desire or indifference. And by giving up their fear-inspired resistance toward the symptom, the irresistible force of anticipatory anxiety is finally enfeebled and put to rest. Commenting on the temptation besetting many behavior therapists to prescribe additional self-control techniques when initial attempts at eradicating symptoms have failed, Ascher (1980) observes how such procedures might function directly to maintain client discomfort by inadvertently helping to perpetuate the whole performance anxiety process. To interrupt the cycle that may be "feeding" the symptom, clients need to be induced *not* to try harder but, paradoxically, either to try something diametrically opposed to their former "rational" efforts, or to give up trying completely.

A number of theorists have sought a neurophysiological explanation for the phenomenon of anticipatory anxiety, as well as for its paradoxical antidote—perhaps the earliest of these being logotherapist Hans Gerz (1962, 1966, 1979). Their reasoning is based on what is generally known about the nature of the voluntary and involuntary (or autonomic) nervous systems. Although certain bodily functions are controllable through one's musculature, others are ordinarily not subject to such control—that is, those operations regulated by the autonomic nervous system. This system controls not only such functions as respiration, heartbeat, and digestive processes, but *also* normal emotions (such as love, anger, and fear) and pathological emotions (such as phobias and obsessions). Given that both types of emotional responses are controlled by the autonomic nervous system, they cannot be governed by will or decision (Gerz, 1979). By *intentionally* seeking to produce, or "manufacture," symptoms, this argument goes, patients cannot help but fail, since they lack voluntary control over their involuntary nervous system. Erythrophobics consciously endeavoring to blush, for example, will find themselves unable to do so; and this failure is viewed as enabling such individuals to relinquish their fear associated with uncontrollable blushing. For whenever they reexperience this fear, they need only try to *will* it into manifesting itself (i.e., determining to flush bright crimson) to experience its eventual disappearance.

This tactic of willfully trying to produce the feared symptom usually impresses clients as absurdly incongruous when the therapist first proposes it. And their bemused reaction tends to introduce an element of humor into the therapy, particularly since—if the clinician has followed Frankl's recommendations on "administering" paradoxical intention—the symptom-prescribing suggestion is carefully formulated and delivered in the most humorous manner feasible. Such an injection of humor is designed to help clients detach themselves from their symptoms through the very act of smiling or laughing at them. As Kaczanowski (1967) has observed, it is impossible to laugh spontaneously and feel afraid at the same time.

Once aware of the humor in their previously enslaving problem and able to distance themselves from the symptomatic concerns with which they have come increasingly to identify themselves, clients begin to experience a change of attitude, or new sense of freedom and self-determination. It is this expanded viewpoint toward their dysfunctional condition—which Frankl refers to as nothing less than an "existential reorientation" (1960, p. 530)—that is the key to improved or nonsymptomatic functioning. In fact, to Frankl the effectiveness of his seemingly illogical technique comes directly from the human ability to detach oneself both from the world *and* oneself; and this self-detachment is what allows individuals to regain control over their lives. Consequently, in its facilitating a "lighter," and finally liberating, attitude toward their previously oppressive symptoms, humor is deemed an essential component in the successful application of paradoxical intention. And much more than an important therapeutic ingredient, it is actually an intrinsic part of Frankl's *theoretical account* for the efficacy of the technique.

As Fabry, Bulka, and Sahakian (1979) and Gerz (1979) have suggested, in learning to laugh at and place themselves at a distance from their symptoms, clients are empowered to treat themselves. Since dependence on the therapist for cure ceases to be tenable when that therapist is constantly instructing them to take the initiative for "getting worse," clients are prompted to take responsibility for their destiny by adopting an attitude of indifference or control over the undesired condition that brought them into therapy. When the symptomatic pattern (or vicious circle) is broken, it is clear to clients that *their* resources—not the therapist's—have been the cause. For it has been their own courage and self-trust that has allowed them to grapple directly with their fears and thus realize their inner freedom.

Other Theoretical Explanations of Paradoxical Intention

Alternative theoretical accounts for the effectiveness of paradoxical intention, generally compatible with Frankl's thesis though stressing somewhat different mechanisms of change, have been proposed. Gerz (1962, 1966), whose principal rationales relating to neurophysiology and self-dependence have already been cited, also offers two primarily psychodynamic explanations. He suggests first of all that the therapist's approach to the client's symptom—humorously detached and free of anxiety (though not unconcerned)—is somehow imparted to the client, who thereby comes to adopt the therapist's ego strength (an interpretation that includes a distinct behavioral, or "modeling," component). Secondly, assuming that phobic behavior may represent displaced hostile impulses, Gerz proposes that by instructing clients to carry out precisely that which they fear, the therapist is allowing them symbolically to act out their hostile impulses. In brief, Gerz's speculations cover the theoretical gamut: behavioral (and psychophysiological), humanistic, and psychodynamic.

Richard Rabkin, in *Strategic Psychotherapy* (1977), also reveals something of this eclecticism in theorizing on the effectiveness of paradoxical intention—at one point discussing Freud's idea of "counterwill" as providing a possible explanation. To Freud, a distressing ego-alien idea becomes split off from consciousness, develops its own power, and operates as a *counterwill*, inducing the individual to act out the distressing idea, despite efforts of the conscious will against such expression. Paradoxical intention, as Rabkin conceptualizes it, is capable of fostering a process directly opposed to the counterwill prompting the symptomatic behavior. As he hypothesizes:

> If I am worrying about fainting and my intention to attempt not to faint is causing me to become more faint, then, if I try to faint, the same mechanism, whatever it is, will operate in reverse by preventing me from fainting. (p. 150)

Finally—as the phrase "whatever it is" suggests—Rabkin is less than satisfied with the explanatory supposition of counterwill, since it hinges on what strikes him as clearly an outdated notion of mental faculties. As an alternative to this concept, therefore, he proposes the behavioral (and much more contemporary) idea of "stimulus management," postulating that the phenomenon which Freud called "counterwill" might better be understood as a failure on the part of the individual adequately to handle incoming stimuli. For example, in studying for an examination one's focus must be on the course material, not on the consequences of failure. To the extent that such thoughts of failure (covert stimuli) dominate the individual's mind, the ability to study will be impaired. The humorously devious technique of paradoxical intention is regarded as useful in its helping individuals learn how to keep such unwanted stimuli under control.

Paradoxical intention as a "learning technique" has been stressed by several writers. Lazarus (1971), who describes a procedure he calls "blow-up" but which appears essentially identical to Frankl's technique, hypothesizes that relinquishing the response of avoidance to irrationally phobic stimuli creates the opportunity for such stimuli to become extinguished. Presenting a social learning theory of pathogenic obsession, Sahakian (1969) also speaks of extinction, arguing that paradoxical intention is a process of reversing the pattern of the client's conditioning. And, to give one last example of an attempt to explain Frankl's technique in generally behavioral terms, Solyom, Garza-Perez, Ledwidge, and Solyom (1972), in a pilot study using paradoxical intention to treat obsessive thoughts, conclude that the improvements they observed might be associated with (1) a genuine attitude change induced by the procedure, (2) the gradual extinction of the avoidance response caused by preventing its occurrence, or (3) the process of habituation related to the symptom. These authors circumspectly add: "These possibilities are not mutually exclusive but may describe the same phenomena on different levels of complexity" (p. 296). Somehow this verdict seems related to Rabkin's "whatever it is" and suggests that the ultimate Why of anything intricately human must remain tantalizingly hypothetical, particularly since multidetermination in matters both pathological and therapeutic seems much more reflective of psychological reality than any exclusive "single" interpretation of that reality might be.

Research on Paradoxical Intention

The substantial number of therapists reporting success with paradoxical intention in the past fifteen years has resulted in the technique's increasing popularity. Nonetheless, an examination of the literature reveals that only about half of the studies devoted to it can be regarded as controlled experimental investigations. For a good number of published writings on its effectiveness represent largely anecdotal case descriptions (e.g., Frankl, 1960, 1975; Gerz, 1962; Lamb, 1980; Lamontagne, 1978; Macaruso, 1979; Victor & Krug, 1967). Moreover, many practitioners of the technique do not employ it alone but combine it with drugs or a variety of other change strategies—such as systematic desensitization, implosion, stimulus control, satiation, assertiveness training, modeling, and cognitive restructuring (e.g., Goldstein, 1978; Jacobs, 1972; Nystul & Muszynska, 1976; Saslow, 1971). In short, given the nature of most of the clinical data supporting the utility of paradoxical intention, accurately assessing its value has been, until recently, extremely difficult.

As noted by Ascher (1980), the abundant case studies on the efficacy of paradoxical intention, rather than confirming its usefulness, may actually have succeeded primarily in offering suggestive hypotheses for future experimental inquiry. Had these studies included scrupulously detailed descriptions of the technique's administration, they might also have served as models for its effective implementation. However, reports of therapy based on paradoxical intention typically have *not* adequately described the specificities of the procedure—certainly not as regards its utilization in a behavioral context. Important aspects of its administration have not been mentioned, nor have the steps essential in assuring the *maintenance* of improved functioning. Because paradoxical intention has typically been carried out in a somewhat impromptu, even unpredictable, manner (relating to its humorous, detached character), its use in carefully controlled experiments has been problematic. Still, a number of behaviorally oriented researchers have recently managed to adapt the procedure to accomplish this purpose. The demands necessitated by sound experimental design have led to the administrative deletion of some of the therapy's unpredictable elements but, as Ascher notes (p. 268), the explanation of the method's overall rationale (including the need for self-initiated "homework") has remained generally intact.

Ascher's (1980) lengthy chapter on paradoxical intention represents the most thorough introduction to the procedure in print (including a 26-page case study meticulously detailing the method's actual administration). To Ascher, paradoxical intention can be used within a behaviorist orientation in two ways. It can be turned to when the original treatment regimen has failed, and it can be employed as itself the primary treatment (supplemented by more orthodox behavioral methods). Because the performance anxiety of some clients relates to their inability to change the dysfunctional frequency of their behavior—thereby rendering them incapable of benefiting from a conventional behavioral program— the use of paradoxical intention, by expressly alleviating their anxiety about improvement, may help to reverse this behavior's frequency. As examples of discomforting responses occasionally resistant to treatment because of anxious attempts by clients to control their autonomic nervous system, Ascher lists excessive perspiration or blushing, sleep disturbances, sexual dysfunctions, and psychogenic retention of urine and fecal matter. It should be added that beyond such *unwitting* oppositional responses on the part of basically compliant clients, Ascher is cognizant of the usefulness of paradoxical intention as a defiance-based technique as well. For, as he suggestively remarks, "Clients who appear to be uncooperative, resistive, or rebellious pose a problem for any therapeutic program" (p. 283).

Having, preliminarily, suggested something of the nature and limitations of case histories using paradoxical intention, and also the beginnings of experimentally more sophisticated studies in this area, it remains to review briefly the controlled research now existing on the technique.[*]

One precursor to present-day research on the technique is Gerz's (1966) essentially nonexperimental report of its employment with 51 phobic and obsessive-compulsive patients over a six-year period. Gerz's perspective, or bias, is much more that of a therapist than a researcher, as the first words of his article's title ("Experience with") should indicate. Although all the patients reported on received messages that might well be conceived as paradoxical intention, the technique was used primarily in conjunction with "reconditioning therapy" and as an adjunct to dynamic therapy generally, and drugs were frequently administered. Given this therapeutically complex situation, the meaning of Gerz's impressive claim that about three-fourths of his phobic patients and two-thirds of his obsessive and pseudoneurotic schizophrenic patients recovered, and that almost 90% improved overall, is impossible to evaluate as regards the specific effectiveness of paradoxical intention. Moreover, to complicate matters further, Gerz's study apparently involved no screening procedures, employed no control groups, dealt mostly with patients that had been exposed to prior treatment, did not report the length of treatment for different patients (nor make any attempt to equate the duration of this treatment), and determined recovery/improvement rates by his clinical judgment alone. None of these observations is meant to detract from Gerz's undertaking as a serious, and very possibly successful, therapeutic endeavor, but only to suggest that its value as empirical research must be viewed as nil.

A pilot study reported by Solyom, Garza-Perez, Ledwidge, and Solyom in 1972 represents the first attempt to adapt Frankl's technique to an experimental context. Despite its methodological shortcomings (some of which are freely admitted by the authors), the experiment's design and execution make its results far more interpretable than Gerz's ambitious but unsystematic effort. This study, focusing on ten patients with multiple obsessions, sought to reduce the effect of extraneous variables by having

---

[*]It has, however, not been feasible to make the present review "exhaustive." Published studies omitted from consideration here—almost all of which report very positive results—are those by Ascher (1981b), Bornstein et al. (1981), Lacks et al. (1983), Last, Barlow, and O'Brien (1983), Mavissakalian et al. (1983), Milan and Kolko (1982), and Relinger and Bornstein (1979).

participants serve as their own controls. That is, two different obsessive thoughts judged as approximately equal for each patient in frequency and importance were selected, and paradoxical intention was limited to one of these thoughts—the other serving as a control. The rationale of the procedure was uniformly explained to patients, as was its self-application. Several objective rating scales were included in the pretreatment assessment; and final data collection, unlike Gerz's, was objective. At the conclusion of the six-week treatment period, during which all patients were seen for one hour a week, two patients reported total elimination of the target obsession and three judged it much less frequent—as compared to the control obsession, which in four out of these five cases continued unabated. Three of the patients reported no change, and two others had to be excluded because of their inability to apply the technique. No evidence of symptom substitution was found, nor did new obsessive thoughts replace those that had been eliminated. However, the 50% improvement rate reported was essentially the same as that claimed for other therapeutic methods.

Focusing on the problem of psychogenic urinary retention, Ascher (1979) attempted to apply paradoxical intention to five cases that failed to improve significantly after eight weeks of participation in a more conventional behavioral program emphasizing systematic desensitization. Ascher hypothesized that these clients were resistant to the treatment of choice because of performance anxiety. Thus he sought to counter this anxiety by explaining to them the rationale of paradoxical intention, and then instructing them to enter as often as feasible the fear-provoking bathrooms (typically those in public facilities) and engage in all activities ordinarily associated with urinating. Under no conditions, however, were they actually to urinate. Ascher assumed that when performance anxiety sufficiently decreased—and urgency became sufficiently great—clients would violate his directive. Presenting the results of this study in a table recording these clients' reported discomfort level in weekly intervals— from the time of initial assessment through the eight weeks of their participation in the conventional behavioral program, and then through the additional sessions (ranging from one to six) utilizing paradoxical intention—Ascher was able to show dramatic improvement in *all* clients following the introduction of paradoxical treatment. Follow-up information obtained six months after each client's final session indicated that no clients had experienced a return of previous discomfort levels linked to urinating in public places. Given the various measures Ascher took to keep this study reasonably simple and methodologically sound, it might be concluded that the data presented, though limited as regards the number of cases reported, provides at least preliminary evidence for the efficacy of the technique in cases where other, more straightforward, behavioral techniques have already failed.

Six other research undertakings on paradoxical intention center on its use in treating insomnia. The first, a time-series analysis of the technique's effectiveness by Relinger, Bornstein, and Mungas (1978), involved a 31-year-old housewife solicited for the project through a radio announcement. This respondent had suffered constantly from noncyclical insomnia for 20 years, and her only form of prior treatment was over-the-counter drugs. Dependent measures in this study included eight different sleep dimensions, which the client was instructed to chart daily. Her program involved a three-week baseline period, one week of treatment for a half-hour each day, and a one-month follow-up. Additionally, at 3- and 12-month posttreatment intervals, the client was asked to record sleep data for seven continuous days and forward it to the experimenters. Her paradoxical instructions were to stay awake as long as possible, so as to become more aware of the thoughts and feelings preventing her from falling asleep. To control for the treatment's demand characteristics, counterdemand instructions were regularly administered: namely, that the client was not to expect any improvement till the end of treatment. Following her treatment period, time-series analysis was done on each of the dependent variables to test for treatment effects, and least squares analysis t-tests were then performed to assess changes in the eight different sleep dimensions. Significant improvement was found in five of these dimensions, and a sixth ("number of times awakened during the night") improved significantly one month following treatment. Follow-up analysis revealed that not only did treatment gains persist but, at the end of twelve months, they actually improved. Concluding that this single-subject investigation clearly revealed the efficacy of paradoxical intention applied to insomnia-related behaviors, these authors suggest that future research might well seek (1) to obtain both autonomic arousal measures prior to sleep and any objective changes in sleep patterns, so as to evaluate the active therapeutic agents associated with the paradoxical procedure; and (2) to evaluate the usefulness of this procedure with clients revealing a variety of insomnia symptoms, so as better to measure the technique's range of application.

In a multiple case study, Ascher and Efran (1978) attempted to assess the utility of paradoxical intention within the frame of a behavioral change program for sleep-onset difficulties. The technique was introduced as an adjunct to other behavioral methods—primarily deep muscle relaxation and systematic desensitization—in five cases that had shown unusual resistance to treatment. These five cases represented about 10–15% of the clients seen for sleep disturbances during a four-year period. Following their two-week baseline period and ten-week behavioral program (where "some improvement" was reported, though deemed unsatisfactory by the participants), these five individuals received two weeks of paradoxical intention. Three of these clients were instructed to remain awake as long as possible to experience and report back their thoughts prior to sleep onset, and the remaining two were told to lengthen substantially the number of steps (and hence the duration) of their previous relaxation exercises, even if such extension meant resisting the mounting urge to sleep. Treatment was discontinued after the two-week period for four of the five clients. The fifth client was asked to return to his previous program for three additional weeks to work further on reducing anxiety-provoking thoughts preceding sleep onset, after which his former paradoxical instructions were readministered for a final three-week period. A table presenting the average number of minutes to sleep onset for each week the treatment program was in effect showed a far more rapid reduction in onset latency during the period when paradoxical intention was employed. The fifth client, whose treatment consisted of two extra phases, reverted from an average 6-minute onset latency during phase three to a 28-minute latency during the return to his earlier treatment procedure, and then back to a 7.5-minute latency once paradoxical instructions were reintroduced. The two different rationales provided for the keep-awake directive characterizing phase three for all participants made no discernible difference in the technique's effectiveness. And an informal follow-up one year later indicated that all five clients remained satisfied with their improvement.

An unusually well-controlled experimental study—and the first controlled *group* study—investigating the comparative clinical efficacy of paradoxical intention was undertaken by Turner and Ascher (1979). Of 115 individuals initially responding to a newspaper article, 50 were finally selected for the experiment (25 men and 25 women). These individuals, revealing clinically significant sleep-onset insomnia (i.e., requiring one hour or more to fall asleep at least three nights a week), were randomly assigned to one of five groups: progressive relaxation, stimulus control, paradoxical intention, placebo control, and waiting-list control. After a baseline period of ten days, clients received 30–45 minutes of therapy once weekly for four weeks. Thorough analysis of the data—which included a daily sleep questionnaire, a spouse/roommate reliability check, and instruments for discriminant validation—indicated significant improvement in each of the treatment groups, though no differences between the two control groups, and a significant difference between both control groups and the three treatment groups. The degree of improvement in sleep onset experienced by clients in the treatment groups was judged by them sufficient to render unnecessary any additional therapy. Inasmuch as paradoxical intention did as well in alleviating insomnia as did progressive relaxation or stimulus control—procedures already amply validated as regards their effectiveness with sleep disturbances—this experiment seemed to Turner and Ascher to provide important support for the inclusion of this technique in the group of effective behavioral (as contrasted to medical) treatments for insomnia. Two cautionary notes, however, are in order. First of all, as the authors themselves hypothesize, it is possible that the random assignment of clients to groups might have resulted in a mismatch between specific sleep problems and treatments. (The possibility of such a fortuitous circumstance should remind us of the extreme difficulty of contriving *any* experiment that might, "once and for all," globally demonstrate the efficacy of a therapeutic technique.) And, much more important, a follow-up investigation of this study, reported by Turner and DiTomasso (1980), found significant differences between progressive relaxation and stimulus control versus paradoxical intention, the last group failing to maintain the improvement earlier shown.

Since before this discouraging follow-up was completed, the Turner and Ascher experiment represented the most elaborate—and convincing—empirical evidence for the clinical effectiveness of paradoxical intention to date, Ascher and Turner (1979) attempted a partial replication of it. This undertaking, on the whole extremely similar to these two researchers' previous experiment in design, outcome measures, and procedure (including the use of two control groups), was limited to only a single treatment group: paradoxical intention. Twenty-five clients, whose mean latency to sleep onset was 65 minutes and whose complaints had endured for an average of eight years, participated in the study. Results indicated significant improvement on the part of clients randomly assigned to the paradoxical intention group on three of the four sleep-related behaviors measured, but no change in either of the two control groups. Thus this experiment successfully replicated treatment effects found in these two investigators' earlier controlled group experiment. However, the fact that no follow-up data on this undertaking was provided precludes any final assessment of its results.

Ascher and Turner (1980), in yet another experiment using paradoxical intention to treat insomnia, compared two methods of administering this technique. Again, very similar in overall design and execution to these authors' two earlier collaborations, this experiment consisted of 40 insomniacs, with a mean sleep onset latency of 70 minutes and a mean problem duration period of nine years. Since experimental work on the treatment of insomnia through paradoxical intention employed one of two varying sets of instructions, Ascher and Turner determined in this study to investigate possible differences in the effectiveness of these two procedures. Studies randomly assigning clients to treatment groups (i.e., these authors' prior experiments on insomnia) have offered clients a straightforward rationale for the use of this technique based on the popular hypothesis that voluntary attempts to control an involuntary system engender anticipatory, or performance, anxiety—a viciously spiraling process which succeeds only in exacerbating the problem. In contrast, controlled case studies have employed a reframing procedure conveying the need for this paradoxical device in a way most appropriate to the understanding of the particular individual. This latter explanatory method—which in this experiment consisted of telling clients that anxiety-provoking thoughts were disturbing their sleep and that they needed to try to stay awake as long as possible to become more cognizant of them (so that they might later be treated in a systematic desensitization program)—was designated type B administration. The former performance-anxiety rationale for keeping awake constituted the type A method. In both groups, though the rationale for using paradoxical intention differed, instructions were to lie in bed under conditions natural for sleep onset and maintenance. The 40 participants were randomly assigned to these two treatment groups, and to the two control groups (placebo and waiting list). Final analysis of the results indicated that the type A procedure was superior to the no-treatment control on all five variables measured, and to both the type B and placebo control methods on three of these variables (including reduction of sleep-onset latency).

Ascher and Turner attempt to explain these results by pointing out that the strategy of reframing is typically employed to enhance the cooperation of resistant clients by altering their viewpoint toward their problem so as to facilitate the possibility of change. The general ineffectiveness of reframing in this experiment is therefore considered as quite possibly related to its not being well suited to the individuals in the group. Moreover, the probable compliance of most of these individuals could itself have undermined their treatment, since they were told they needed to keep themselves from falling asleep in order to collect the data on which future treatment in systematic desensitization depended. The authors consequently conclude that the results of their study should *not* be taken as implying the superiority of type A administration over type B. Instead, the choice of administration should be decided on the basis of setting and the client's individual needs. What their experiment does suggest is that reframing is not an effective method when identical instructions must be given to a randomized group of individuals.

The latest collaboration of these two researchers (Turner & Ascher,

1982) is quasi-experimental in design, comparing new treatment data with data previously collected. The investigation sought to replicate the earlier experiment of Turner and Ascher (1979), which compared progressive relaxation, stimulus control, and paradoxical intention in the treatment of insomnia. Several methodological features are seen as restricting the external validity of this study, the most important being that a single therapist conducted all treatment sessions. The authors perceive this circumstance as introducing the possibility that the outcome of their study may have been determined by differential therapist expectancies, even though several experiments on progressive relaxation and stimulus control procedures have failed to demonstrate this effect. Consequently, their replication used several clinicians-in-training as therapists. Results indicated that paradoxical intention did not lead to therapeutic change; on the other hand, progressive relaxation and stimulus control were again shown to be effective. Additionally, a significant therapist effect was indeed found, which the authors regard as quite possibly related to the level of experience and expertise of the therapists employed. As regards the ineffectiveness of paradoxical intention, two explanations are offered. First, clients randomly assigned to this treatment group were significantly less disturbed than the other clients and might have failed to exhibit change in such short-term (four-week) treatment because of a high floor effect. Second (as already suggested in Ascher and Turner's earlier papers), random assignment of clients to experimental conditions might have led to a mismatch between individual clients and treatment programs. Finally, the experimental analogue of paradoxical intention utilized in this study and presented uniformly to clients—which the authors concede was a "pale shadow" (p. 40) of the method as described by Frankl—could hardly be expected to lead to substantial improvement in a group of insomniac clients not presenting with a high level of disturbance.

"Instructed Helplessness": A Postscript on Behavioral Paradox

In an intriguing article entitled "Learned Helplessness and Learned Restlessness," Dale Fogle (1978) considers whether the popular learned-helplessness model may not have become overgeneralized. He argues that coping responses to threat involving escape, avoidance, or other control methods are not always the most adaptive behaviors. In fact, as has already been suggested here, such unwanted conditions as insomnia, stuttering, and some sexual difficulties are frequently maintained or aggravated by the individual's anxious attempts to deal with them directly. As opposed to learned-helpless animals, who because of past experience resist finding out that a coping response is now available, chronically anxious, unrelenting avoiders fail to learn that their inflexibly evasive behaviors may no longer be necessary. And hence the half-facetious term, "learned restlessness."

Ineffective coping responses in humans are seen by Fogle as having an experimental analogue in the stubborn persistence of punished escape/ avoidance behaviors in laboratory studies on vicious-circle learning. These studies, almost diametrically opposed to the learned-helplessness model, show how animals who have discovered the proper response to escape or avoid shock cling "superstitiously" to this response long after experimental contingencies have changed and their previously effective coping behavior now regularly precipitates the feared shock. In such cases, where instrumentally effective coping responses may not be available, learned helplessness may indeed be seen as an adaptive reaction: that is, what cannot be controlled externally is better disregarded, left alone, or endured.

To Fogle, effectively treating "learned restlessness" demands a paradoxical strategy emphasizing response prevention, or "instructed helplessness," that influences clients to renounce their escape/avoidance efforts and either risk, or simply accept, the previously dreaded consequences. This "giving up" approach—expressly designed to undo the symptomatic complications of clients' "trying-too-hard" syndrome—is seen as related to Frankl's technique of dereflection, which determinedly seeks to refocus attention away from clients' counterproductive problem-solving attempts. It is also viewed as similar to Masters and Johnson's sensate focus exercises, which are calculated to prompt sexually dissatisfied couples to relinquish self-defeating efforts to accomplish through sheer force of will the orgasmic success which eludes them, and to focus instead on other components of sexual pleasure. As Fogle accurately notes, such a passive orientation of total resignation or surrender is far less frequent in paradoxical interventions than are other, more confrontive, paradoxical approaches—such as negative practice, paradoxical intention, implosion, and flooding. These change strategies, despite differing theoretical rationales, all have in common their actively encouraging clients, whether imaginally or in vivo, to encounter or produce the feared event. Yet it may be possible that the "active ingredient" in such methods is simply in their inducing clients to abandon their avoidance efforts. If this be the case, then mere giving-up tactics could conceivably prove as efficacious with some problems as symptom-prescribing, or "trying-the-opposite," approaches. For the voluntary decision to relinquish all deliberate avoidance attempts and simply allow the feared event to occur might itself foster a more benign perception of that event. In support of this viewpoint, Fogle cites two experimental confirmations that a negative stimulus is perceived as less aversive when voluntarily tolerated than when voluntarily terminated—adding that direct experience of the previously avoided event (if in fact it takes place) may further disconfirm the calamitous expectations associated with it. More-over, in the endeavor to furnish some empirical support for his "giving up" hypothesis, Fogle has recently published the findings of a controlled experiment on insomnia which, indeed, does just that (Fogle & Dyal, 1983).

Perhaps it is suggestive of the Western mentality that techniques advocating an active approach to problem-solving should have almost completely overshadowed an orientation counselling the capitulation to problems precisely so that they might be fully experienced, and thereby change their dimensions—or become dimensionless and disappear altogether. Fogle himself, realizing that his provocative discussion has very likely raised more questions about the appropriate administration of instructed helplessness than it has answered, is led to conclude: "One thing is clear: Any therapeutic application of instructed helplessness as an antidote for learned restlessness will have a paradoxical appearance, whatever specific form it takes" (pp. 45–46). And these words return us directly to *all* the techniques so far described. For whether clients are told to enact their undesired behaviors, "get into" their anxieties, or embrace their helplessness, it is obvious that these strategies do not readily pacify troubled individuals or cater to the almost universal human need for succor and support.

CHAPTER 4

Gestalt Therapy

Today, within the realm of humanistic-existential psychotherapies, gestalt therapy is probably the most prominent. It is similar to other "third force" therapies in its strong conceptual emphasis on self-fulfillment and the development of authenticity and self-responsibility. These and other growth-related characteristics serve to define it as an entity separate and distinct from other schools of therapy. Nonetheless, it bears significant (though not commonly acknowledged) resemblances both to psychodynamic and, to a somewhat lesser extent, behavioral models.

AFFINITIES BETWEEN THE GESTALT AND PSYCHODYNAMIC APPROACH

Fritz Perls, the spiritual grandfather of gestalt therapy, may be one of the most vocal defectors from Freud's theoretical camp, but the psychoanalytic origins of many of his basic assumptions about humanity and the etiology of personal dysfunctions are—despite the pronounced humanism of his orientation—fairly evident. Perls' focus on developing self-awareness and his notion that such awareness plays a critical role in stimulating one's personal evolution, recalls Freud's prevailing concern with helping patients acquire insight into the primal cause of their neurotic behaviors so that they might be liberated from them. Perls' realization that for clients to attain new levels of insight their resistances needed to be meticulously examined and actively dealt with likewise reflects Freud's earlier appreciation of resistances and the devious ways they functioned to obstruct treatment. Dublin (in E. W. L. Smith, 1976) speaks of Perls' borrowing from, but ultimately revising (or even transforming), such Freudian concepts as anxiety, the ego, oralism, introjection, and projection. And, indeed, it is difficult to read the works of Perls without being struck by how the humanistic (at times, phenomenological) language of gestalt therapy somehow manages to accommodate, or subsume, the much more biological and deterministic vocabulary of psychoanalysis.

The gestalt approach warrants particular comparison with paradigmatic therapy, which amends or "modernizes" psychoanalysis in ways that obscure some of the chief differences between psychodynamic and gestalt practices. In paradigmatic therapy practitioners avoid interpretation in much the same manner as do gestalt therapists, preferring to cultivate self-insight through tactics having a dramatic immediacy not typical of traditional analysis, where the client's role in the face of intellectualized interpretation is generally more passive. Although paradigmatic therapists, in contrast to their gestalt counterparts, may finally be more interested in having clients explore *why* they act as they do and less concerned with clients' discovering the more concrete *how* of their behavior, they resemble gestalt therapists in the attention they pay to the here-and-now interpersonal tensions of therapy—and the rich opportunities these situations present to "surprise" clients into an emotional/intellectual awareness till then resisted. For as past conflicts and circumstances are instantaneously "recreated" in the present, clients may develop productive insights into their self-defeating behavioral patterns.

AFFINITIES BETWEEN THE GESTALT AND BEHAVIORIST APPROACH

The somewhat mechanistic underpinnings of traditional (or precognitive) behavior therapy would seem far less comparable to gestalt ideas and practices; and clearly major differences do separate the two therapeutic perspectives. All the same, several concepts and procedures in gestalt therapy are suggestive of basic operations in behavior therapy. For instance, the two approaches are similar in the comparatively little attention they give to the client's past history and their marked emphasis on present behaviors and experiences. Gestalt therapy may have little interest in quantifying a client's current, observable behaviors, but its pervasive focus on the here and now reflects the behaviorist's abiding concern with concrete, present-day specificities in the client's life.

The well-known behaviorist technique of systematic desensitization, in its taking phobic situations in the client's life and endeavoring directly to reproduce their affect through appropriate imagery, also may be compared to gestalt methods that strive to have clients confront their irrational fears and, through allowing them full and spontaneous expression, to resolve or "transcend" them. As will later be discussed in more detail, the common gestalt technique of encouraging clients to "stay with" (or even exaggerate) anxiety-producing thoughts and feelings fits well within a paradoxical frame—and bears resemblance not only to systematic desensitization but to the more intensive behaviorist techniques of implosion and flooding. Both approaches regard the client's self-hindering avoidance behaviors as the target for intervention, and seek to "decondition" phobic reactions through prompting clients freely to "relive" and "experience out" the phobia as it is intentionally evoked by subjective imagery. Doubtless it is clumsy to describe the commonalities in gestalt and behaviorist orientations in a language that combines both perspectives. But despite the obvious incongruities of using such a hybrid vocabulary, the positive relationships between these two philosophically divergent (if not exactly diametrically opposed) viewpoints should be apparent.

Broad similarities between the gestalt approach and other therapeutic methods and disciplines have been pointed out with some regularity. Indeed, the literature on gestalt therapy contains many efforts to link it conceptually to a miscellany of change procedures routinely viewed as independent from it. To offer just a brief sampling of these attempts: Scanlon (1980) reflects on ways that gestalt procedures can be employed within a psychodynamic model; Close (1970) portrays gestalt's "gross exaggeration" techniques in terms of the double-bind theory of schizophrenia closely tied to the communication-systems approach to therapy; Levitsky (1976) explains how gestalt methods may be integrated with and utilized within a hypnotic context; and Greaves (in E. W. L. Smith, 1976) expands on the spiritual and technical affinities between gestalt therapy, Tantric Buddhism, and Zen.

The reason that this section concentrates on paradoxical strategies specifically in gestalt therapy (as opposed to, say, Rogers' client-centered therapy) is that, among all the related humanistic psychotherapies, gestalt concepts are probably the most fully delineated and their corresponding techniques the most vividly illustrated. If this section is briefer than those expounding paradoxical elements within other major therapeutic orientations, it is because the literature on gestalt therapy is much less abundant and its particular use of paradoxical techniques limited essentially to a single paradoxical intervention, even though this intervention comes in several forms and gradations and is identified by a variety of different (though almost synonymous) phrases. Since gestalt therapists have tended to eschew the whole notion of paradox in describing this technique (because of the implications of manipulativeness this term unfortunately has come to carry), only a small fraction of the literature explicitly links gestalt method to paradoxical practices in psychotherapy.

GESTALT THERAPY AND THE DIALECTICAL THEORY OF CHANGE

To the extent that writers on gestalt therapy refer to paradox at all, they do so primarily in discussions of the dialectical principles underlying gestalt tenets. And these discussions strongly suggest that the theory behind the actual practice of gestalt therapy is steeped in paradox. In a short but seminal essay entitled "The Paradoxical Theory of Change," Beisser (1970) articulates the dialectical premises of gestalt therapy; and several later essays have alluded to the usefulness of Beisser's succinct explication of gestalt procedures in paradoxical terms (e.g., Latner, 1974; Levitsky, 1976; Scanlon, 1980; Weeks, 1977).

To Beisser:

> *Change occurs when one becomes what he is, not when he tries to become what he is not.* Change does not take place through a coercive attempt by the individual or by another person [i.e., the therapist] to change him, but it does take place if one takes the time and effort to be what he is—to be fully invested in his current positions. . . . The premise is that one must stand in one place in order to have firm footing to move and that it is difficult or impossible to move without that footing. (p. 77)

As Beisser observes, although Perls did not express his change theory in quite this way, the paradoxical foundation of many of his ideas and practices are easily inferred. The wisdom of the French expression "*plus ça change . . .*" (or here, "the more one changes, the more one stays the same") has its paradoxical corollary in Perls' implicit notion that the more one stays the same, the more one is *then* able to change. Change is grounded in precisely that acceptance of self which has previously been resisted; and only through such acceptance can the internal energy making self-evolution possible be unleashed. The paradox of this theory of change—or better, growth—is at least partially resolved when it is realized that acceptance of one's "sameness" represents a radically different *attitude* toward the self, which provides the necessary impetus for self-transcendence.

To portray this situation using yet another paradox, one cannot begin the difficult (and basically infinite) journey of *becoming* until one fully *is*. And such in essence is the humanistic doctrine of "self-actualization," perceived idealistically by its exponents as a never-ending process of personal revelation and unfolding. The stimulus for this process of psychological and spiritual evolution is self-awareness, an awareness that can be developed only through focusing unflinchingly on the Now of one's existence. Perls' emphasis on facilitating the client's getting more fully in touch with present, moment-to-moment realities is a consequence of his enduring belief that change stems from just such a commitment to "stay with" one's thoughts and feelings, and thereby discover the inmost truth of one's being. Transcending the limiting circumstances of one's life is viewed as viable only after one has emotionally understood—or "become"—the different facets of one's self which serve to create these circumstances in the first place.

Perls (1971) has written that "any intention toward change will achieve the opposite" (p. 18). Given this reasoning, therapists who seek directly to be helpful are actually setting into motion client resistances to being helped. Perls' dialectical notion that one force inevitably creates a counterforce explains his unwillingness to advise clients straightforwardly to alter their behavior. Rather, he encouraged clients to become *more* of what they were—so as, ultimately, to foster the emergence of *their own* counterforce. Regarding clients (and people generally) as containing within them an endless number of polarities, he sought to evoke change obliquely, by making individuals more aware of impulses they already had but which had not yet been recognized and expressed to the point whereby the antithetical, and potentially liberating, impulses might also be generated.

As a humanistic—and holistic—psychotherapy, gestalt procedures are concerned with *both* poles of a client's personality and seek through their very inclusiveness to prompt clients to push beyond the incessant "shoulds" that thwart their full functioning. Committed to assisting individuals to express self-forbidden thoughts and feelings (regardless of their immediate unpleasantness), gestalt interventions are explicitly designed to maximize the client's opportunities to become more fully, more creatively, human. Accepting and expressing both poles of one's personality is in fact viewed as a key prerequisite to achieving the gestalt ideal of being "centered."

GESTALT THERAPY AND EASTERN THOUGHT

Most of the above ideas can be seen as remarkably similar to those espoused centuries earlier in Eastern philosophy. In particular, the many paradoxes inherent in gestalt theory and practice have Eastern antecedents difficult to ignore in any extensive examination of therapeutic paradox. Smith (1976) refers to Perls' notion that humans can transcend themselves only through realizing their true nature. They cannot deliberately decide what to be and make themselves over to fit their preconceived image, for such efforts only lead to the loss of self. As in Eastern thought, especially in Taoism and Zen, the single way toward fulfillment is through coming to understand one's nature and permitting that nature to flow forth unimpeded, to simply "be." Paradoxically, humans can move beyond themselves only by remaining steadfastly what and where they are in the present. Growth is the outcome not of efforts to change but of allowing oneself to be more completely and knowingly what one already is.

In an essay called "Gestalt Therapy, Tantric Buddhism, and the Way of Zen," Greaves (in E. W. L. Smith, 1976) outlines a wide variety of commonalities shared by these approaches to human evolution. At least two of these points of kinship have paradoxical ramifications that have already been discussed: (1) the endeavor to resolve polar opposites and conflicts through the integrative process of centering, and (2) the acceptance of (or immersion into) experiences rather than the detached, intellectualized analysis of them. Smith (1976), commenting on a key similarity between the gestalt therapist's and Zen master's approach, observes that both change agents are acutely aware that growth emerges from frustration and that merely telling individuals about reality cannot substitute for firsthand life experiences. As a consequence of this skepticism toward straightforwardly cognitive or didactic orientations, both gestalt therapist and Zen master adopt cruel-to-be-kind teaching devices. They strive to facilitate growth by *rejecting* the role of "changer" and responding negatively to all requests and manipulations to get them to do the student's, or client's, own thinking, feeling, or acting. Despite all the individual's frustrations and despite the many entreaties for help, they throw the individual time and again back upon his own resources, realizing that there are no convenient shortcuts for the kind of essential, self-liberating knowledge their subjects impatiently crave.

PARADOX IN GESTALT PROCEDURE: CHANGE THROUGH BEING MORE OF THE SAME

From what has now been said about the paradoxical base of several gestalt tenets, the correspondingly paradoxical nature of one of gestalt therapy's main techniques should be almost axiomatic. This technique goes by a variety of closely linked descriptive phrases. But whether it is characterized as identifying with, or "becoming," what one has previously denied; accepting, or "staying with," one's unwanted thoughts or feelings; or purposely accentuating or exaggerating elements of self previously held in check, it always involves the individual's actively confronting in himself that which has been resisted. The "objects" of one's avoidance—feared because associated in the mind with unpleasantness or catastrophe—become, paradoxically, objects to embrace, to take to one's self as though they were not cast off but, indeed, coveted.

Identifying with, or "Becoming," Dissociated Parts of the Self

Beisser (1970) underscores the gestalt therapist's renunciation of the traditional "changer" role by noting the practice of "encouraging the patient to enter and become whatever he is experiencing at the moment"—governed by the belief that (as Proust long ago put it) "'to heal a suffering one must experience it to the full'" (p. 78). Such "healing," typically regarded as a process of self-integration, may require the client to undertake a number of experiments without personal precedent. For example, in cases where the individual appears defensively to have fragmented his self into separate, mutually alienated parts, the therapist may request that these parts begin openly to communicate with one another—the assumption being that once the client can allow himself to identify with fragments of self till then resisted, the self may become reintegrated and the individual's full functioning restored.

Dealing concretely with disowned parts of the self is made tenable by the therapeutic contrivance of having the individual "act out" these parts. By imaginatively dramatizing the implicit, what has been hidden and covert may become explicit and "real." By having the client dialogue with split-off parts of the self—which, conceptually, can be understood as "prescribing" the symptom of self-alienation—the client's internal disunity, or self-dissociation, may be *reassociated* and a harmonious integration of the self (or new "whole") become possible. As Beisser (1970) paradoxically describes the results of this reconciliation procedure: "By being what one is—fully—one can become something else" (p. 78). Or, to rephrase this belief somewhat more accurately (since one cannot actually become other than what he is), to evolve as a human being, one must first "reclaim" the dissociated parts of himself. Therapeutic cure isn't really in becoming different as such but in regaining the birthright of one's mental/emotional health. Thus the ideal of being centered in gestalt therapy is best understood as recovering one's true psychological balance or equilibrium, and by so doing getting in touch with one's natural control and competence as a human being.

In Stevens' *Awareness* (1973), there is an experiment or exercise called "Symptom Dialogue" (pp. 92–93), which instructs participants to explore troubling symptoms openly. Individuals are requested particularly to attend to feelings of pain and tension, to try to accept any discomfort which they may feel and allow it fully into awareness, to see whether they can increase their symptom, and finally to *become* the symptom and—as symptom—initiate a creative verbal interchange with the person they are, in a sense, serving. Such candid dialoguing is implicitly viewed as helping to alleviate the accumulated anxiety and stress associated with the habit of denial. It is also regarded as facilitating the long-term stability achievable only through expressing, experiencing out, and ultimately reconciling, the deep personal conflicts that have caused one's psychological fragmentation in the first place.

Accepting, or "Staying with," the Symptom or Unwanted Experience

In Perls, Hefferline, and Goodman's *Gestalt Therapy: Excitement and Growth in the Human Personality* (1951)—which might well be regarded as the earliest "text" delineating this humanistic approach to change—the authors enunciate the rationale behind exercises that propose to permit the symptom its say in order to integrate it with the self (and thereby render it superfluous). In their own words:

> The notion of accepting the symptom—precisely what you feel you want to be rid of—always sounds preposterous. . . . You may ask, "If I have a symptom that is painful or some characteristic that is undesirable, should I not try to get rid of it?" The answer is, "Certainly!" . . . [But] the direct means of condemning the symptom, of regarding it as something which has been imposed upon you, of appealing to others for help in making it disappear, will not work. The only way that will work is an indirect one: become vividly aware of the symptom, accept both sides of the conflict as *you*—this means to re-identify yourself with parts of your personality from which you have dis-identified yourself—and then discover means by which both sides of the conflict, perhaps in modified form, can be expressed and satisfied. . . . You must, where necessary, learn to face pain and to suffer, in order to destroy and assimilate the pathological material contained in the symptom. (p. 166)

Besides clarifying the general purpose of *most* gestalt techniques, this quotation suggests the paradoxical kinship between such a tactic of "prescribing the acceptance of a symptom" and the behaviorist, "symptom-immersion" devices of implosion and flooding. All these procedures seek to enable clients to neutralize their symptoms through a sort of active incorporation of them, rather than the passive deference to them which has typified their former avoidance behavior. Transcending what has been feared through accepting the fear and granting it total expression is in the end synonymous with Perls' frequently repeated insistence on the need not to resist—or "interrupt"—one's experience but to let it flow unobstructed, so that space might be created for a *new* experience and the individual evolve as nature dictated.

Levitsky and Perls (1970) discuss the gestalt directive to "stay with" one's unpleasant feeling, mood, or state of mind as a way of confronting the neurotic's habitual attempts to flee from such emotional or mental discomfort. The phobic avoidance pattern seen as crucial in maintaining neurotic behavior is challenged by the instruction to stay with the feared experience until the anxiety associated with it begins to dissipate. To Levitsky and Perls, individuals successfully encouraged to assimilate dimensions of their life till then "unpleasant to the taste, difficult to swallow, and impossible to digest" (p. 149), are able to increase their self-confidence and greatly expand their capacity for self-governance and effective coping with the daily frustrations of life.

The imaginative acting out of incompleted behaviors in therapy sessions—one of the trademarks of gestalt practice—relates directly to Perls' (1976) notion that until individuals achieve full awareness of the meaning of their actions, they are compelled endlessly to repeat them. Such repetitions constitute their "unfinished business." These repetitions cannot lead to any final solution because they are regularly accompanied by interruptions—the going so far and no farther that keeps these individuals psychologically stuck. Therapy, consequently, is devoted to helping such persons discover the moment at which they interrupt the natural flow of their experience. The ultimate hindrance to productive self-realization is, to Perls, personal confusion; and Perls therefore sees the struggle against neurosis as being won only when clients are first assisted in developing awareness of, tolerating, and most of all, *staying with* this confusion. However unpleasant the feeling may be, permitting it to exist and getting into it is judged far safer than interrupting it and thereby prompting its spontaneous manifestation through inappropriate behavior. Similar to other feelings, confusion, if left to "flow" freely, will not last indefinitely but eventually be transformed into a more positive emotion capable of fostering suitable action.

Perls' recommendation to stay with one's internal fog in order to dispel it is perhaps most vividly—and paradoxically—portrayed in what he describes as the final step in dealing with one's confusion: the "withdrawal into the fertile void" (1976, p. 100). Such withdrawal, ironically, is made possible through one's becoming able to focus on the avoidance techniques which routinely interrupt it. Experiencing the void—which is tantamount to "participating" in one's confusion to the utmost—promotes in turn an "aha" experience yielding an insight, realization, or solution to problems not previously available. Perls compares this creative process of self-revelation to a state resembling a trance, or "hypnogogic hallucination"—even to a "schizophrenic experience in miniature"—but argues that those who find the confidence to enter this void return more sane than when they first undertook this intense inward journey. The potentially self-purifying aspects of Perls' "void" is suggested by his description of it as serving to cultivate an awareness far transcending any intellectualization (which in fact can only interrupt this process). For Perls, it is in the fertile void that "confusion is transformed into clarity, emergency into continuity, [and] interpreting into experiencing" (p. 101). Moreover, this experimental retreat indirectly aids the individual in achieving the foremost therapeutic goal of self-support, since returning from it more intact than before furnishes potent evidence of the individual's inner resources.

Cohn (1970) sees the personal blankness or confusion that occurs in gestalt therapy as resulting from the therapist's careful separation of the client's presenting conflicts into dualities and the subsequent instruction that these dualities be enacted in a series of dialogues. The ultimate *impasse* deriving from the expression of internal impulses which pull the individual in opposite directions is experienced, phenomenologically, as confusion; and once the client can adequately assimilate this confounding experience, the way is paved for essential organismic change. It might be added that before such an experience can become digested and thus self-nourishing, the individual must allow himself to give up all efforts at control.

The stubborn attempt to control by self-interruption or avoidance that which is feared has, of course, characterized the individual's response pattern all along and kept him from developing any sense of his native ability to confront reality openly. As Becvar (1978)—describing the gestalt procedure of having the individual immerse himself in feelings that parental injunctions and one's own protective psychology have repressed—is led to conclude: "By losing control, a person survives and ultimately thrives in a new self-acceptance, in acceptance of others, and derives a new set of rules for being in control" (p. 38). Such a conclusion is remarkably similar to Kopp's (1976) delineation of the "pilgrimage" of psychotherapy clients in general. Kopp, deeply influenced by his reading of Eastern philosophers, emphasizes the need for the client to unrestrainedly give in to himself if he is ever to become wholly liberated from the prison he has himself constructed. As he paradoxically conceptualizes it: "You cannot get out of a trap unless you first get into it. Overcoming by yielding is the only escape" (p. 64). The solution, then, for feeling stuck and confused is to *stay* stuck and confused—indeed, become *more* so—for only through such unfettered experiencing of one's blurred reality will that alienated part of one's self causing the internal fog be reclaimed and one's life at last become translucent.

Accentuating or Exaggerating Submerged Elements of the Self

Penetrating one's interior mist by first becoming engulfed in it vividly suggests the paradoxical logic informing the general gestalt directive not to fight an unpleasant experience but to surrender to it, precisely so that one may not forever be enslaved by it. Accepting one's experience is taken even a step further in the closely related gestalt technique of having clients accentuate, or exaggerate, what they would like to be rid of altogether. Referring specifically to physical tensions, Zinker (1978) speaks of his encouraging clients "to flow with the resistance, to lean into it [and] exaggerate it" (p. 26), observing that such exaggeration of tautness typically results in a loosening of the musculature that enables a fuller, more positive expression of movement. As Polster and Polster (1973) explicate the basic principle behind the familiar gestalt practice of overemphasis or amplification: "Any focus which highlights what is already happening provides a foundation for change" (p. 163). Zinker himself explains the rationale of such intensification procedures with picturesque precision in his comment that "if you keep flying north long enough, you'll eventually be heading south" (p. 202).

If gestalt therapists attend so much to unhealthy polarities within an individual, it is because of their conviction that helping a person get better in touch with one of these poles and then magnify it actually prompts this person to bring into focus the complementary, though submerged, opposite pole of his personality. Through dramatically heightening the characterological imbalance, reintegration—or "self-centering"—can occur spontaneously, as the individual softens and assimilates the no-longer-antagonistic extremes of his personality. Exaggeration can also be fruitfully employed to enable an individual to move beyond expression-inhibiting incongruities in his self-presentation. Zinker (1978), for example, describes how clients may render a tale of misfortune while wearing a frozen smile totally discrepant to it. Assuming that this conflicting message reflects a similar internal confusion or block, he has such clients exaggerate their contradictory behavior to the point that hysterical laughter may dissolve into authentic weeping and the individual become aware of feelings till then repressed. Clearly implied here is the idea that only through fully expressing feelings which have been denied because of fears they would be overwhelming can clients begin to experience some relief from self-inflicted tensions.

EMPIRICAL RESEARCH ON PARADOX IN GESTALT THERAPY

As with the paradoxical techniques in psychodynamic treatment, the symptom-accepting and -exaggerating procedures of gestalt therapy have not yet been subject to any meaningful empirical examination. Although in recent years preliminary research efforts to explore the effectiveness of certain gestalt methods have been initiated (particularly within a counseling context), at present no studies exist which concentrate specifically on the paradoxical strategies delineated here. As Fagan and Shepherd (1970) have pointedly remarked: "While the Gestalt therapist attempts personally and in his work with his patients to be open to experimentation in the true sense of the word, in the more scientific sense this is still to be accomplished" (p. 241). Despite the obvious difficulties of such a task—including all the measurement-defying subtleties of therapeutic procedure and interaction—the potential importance of such research should be obvious. And despite the *personal* confirmation experienced by gestalt therapists using the paradoxical interventions described here, the *scientific* confirmation that can come only through accepting the hard challenge of rigorous experimental scrutiny still remains to be undertaken.

CHAPTER 5

The Systems Approach—
Theory and Therapy

SYSTEMS THEORY AS APPLIED TO THERAPY

Sluzki (1978) has spoken of the systems orientation to therapy as constituting "a major epistemological shift in the behavioral sciences" (p. 392).
Although the paradoxical techniques deriving from this theoretical stance
may, in the end, bear fairly close comparison to therapeutic methods already discussed, this approach (as Sluzki observes) involves crucial differences both in the unit and process of observation and analysis and in the
basic goals of treatment. Moreover, the logic behind systemic interventions
is grounded in a set of assumptions (or "epistemology") that stands clearly
apart from earlier models of human behavior, particularly the psychoanalytic. These assumptions result in widespread shifts in emphasis, which
encompass both the therapist's conceptualization of problems and the
specific interventions used to deal with them. Sluzki categorizes these
frequently dramatic shifts as from (1) "individual to larger systems"; (2)
"content to process"; (3) "interpretations to prescriptions"; (4) "intentions
to effects"; (5) "origins to present, self-perpetuating loops"; (6) "roles to
rules"; (7) "symptoms to functions"; and (8) "linear causality to cybernetic
circularity." This compendium suggests essential differences between the
systems perspective and earlier theoretical viewpoints. By way of further
clarifying what is "new" in this therapeutic approach, it will be useful to
compare it to the other major outlooks on the foundation and solution of
perennial human problems.

Systems Theory versus Psychodynamic,
Behavioral, and Gestalt Theories

It should be stressed that exponents of the systems perspective have shown
little interest in repudiating earlier theories about the sources of dysfunctional behavior. Rather such theorists have concentrated pragmatically on

84

how such behavior is maintained through present-day interactive sequences and cycles. Attention is placed on breaking the problem-perpetuating chains, not on helping individuals better grasp their origins.

In general, systems theory (and the "strategic" interventions closely tied to it) contrasts most sharply with the psychodynamic approach—although again, as Stanton (1981b) notes, the existence of intrapsychic events and the role of past experience in determining current behaviors is not actually denied by systems-oriented therapists. What *is* directly challenged is the psychodynamic emphasis on such occurrences as the most effective, or efficient, way of inducing therapeutic change. Strongly reacting to the painstaking cultivation of client insight into the historical origins of present-day problems, therapists working within a systems framework tend to eschew interpretation of unconscious processes. If interpretation is employed at all, it is for the purpose of "reframing" a situation so that clients may be prompted to reevaluate it; it is not designed to heighten intellectual awareness or assist clients in getting in touch with repressed thoughts and feelings. The seminal psychoanalytic concept of transference, while not actively contested, is ignored as a vehicle for implementing change.

In Fisch, Weakland, and Segal's *The Tactics of Change* (1982), a key work on strategic techniques in therapy, the authors point out that their model is in essence nonpathological. It is not concerned with the presumed intrapsychic dynamics of problematic behavior but with its interactional components and the "rules" that govern its repetition. It does not focus on an individual's buried past, or the primal causes of current effects, but on the here-and-now, *observable* manifestations of the presenting complaint. Inferences about origins and their intimate connection to enduring personality deficits are abandoned as the therapist's attention abruptly shifts from making the patient more "insightful" about his condition toward altering the interpersonal *context* serving to perpetuate it.

The marked interpersonal emphasis of strategic therapists is a direct result of their involvement in the family therapy movement of the 1950s and 1960s, which came to recognize the inadequacies of viewing a family member's problems in isolation and began to explore these problems in relation to the specific behaviors of other, "nonsymptomatic" members. Echoing the words of Sluzki (1978), Fisch et al. (1982) reiterate that the whole idea of conceptualizing problems in their immediate relational context comprises a major epistemological shift in that the therapist's quest for knowledge is transferred from the domain of "linear cause-and-effect chains to a cybernetic or systems viewpoint . . . involving feedback and reciprocal reinforcement throughout" (p. 9). Attempts to link symptomatic behavior to unconscious motives, secondary gain, and early characterological fixations give way to the methodical investigation of how such behavior operates to maintain family homeostasis and provide the individual with certain interactional advantages, particularly around matters of control. The largely unprecedented vocabulary of systems theorists suggests their radical departure from psychodynamic formulations, which are based on notions of mental and emotional deficits, and the etiology of problems as originating from internal—rather than interpersonal—factors. Far from attributing the persistence of a problem to an individual's deep-seated irrationality, systems theorists subscribe to the belief that humans are, indeed, logical to a fault in the sense that they strive to solve their difficulties through actions rigorously adhering to logical principles. The problem is simply that the *premises* behind the logical deductions informing their behavior are incorrect or inapplicable.

Behavioral theorists, unlike systems theorists, tend to conceptualize problem-maintaining behaviors as resulting not from logically faulty premises but from faulty learning experiences. All the same, the behaviorist approach to therapy bears much closer resemblance to the systems orientation than does the psychodynamic. For it, too, is symptom-focused and typically disregards as inessential to therapy the underlying, or unconscious, causes and motivations of maladaptive behavior. Efforts to foster client insight into these often murky origins are also viewed as peripheral to promoting therapeutic change. Although to varying degrees interventionists from both schools are willing to concede the utility of acquiring a firm grasp of the dynamics behind specific problem behaviors in formulating an effective treatment plan, neither orientation considers imparting such awareness to clients a prerequisite for effective therapy. The stress is purely pragmatic, centering on techniques carefully devised to induce clients to alter habitually self-defeating behaviors. Given the typical difficulty of this task, helping clients additionally to understand just *why* they have acted, reacted, or interacted self-defeatingly is judged a goal hardly worth pursuing. In fact, in both behavioral and systems-oriented therapy the goals of treatment are far more confined, concrete, and even "operationalized" than are the more subjective and far less delimited goals of psychoanalysis.

Therapy grounded in a systems perspective does differ, however, from behavior therapy in its generally being much less cognitively or behaviorally direct: it tends to show comparatively little interest in transmitting to clients the misconceptions behind their problems or in teaching them particular methods and skills to overcome them. Dedicated to effecting systems change through restructuring broadly symptomatic communica-

tion patterns, its focus goes beyond predominantly linear ideas of reinforcement and causality to circular notions of self- and system-preserving
feedback loops. Moreover, as Madanes and Haley (1977) observe, "the
behaviorists who classify a symptom as a 'bit' that can be counted as
present or absent are thinking differently from therapists who consider a
symptom to be a communication about a person's life situation and therefore an analogy about something else" (p. 91).

   The gestalt approach to therapy would appear, as regards its affinities
with the systems viewpoint, to fall somewhere midway between behavioral
and psychodynamic perspectives. Similar to systems theory—and to behavior therapy as well—its methods concentrate on the here-and-now
aspects of problematic behavior. Much more essential, however, as a link
between systems and gestalt theory is their metaphysical view of reality as
dialectical, and their similarly dialectical perception of behavioral change:
that is, clients—or individuals within a system—are seen as enabled to
change precisely through their being encouraged to remain the same. Even
more paradoxically, instructing clients (particularly rigid or resistant
ones) to become *more* of the same is seen as frequently capable of accelerating this change. Such a summary of the dialectical essence of the two
theories admittedly borders on the simplistic, since what defines both
theories as dialectical is their emphatic denial of "either-or" conceptions
of human behavior and their insistence that psychological reality is in a
constant state of flux. Moreover, this reality, arbitrary in the sense that it is
knowable only through individual perception, cannot be adequately portrayed by any single label or frame of reference. From this modernist
vantage point, symptoms themselves need to be appreciated as *both* positive and negative. Despite their acting overall as hindrances, they serve
certain practical functions and must therefore be befriended—indeed,
supported—if therapy is to help the client relinquish, or "transcend,"
them.
   In a sense, systems theory—most notably in its emphasis on the family
as a unit—may be seen as taking up where gestalt theory leaves off. Both
approaches may be broadly understood as comprehensive, or "holistic,"
but the *context* of systemic interventions differs radically from that of
gestalt. In *The Gestalt Approach and Eyewitness to Therapy* (1976), Perls
proclaims that what gestalt practitioners wish to accomplish is "to integrate all the dispersed and disowned alienated parts of the self and make
the person whole again" (p. 181). This statement suggests not only that
which connects gestalt and systems viewpoints but what clearly separates
them as well. Both orientations may have an integrative—or "organic"—

emphasis, but the systems approach focuses sharply on the collective and interpersonal rather than the individual and internal. Further, the systems approach is devoted to *reintegrating* an already existing unit rather than bringing together a unit whose parts have become fragmented and dissociated. To systemic thinkers, all units, or subunits, are integrated by definition. The problem is that the *manner* of integration does not permit parts of the whole to function without considerable friction and discomfort, requiring the therapist to somehow take apart and reassemble subunits so that the larger unit may begin to operate more harmoniously—no longer, for instance, necessitating a symptom-bearer, or "scapegoat," to maintain its precarious balance.

It should, additionally, be noted that unlike gestalt practitioners, who give special consideration to the expression of repressed feelings, systems-oriented interventionists concentrate their attention on behavioral chains and sequences. The complicated array of feelings that may underlie family interactions is considered tangential to the primary business of realigning different components of the system so that it may operate more effectively and the family's presenting problem be, in effect, "rearranged" out of existence.

Stanton (1981b) offers a pithy summation of how the systems—or strategic—approach to symptoms and symptom change differs radically from both individually, and intrapsychically, focused accounts of dysfunctional behavior. Reducing the many theoretical and practical discrepancies between therapeutic schools to four major points, he concludes that "1) 'symptoms' can be viewed simply as particular types of behavior functioning as homeostatic mechanisms which regulate family transactions . . . ; 2) problems in an identified patient cannot be considered apart from the *context* in which they occur and the *functions* which they serve; 3) an individual cannot be expected to change unless his family system changes . . . [and] 4) 'insight' per se is not a necessary prerequisite for change" (p. 365).

The Bateson Project, Family Systems Theory, and the Double-Bind Concept of Schizophrenia

Having indicated, by way of introduction, a few of the more salient relationships between systems theory and earlier formulations of human behavior and therapeutic process, it will be useful to suggest how general systems theory came to be applied specifically to family treatment. The grant that anthropologist Gregory Bateson received in 1952 to study certain intricacies of human communication culminated in what is now commonly referred to as "The Bateson Project" and marks the formal beginning of the systems approach to therapy. Including such coworkers as Jay Haley, John Weakland, and William Fry, and employing Don D. Jackson as psychiatric consultant, this group conducted its research in a Veteran's Administration hospital in Palo Alto and adopted a cybernetic language in its efforts to understand seriously dysfunctional families.

Postulating that the complexities of family interaction were best understood in terms of general systems theory, as seminally enunciated by Von Bertalanffy (1968), the Bateson group sought to develop theoretically the multiple analogies between family dynamics and other cybernetic systems. Perceiving the family as, in essence, an "organism" and therefore a vibrant, though highly structured, system of reciprocally interacting parts and processes, the group came to see the families it studied as bound by particular rules dictating both internal and interpersonal behavior. As Sluzki (1978) points out, the emphasis on *rules*—a system attribute describing members by the way they interrelated—replaced the earlier conceptual focus on *roles*, with all its individual connotations. Defined interactionally, family systems were seen as nonlinear (i.e., operating in accordance with cyclic, rather than causal, principles) and as comprised of interlocking feedback mechanisms designed to maintain homeostatic functioning. The fundamental notion of interlocking behaviors among family members and their conformance to prevailing rules suggested to the Bateson group the means by which change might best be facilitated. And the various tactics of what later was identified as "strategic therapy" all involve the attempt to alter individual behavior through modifying the family system—or, more accurately, modifying the specific *transactions* among members (or subunits) of this system.

In studying schizophrenic patients in terms of family transaction, the Bateson group concluded that their pathological behavior was best understood as a natural, even appropriate, means of communication in a system which itself required designation as pathological. In short, the patient's "symptomatic" behavior was seen as representing a desperate, yet almost heroic, attempt to adapt to a seriously disturbed interpersonal system. Reacting to paradoxical messages that served to place him in what the Bateson group termed a "double bind," the schizophrenic patient exhibited behavior logically reflecting his damned-if-you-do-and-damned-if-you-don't position in the family (Bateson, Jackson, Haley & Weakland, 1956). As Watzlawick, Beavin, and Jackson (1967) pointedly remark: "If . . . the schizophrenic is attempting *not* to communicate [which, according to communication theory, is not actually possible], then the 'solution' to this dilemma is the use of undecidable messages which say of themselves that they are saying nothing" (p. 224).

Elaborating upon and slightly modifying the Bateson group's theoretically unprecedented description of the interpersonal (as opposed to intrapsychic) etiology of schizophrenic behavior, Watzlawick et al. (1967) indicate three essential ingredients of a pathological double bind:

> (1) Two or more persons are involved in an intense relationship that has a high degree of physical and/or psychological survival value for one, several, or all of them. . . . (2) In such a context, a message is given which is so structured that (a) it asserts something, (b) it asserts something about its own assertion and (c) these two assertions are mutually exclusive. . . . (3) . . . the recipient of the message is prevented from stepping outside the frame set by this message, either by metacommunicating (commenting) about it or by withdrawing. . . . (p. 212)

Watzlawick et al. also allude to the bidirectional nature of this self-perpetuating, vicious-circle phenomenon. That is, the paradoxical communication induced by a double bind in turn "double-binds the double-binder" (p. 214), so that the ultimate pathogenicity of such binds cannot adequately be understood by any straightforward cause-and-effect reasoning. Moreover—as Watzlawick et al. (1974) later observe—familial double binds may lead to dysfunctioning other than schizophrenia. Depending on the variables governing the situation, double binding can culminate in a variety of pathological behaviors and interactions, not all of which warrant classification as psychotic.

The Therapeutic Double Bind

Since resisting a double bind in a homeostatic system has the paradoxical effect of sustaining it, members of the Bateson group seized upon the idea of prescribing the double bind—or rather the *symptom* resulting from this bind—as an antidote for disturbed family transactions. They coined the term "prescribing the symptom" to underscore the counter double-binding nature of their stratagem. The *therapeutic* double bind seen as deriving from such purposeful symptom prescription was later conceptualized by Watzlawick et al. (1967) as representing the "mirror image" (p. 241) of a pathogenic double bind.

A central assumption behind the use of symptom prescription is that many family systems—by homeostatic definition—are strongly impelled to resist change and outside influence. Such systemic resistance is viewed as markedly susceptible to a therapist (or external agent) who either explicitly prescribes it or promotes it indirectly—through encouraging the family's symptomatic member to maintain (or even accentuate) pathological behavior. The family's dilemma in this situation should be clear: either it resists the therapist by deciding to continue to do what it has already been doing, thereby subjecting itself to the therapist's authority and control, and establishing a norm for following future directives; or it resists the therapist by altering its dysfunctional communication pattern in the direction of healthier (i.e., less symptomatic) behavior. Whichever the case, the family's resistance to change has been strategically converted into a vehicle of change (see Watzlawick et al., 1974). As Stanton (1981b) notes, the family's very confusion as to how best to resist can lead to "new patterns and perceptions and thus to change—at the very least [as Hare-Mustin, 1976, is cited as pointing out earlier] it can help [the family] to achieve a certain amount of detachment from the disturbing behavior" (p. 374).

Such adroit maneuvering of the family's resistance back upon itself is, of course, at the heart of the therapeutic double bind. And it should be noted that a therapeutic double bind is not simply one in an arsenal of paradoxical techniques (as the literature on therapeutic paradox has commonly asserted or implied), but the frequent *result* of such techniques, at least when they are employed successfully. Accurately understood, the therapeutic double bind is a hypothesis used to explain how and why certain paradoxical techniques—especially symptom prescription, with which it is often confused—are capable of introducing change into rigid systems. Further, it needs to be stressed that therapeutic double binds may occur within individuals, or self-systems, as well as within family groupings. All that is required for such binds to take place is a directive which, as long as the client reacts to it and does not leave the therapeutic field entirely, obliges that client either to alter his viewpoint or behavior. In short, in a well-planned and executed double-binding situation, the client cannot *not* be influenced.

Watzlawick (1978) cites an exceptionally elegant example of a double bind—which is no less illustrative by the fact that his own explanation of its dynamics confounds the device of symptom prescription with what we might label "symptom confrontation" (its diametric, and *nonparadoxical*, opposite). The case, originally reported by Bandler and Grinder (1975), involves a member of a therapy group whose symptom was that she could not say "no." She was able to trace the origins of this problem-engendering behavior to the childhood circumstance that she once refused to stay home with her father and later returned to find him dead, thereafter becoming terrified of the disastrous consequences of denial. The therapist, by insisting that this woman say "no" to every member of the group, contrived to place her in a double bind. Her desperate, though predictable, reaction to the therapist's command was to refuse to follow the directive, adamantly protesting that it was impossible for her to say "no" to people. Only after several minutes of rejecting the therapist's request and the therapist's eventually informing her that in fact she had been saying "no" to him all along could she realize that it was possible for her to deny something without harmful consequences. Watzlawick sums up this double bind as follows:

1. Symptom: "I cannot say 'no'."

2. Symptom prescription: "Say 'no' to everyone present!" [Note: contrary to the author's schema, prescribing a symptom here would actually necessitate telling the woman to say "yes" to all the group members, since her symptom has been defined as *agreeing to*, rather than refusing, any and all requests from others.]

3. Double bind: Two alternatives (either to say "no" to everybody or to say "no" to the therapist) which both lead to the desired outcome. (p. 105)

As Watzlawick concludes, opposed to the damned-if-you-do-and-damned-if-you-don't predicament of the individual placed in a pathogenic double bind, in the therapeutic double bind the individual is changed *regardless* of whether or not he chooses to obey the therapist's directives.

Finally, this process of change is much less dependent on the content of the therapist's interventions than on the *relationship* between the therapist and client(s). The delineation by Watzlawick et al. (1967) of the underlying structure of the therapeutic double bind, besides calling attention to its being the exact counterpart of the pathogenic double bind, emphasizes the interactional vantage point of systems-oriented theorists. For the three prerequisites of a therapeutic double bind are described as including (1) an intense relationship between therapist and client, based on the high survival value and expectations that the client typically attaches to this alliance; (2) the therapist's paradoxically enjoining the client to change by not changing, with the implicit understanding that such a directive will eventuate in change; and (3) the circumstance that the client is prevented by the therapeutic context from withdrawing from the situation or commenting upon the paradox. As Watzlawick et al. remark, given such an interactional state of affairs—and the "pragmatic reality" of the therapist's "logically absurd" injunction—"the patient cannot *not* react to it, but neither can he react to it in his usual, symptomatic way" (p. 241). Contemplating the logistics of a double bind (whether pathogenic or therapeutic) at a more abstract level, Erickson and Rossi (1975) hypothesize that double binds permit free choice on a primary level, which is recognized by the individual, but—on a secondary level *not* generally perceived—they so highly structure behavior as virtually to bankrupt choice.

First- and Second-Order Change

Elaborating on the theory of the therapeutic double bind, Watzlawick et al. (1974) postulate that this interactional phenomenon leads to "second-order change"—a term that since its inception has been employed frequently in family systems literature. As contrasted to "first-order change" which, when it takes place within a system, leaves the system itself unchanged, "second-order change" results in a fundamental alteration of the system. Whereas first-order change is powerless to modify the system because it is brought about through behaviors that conform to the system's prevailing rules, second-order change is able to effect basic changes in the system by *overriding* the rules which, in fact, have defined the system.

A useful summation of differences between first- and second-order change has been offered by Weeks and L'Abate (1982). Alluding to earlier studies on the dialectical approach to counseling (Adams, 1977) and certain dialectical aspects of the family life cycle (Weeks & Wright, 1979), they observe that:

> First-order change appears to be linear, stepwise, or mechanistic . . . a change in quantity, not quality. [It] involves using the same problem-solving strategies over and over again. Each new problem is approached mechanically. If the problem resists resolution, more old strategies are used and are usually more vigorously applied. There is either more of a behavior or less of a behavior along some continuum. . . .

> Second-order change refers to a change in the system itself. The system is transformed structurally and/or communicationally. Second-order change tends to be sudden and radical; it represents a quantum jump in the system to a different level of functioning. [It] is discontinuous and qualitative. It is not logically predictable and often appears abrupt, illogical, and unexpected. (p. 19)

The authors go on to link second-order change to paradoxical interventions, since these tactics are typically contrived to confuse and unbalance a rigid system, and to disarm family members of their resistance toward exploring new and (at least to them) noncommonsensical approaches to old problems. However, it is important to note that although so-called "paradoxical change" is virtually synonymous with second-order change, this type of change is *not* limited—as Weeks and L'Abate suggest—to exclusively paradoxical strategies. It may occur through the use of more conventional therapeutic methods as well.

Additionally, as Musliner (1980) in particular has pointed out, second-order change is not necessarily superior to first-order change. If a family's rules enable its members to interact with relatively little friction, first-order change may well be sufficient to resolve a conflict. First-order change is in fact the usual way that families (here seen as homeostatic systems) settle their problems: that is, norm-deviating behavior in a member supplies the system with negative feedback automatically triggering a corrective counterreaction. If parents, for instance, become too lax in enforcing boundaries, eventually the child will act out and the parents will come to attention, jointly pulling taut the disciplinary slack. It is at times when the family's rules have themselves created the problem, that first-order change is powerless to effect a satisfactory solution—and in fact only exacerbates the problem. For example, if the child's acting out is a result of father's authoritarianism and mother's passivity, the first-order "solution" of father's becoming stricter may prompt the child toward further rebellion, and so on. In this case, the system itself requires correction—such as the father's altering his dictatorial stance and requesting help from the mother. Although such a second-order change may occur from within the system, frequently its "engineering" is dependent upon an outside observer, whose very detachment is able to bring to it an unprecedented perspective on issues that, from within, have come to seem well-nigh irresoluble. If change based on the introduction of an external agent's vantage point appears paradoxical to those directly involved, it is because this change has been caused by disrupting precisely those refractory rules that have served to stabilize the system and keep it functioning "logically." Moreover, this change is frequently facilitated in therapy through adopting such specifically paradoxical devices as reframing and symptom prescription, since both these tactics tend to undermine interactive sequences maintaining the system's dysfunctional status quo.

The Mental Research Institute

The most prominent group of theorists/practitioners that have focused on producing second-order change through reframing and prescribing symptoms and problem-engendering behaviors is the group heading the Mental Research Institute (MRI), originally established in Palo Alto by Don D. Jackson in 1959 and including since its beginnings such staff members as Virginia Satir, Jules Riskin, Paul Watzlawick, Jay Haley, John Weakland, Arthur Bodin, Richard Fisch, and Carlos Sluzki. The importance of MRI (whose functions have broadened markedly over the years) in promulgating the use of paradoxical tactics in therapy is best suggested by Bodin's (1981) recounting that by 1979 the Institute had offered advanced training courses to over 30,000 medical and mental health professionals. During its first twenty years the Institute also sponsored 52 research projects, 21 books (many appearing in foreign editions), more than 300 other publications, and five national conferences. As Bodin (MRI's "official" historian) observes, all these activities bear testimony to MRI's pioneering research and training on the family and problems in communication, as well as to its developing practical models for family therapy, brief focal therapy, and emergency treatment.

When Bodin discusses the key influences on the MRI staff, he refers to Frankl's "paradoxical intention" (1960); Rosen's "reductio ad absurdum" and "reenacting an aspect of the psychosis" (1953); and the devious framing and linguistic tactics found in Erickson's ingeniously creative mode of hypnotherapy—particularly as expounded by Haley (1963, 1973). Bodin's frank acknowledgment of MRI's conceptual and strategic debt to these eminent practitioners—all of quite divergent theoretical persuasions—should suggest something not only of the eclecticism of MRI's staff but also of their pragmatic focus, especially as manifested by their increasing concern with more effective methods of short-term treatment.

Complementing several statements made earlier in this section about the relationship between the communication-systems orientation and more established approaches to therapy, Bodin explicitly compares MRI's clinical stance to those of psychoanalysis and behavior modification. Although central ideas in psychoanalytic theory, involving the role of internal (or intrapsychic) mechanisms in determining thought and behavior, are seen as generally respected by MRI members, these latter-day theorists deny the "knowability" of another's inner perceptions. Consequently, the most that can scientifically be achieved is to study actual performance and behavior, and to devise specific treatments based on such concrete, observable phenomena.

It needs to be stressed, however, that while MRI therapy is a *kind* of behavior therapy, it differs significantly from the at once more popular and narrower brand of behavior therapy familiarly known as "behavior modification," which is firmly grounded in learning theory and largely ignores the interactional origins and complexities of human problems. Citing G. S. Greenberg (1977) on these important distinctions, Bodin further notes Greenberg's observation that (to use Bodin's own paraphrase) "neither family therapy nor behavior therapy has integrated within its boundaries the fundamental components of the other" (p. 293). Finally, the lack of impact of behavior modification on typical MRI interventions is attributed to the circumstance that (1) MRI pioneers have had backgrounds in fields other than psychology, and (2) MRI tactics are frequently indirect, even counterintuitive, to a degree so foreign to orthodox behaviorists as, indeed, to elicit disapproval (if not downright alarm) from them.

In delineating the basic premises behind MRI's interventions, Weakland et al. (1974) underscore their conviction that regardless of the origins and etiology of the problems people bring to therapy, these problems endure only because they are maintained by ongoing behaviors of the client and others in his interactive context. Correlatively, if such problem-perpetuating behaviors can be altered or eliminated, the problem itself will be resolved or simply disappear; and such resolution will occur notwith-standing the nature, duration, or origin of the problem.

In *Change* (Watzlawick et al., 1974), common notions about problems and their solutions are rudely punctured in the authors' contention that from a second-order change perspective, conventional solutions (i.e., solutions deriving from a first-order change viewpoint) frequently represent the keystone of the problem. To genuinely resolve the problem, therefore, the authors imply that a paradoxical approach is needed. For the ineffective (or pseudo-) solution already attempted by the client(s) must be redefined as *itself* the problem—while the problem, reframed and/or prescribed, actually represents the vehicle of change. From this vantage point the therapeutic double bind deriving from symptom prescription is curative not because it successfully undercuts an earlier pathogenic one but, more broadly, because it obstructs precisely those interactional sequences which have created the problem and kept it intact. For instance, vehement though well-meaning struggles to "cheer up" a depressed person whose depression is a temporary and normal reaction to some important loss may inadvertently aggravate this prepathological condition to the point that it assumes truly pathological proportions. Having clients take the paradoxical posture of endorsing, or even intensifying, this depression may then become the best antidote for it.

It should be apparent that relabeling or reframing problem behaviors, usually as preparatory to prescribing them, is geared either toward altering the cognitions maintaining the vicious-circle interactions or exactly the reverse. In either case, what is facilitated is a new mode of interaction which renders extraneous the undesirable behavior. Acutely contrasting with a psychodynamic approach, the therapist's calculated reframings are *not* contrived to impart insight into dysfunctional behavior (the value of which is regarded as dubious) but simply to eradicate it. Paradoxical prescriptions to clients, intended to disrupt their subjectively logical, but routinely self-defeating "solutions" to problems, are viewed by Weakland et al. (1974) as "probably constitut[ing] the most important single class of interventions" (p. 158) utilized by MRI's Brief Therapy Center. Although these noncommonsensical prescriptions run strongly counter to client expectations and may well seem perverse in their apparent opposition to mutually agreed-upon treatment goals, they may be appreciated as succeeding where "sweet reason" has blatantly failed. Through encouraging, or *seeming* to encourage, symptomatic or generally problematic behavior, they either reduce or remove such behavior or help the individual(s) to gain final control over it.

The Milan Center for Family Studies

Further developing many of the ideas germinated in this country by The Bateson Project and Mental Research Institute, the Milan Family Therapy Group* is probably best known for its innovative treatment of families whose ill-conceived rules have produced a schizophrenic member. Comprised of four psychiatrists originally trained in psychoanalysis, this group was formed in 1971 under the leadership of Mara Selvini Palazzoli—who earlier, in 1967, founded the Milan Center for Family Studies—and included in its research team Luigi Boscolo, Gianfranco Cecchin, and Giuliana Prata. The group's most significant contribution, cited regularly in family systems literature, is *Paradox and Counterparadox* (1975/1978), which methodically elucidates a systemic model for working with schizophrenic and other seriously disturbed families. Avoiding analytic interpretations as only fueling a family's resistance, and concentrating instead on devising paradoxical prescriptions expressly calculated to loosen the rigidity of family members' transactions, the Milan group is plainly indebted to the so-called Palo Alto group and its pragmatic orientation toward change. In fact, at one early point in its development, the group employed Paul Watzlawick as its consultant.

The Milan group's two key strategies—both of which will be taken up later in somewhat greater detail—have a decidedly paradoxical flavor. Similar in essence to the therapeutic tactics employed by the Mental Research Institute in their brief treatment model, the *scope* of these methods is significantly enlarged. The group's generous use of "positive connotation" takes care to reframe, and thereby support, not simply the symptom but the entire system which has given rise to it, so that fuller access to the family may be gained through neutralizing, or inverting, its homeostatically motivated opposition to outside influence. Both the individual's symptom *and* family members' reaction to it are construed in a favorable light: as functioning purposively to hold the family together. The result of such apparently benign reframing is that the whole family system (which may include several generations) is subtly implicated in the problem. Thus induced by the therapists' positively connoting all aspects of the system to "share in" the individual member's symptom, each family member (or

*Presently disbanded.

better, the intractable system underlying the symptom) becomes susceptible to treatment.

Once the therapeutic alliance has been established through positive connotation, the Milan group's second principal technique, *paradoxical instruction*, is ready for implementation. This technique, closely linked to the symptom prescription tactics of MRI, is nonetheless distinguishable in its being directed less to the identified patient or symptom than to the family system as a whole. Following the irresistible logic of the group's earlier positive connotations, the paradoxical instruction basically requests that the family remain the same. As a consequence of this unexpected endorsement of its pathology, the family—threatened by anything that might interfere with its homeostasis yet needing to view its now "collective symptom" negatively—is prompted to consider change in a totally new context. Their stubborn reluctance to behave differently, severely weakened (or even perverted) by their being told *not* to behave differently, is transformed into a powerful vehicle for change.

The Role of Symptoms in Systems

What theoretically unites The Bateson Project, The Mental Research Institute, and The Milan Center for Family Studies is their conviction that symptoms are not accidental but skillfully fabricated to achieve particular systemic purposes. Although these symptoms may be generated far below the level of individual awareness and conscious intention, they are yet remarkably suited to preserve or protect certain aspects of the system. As such, all members of the system need to be appreciated as in some way sharing responsibility for their continuance.

Conceptualizing symptoms from a communications perspective, Haley (1963) regards them as "interpersonal power tactics," or attempts to gain control over others. Specifically, in the therapeutic arena the patient is viewed as exploiting symptoms to exert power over the therapist, thus sabotaging all well-meaning endeavors to help him. Seen in the more intricate context of family systems theory, where so-called "dysfunctioning" actually represents a cooperative effort—or collusion—among family members, symptoms are best apprehended as yielding a measure of control to *everybody* involved in their operation. In the context of therapy, what might practically be identified as the *family's* symptom may be regarded as the key instrument of its resistance. That is, one primary function of symptom maintenance in therapy is its enabling the family to assert control over the therapist. The family can conveniently strip the therapist of his potential power to foster change by adhering precisely to those interactions that have kept the maladaptive behavior in place.

Such stubborn adherence to supposedly undesired behaviors is perceived (and often professed) by family members to be innocent, since their central contention all along has been that the behavior or behaviors in need of changing are involuntary. But, as Jacobson and Margolin (1979) observe, from a systems perspective one of the two assumptions justifying the use of paradoxical interventions is the notion that a discrepancy exists between the family's claim that target behaviors are nonvolitional and the reality of their being voluntary. The second assumption which supports the use of paradoxical directives is that maladaptive behavior in a marriage or family exists chiefly for its communicative value. Serving as a statement, or metaphor, about current power relationships among family members, it succinctly symbolizes the terms, or rules, of family transaction. To disrupt these symptom-perpetuating rules, the therapist must find a way of gaining control over them. Typically, symptom prescription techniques are adopted as providing the most efficient means by which the therapist may usurp the curiously tyrannical power linked to these dysfunctional interpersonal rules. Prescribing symptoms directly, or at least finding some plausible reason to sanction their continued use, impairs their utility as power tactics and thus increases the chances of nonsymptomatic change.

Erickson and Systemic Paradox

Doubtless one of the most important precursors of strategic therapy is Milton Erickson, whose innovative methods have been widely promulgated from a systems vantage point. As Stanton (1981b), among others, has pointed out, besides the strong theoretical impact of Gregory Bateson, Erickson is the other major figure foundational to the full development of the strategic orientation to therapy. In fact, Jay Haley—generally recognized as the leading expositor of this approach—is cited by Stanton as openly confessing that almost all his ideas originate in some form from Erickson's highly individualistic approach. Before describing the general tenets behind strategic therapy and the subtle ways this treatment contrives to turn presenting symptoms back upon their "presenters," it may be useful briefly to suggest how Erickson's provocative conceptions of the nature and purpose of client symptomatology stimulated the thinking of the communication-systems theorists who studied him—foremost among them (and by far the most industrious in disseminating his working principles) being of course Haley himself.

Most of Erickson's ideas center around the importance of accepting and utilizing that which the client brings to therapy. Specifically, many of his methods are only marginally paradoxical. Yet the almost routinely devious tactics he employed in his therapy, in their profound understanding of the positive functions served by symptoms, deserve to be viewed as broadly paradoxical. For, taking thoroughly into account the personal benefits deriving from symptoms (or generally troublesome behaviors), Erickson sought to "adjust" these symptoms so that they would either disappear as superfluous, be substantially altered, or remain intact but cease to disturb the individual(s) concerned. As opposed to treatment striving in one way or another to confront and ultimately vanquish client symptomatology, Erickson chose a much more cordial stance toward symptoms, thereby winning the client's permission to "tamper with" them therapeutically. This essential principle of consciously "utilizing the symptom" (as Erickson himself frequently put it) may be seen as informing virtually all the different symptom prescription techniques subsequently developed by systems practitioners. And it is in the therapeutic empowerment gained from the employment of such skillfully wrought interventions that many methods inspired by Erickson's distinguished example have come to be designated "strategic."

In an article entitled "Special Techniques in Brief Hypnotherapy" (1954b), Erickson expounded on how the unique needs of patients not amenable to comprehensive treatment could be met through utilizing their neurotic symptomatology. Postulated on the notion that some patients' "total pattern of adjustment is based upon the continuance of certain maladjustments which derive from actual frailties," he endeavored in his treatment planning to "provide adequately for constructive adjustments aided rather than handicapped by the continuance of neuroticisms" (p. 109). Again, the broadly paradoxical flavor of Erickson's thinking should be evident since, though it stops short of actually *prescribing* the client's symptom, it is grounded firmly on the assumption that symptoms may need both to be viewed and handled positively if therapy is to proceed unhindered. The work of therapy is conceived not simply as exterminating symptoms but as somehow contriving to *reconstitute* them.

Describing complementary hypnotherapeutic tactics—all of which are differentiated from straightforward attempts at symptom removal in their "full respect" (p. 127) for patient symptomatology—Erickson delineates the obliquely curative functions of "symptom substitution" (which satisfies the patient's needs for neurotic defenses while helping him achieve a more satisfactory adjustment), "symptom transformation" (which utilizes a patient's neurosis by converting the personality functions it serves without interfering with the symptomatology itself), and "symptom amelioration" (which safeguards, or protects, an "overwhelming, all-absorbing symptom-complex" (p. 117) in order to effect the only symptom improvement realistically tenable). In all these stratagems, Erickson can be seen as tolerantly "supporting" client symptoms in his keen awareness of their uniquely adaptive qualities. Finally, as Erickson take pains to emphasize, treatment needs to concentrate more on altering the patient's current and future behaviors than on understanding and communicating how long past events have led to the patient's present maladjustments. Such a refocusing of therapeutic attention away from the etiology of symptoms to their here-and-now manifestations is also precursory to the stress placed on present-day events by later strategic therapists.

Erickson's indirect methods, frequently calculated to foster change through accepting and positively relabeling symptomatic behavior, may be viewed additionally in a communications context. Particularly as presented by Haley (1967, 1973), Erickson's indirect techniques are guided by the awareness that patient symptoms are emblematic of a personal decision on how best to interact with others, the therapist included. Thus, regarding patient symptomatology largely as an interpersonal strategy deeply woven into the social fabric of the patient's past and present life, Erickson's theoretical convictions may be appreciated as systemic. And the interventions correlative to these basic assumptions are best apprehended as closely kindred to those techniques most often described as "strategic."

Some Theoretical Undercurrents of Strategic Therapy

It should be noted that strategic therapy has at times also been referred to as "directive therapy." By way of characterizing this treatment perspective generally, the term "directive" warrants some clarification, for it is unintentionally ambiguous about the approach it is meant to identify. As contrasted to the more passive, or noninitiative, techniques of psychoanalysis, it attempts to influence, instruct, or "direct" the client both cognitively and behaviorally. In fact, it might be said that this approach actually *hinges on* therapist directives to clients. On the other hand, as contrasted to most cognitive, cognitive-behavioral, and conditioning-type therapies, this approach is anything *but* direct, relying not on straightforward explanations to prompt clients to adopt new behaviors but rather on a variety of *indirect*, subtle, and at times even devious reframing devices. These devices are designed much more to shake up the dysfunctional system seen as "nurturing" the problem than to frankly educate clients on the irrationality of their behavior. Finally, the strategic or directive approach is distinguished in the paradoxical way it accommodates—rather than challenges or confronts—client symptoms and their special communicative functions. Therapy, although it might accurately be described as symptom- or problem-focused, does not really seek to remove symptoms as such but to *indirectly direct* the client's life so that maladaptive behaviors are no longer communicationally feasible or subjectively required.

In addition to suggesting something of the "indirect directiveness" of strategic treatment, another point of clarification may be in order. For the term "strategic therapy" is occasionally used as synonymous with "systems therapy," "systemic therapy," or "family systems therapy," while at other times some sort of differentiation between these terms is implied. What would seem the most *practical* distinction to make here is to see the employment of some form of the word "system" as intimating that the therapeutic context involves at least two people, whereas "strategic therapy"—in a sense the more general term—alludes less to the number of clinical recipients than to the nature of the intervention, which seeks to effect second-order change through therapist-initiated tactics designed to fundamentally alter undesirable behavioral sequences. Closely tied to this discrimination is the corollary that strategic techniques, though they may be therapeutic, do not in themselves constitute a therapy (as has already been suggested, e.g., by Haley, 1963, 1973, and Musliner, 1980). It is the underlying theory which supports the use of such techniques that ultimately defines the clinical orientation; and this theory is best appreciated in terms of systems. Strategic methods, therefore, need to be understood as the tools, or vehicles, for achieving beneficial systemic change.[*]

The systemic assumptions behind working strategically, adapted specifically to a family context, are concisely delineated by Musliner (1980) in an article called "Strategic Therapy with Families and Children." Here the author enumerates the premises of his conceptual framework as including five major points:

> (1) a child-focused problem reflects both individual and family dysfunction; (2) the child's symptom serves an essential function in the family system; (3) the symptom is embedded in a cycle of interactions in the family; (4) in order to change problem behavior one must consider all components of the cycle and deal specifically (though not necessarily directly) with any or all of them; (5) there are consequences, often significant, of altering the system by changing the behavior or functioning of any part of the system. (p. 104)

Musliner's second premise, which recalls the earlier section here on "The Role of Symptoms in Systems," hints at the difficult task confronting the therapist. For the problem brought into therapy originates from, and is

---

[*]By the same token, the title of Weeks and L'Abate's book on paradoxical methods, *Paradoxical Psychotherapy* (1982), must be seen as an unfortunate misnomer, for it implies that paradoxical strategies used in therapy are themselves the therapy—an implication that even the authors would probably feel obliged to deny, since they view such techniques as employed *across* major schools of therapy.

complicated by, the unavoidable circumstance that the system routinely reinforces the symptom, which in turn reinforces the system, and so on. The reciprocal and circular relationship between symptoms and systems in fact points to the utility of treating symptoms within the systemic context that sows and sustains them. The task of devising specific therapeutic interventions is perhaps all the more difficult in that the strategic therapist maintains a dialectical stance toward symptoms. Apprehending their positive as well as negative functions—particularly their serving as a much needed stabilizing force—necessitates that therapy not actively oppose them, regardless of their possibly serious repercussions. As has already been suggested, the systemic approach to treatment is grounded in the notion that human reality is circular and that the clarity derived from convenient cause-and-effect assumptions about the determination of events is basically a fiction. This systemic, nonlinear orientation toward therapy is inevitably paradoxical in much the same sense that a dialectical metaphysics, founded on certain principles of negation, is also paradoxical. And a therapeutic model which subscribes to the radically relative idea of reality as dependent on one's personal frame of reference ultimately dictates interventions that run sharply counter to "common sense." For such perceptual relativity leads to the popularly unacceptable notion that a conventional solution (e.g., direct attempts at cheering up a depressed person) may—from the vantage point of an outsider apprehending the nonpolar relationship of supposed opposites— be viewed as part and parcel of the problem and *itself* require abandonment.

Most of the reframing and symptom-prescribing devices employed in strategic therapy derive logically from the dialectical posture inherent in a systems view of human relationships. Offering a theoretical justification for their "illogical" change tactics, Fisch et al. (1982) state that "if problem formation and maintenance are seen as parts of a vicious-circle process, in which well-intended 'solution' behaviors maintain the problem, then alteration of these behaviors should interrupt the cycle and initiate resolution of the problem" (p. 18). The following section, which elucidates the various methods involved in "strategic paradox," should clarify the rigorous logic behind interventions that, to the layperson, must appear chaotic or confused.

TECHNIQUES AND TACTICS OF STRATEGIC THERAPY

Introduction

It should be admitted at the outset that the large number of paradoxical tactics enumerated below do not belong exclusively to the domain of communication-systems theory. Discussing therapeutic paradox in accordance with the major theoretical orientations inevitably leads to a certain arbitrariness, since in actual practice most of these methods, regardless of their "generic" tags, are positively related. Still, while many methods specifically linked to strategic therapy are not necessarily peculiar to this approach, such techniques are stressed far more in this treatment mode, as well as justified in terms that differentiate practitioners working within a systems framework from therapists with disparate theoretical commitments. Both the interventions and explanations of strategic therapists emphasize the interactional dynamics of behavioral dysfunctioning (and its complementary interactional solution) to a degree that clearly defines their focus as distinct from other persuasions.

Finally, however, as is recognized with increasing frequency (see, e.g., *Converging Themes in Psychotherapy*, M. R. Goldfried, ed., 1982), therapeutic approaches traditionally distinguished from one another may have a good deal more in common than theoretical purists would like to concede. If the position taken here is that it is nonetheless useful to divide the discussion of paradoxical strategies along familiar theoretical lines, it is because the bewildering heterogeneity of these tactics may otherwise make the subject appear forbiddingly complex. As Selvini Palazzoli (Barrows, 1982) soberly reflects in a recent interview: "There are many, many discussions concerning paradox—many, many kinds of paradox" (p. 67). And this observation hints at both the oversimplifying hazards of seeking to clarify an extremely complicated subject on which perhaps too much has already been said, and the importance of at least making an earnest attempt at such clarification. For to the extent that the enormous variety of paradoxical methods can be conveniently and accurately elucidated, to that extent will these potentially valuable devices become more accessible, or "available," to the interested practitioner.

From a systems vantage point alone, something like twenty different names and phrases have been employed to label paradoxical strategies. Rather than risk getting lost in the maze of such nomenclature, it may be helpful to classify all these titles as belonging, finally, to one of either two general headings—*reframing* or *symptom prescription*—the two terms used earlier in discussing therapeutic paradox from a systems orientation. In contrast, Tennen, Press, Rohrbaugh, and White (1981), in their effort to categorize paradoxical strategies across theoretical orientations, offer a threefold classification system: specifically, *prescribing*, *restraining*, and *positioning*. Whereas "prescribing" tactics encourage or direct clients to engage in the behavior targeted for elimination, "restraining" methods discourage change or even deny that change is possible. Lastly, "positioning" techniques involve altering a problematic perspective (or "position") by accepting and exaggerating it. In addition, based on whether clients are expected to cooperate or resist the therapist's directive or viewpoint, these three essential paradoxical strategies are also conceptualized in terms of their rationale, as being *compliance*- or *defiance*-based (see also, Rohrbaugh, Tennen, Press, & White, 1981). This secondary classification—a most useful one in devising appropriate paradoxical tactics—posits that prescribing and restraining may either be compliance- or defiance-based, while positioning tactics clearly anticipate client resistance.

Despite the comparative elegance, and comprehensiveness, of Tennen et al.'s schema, the decision here has been to describe the techniques of strategic therapy exclusively from the twofold classification of *reframing* and *symptom prescription*. The reason for this choice is that so-called "restraining" devices can hardly be seen as discrete or discontinuous from "prescribing" tactics: they actually represent a variant of such tactics, since discouraging a change in behavior is closely related to encouraging clients to maintain the *same* behavior. The fact that both these strategies may be either compliance- or defiance-based also suggests their essential kinship. Tennen et al.'s third category, "positioning," largely overlaps with that stratagem more familiarly known as "reframing"; and reframing may be the more useful term in its definitional capacity to include interventions understandable as *either* compliance- or defiance-based. Finally, the bipartite, reframing-symptom prescription division of paradoxical strategies may be the more practical in that, in actual practice, *both* these interventions are usually employed—the former device applied to increase the credibility of the latter. Or, put in somewhat different terms, paradoxical strategies may be seen as involving both a cognitive and behavioral component: reframing devices strive to alter the clients' way of thinking about their problematic behavior, whereas symptom prescription techniques (which are typically "set up" by such reconceptualizations, and which may be either implicit or explicit) seek to effect a change in the behavior itself. Although for the sake of clarity and convenience reframing and symptom prescription tactics will be reviewed separately, it should be kept in mind that as commonly implemented these two interventions represent complementary parts of a single treatment plan.

Reframing, Relabeling, and Redefinition

As centrally defined by Watzlawick et al. (1974), *reframing* involves fundamentally altering the meaning attributed to a situation through changing the conceptual and/or emotional context (i.e., the "frame") in which this situation is experienced. Such therapist-initiated "interpretation" (which has almost nothing to do with traditional psychoanalytic interpretation) is contrived to fit the facts of the problematic situation, or symptom, so well that recipients are prompted to react to it anew—and in such a way that the situation is bound to undergo transformation. What is essential for successful reframing is that the new frame be chosen with special care, so that it will be congenial to the recipient's (s') way of thinking and conceptualizing about reality. For if a family with an anorectic child, for example, is able to accept a therapist's perception that the problem is not in the parents' inability to influence the child to eat but in the child's self-sacrificially losing weight for the family, then the thoughts and behaviors which have created and maintained the problem must change. And such change cannot but affect the problem itself. In short, since the problem is the result of the prevailing cognitive-emotional situation, to modify that situation is inevitably to modify the problem as well.

Grunebaum and Chasin (1978) have suggested that a distinction be drawn between "reframing" and "relabeling"—the latter term introduced and made popular by Haley (1963). To these authors, whereas reframing involves a change in the context, or frame of reference, used to understand a particular behavior (e.g., altering one's point of view from moral to medical), relabeling involves no such change (e.g., altering one's diagnosis from "psychotic" to "neurotic"). Whereas relabeling as such does not lead to a change in frame of reference, reframing does regularly result in a change of label. As regards the example alluded to above, Grunebaum and Chasin remark that in moving from an individual to a family frame, although the label "anorectic child" is changed to "family with a parent–child coalition," the essential process is best apprehended in terms of reframing, since "the change of frame is the primary event and the change in label is a secondary consequence" (p. 454). Notwithstanding this potentially useful distinction, it must be frankly conceded that in the literature "reframing" and "relabeling"—and "redefinition" also (an appellation brought into use mainly through the work of Andolfi and his colleagues)—have been treated generally as synonymous therapeutic terms and used interchangeably. No differential employment of these terms will be attempted, therefore, in discussing this key paradoxical device—although "reframing," in its being probably the more generic and widely adopted designation, will be used preferentially.

Clarifying the therapeutic function of reframing is difficult for two reasons. First, what reframing *is* and how it serves to effect change are frequently described in the same terms. That is, reframing is typically seen not just as a technique but as an explanation for a technique. It is something like saying that reframing is effective because it reframes—and this confusing circularity seems somehow inherent to the whole concept of reframing. Another problem in clarifying the rationale of reframing is that reframing and symptom prescription are often used in tandem and therefore elucidated as a single mechanism of change. Consequently, the two complementary devices are not always distinguished theoretically and reviewing the explanations for their use inevitably involves a certain amount of repetition. It is, nonetheless, advisable to explain the functions of these two devices separately. But it should be noted at the outset that some explanatory overlap and reiteration is unavoidable.

One of the most obvious characteristics of reframing, or relabeling, is its tendency to confuse, startle, or "shake up" the individual or family to whom such perceptual alteration is proposed. As the therapist questions old labels or tactfully dismisses them—say, by redefining a family's fighting as actually an expression of caring—the response chain tightly linked to these labels begins to loosen. For the rationale justifying these responses is undermined along with the no-longer-appropriate label, the label in fact being practically synonymous with the rationale (see, e.g., de Shazer, 1975). The assumption underlying the use of reframing methods is that if the problem can be seen from an alternative standpoint it must be reduced or eliminated, since its very existence is intimately associable with the perspective of those involved. If, again, a family's fighting is reperceived by its participants as an attempt—though inadequately realized—at closeness, then the ill will implicitly understood as fundamental to such antagonistic behavior must be transformed into a much more positive interpersonal point of view. And, as a result of such modified perception, fighting can no longer be regarded as a tenable, or appropriate, response.

Examining the device of reframing within a family therapy context, Papp (1980a) argues that systemic redefinition creates a "perceptual crisis," which makes the family's "regulat[ing] itself through a symptom" increasingly difficult and thereby facilitates its moving toward a new means of self-regulation (p. 46). Complementing this explanation is Andolfi's (1979a), which postulates as the key objective of reframing methods their making it possible for the family to become the initiator, or "protagonist," of its own change. Similarly, Keller and Elliot (1982) view reframing in terms of the therapist's "selling" the family a "new reality," which prompts it to undertake correction of its "homeostatically-based vicious cycle" (p. 119). In all these authors, and in many others as well, there is a conviction (often left unstated) that essential cognitive change must have behavioral repercussions that, in turn, reinforce the new cognitions. Or, regarded somewhat differently, a pathogenic cycle fundamentally reconceived must eventuate in a therapeutic cycle, yielding a new and substantially more adaptive homeostasis to all concerned.

The important point, of course, is that if the *meaning* of a problematic situation is altered through changing its conceptual (and therefore emotional) context, the situation itself cannot but be experienced in radically divergent terms. And experienced dissimilarly, the situation need no longer be problematic. It should, moreover, be emphasized that the problem-ameliorating aspects of successful reframing are *not* dependent on whether the actual situation is altered. In fact, the situation in some cases may not even be alterable. But as long as it is *perceived* differently, its consequences will be different as well. As Watzlawick et al. (1974) point out, such an idea is hardly new: it has, indeed, been enunciated as early as the first century A.D., when Epictetus observed that "it is not the things themselves which trouble us, but the opinions that we have about these things" (p. 95—original source not given). When such options are affected by the introduction of new frames, labels, or definitions, the individual's way of thinking and feeling are also affected. In a family context, the new perceptual frame—focusing on the symptom or problematic behavior as an expression of the family *system*—alters both the identified patient's conception of the problem and the rest of the family's conception of the identified patient (see, e.g., Weeks & L'Abate, 1982). As a result, the particular functions served by the symptomatic behavior are undercut, and the habitual interactional sequence perpetuating this behavior is relinquished as no longer necessary.

Besides the central purpose of reframing techniques to change or eradicate dysfunctional behaviors through changing the perceptions underlying these behaviors, a number of additional uses for these devices have been proposed. Bergman (1980), Madanes (1980), and Jessee, Jurkovic, Wilkie, and Chiglinsky (1982), for example, discuss reframing in the context of a therapeutic system, and stress its ability to beneficially alter the existing power hierarchy. Particularly in treatment settings involving children, the therapist's tactical reframings of symptomatic behavior are seen as enabling him to gain control of it and reestablish his normal superordinate status in the therapeutic relationship, without which change can hardly be feasible.

In quite a different context, relabeling symptomatic behavior has been viewed as helping to provide clients with a greater sense of *self*-control. For when clients are more upset by the out-of-control feelings engendered by the symptom than by the symptom itself, positive relabeling of the symptom may induce them to conceive it as far less suggestive of personal powerlessness (see, e.g., Weeks, 1977; Weeks & L'Abate, 1982). Finally, relabeling—by implying that the symptom is actually the *vehicle* of change—may be instrumental in prompting clients to adopt "an expectational set that change is imminent" (Weeks & L'Abate, 1982, p. 107).

Positive Connotation

As mentioned earlier, the term "positive connotation" derives from the work of Selvini Palazzoli and her associates in Milan. Basically a form of reframing, it can be distinguished in part by its invariably identifying symptom-related behaviors as positive. Reframing, relabeling, and redefinition, on the other hand, in their attempt to jolt client perceptions, may occasionally interpret behaviors or events presumed to be positive in an unprecedented pejorative manner. Additionally, positive connotation stands somewhat apart from reframing in its being used always within a family context and directed much less toward the symptom than toward the entire system which has given rise to it—thus *defining* the symptom as systemic. A stance of approval is adopted toward *all* the behaviors exhibited by the family that pertain to the symptom, particularly those traditionally viewed as pathological. As Selvini Palazzoli et al. (1975/1978) stress, what at bottom is being positively connoted is "the homeostatic tendency of the system, and not its members"—although individual behaviors may be specifically approved in their "denot[ing] the common intention toward the unity and stability of the group" (p. 58). In short, both the symptomatic behavior and the family's *response* to it are construed positively—and complementarily—as serving to bind the family together.

Generally, the therapeutic purposes of positive connotation overlap with those already delineated for reframing, although the explanations supporting its employment usually carry a more elaborate systemic emphasis. To begin with, concentrating on family relationships and elucidating them in a positive way serves both to shift the context of therapy to a systemic level and to help the therapist avoid taking sides between family members, especially between the identified patient and the rest of the family (Weeks & L'Abate, 1982). Perhaps even more important, positive connotation permits the therapist to be accepted by the entire family system. For negative evaluations, particularly those directed toward the parents, regularly produce discouraging results—whether the subjects of criticism respond with defensive indignation and disapproval or, even worse, with a despondent type of depressive self-criticism that effectively operates to leave the therapist(s) impotent (Selvini Palazzoli et al., 1974).

By averting family resistance and thereby gaining access to the family system, the *therapeutic* system—and Selvini Palazzoli's model is a conjoint one—can proceed to exert its influence for change. Having, moreover, aligned itself with the family's inevitable homeostasis (since all systems, by definition, are characterized by a homeostatic tendency), the therapeutic system may begin to undermine the factions and alliances maintaining the dysfunctional behavior which the family, purportedly, wishes to eliminate. And, paradoxically, it is precisely through therapist efforts to *strengthen* the family's homeostatic tendency that the capacity for transformation inherent in living systems is activated (Selvini Palazzoli et al., 1974). To do otherwise—that is, to reject the family's pathogenic system by implying through negative evaluation that it needs to change—would only be to prompt the family to reject in turn the possibility of allowing the therapist "admission" into this system, obviously a prerequisite for successful treatment (Selvini Palazzoli et al., 1975/1978).

Once the family has been induced, through the therapist's sanctioning its homeostatic tendency, to accept an external perspective on its problems, it finds itself in an extremely uncomfortable position. For confronted with positive interpretations that include the very symptom it has determined should be removed, it is forced to ask itself whether its cohesion and stability must in fact depend on one member's symptomatically sacrificing himself. As Dell (1981b) observes, the therapist's stance is paradoxical in its being at once "benevolent" and "toxic": benevolent because of the loving and charitable motives it ascribes to the family and its symptom bearer, and toxic because "it radically (and unacceptably) contradicts family members' premises as to what is actually happening in the family." In such a context (as provocative as it is unprecedented), Dell perceives the family as changing "in the process of trying to rid themselves of the toxic and stupefying reframing of their family game" (pp. 49–50). It might be said, in summary, that the same benevolence that has permitted the therapist to be received into the system operates to unbalance this system—and so badly that equilibrium can be restored only through self-initiated adjustments which ultimately transform the system and render the symptom unnecessary.

Symptom Prescription

At the same time that a reframing device can be viewed as itself a paradoxical strategy, it is often expressly employed to help clients accept the logic of the paradoxical instruction, task, injunction, or (to use the most common term) "symptom prescription" that follows in its wake. In fact, the key distinction between the complementary techniques of reframing and symptom prescription is that the former is implicit whereas the latter is explicit (Weeks, 1977; Anderson & Russell, 1982). For even though reframing as such does not involve directing clients behaviorally, any unwanted behavior or behavioral sequence positively relabeled must be worth continuing—just as any presumed *desirable* behavior, redefined negatively by the therapist, carries the implication that it ought in some way to be changed. Again, reframing does not specify that clients *do* anything differently; indeed, it can sometimes effect change regardless of whether the individual or family consciously agrees with it. Symptom prescription, however, does endeavor to enjoin clients behaviorally, although (depending on whether it is compliance- or defiance-based) it too may be successful even when the therapist's instructions are not obeyed. In fact, in cases where the directive puts clients in a double bind from which they cannot escape *without* changing, the actual willingness of clients to follow therapist instructions may be irrelevant to their effectiveness.

Simply defined, symptom prescription involves encouraging or instructing clients to maintain their symptomatic behavior—or, more broadly, their presenting problem or complaint. The paradoxical flavor of such an approach should be obvious since, within the context of therapy, practicing the undesired behavior is tacitly regarded as the means toward altering or eliminating that behavior. The underlying message of the directive is that symptoms can be removed by being intentionally adhered to, or that through consciously willing to occur problematic behaviors thought to be involuntary, their control will eventually be delivered into the client's hands.

It should be emphasized that there are numerous variants of symptom prescription—such as symptom modification, symptom exaggeration, and even *system* prescription—and that these closely linked methods are not really synonymous with symptom prescription in that they do not request that clients *literally* repeat symptomatic behaviors. Although the literature on therapeutic paradoxh as tended to use the term "symptom prescription" rather loosely to include a variety of its extensions, in the present discussion an attempt will be made to distinguish among the many variants of instructing clients to move toward change through somehow avoiding it. Before elaborating on the many varieties of symptom prescription, however, it will be useful to summarize the many theoretical explanations offered for the effectiveness of the basic technique.

One frequent justification for prescribing symptomatic behaviors is that the very novelty of this approach is capable of increasing the potential for therapeutic change. Straightforward interpretations, in contrast, are judged much easier to ignore, particularly since they may have been anticipated in advance and, as a consequence, already discounted. Addressing the utility of intervening unexpectedly with seriously disturbed families, Selvini Palazzoli (Barrows, 1982) picturesquely remarks in an interview that "counseling the family . . . what the concierge could also counsel does not have a therapeutic effect at all." To disrupt obstinately fixed family patterns, the therapist's tactics must manage to surprise—and even shock—their recipients. As Selvini Palazzoli describes her own clinical objectives, rather than search for paradoxical methods as such, it is preferable "to seek what is unexpected or what is so cryptic but at the same time so disorganizing for the family, that it upsets their rigid or their dysfunctional organization" (p. 67). In short, the impact of an unexpected prescription comes from its *shaking up* the recipient's habitual view of reality. It is compelling in a way that makes it exceedingly difficult to disregard and, once responded to, it can hardly help but play havoc with the individual's cognitive and behavioral equilibrium.

Another rationale frequently proposed for encouraging the continuance of symptoms is that such encouragement functions to give the therapist instrumental control over treatment, without which the therapist is impotent to effect change (see, especially, Haley, 1963). Directing clients to behave symptomatically makes it impossible for them to exploit their symptoms to gain power over the therapeutic relationship. And (as this argument typically goes) the basic purpose of symptoms to begin with is their enabling the individual to exert control over social interactions. Besides undermining the usefulness of dysfunctional behavior in dominating others, the therapist's bold assumption of control over this behavior serves to impart to the client the message that the therapist may, indeed, be in a position to extinguish the symptomatic behavior altogether. That is, if the therapist can evoke the symptom, the possibility must exist that he can also eradicate it—especially since such intentional evocation is done within a context mutually understood as therapeutic.

Closely allied to this explanation of beneficial therapist control is Haley's (1963) notion that symptom prescription permits the therapist to create for the client a "benevolent ordeal." Such an ordeal decreases the attractiveness of behaving symptomatically while at the same time increasing the desirability of alternative, and symptom-free, responses. As Haley paradoxically characterizes the situation:

> If a therapist was merely benevolent, the patient could deal with him. If he was merely a man who provide[d] punishing ordeals, the patient could righteously seek the company of someone else. Yet when the therapist benevolently provides a punishing ordeal which will continue until the patient changes, the appropriate response for a patient is to undergo "spontaneous" change. (p. 187)

Placed at an interpersonal disadvantage as long as symptoms persist, the patient can regain control of the relationship only through abandoning dysfunctional behavior. Translating such an idea into psychoanalytic terms, it might be said that at this point the therapist's maneuvers have succeeded in divesting the patient of the most important secondary gain provided by his symptomatology.

As commonly theorized, prescribing the client's symptoms fosters another level of control in addition to the interpersonal. This control—ultimately the crucial one—is the *self*-control that the client is able to achieve through deliberately practicing the symptomatic behavior. As first elaborated by Watzlawick et al. (1967), symptoms are by nature unwilled and therefore experienced as autonomous. Nonvolitional, they are also spontaneous in that the individual "falling victim" to them feels no control over their occurrence. Rather, they are reacted to hopelessly, as somehow having their own indomitable authority. Viewed from this perspective, "successfully" prescribing symptoms must undermine their coercive power, since a client who deliberately performs his symptomatic behavior cannot do so without seriously interfering with its former spontaneity. And here, of course, is the famous "be spontaneous" paradox in therapeutic action. For the client cannot intentionally engage in behaviors thought to be unintentional (or "spontaneous") without coming to realize that these behaviors are not really as beyond personal control as had been assumed. In short, once the client practices the supposedly spontaneous behavior *on demand* this behavior can no longer be regarded as involuntary. And, complementarily, no longer can the client claim irresponsibility for a symptom that can be produced at will, even if initially such production has been at the therapist's bidding. In the theoretical language characteristic of Watzlawick et al.: "By subjecting himself to the therapist's injunction the patient has stepped outside the frame of his symptomatic game without end, which up to that moment had no metarules for the change of its own rules" (pp. 237–238). Similar to other paradoxical tactics which create therapeutic double binds, symptom prescription obliges clients to remove themselves from the "frame" that has created their perceptual-behavioral dilemma and kept it fixed.

Besides this elegantly simple idea that demanding spontaneous behavior effectively precludes it, there is the related explanation of attribution theory. According to this vantage point, when individuals come to ascribe to themselves the capacity to control behavior formerly perceived as out of control, they will begin to exert increased control over it. Subsequent to symptom prescription, behavior once considered spontaneous is now held to be self-controllable, as they become convinced of the voluntary essence of this previously "involuntary" behavior (Fish, 1973). And so redefined, the symptom must lose its firm hold on them.

Discussing the rationale of symptom prescription with families, Herr and Weakland (1979) observe that such tactics prompt members to develop insights into themselves and their mutually unsatisfying interactive sequences through helping them discover the volitional aspects of these seemingly automatic transactions. By a therapist's urging contentious family members, for example, to fight *more* so as, eventually, to fight less, these members are given an ideal opportunity to find out that they have actually been controlling the frequency of their fighting all along. And once members are forced to recognize that they are hardly innocent about how to start (and intensify) family quarrels, they are obliged to take responsibility for the intentionality of these fights. Herr and Weakland see symptom prescription as additionally valuable in its teaching family members more closely to attend to each other's behavior. Once cognizant of their own power to instigate problems, members begin to understand how others in the family similarly exert their power in negative ways, *as well as* how they can negate this power by not responding "reflexively" when provoked.

Yet another justification for symptom prescription is offered by Herr and Weakland in their pointing out that the frequent information-gathering pretext of such seemingly perverse directives permits the family to renounce its symptomatic behaviors only as quickly as it feels comfortable in doing so. Enjoining a family, on the other hand, to acknowledge its control over dysfunctional interactions and to proceed at once to behave more harmoniously with one another is much more likely to lead to failure and consequent feelings of hopelessness. An adequate amount of time must be allowed for major readjustments in a family system; and symptom prescription, which "inoculates" the family against failure through creating a therapeutic double bind, is beneficial in helping the family set its own appropriate pace for change.

Of all the arguments advanced for the use of symptom prescription— and, it should be added, for other paradoxical devices as well—doubtless the most prevalent is the rationale of resistance. The reasoning here is that many clients who come to therapy actually feel compelled to oppose all therapist efforts on their behalf. Relating to the closely aligned "control" rationale already discussed, it might be said that these clients, however unconsciously, recognize that to the extent they can "provoke" the therapist to try to help them and successfully resist his various attempts, they will remain in control of the relationship—however self-defeating and countertherapeutic this control may be. To nullify or therapeutically "appropriate" this negative set, the therapist needs to *join* client resistance in such a way that clients can continue to assert their need for interpersonal power only by resisting their former resistance and moving in the direction of change.

It is imperative to stress that there are several other resistance explanations for symptom prescription independent of the need-for-control hypothesis. The social-psychological principle of *reactance*—which postulates that explicit or implied threats to restrict or eradicate some important aspect of an individual's freedom will prompt the individual to react negatively and reassert that freedom—has occasionally been proposed to account for the effectiveness of symptom-prescribing techniques (Brehm, 1976; Brehm & Brehm, 1981; Fish, 1973; Seltzer, 1983). Here the rationale pertains less to interpersonal control than to the personal control restored through the individual's doggedly resistant stance. Ironically, with a well-calculated symptom prescription clients may begin to fear for the elimination of their *asymptomatic* behaviors and feel constrained to behave more normally so as to protect or reestablish these latent freedoms. The anxiety associated with change, and sometimes suggested as itself the primary reason for client resistance (e.g., Lantz, 1978), may well be understandable as deriving from the individual's, or family's, fear that behaving differently may eventuate in a serious forfeiture of freedom and control, both personal and social. In such a setting, for a therapist to ask for *no* behavioral change is substantially to lessen client feelings of risk.

Principles of communication and cybernetics have been adopted to account specifically for the dynamics of *family* resistance to change. As explained by Weeks and L'Abate (1982), families are best seen as circular (as opposed to linear) systems. In such systems negative feedback inhibits change because it elicits a counterforce that functions to restore the family's status quo or homeostasis. Contrariwise, positive feedback serves to promote change (or disequilibrium in the system) through its amplifying divergences from the family norm. In this conceptual scheme, paradoxical directives are seen as mechanisms of positive feedback operating to "topple the dysfunctional system of behavior by forcing it to recalibrate" (p. 20). And such recalibration culminates in what has earlier been characterized as second-order change. Although the system itself remains intact (for a certain homeostatic combination of positive and negative feedback continues to be present), it can no longer abide by its old—and now obsolete—behavioral rules. Indeed, it is in the family members' endeavors to escape the confusion introduced into the system by such positive feedback that they are led to resist their former reluctance to try out new behaviors.

Besides inducing the family to take a stand against its own habitual resistance to change, symptom prescription appeals to the family's need to assert its resistance to outside influence. It has regularly been pointed out that families often reveal themselves as antagonistic to therapist efforts to modify their behavior. Driven to react negatively to external directives that threaten their homeostatic operations—which are unconsciously perceived as vital to maintaining internal stability—they are particularly vulnerable to injunctions that *require* them to continue dysfunctional behavior. As Jacobson and Margolin (1979) put it: "Since the family's collusive defensiveness leads to the adoption of a stance which resists outside attempts to influence it, when the therapist instructs them to behave pathologically, the only way to resist . . . is by changing for the better" (p. 151). Seen in somewhat different (though complementary) terms, the therapist's push for no change sets into motion the family's homeostatically induced negative feedback, which in this instance provokes the family to change. Through the use of symptom prescription, the balance or stability of the family is temporarily thrown into disarray, and the family is forced to defy the therapist (and, inadvertently, its own "symptom-making" rules) by adopting less dysfunctional behaviors. Only through reconstituting its collective self can the family defeat the therapist, whose unanticipated request for no change has ironically *increased* his power in relation to the family, since his encouragement and support of symptomatic behavior is implicitly feared as endangering family homeostasis.

Stanton (1981b) attempts to summarize the effectiveness of paradoxical instructions delivered to a family in terms of a "compression" mechanism. According to his rather intricate theorization (based on his extensive work with addict families):

> Dysfunctional nuclear families and subsystems [vacillate], in cyclic form, between an overly-close, "undifferentiated" or "fusion" state, through a disintegrating/expansive or "fission" state directed outward, to another fusion state with the family of origin. In other words, when the nuclear family implodes toward a point of near fusion, a counter-reaction occurs outward, away from fusion with the immediate family member(s) and toward a fusion state with the family of origin. . . . The paradoxical intervention, by compressing either the nuclear family or the family of origin toward fusion, accelerates the process and causes an explosive counter-reaction. (pp. 375–376)

In this situation the therapist's "strategic" role is to obstruct the usual course of such a counterreaction and redirect its movement in such a way that new responses become imperative. Ideally, the result of this crisis-creating intervention is to break the family's pathological pattern and, through provoking an expanded behavioral repertoire, lead it toward healthy transformation.

A final systems-based explanation for symptom prescription methods which might be mentioned here is that proposed by Hoffman (1981)—

who actually offers *three* separate, though ultimately translatable, nonlinear analyses to account for the usefulness of such methods. Considering paradoxical prescription in terms neither of the individual nor of opposing family "branches," Hoffman explores the larger context of the family system interacting with (or cognitively "assaulted by") the therapist. Viewing symptoms (or dysfunctional behaviors generally) as essentially the result of desperate family maneuvers to maintain a subjectively required interactive balance, this author argues that therapists can advantageously tip this balance by throwing their authoritative weight on the side of symptomatic behavior. In the family's reaction—or overreaction—to what we might only half-facetiously term the therapist's dexterous "unbalancing act," the symptom sustaining the dysfunctional system must defensively be abandoned. For its key role in preserving the family's equilibrium has been seriously undermined by the therapist's "unstabilizing" support.

Discussing a specific case involving marital imbalance, Hoffman seeks to elucidate the curative function of the therapist's paradoxical advice—advice which both members of the couple felt obliged to reject, and in so doing moved closer together, beneficially altering their relational balance. In the author's words:

> The point is that the forces that accomplished these changes were the potentials for recoil built into the relative balance of the relationship. When the therapist tried to even out the seesaw [through straightforward interventions], the couple, answering to interior laws, could not do so. But when he pushed the seesaw too far, it rebalanced itself, so to speak, empowered by a recoil from five relationship arcs: husband/wife; wife/husband; wife/therapist; husband/therapist; and (finally) couple/therapist. (p. 309)

Such a "rebalancing" explanation strikes Hoffman as finally a more serviceable way of accounting for the success of paradoxical directives than any alleged resistance-toward-external-control interpretation that focuses on individual respondents. And, indeed, from a systems perspective the more relationship elements that a hypothesis can account for, the more closely it comes to reflecting the complex multidimensionality of human interaction.

Some Extensions and Variants of Symptom Prescription

Besides literally instructing clients to continue with symptomatic behavior, there are a large variety of paradoxical strategies which, either in their encouraging dysfunctional behavior or discouraging healthier behavior, come under the general rubric of symptom prescription. In this section ten such techniques are briefly reviewed, although this number could probably be halved or doubled depending on the nature and specificity of categories employed. For example, "symptom modification" and "symptom exaggeration" are taken up separately because the dynamics of the latter tactic have generally been discussed in terms somewhat different from those of the former. Yet there is no denying that symptom exaggeration is actually a subset of symptom modification and could thus be considered within this broader heading. As might be expected, theoretical accounts for the effectiveness of all these kindred techniques involve considerable repetition and overlap. In seeking to avoid as much of this explanatory redundancy as feasible, the following exposition focuses on the most distinguishing aspects of these many "variations on a paradoxical theme."

Symptom Modification

As symptom exaggeration is a special type of symptom modification, so is symptom modification a particular kind of symptom prescription. In symptom modification, rarely discussed independently of the main strategic technique of symptom prescription, the symptomatic behavior is prescribed in slightly altered form. To use Zeig's (1980b) classification scheme, modification in the symptom, or symptom complex, may take place on many different levels—including the cognitive, affective, behavioral, contextual, relational, attitudinal, or symbolic. To give just one simple example, the therapist might specify that the problematic behavior (say, a compulsive act) be fully engaged in, but at a time and place other than that in which it occurs ordinarily. The resultant disruption, however minor, of the symptom pattern may have a cumulative effect similar to removing a single pillar from a building's foundation, although in the therapeutic setting the intent is much more to promote systemic reconstruction than to instigate mere annihilation.

As emphasized particularly by Erickson (Haley, 1973), prescribing a symptom in somewhat modified form can function therapeutically to put individuals in closer touch with their own resources to adjust to, control, or overcome frustrating problems. And Erickson, throughout his influential career, maintained the importance of the therapist's contriving to elicit the cure from *within* the patient's cognitive/behavioral framework, rather than striving to change the patient by imposing upon him some external ideational perspective. Related to this notion of fostering nonsymptomatic self-control is the idea that prescribing slight changes in the expression of the symptom indirectly empowers the therapist to gain productive control of it. This hypothesis has been expounded at length by Haley (1963), who appears to view such symptom modification as even more likely to help the client alter his dysfunctional behavior than a literal prescription of symptoms. The central contention here is that if a client can in any way be induced to alter his symptom pattern at the therapist's behest—and this even includes following a request to *exacerbate* symptomatology—then the client is likely to attribute to the therapist the ability to govern his symptom.

Moreover, the client, by setting a precedent for following the therapist's directives, is more apt to comply with a later directive that specifies a greater (and generally more beneficial) alteration in the symptom. This rationale for symptom modification is vaguely reminiscent of the old "foot-in-the-door" ploy of the experienced salesperson, which should suggest its additional value in minimizing client resistance. For permitted in a context of change (i.e., the therapeutic relationship) essentially to continue symptomatic behavior, the client is caught off his defensive guard and prompted to comply with future requests for seemingly benign symptom "adjustments." Subtly comforted into adopting a cooperative set, the client's rigid maintenance of symptomatology must weaken as the therapeutic alliance strengthens. Finally, since the therapist has, through his fundamentally permissive attitude, contrived to "befriend" the symptom, the client cannot actively resist the therapist's directives without taking a stand against his own dysfunctional behavior. And this of course returns us right back to the elegant communications concept of the therapeutic double bind, where the very *context* of therapy may be seen as obstructing a pathological outcome.

Symptom Exaggeration

Asking clients purposely to magnify, or enlarge upon, their problems is frequently referred to in strategic literature as *exaggerating the symptom*. This deliberate intensification of behavior previously regarded as involuntary is viewed as serving to demonstrate to the client its ultimate controllability. For if the behavior can willfully be regulated in one direction— even if this is the *wrong* direction—the possibility must exist that it can be rerouted in a more positive direction as well.

Several other rationales have been specifically proposed for this amplification technique. Farrelly and Brandsma (1974), whose innovative treatment approach cannot really be classified as systemic, discuss the utility of having clients intentionally accentuate their symptoms so that they will begin to realize first-hand the foolishness or absurdity of some of their self-assumptions or beliefs. Aponte and Van Deusen (1981) contend that symptom exaggeration can increase the magnitude of the symptom beyond the point that it can continue to serve a compensatory function, with the result that it must eventually be abandoned.

Finally, a justification for magnifying symptoms that focuses not on the symptomatic client but on the symptomatic *relationship* might be mentioned, even though the authors here choose to conceptualize their method of exaggeration in structural, rather than strategic, terms. As a means toward "creating boundaries in overinvolved dyads," Minuchin and Fishman (1981, p. 155) propose that the therapist consider recommending or prescribing an augmentation in the proximity of family members whose enmeshed relationship is already of pathogenic proportions. An overprotective mother, for instance, may be instructed to attend more closely to her child's *minor* needs, or an overinvolved husband may be directed to monitor even more closely his wife's whereabouts. Ideally, such deliberate intensification of already disproportionate behaviors brings to the surface or deepens the conflict between participants—and to such a degree that they are forced, therapeutically, to increase their mutual distance.

System Prescription

Whereas techniques involving some sort of symptom prescription can be identified within every major theoretical orientation, the strategy of prescribing an entire malfunctioning *system* is uniquely related to the systems approach. In *system prescription*—a device generally seen as originating in the work of Selvini Palazzoli and her associates—what is in essence prescribed are the very rules that have resulted in a symptomatic family member. Positively reframing these rules and then benignly requesting their repetition profoundly challenges the family's symptom-maintaining adherence to them. Indeed, system prescription (or "systemic symptom prescription," as de Shazer, 1978, 1979b, 1980, refers to it) can be viewed as turning the family's conceptual and behavioral universe on its head. As Sluzki (1978) states: "The illegitimate, spontaneous, parasitical behavior becomes legitimate, non-spontaneous and a useful part of the process. The complaint becomes the compliance and the disappearance of symptoms a non-compliance" (p. 383).

This idea of "cure through noncompliance" echoes the resistance rationale of symptom prescription discussed earlier, though it should again be stressed that from a family systems perspective resistance is generally seen in terms of the family members' need to oppose any outside attempt to influence its homeostasis. In fact, direct efforts to alter the rules underlying the family's dysfunctional behavior are usually dismissed by the therapist in the conviction that such "tampering" can only serve to incite a countermovement by the family to uphold its status quo (Selvini Palazzoli et al., 1975/1978). Despite the hardship exacted by the family's symptomatic equilibrium, it is yet implicitly perceived by the family as the only viable alternative for its interpersonal difficulties and will therefore be defended at almost all costs. In such a problematic situation, the therapeutic antidote is simple: the therapist must "outdo" the family by pressing for more homeostasis than it can comfortably tolerate. By successfully "one-uping" the family's resistance, the family is compelled to retaliate by renouncing those same rules that have brought it into treatment. Indirectly provoked to rebel against its own dysfunctional rules, it is able to instigate the healthy process of change previously obstructed by its ambivalently maintained equilibrium (Andolfi, 1980).

Seen from the opposite vantage point, should the family choose to cooperate by engaging in its malfunctional behavior *under the therapist's explicit direction*, it will be violating one of its cardinal rules and thereby establishing an important precedent for further systemic infractions. Specifically, the therapist's prescribing the varied interpersonal components of problem-perpetuating behavior serves to make overt the concealed rules controlling the family's interaction. And once family members become aware of how the *roles* dictated by their self-defeating rules contribute to—or even define—their ongoing problem, it is difficult for them to continue abiding by these rules. As their painful inappropriateness is increasingly exposed, they must eventually be relinquished.

Perhaps, as Papp (1980a) has observed, the key aspect of system prescription is that in following the therapist's advice to engage in its symptom-producing interactive cycle, the family is confronted with its own perverse logic. By "joining" the family system through positively reframing its presenting problem, the therapist paradoxically undermines, or sabotages, this system. For once the family is induced to reenact its vicious cycle *consciously*, the dynamics behind the symptom are fatally altered such that the cycle and symptom become split off from one another. Moreover, the family cannot carry out the therapist's paradoxical directives without coming to recognize its own fundamental responsibility both in generating and sustaining the symptom. And, in the end, therapeutically prompting clients to accept responsibility for their problems and fully "own" them is the goal of virtually all therapy, regardless of emphasis or theoretical title.

Paradoxical Family Rituals

Closely connected to prescribing the problem-engendering family system is prescribing a paradoxical ritual designed to induce family members to forsake the longstanding myth at the foundation of their complaint. This technique, too, is regularly associated with the work of Selvini Palazzoli and her coworkers, who have repeatedly stressed the importance of the therapist's intervening on the *concrete behavioral* level as a way of effecting decisive change—as opposed to more "direct" attempts to rid a family of its collective problem by authoritatively imparting insight about it to them.

Prescribing precisely the stubborn, ritualized behavior that has culminated in the similarly stubborn symptom not only evokes in family members a surprised, or paradoxical, reaction: it is itself paradoxical in the sense that the prescription is at once uncannily blunt yet remarkably subtle. Concerned with essence rather than substance, it does not prescribe the actual *content* of the family's ritualistic behavior, but a highly detailed though circumscribed *form* of this behavior. Through such indirect direction, the family is "seduced" into uncomfortably close contact with its own maladaptive transactional pattern. And this self-confrontation is frequently all that is needed to persuade the family to adopt more functional interpersonal behaviors. The therapist's paradoxical goal in such instances is to explode the family's pathogenic myth once and for all by being rigidly faithful in prescribing its crucial components. At the very least, the ritualized prescription can serve as an extremely useful diagnostic device: whether literally obeyed or largely ignored, it helps the therapist better assess the nature and severity of the family's problem.

As theorized by van der Hart (1978/1983), prescribed rituals are valuable in undermining the function (or symbolic usefulness) of the symptom. Because the troublesome behavior is now controlled by the therapist—who after all has set the particular conditions for it—the family may feel obliged to begin acting asymptomatically. Selvini Palazzoli et al. (1975/1978) speak about the impact of prescribing family rituals in terms of their eliciting surprise and confusion in family members. For such prescriptions operate to align the therapist with the family's homeostatic tendencies at a time when the family anticipates having its modus operandi strongly challenged. Such alignment obliquely functions to prompt the family to obey the prescription and in so doing confront—and ultimately transcend—its own pathogenic rules. As Selvini Palazzoli et al. conclude, arguing for the action-based, noninterpretive advantages of ritual prescription:

> Every ritual becomes valid . . . because of its normative function, which is inherent in every collective action where the behavior of all the participants is directed toward the same goal. . . . Our prescription of a ritual [and not necessarily, it should be added, a *paradoxical* one] is meant not only to avoid the verbal comment on the norms that at that moment perpetuate the family play [which would only arouse the family's resistance], but to introduce into the system a ritualized prescription of a play whose new norms silently take the place of old ones. (pp. 96–97)

Paradoxical Written Messages

It should be noted that paradoxical written messages are not, at least in content, any different from antiexpectational communications delivered orally. But while such messages almost always contain some type of reframing and symptom prescription, the fact that they are conveyed in epistolary form affects their potency and dramatic impact on recipients. Usually employed with particularly difficult couples and families, these letters (similar perhaps to formal or "official" communications generally) tend to be given considerable weight and authority by those receiving them. And the very importance attributed to these unanticipated documents can compel individuals seriously to reflect on their role in maintaining symptoms or complaints, in sharp contrast to their previously resistant attitude.

Probably foremost in advocating the use of paradoxical written messages and directives are Selvini Palazzoli and her associates in Milan and, in this country, L. L'Abate and his colleagues at the Family Study Center at Georgia State University—who have for several years now investigated the various applications of such missives. As Weeks and L'Abate (1982) describe it, paradoxical letters are almost always reacted to as "cryptic, obscure, confusing, perplexing, or noncommonsensical"; and this initially mystified reaction "helps to secure the client's involvement, since the person or system receiving the letter must work on deciphering its meaning" (p. 156).

Besides the sheer attention-getting value of paradoxical written messages, Weeks and L'Abate enumerate three other functions that such letters can serve. First, therapist communications specifically recorded for clients and then given to them (or sent to them by mail) are much less likely to be ignored, distorted, disparaged, or repressed than are such communications delivered orally. Second, a written message has a permanence to it that encourages its being read and thought about repeatedly *outside* the therapy sessions, leading to a cumulative effect that may go considerably beyond the single transmission of this same message during a treatment session. The letter, in fact, may contain as part of its message the explicit instruction that it be read (silently to oneself or aloud to others) a specific number of times between interviews. Finally, as has already been suggested, written communication has a certain "binding" quality about it that may make it more difficult to resist than the identical communication delivered orally. In sum, used as an ancillary paradoxical strategy—especially in cases where an impasse or deadlock has been reached—written messages can be extremely helpful in facilitating or reviving therapeutic movement.

Restraining Change

In *restraining change* the therapist actively discourages the individual, couple, or family from modifying troublesome behavior by suggesting that such change is not really a feasible alternative. This paradoxical maneuver is generally adopted when therapeutic change is noticeably slow in occurring. As Watzlawick et al. (1974) observe, restraining tactics flagrantly violate the dictates of common sense, since when progress is slower than expected, the popular notion is to accelerate it through supportive prodding or encouragement. Further, when initial signs of improvement do appear, its augmentation is commonly felt to be best fostered by an attitude of commendation and hopefulness. Yet in a great number of cases the most productive response to incipient change is cautiousness—with a "go slow" directive being the treatment of choice.

Weakland et al. (1974), in characterizing the methods of MRI's Brief Therapy Center, emphasize that despite their ten-session limit they regularly recommend at the outset of treatment that clients not change too fast. And later, when clients begin to share their progress, they respond with worried concern and a guarded suggestion that this improvement be intentionally slowed down. These warnings are viewed, paradoxically, by the authors as distinctly advantageous to rapid progress. Their speculations as to why this should be so are that such hesitancy (1) reduces, or keeps in check, the almost inevitable anxiety associated with change, and (2) enhances client motivation to build further on therapeutic achievements so as to counter the therapist's supposedly exaggerated circumspection. The second of these two hypotheses, it might be added, clearly warrants appreciation as "defiance-based" in that it justifies restraining in terms of its effectively mobilizing whatever resistance the client might harbor toward the therapist's authority (see Rohrbaugh et al., 1981).

Considering the use of restraining devices in a family systems context, Papp (1980a) argues that if the symptom is understood as essential to the operation of the family system and the therapist maintains a basic respect for this system, then change is, indeed, a cause for some negative concern. Consequently, when signs of change become evident it is appropriate to counsel restraint. Such carefully measured opposition to progress enables the therapist prudently to regulate its pace, as the family resists the unexpected attempt to hold it back and pushes onward (and perhaps with redoubled effort) for more change. It may be assumed that despite any family impatience to "get on with it," it is yet reassured by the therapist's scrupulosity in warning of the possible repercussions of change. Finally, despite a most cautious attitude and constant reminders that progress be gradual, the therapist does "allow" the family (however begrudgingly) to continue to change.

As a sort of footnote here, it might be mentioned that Weeks and L'Abate (1982) briefly examine, in their discussion of restraining change, the closely related techniques of "inhibiting change" and "forbidding change." But for almost all practical purposes these two stratagems can hardly be distinguished from the basic device of restraining, and in fact are justified by very much the same reasoning. Obviously any tactic which seeks to place change (and its attendant risks) under therapeutic "protection" obliges the therapist to painstakingly evaluate just *how much* restraining is likely to elicit the most beneficial reaction from a given client.

Relapse Prediction

A most noteworthy variant of restraining is the tactic of predicting a relapse. Such prediction is done when, as a result of the therapist's successfully prescribing the presenting complaint, it seems miraculously to vanish. By informing the client that the problem will, in all likelihood, as suddenly reappear, the therapist generates a therapeutic double bind. For if the symptom recurs, its doing so fulfills the therapist's prediction—and thus is redefined as under the therapist's control. And if it does *not* recur, it is now under the client's control—and thus ceases to exist independently of the client's will. In either case, the involuntary, noncontrollable, spontaneous character of the symptom is critically undermined. Moreover, by losing much of its former "autonomy," it also loses its power to elicit the same degree of concern or anxiety in the client, enabling him to deal more confidently with the situation *underlying* the symptom.

Relapse prediction also has special utility with the recalcitrant client. When the client's relationship to the therapist is predominantly oppositional, the relapse prediction will be regarded as a challenge to continue to be asymptomatic, so as to deny the validity of (and external control implied by) the therapist's pessimistic forecast. Weeks and L'Abate (1982) describe, for example, a therapist's telling a couple who have just had a "fightless" week (in reaction to the therapist's prescription for continued fighting) that they could expect to double their usual number of fights the following week. This provocative forecast evoked laughter from the couple and the bet that they would prove the therapist wrong—which they proceeded to do.

Finally, to further capitalize on the predilection of certain clients to defy authority, Weeks and L'Abate suggest that the therapist might well choose to discuss with the client all the things that might consciously be done to *ensure* the occurrence of a relapse. Such a suggestion contrives to take full advantage of the client's potentially sabotaging negativism. But, equally important, it also serves to increase the client's awareness of the many ways he has himself contrived to perpetuate his symptom in the past.

Relapse Prescription

Beyond predicting symptom recurrence is actually prescribing it. So-called *relapse prescription* can be seen as a natural extension of relapse prediction and is at times used in conjunction with it to moderate or neutralize impediments to change. Prescribing a relapse is viewed by Watzlawick et al. (1974) as especially indicated when a client has just overcome a substantial obstacle and, notwithstanding his elation, is now apprehensive that his success may be merely accidental. If at this point he is told that there is bound to be some sort of falling back (i.e., given a relapse prediction), and that such "slippage" is really desirable because it will help him better understand his problem, the treatment stage has been set for *directing* him to bring about a relapse.

The therapeutic double bind generated through prescribing a relapse is that (1) should the client experience a relapse, such an event can be seen as proof that he now has sufficient control over his problem to produce it deliberately, and (2) should he *fail* to produce a relapse, such nonrecurrence demonstrates that he now has sufficient control to avoid this problem deliberately. Additionally, Sluzki (1978), in describing relapse prescription implemented within a marital treatment setting, contends that once the generally symptomatic behavior is reframed as under the individual actor's control, its "main interactional value . . . its being there *in spite of* the participants, is lost, and, with it, the symptom itself" (p. 384).

Similarly, Weakland et al. (1974) speak of the therapist's prescribing a relapse—particularly in cases where the client has improved with dramatic rapidity—as helping the client further strengthen control over problematic behavior. This tactic is thereby likened to Rosen's "reenacting an aspect of the psychosis" (1953) and to related techniques of Erickson, all of which somehow manage to redefine in advance any possible relapse as yet another step forward. A famous example from the work of Erickson is cited in this respect by Stanton (1981b), who quotes the following "nostalgic" directive given by Erickson to the too-rapidly-improving client: "I want you to go back and feel as badly as you did when you first came in with the problem, because I want you to see if there is anything from that time that you wish to recover and salvage" (originally in Haley, 1973, p. 31). This unusual ploy not only exhibits Erickson's compassionate understanding of a symptom's more positive aspects, and the deeply personal (though largely unconscious) fear that may therefore follow the symptom's sudden amelioration, but also evidences Erickson's ingenuity in anticipating any resistance on the client's part. For—and this, incidentally, represents a *second* level of therapeutic double bind—the client can now resist the therapist's injunction to have a relapse only by continuing to improve.

Declaring Helplessness

Some clients do not appear to improve because, finally, they are more motivated to defeat the therapist than to change their behavior. Their manifestations of resistance soon become painfully obvious: they begin to miss appointments, cease to follow (or even *attempt* to follow) homework assignments, counter every therapist suggestion or interpretation with a "yes, but . . ." response, and so on. When a therapist reacts to the ensuing stalemate by trying even more assiduously to effect change, he succeeds only in setting himself up for more failure (or, to use an increasingly popular term, "burnout"). As Selvini Palazzoli and her colleagues (1975/ 1978) have observed, since the therapist's continuing efforts in such situations can only lead to additional frustration—given, that is, the nature of the clients' "game"—what is called for is a radical change in professional stance. Namely, the therapist must frankly and humbly admit his own inadequacy to help facilitate the (supposedly) desired change.

Selvini Palazzoli et al., who are responsible for formally introducing this last-ditch strategy into the literature, describe the tactic at length in a chapter of their book provocatively entitled "The Therapists Declare Their Impotence without Blaming Anyone." Describing the family's reaction to this unanticipated confession of therapist confusion and incapability, they comment:

> The immediate reaction is always one of astonishment, often followed by intense agitation and requests for help. The fear of losing their "adversaries" forces the family to do something, anything, to keep the game going— "so . . . then, what about us, what can we do?"—and often brings them to the point of making a generous self-accusation: "But couldn't it all be *our* fault?" (p. 148)

The important point here is that the family, despite their resistance (which derives from their fearful sense that the family's survival may actually hinge on continuing to interact symptomatically), also cannot resist such an external challenge to their game. They are, after all, "involved" in therapy—though after their own ambivalent fashion—and the therapists' declaration of impotence and the consequent need to terminate treatment constitutes a severe threat to their position.

Paradoxically, the official pronouncement of failure places the therapists one-up in relation to the family. For such capitulation serves to end, *on the therapists' terms*, the impasse which has served to define the family's triumph and which the family has "valiantly" fought for, even at the expense of their own improvement. In at once surrendering to the family and threatening through such forfeiture to "cut them off," the therapists in fact achieve a vital control of the relationship. For the family is then obliged to convince the therapists that they can in fact make advantageous use of treatment. Given their own tyrannical rules, they are simply unable to resist the challenge to get better in order to have another "round" with the therapists. As Selvini Palazzoli et al. elegantly put it: "This tactic . . . exploits one of the fundamental rules of the family game: never permit the collapse of the enemy" (p. 150).

It should be evident from the above description that the central justification for this last-resort tactic is that it permits therapists indirectly to assert control in cases distinguished by a resistance so extreme that without drastically nullifying it no therapeutic change is possible. The symmetrical game in which both therapists and family have become entrenched is thus broken and reconstructed as complementary so that therapy may at last become tenable. A second justification for declaring helplessness relates to many other reframing-symptom prescription techniques: that is, the therapists' willing self-disqualification forces the family to take the initiative for their own change. Further, through thereby defining themselves as aligned with the family's homeostatic tendencies, the therapists avoid being perceived by the family as threatening their status quo. In paradoxical summary, there are times in treatment when change is possible only after it is solemnly declared impossible, when situations can be improved only after they are professed hopeless, and when symptoms can be extinguished only after they are "decreed" to be permanent.

"The Confusion Technique"

One final, and especially curious, version of restraining change might be mentioned here. Referred to as "the confusion technique," it is in its own way quite as extreme a paradoxical strategy as declaring helplessness. First expounded in the literature by Erickson (see Haley, ed., 1967) as a method of inducing hypnotic trance, this device involves the hypnotist's showering the subject with a steady stream of words in an ever-evolving frame of reference. In such a baffling linguistic situation—which also incorporates intentional ambiguities and language as elliptical as it is incoherent—the subject is simply unable to focus meaningfully on the sender's vocalizations. The ultimate effect of such verbal obfuscation is for the subject to experience confusion and an increasingly desperate need to receive a communication that is complete and unequivocal—thus making him particularly susceptible to the trance-inducing message that follows.

De Shazer (1979b) discusses this innovative hypnotic strategy as precursory to his own analogous endeavors in therapy with couples who prove themselves rigidly resistant to setting concrete and realistic treatment goals. Adapting Erickson's devious maneuvers, he proceeds unquestioningly to accept every topic the couple presents as just another entry in the couple's ongoing list of problems and even refuses to allow the couple to focus on any single topic. Moreover, he suggests various problem areas of his own that might evoke additional complaints. As the couple becomes more and more bewildered by the systematic aborting of each and every item brought up, the therapist goes on to assure them of the significance of all their discussions and the utility of this elaborate history-taking in helping him better understand their relationship. At this juncture yet another topic is introduced. In fact, the therapist continues with this tactic until the couple eventually reacts in their mounting frustration by openly rebelling against what initially began as their own resistance toward articulating essential problems and using treatment productively.

In the case that the couple complains about the therapist's meandering methods but *still* fails to focus meaningfully on the work of therapy, the therapist bewails his own confusion and questions why they have not already terminated treatment, given their obvious lack of progress. The couple's reaction, de Shazer notes, is one of total befuddlement because they have come to assume that in their diverting treatment through bringing up countless side issues they have actually been complying with the therapist's directives all along. The ultimate outcome of the therapist's baffling intervention is frequently that the couple "spontaneously" becomes much more explicit about their primary problem and goals, so that their basic situation finally becomes comprehensible—and workable.

Again, citing Erickson (Haley, 1973) as his source, de Shazer argues that through implicitly endorsing a couple's "set" of withholding crucial information, the therapist gains control of therapy. For if the therapist can give them permission to withhold, it follows that he also has the power to permit them to broach even the most "loaded" of subjects. As already suggested, the confusion technique—conceptualized as an extension of sanctioning or encouraging client resistance—is also supported by the contention that it prompts clients to reveal and begin to grapple with very sensitive, and therefore zealously protected, issues in their relationship. Similar to virtually all paradoxical strategies that avoid opposing client resistance to change, it creates for the couple a therapeutic double bind. It leads them, unsuspectingly, not out of but more deeply *into* a corner from which there can be no tenable route of escape other than their venturing the previously resisted step of *self*-liberation. Once artfully enticed to lay claim to their own inherent ability to "cure" themselves, they are at last able to achieve the asymptomatic control of their lives which till then has eluded them.

EMPIRICAL RESEARCH

Introduction

Without doubt empirical investigations of paradoxical methods applied within a systems framework are still in the embryonic stage. Given the considerable bulk of articles and books that directly address the value of employing such techniques "strategically," the published experimental literature supporting their use seems particularly scant. Moreover, these empirical examinations have important limitations, so that they really cannot be regarded as confirming the comparative superiority of paradoxical to nonparadoxical methods in prompting therapeutic change.

It needs, preliminarily, to be stated that all of the eight studies reported on here fall short of reflecting the systemic use of paradox—especially as it is (and must be) tailored to fit the biases and needs of individual clients. Such an admission is meant less as a negative judgment on these beginning efforts to justify strategic paradoxical interventions than as a reminder of the immense practical difficulties involved in attempting, experimentally, to validate these rich and multifaceted therapeutic devices.

Choosing which studies to discuss in this section has been complicated by two factors. First, none of these investigations really succeeds in adhering to the clinical conditions of a systemic paradoxical intervention and, at the same time, employing the experimental controls without which the significance of reported results must remain debatable. Second, the artificial simplification of several of the better controlled studies (most conspicuously in the administration of their paradoxical interpretation or directive) raises the question of just how "systemic" the approach actually was. It should be recalled that just about *all* paradoxical strategies, regardless of the therapist's assumptions in using them, encourage clients to maintain dysfunctional behavior. In order to identify these techniques, therefore, as belonging to a systemic orientation rather than some other theoretical persuasion, it has been necessary to consider not only the nature of their implementation but also the explanations offered for their effectiveness.

Such considerations can at times become a bit tricky. For example, one study reviewed here (Hsu & Lieberman, 1982) is, if we are to take its title literally, not on systemic paradox at all but on paradoxical intention—essentially a behaviorist strategy. But if we look closely at how this clinical report characterizes the technique it explicitly designates "paradoxical intention," we find that its depiction simply does not conform, either procedurally or theoretically, to the basic description provided for it by its founder, Viktor Frankl, or by his successors. Indeed, one of the most reliable guides in determining which theoretical category best fits a paradoxical technique used in an empirical examination is the reference list which concludes the study. For such a list generally suggests the theoretical and technical sources and commitments of the author(s). In fact, the therapy outcome study just alluded to, which purports to be on paradoxical intention, cites in its reference section only a single article by Frankl, while including (as part of its conceptual framework) works by Erickson,

Haley, and Watzlawick, three key figures in the communication-systems approach.

Since paradoxical intention is frequently confounded with what in systems literature is typically termed "symptom prescription," it may be advisable, briefly, to distinguish the two techniques—if only by way of clarifying what makes the latter intervention fit best within a systems, or "strategic," approach. Although symptom prescription is obviously reminiscent of behaviorism in its endeavoring to remove the reinforcement supplied by symptomatic behavior, it conceptualizes the *dynamics* of this reinforcement very differently. Postulating that symptoms are maintained because of the interpersonal control they indirectly afford clients, strategic therapists see their directly instructing clients to practice symptoms as seriously undermining this control. Indeed, the therapeutic double bind regularly associated with symptom prescription is perceived as resulting from the therapist's maneuvering clients into a position that prompts them, whether they comply with the paradoxical directive or not, to abandon their symptomatic behavior. For if they effectively comply with the therapist's injunction to act symptomatically, they can no longer deny responsibility for "nonvoluntary" behavior. And if they *resist* the therapist's directive (as is the more likely alternative) and assert their need for interpersonal control by behaving nonsymptomatically, they are also obliged to admit to themselves the willfulness—and changeability—of their behavior.

Moreover, whereas symptom prescription is rooted in conceptions relating to interpersonal communication and control, paradoxical intention is grounded on *intrapersonal* ideas about the nature of anxiety and avoidance. The latter technique—compliance-based, almost by definition—is postulated as valuable primarily because it confronts, head-on, the anxiety serving to maintain the symptom. Having clients intentionally "surrender" to the symptom—whether this entails deliberately giving in to a murderous obsession, consciously trying to faint at the sight of a snake, or trying *not* to fall asleep at night—is hypothesized as disrupting the vicious cycle that is anticipatory anxiety and thus severing the link between the feared behavior and the general symptom of avoidance. In short, one gains power over the symptom (i.e., intrapersonal control) through inviting or practicing it intentionally. In no longer attempting to flee the anxiety-inducing situation (or, in the case of insomnia or sexual dysfunction, to exert influence over that which can only be spontaneous), one paradoxically regains control over it.

Admittedly, the tactics of symptom prescription and paradoxical intention may be closely tied in their common assumption that a symptom's spontaneity must be reduced when deliberately practiced. But the two techniques are readily distinguishable when it is kept in mind that the therapist employing paradoxical intention is dealing primarily with the *anxiety* intimately associated with the symptom, whereas the practitioner of symptom prescription is principally involved in altering the *system* (whether self-, marital, or family) in which the symptom occurs—and in such a way that the interpersonal advantages of the symptom are either nullified or no longer needed. In further contrast to paradoxical intention, symptom prescription typically makes more elaborate use of the therapeutic relationship to induce clients to alter behavior patterns and begin to assert themselves less symptomatically. Because symptomatic behavior is viewed as fundamentally a misguided strategy of communicational control, treatment in various ways centers on reducing its transactional value.

Clinical and Quasiclinical Studies

The recency of efforts to evaluate the effectiveness of symptom prescription techniques is best suggested by the fact that prior to 1980 only a single article can be identified that seeks to make some sort of empirically derived statement about their usefulness. This essay, authored by Weakland et al. (1974), is devoted mainly to expounding the strategic therapy practiced by MRI's Brief Therapy Center. Such treatment, though unquestionably highlighted by symptom prescription devices—and the authors pronounce "paradoxical instructions" as "probably constitut[ing] the most important single class of interventions in our treatment" (p. 158)—is not, it should be noted, wholly restricted to these methods. Consequently, the empirical assessment included in this essay (which comprises, incidentally, little more than 10% of its content) cannot be taken as exclusively evaluative of symptom prescription. Rather the reported results are most accurately understood as reflecting a general systems approach to therapy. Indeed, the authors explicitly remark that even in cases where only the "identified patient" was seen, the central complaint was conceptualized as embodying a system of relationships (involving the patient's family, friends, or work environment) which functioned to maintain the problematic behavior.

The data for the authors' initial evaluation of their method was obtained during a six-year period of developing and testing at the Center, during which time 97 individual, marital, and family cases were handled (involving 236 people in all). The results derive from a broad socioeconomic range of clients and an equally wide variety of clinical problems—chronic as well as acute. Employing no screening procedures and making use of many different referral sources, cases included individuals from 5 to 60 years of age and involved a maximum of 10 one-hour sessions, usually scheduled at weekly intervals. In the main, treatment attempted to achieve "limited but significant goals" (p. 142) in alleviating the major complaint of the patient(s). According to this chief objective, about three-quarters of the cases were seen as culminating successfully.

Considering the direct comparison of treatment aims to observable results as their foremost evaluative task, the authors drew their conclusions about each case on the basis of client interviews conducted by a nonparticipating therapist about three months after treatment. In this follow-up interview, clients were asked five questions pertaining to the alleviation of their problem and the occurrence of constructive behavioral change. Responses to these questions led to a final threefold classification of results—which summarily concluded that 40% of the cases obtained complete relief from the dominant problem; 32% demonstrated significant, though incomplete, relief; and the remaining 28% showed little or no change in resolving the main problem (i.e., treatment was deemed a failure). Such a general improvement rate of 72% is very impressive, especially since the average number of sessions per case was only seven.

All the same, the results of this investigation, promising as they are, require cautious interpretation. In fact, the authors suggest as much in their candid admission of several of the study's limitations, including possible errors relating to clinical judgment and what is loosely referred to as "occasional ambiguities" (p. 163) in their method of evaluation. The study is subject to further criticism in its lack of any screening procedure, the absence of any "placebo" or waiting list control group (the Center in fact maintaining no waiting list whatsoever), the relative briefness of its follow-up period, and its failure to take into account the possibility that certain extratherapy variables may in some cases have appreciably influenced the results. This said, however, the results reported do succeed in suggesting the comparative efficiency of strategic techniques in promoting significant behavioral change, especially in more chronic cases.

A multisided investigation by Wagner, Weeks, and L'Abate (1980) proposed, among other things, to determine the differential effectiveness of paradoxical written messages—a subject on which almost no empirical research had previously been attempted. The authors also intended that this research measure the efficacy of "paradoxical psychotherapy" generally—though the particular design of their experiment frankly would seem to have been ill-suited for this purpose. Taking part in this study were 56 married couples—all of whom were *nonclinical* volunteers drawn from introductory psychology classes and whose experimental involvement was determined apparently by the need to obtain course credit for such participation. These couples, whose degree of satisfaction in their marriage was evaluated before and after a six-session program devoted to marital enrichment, were divided equally into four groups: (1) an enrichment group, (2) a group which received enrichment and a *linearly worded* (i.e., straightforward or nonparadoxical) written message following their fourth session, (3) a group, complementary to the second, which received enrichment and a *paradoxically* worded letter (i.e., one which "cryptically" reframed a specific difficulty), and (4) a no-treatment control group.

Although the results of the enrichment program (chosen individually for each couple in all three experimental conditions) could hardly be interpreted as dramatic, the authors' assessment instruments—three separate marital satisfaction scales—did suggest the general effectiveness of all three treatment regimens in promoting marital contentment. No significant differences, however, were found distinguishing the three experimental groups. Also, the group receiving paradoxical letters ancillary to enrichment actually evidenced somewhat *less* overall mean change in their pre- to posttest scores than did either the enrichment-only group or the group receiving enrichment plus a linear letter—which, incidentally, revealed the largest mean change. The authors argue that their rating scales may have "missed the mark" in requiring spouses to assess the degree of felt contentment in various areas of their relationship instead of questioning them about specific problem areas that a paradoxical letter might have been particularly planned to address. Indeed, the authors express the concern that these rating instruments, in being linear and direct, may simply have been inappropriate for gauging the effectiveness of a paradoxical, and oblique, intervention strategy.

In Weeks and L'Abate's *Paradoxical Psychotherapy* (1982), additional arguments are advanced to account for the relatively disappointing amount of change shown by the paradoxical letter group. Noting that a technique may need to be implemented several times in order to adequately assess its validity, the authors point out that only one letter was prepared for couples in this group (though, of course, the same holds true for the "linear letter group"). Moreover—and much more crucial—all the couples in the experiment were basically nonclinical. They did not exhibit specific problems and they demonstrated no resistance toward the program. Given such a population, the introduction of a paradoxical intervention may well have been gratuitous and, in fact, counterindicated.

Supplementing the authors' own reservations, it might be said that besides the unfortunate situation that neither the subjects in this experiment nor the instruments used to evaluate it enabled the researchers meaningfully to measure what centrally interested them, another circumstance (and one *not* recognized by the authors) reduces the bulk of their experiment to something approaching inconsequentiality. That is, the so-called "paradoxical letter" quoted in their article as exemplifying their approach does not, at least out of context, appear to be paradoxical at all but rather to embody far more *innuendo* than its also illustrated nonparadoxical counterpart—which, alternatively, seems at once much less elliptical and much more direct, coherent, and meaningful in its message. Obviously, unless a letter in some way encourages its recipients to continue to practice their damaging or dysfunctional behavior—and is thus *responded to* in a confused or even baffled manner (and the experiment made no attempt to query respondents on their reaction to this letter)—it hardly merits the label "paradoxical." In trying somehow to adapt a paradoxical letter to nonsymptomatic subjects, the researchers may indeed have stretched their "working definition" of the concept to a point beyond any clear recognition—and therefore beyond any practical utility as well.

Two individually oriented empirical explorations of symptom prescription deal directly with clinical patients. The first of these case studies, reported by Zarske (1982), involves the treatment of a cerebral palsied child with temper tantrums. After a five-day baseline period, during which the mother was instructed to chart the frequency, duration, and location of her child's tantrums, two phases of an "encouraging the symptom" strategy were implemented, each lasting for two weeks. Daily measurements of the child's tantrum behavior indicated a dramatic decline in the first treatment phase and a further decline, culminating in the total absence of such behavior, during the second phase. One- and two-month follow-ups revealed that not a single incidence of the child's tantrums recurred.

Despite the very positive results of this study, a few limitations might be mentioned. Since all charting was done by the child's parents (or, during the child's preschool hours, by the aide who served as his daytime caretaker), the investigation could not be monitored or controlled by the experimenter himself. In addition to the second-hand (and thus unverifiable) nature of the reported results, the effectiveness of the paradoxical treatment cannot be evaluated in relation to other possible treatment approaches. And, given the special conditions of the child's therapy and various matters involving family dynamics, the generalizability of the study may well be debated.

Nonetheless, regardless of these limitations, and also the relative brevity of the two follow-up periods, this investigation goes well beyond the vast majority of such studies in providing some form of experimental measurement to demonstrate its treatment's effectuality. Considering the anecdotal nature of almost all the clinical reports on symptom prescription devices, this conscientious effort can only be appreciated. At the very least, this study warrants the conclusion that a well-planned paradoxical intervention may succeed in systematically removing the reinforcements associated with a symptomatic (and highly manipulative) behavior—thereby necessitating that the child develop other, and much healthier, modes of social interaction.

The second largely uncontrolled clinical investigation of symptom prescription containing suggestive empirical data involves eight seriously anorectic patients. Entitled "Paradoxical Intention in the Treatment of Chronic Anorexia Nervosa" (Hsu & Lieberman, 1982), this is the study alluded to earlier as identifying its intervention misleadingly. For, by theoretical definition, compliance-based paradoxical intention works by prodding patients directly to confront the object of their fears; and this report conceptualizes its therapeutic task otherwise, as based predominantly on utilizing the patients' need to assert interpersonal control through resisting therapist directives.

The symptom of anorexia is seen here as representing not only the patients' self-denial and compulsion to be different and special, but also their need to establish a form of control, particularly over others. The therapist, by aligning with the patients' precariously self-sacrificing control mechanism, enters into a coalition with them that, paradoxically, reduces their frenzied need to maintain such control. Additionally, in the therapist's permissively "allowing" the symptom, he is in turn allowed by the patients (however unwittingly) to redefine the interpersonal battle for control. That is, by contriving to support the patients' continued adherence to the anorectic disorder, he not only reduces their resistance toward him but subverts it also, so that it can effectively be expressed only by their countering *their own* former resistance toward gaining weight and becoming physically normal. As the authors put it—sounding far more like disciples of Haley and Watzlawick than of Frankl—"the paradoxical intention provides an interpersonal jujitsu that undermines and destroys the previous interpersonal set and context" (p. 652).

Briefly, subjects in this study were eight chronic anorectic patients (six female and two male) who were admitted consecutively to the hospital where the authors worked and who had not been able to maintain their weight following discharge. Having in the course of their hospitalization received intensive individual therapy, family therapy, and controlled feeding until reaching their targeted weight, these "veteran" patients had *already* undergone similar treatment elsewhere—with similarly unsuccessful results. Given such unyielding allegiance to their symptomatology (and the fact that no patient had experienced a spontaneous or posttreatment remission for more than four months during the past five years), the authors decided to adopt a paradoxical approach in treating them. Patients were informed that the very chronicity of their eating problem indicated their need to keep it; and the advantages of their illness, at least as "perceived" by the author, were explained to them. Unintentionally undercutting the paradoxical nature of their strategy (which seems to center much more on reframing than on any symptom prescription as such), the authors also permitted and even *encouraged* patients to disagree with their favorable interpretation of the benefits afforded by the symptom. In this unprecedented treatment context, all eight individuals were seen (as outpatients) for a minimum of six weekly one-hour sessions.

A follow-up conducted two to four years after the completion of therapy revealed that half of the former patients had maintained a normal weight and that only a single patient was seriously underweight (below 75% of average). At the time of follow-up, none of the individuals was in treatment. The authors describe these results as "gratifying," while at the same time acknowledging that the "personality difficulties" (including the "social and sexual functioning") of these individuals did not appear much improved—suggesting to them the need for further (postsymptomatic) therapy. But since treatment did not really focus on altering the family system maintaining the patients' symptom, it should come as comparatively little surprise that progress in the interpersonal arena was scant.

One might question, additionally, the nature and content of the therapists' follow-up. This follow-up was nonuniform in its assessing the results of the patients' paradoxical treatment both at different posttherapy times and through different evaluative devices (i.e., through personal interviews for six of the patients and through postal questionnaires for the remaining two). Further, the outcome of each patient's therapy was evaluated by questions that apparently failed to check on the all-important matter of symptom substitution. In summary, as the first reported systematic (or at least quasisystematic) attempt to implement a paradoxical strategy in treating an anorectic population, the results of this investigation definitely seem promising. Nonetheless, even more than space permits discussing here, the study exhibits a variety of methodological shortcomings (most of which the authors themselves would probably concede). Also, the improvement of patients, though unquestionably significant as regards both weight gain and stability, appears to have been rather narrowly confined to symptom amelioration rather than encompassing the sort of global social readjustment for which the authors apparently had hoped.

Academic Counseling Experiments

The four experimental investigations reviewed in this section are unusually related. All were published during 1982 in the *Journal of Counseling Psychology*, all were based on doctoral dissertations, and three of the four were coauthored by the same researcher, S. R. Strong. Although these studies seem to subscribe more to the systems approach to therapeutic paradox than to any other theoretical persuasion, it must be stressed that their actual kinship to this orientation is marginal. For one thing their treatment context is at best "semiclinical": indeed, one of these experiments suggests as much by referring to its "student-clients" (Beck & Strong, 1982). Inasmuch as there is no evidence that any of these student participants would, on their own, have taken the initiative or incurred the expense to apply for therapeutic help, they can hardly be seen as reflecting a typical clinical population. Essentially they are student volunteers for an academic experiment. This circumstance needs to be kept clearly in mind when interpreting the results and seeking to estimate their generalizability.

These four investigations also seem to fall short in mirroring a systemic outlook on human problems in that the basic tenets of this perspective, as well as the paradoxical techniques deriving from it, are radically simplified (or streamlined) for purposes of what we might term, only half ironically, "experimental integrity." That is, for the scientific sake of more accurately assessing the data for the specific hypotheses tested, these studies minimize or totally disregard key elements in the systemic orientation.

Not only are the particular clinical indications and counterindications for implementing such a treatment approach ignored, but, far more important, the rich interpersonal dynamic of the therapeutic *relationship*—itself regularly perceived by systems thinkers as fundamental to the effectiveness of symptom prescription—is "standardized" virtually out of existence. Not the relationship but the intervention, pure and simple (or as purely and simply as the experiment could contrive), is assumed to be the mechanism both of change and the maintenance of change. Despite the experimental legitimacy (perhaps even necessity) of isolating the method of change induction from a host of other significant and, in practice, "nonisolatable" variables, the clinical relevance or reliability of the results reported in these generally well-controlled studies must be subject to considerable doubt. The peripheral resemblance of these experiments to a typical clinical situation is further highlighted by the fact that each of them involves only two interviews per student, generally lasting only 30 minutes apiece. Moreover, as already suggested, the function of any particular client-counselor relationship in promoting change was methodically reduced by the experimenters' choice to adopt a basically scripted format—so as to control for this possibly "confounding" variable.

The meaningfulness, or practicality, of these studies is additionally restricted by their total inattention to individual differences among student participants. Plainly these undertakings do not begin to deal with the differential susceptibility to paradoxical interventions based on such factors as client resistiveness. Yet there is a consensus in the literature that the effectiveness of such strategies depends in large part on their ability to provoke certain types of individuals toward new behaviors. More generally, a client's self- and social perspective must be adequately appreciated and appropriately challenged for such tactics to take therapeutic effect. And these studies—by purposely *not* individualizing their interventions—could not begin to take into account (and thereby "control for") dispositional elements that must be seen as substantially influencing the results. Further, since the participants were not asked to indicate their reactions to the researchers' apparently paradoxical reframing and directives, it is impossible to ascertain the extent to which these interventions were *apprehended* as paradoxical, thereby interfering with the students' viewpoint and stimulating them to make beneficial cognitive and behavioral adjustments.

In the end, given the many deliberate depersonalizing and nonclinical aspects of these experiments, it would seem that their prevalent concern was *not* with the selective scrutiny of symptomatic individuals but with the broader exploration of certain social-psychological theories. Powerful interpersonal principles relating to persuasion and influence, which transcend or override personal differences and in fact serve to join otherwise dissimilar individuals, appear to be the focal point of examination. In other words, the thrust of these studies seems directed more toward answering questions in the field of social psychology than toward examining issues of clinical outcome. Dubiously reflective of a prototypical clinical situation, these undertakings—with all their experimental conditions, procedures, and controls—contain findings that can be generalized to a psychotherapy setting only with considerable caution.

Having expressed these general reservations about all four of the academic and semiclinical experiments loosely tied to the systems use of paradox, it remains to briefly describe each one and enumerate its primary results. Despite the many qualifications and caveats made in advance about these studies, it should be emphasized that what is being questioned is not the nature or value of these inquiries but their ability to assess the comparative effectiveness of certain paradoxical strategies as they are implemented within a representative clinical context.

Two of these studies attempt to evaluate the usefulness of paradoxical directives in treating students with serious and recurrent procrastination difficulties. The first, by Lopez and Wambach (1982), assesses over a four-week period the relative effects of paradoxical and self-control counselor directives on subject change. Thirty-two students, all of whom were enrolled in a large introductory psychology course and received credit for participating in the experiment, were randomly assigned to one of two interview conditions, or to a no-interview control group. In the paradoxical directive condition specifically, students were told that to fully observe and grasp the nature of their procrastinating behavior, they needed deliberately to practice it each day. They were thus instructed to schedule a half-hour period each evening to resist studying and focus instead on procrastinating—with the objective of learning how to control their problem through increased awareness. Any studying during these "symptom-prescription" periods was expressly forbidden.

Dependent measures in this experiment included such variables as weekly ratings by subjects of problem frequency, perception of problem controllability, and expectation of change. Results of a repeated measures ANOVA design indicated that in both experimental conditions interviewed students improved significantly more than did their noninterviewed counterparts. Any reported differences between subjects in the two experimental groups as to the *amount* of decreased procrastination, however, were by follow-up inconsequential. One curious finding was that subjects exposed to the paradoxical directive, although they testified to a greater rate of change in their procrastination than did the self-control group during the interval between the first and second interview, did not thereby come to view their problem behavior as significantly more controllable. Since such a conclusion is at odds with what has generally been claimed in the literature on therapeutic paradox, the authors seek to account for this unexpected result in terms of some of the study's specific limitations. Beyond their largely technical explanations (including the experiment's demand characteristics), it might be added that the paradoxical intervention used in the experiment failed to *reframe* the nature of the student's procrastination. If these students did not alter their attitude toward, or cognitions about, their undesired behavior, this failure would seem to have mostly to do with the circumstance that nothing in the message delivered to them was designed to challenge their basic assumptions or beliefs concerning their behavior. In the absence of such provocation, it is little wonder that the experiment's paradoxical directive had so little impact on student self-perception.

The second exploration dealing with serious student procrastination is by Wright and Strong (1982). Perhaps what is most remarkable about this study is that its interest clearly centers on therapeutic issues pertaining to *reactance* and *paradox*, yet not once does it refer explicitly to either of these two concepts, even though they are mentioned in the article's reference section. Its two (only obliquely related) hypotheses are (1a) that directives telling clients precisely what to do stimulate defiance, whereas (1b) directives which offer them a choice of action arouse compliance, and (2) that beneficial change can actually be promoted by instructing clients to adhere to problematic behaviors.

Participating in this study were 30 student procrastinators (again, recruited from introductory college courses), divided equally into two treatment conditions and a control group. Students in the treatment conditions were given two weekly interviews in which they were told (in accordance with "memorized scripts") either to continue procrastinating precisely as they had been doing previously (the experiment's "exactly" condition); or to personally select a few of their procrastination behaviors to continue—all of which, presumably, were identified in the first interview (the "choose" condition). Results showed that students receiving interviews exhibited a substantial decrease in procrastination behavior, regardless of treatment condition. Students in the noninterview (or control) condition revealed no such improvement. The only differences between the two treatment conditions were in their "free response description" of *how* their undesired behavior came to change. Students receiving the "exactly" directive are reported to have perceived their improvement in nonvolitional (or spontaneous) terms, whereas students in the "choose" condition are viewed as tending to emphasize volitional causes for their change.

Limiting, or downright confounding, the results of this study are a variety of circumstances, only one of which the authors see fit to mention. That is, in both experimental conditions interviewers, after tersely explaining in identical fashion why students should not attempt right away to abolish their procrastination behavior, prefixed their final directive to students with the clause "what I *insist* that you do. . . ." Such dictatorial phrasing might well be expected to mask—or better, neutralize—potential differences in the students' attitudinal and behavioral response to the two supposedly contrasting sets of instructions. Using the language of reactance, the students' sense of their behavioral freedom, whether they were in the "exactly" or the "choose" condition, can be seen as similarly threatened by these hardly diametrically opposed instructions. Consequently, employing these two directives with the express intent of eliciting from subjects significantly varying amounts of compliance or defiance seems almost arbitrary, constituting a major weakness in experimental design. The apparent *attributional* differences between the two interview groups in their completion of the free-response form given at posttest may only reflect, as the authors do in fact suggest, different demand characteristics between the two directives.

Other problems in this experiment that undermine its findings may be delineated very briefly. Although it probably is not altogether fair to criticize a study for what it chooses to eliminate from consideration, this experiment does seem regrettably incomplete in its failing to include a treatment group which is directed straightforwardly to stop, curb, or control its various procrastination behaviors. Also, the seeming lack of researcher awareness as to just how *both* interview conditions involved strong elements of therapeutic paradox may relate to the curiously "primitive" nature of the experimental manipulations. A more painstaking inquiry into the relevant literature, both as relates to theoretical framework and practical application, might well have served to increase the sophistication of this investigation and, indirectly, have led to a greater number of significant, and more generalizable, results. Finally, the time elapsed between the second interview and the experiment's posttest—which involved each of the students' filling out several forms and rating scales, and which ostensibly took the place of a follow-up—is nowhere given in the article. Such an omission unfortunately casts further doubt on the ultimate meaning and importance of those few results assessed by the study to be significant.

The other pair of closely linked studies in this section apply paradoxical methods in a two-session treatment of moderately depressed college students. The first of these explorations, by Beck and Strong (1982), compares positive and negative connotative interpretations as they differentially influence therapeutic change. Of the four academic counseling experiments reviewed here, this undertaking seems the most accomplished, both conceptually and methodologically. It is clearly the most thoroughly researched of these experiments, as well as the most sensible, thoughtful, and (in an almost wholly favorable sense) provocative.

This empirical investigation takes as its starting point a recent outcome research report concluding that counseling orientations which employ different ideas and understandings of client problems seem finally about equally effective in producing results.* Considering this conclusion in terms of the systems approach to therapy, Beck and Strong speculate that different kinds of therapist interpretation may foster change in their similarly interfering with the practical utility of symptomatic behavior in social transactions. In other words, the behavioral strategy that is the symptom loses, through the therapist's calculated reconceptualization of it, its power to help the individual dominate or control interpersonal relationships.

Dovetailing with this explanation of symptomatology is the relatively new social-psychological theory of *impression management*. This extremely suggestive formulation contends that people "design" their behavior strategically, in order to persuade others toward certain inferences about their inner qualities and thus structure these others' responses toward them. In this theoretical context, therapist interpretation is viewed by the authors as informing clients that the impression they *intended* to create differs from that which the therapist in fact received. Accordingly, it is predicted that clients will be prompted in their efforts to "correct" the therapist's impression (and thereby engender the interpersonal response they desire) to tactically modify their behavior.

Also corresponding to this theory is the notion that therapist feedback can motivate clients to behave differently, regardless of whether it implies positive or negative characteristics in the individual. For as long as the client's expectations of the therapist's reactions are defeated, the incentive to act differently will be aroused. Although such a motive is easy to appreciate as regards the therapist's interpreting the symptom as reflecting negative qualities in the client, it is less obvious how a therapist's *positive* feedback about the presenting problem (e.g., as actually suggesting the person's inner strength and fortitude) can also propel an individual toward beneficial change. Yet there is substantial evidence from the communication-systems literature which suggests that reframing symptoms positively may operate to stimulate therapeutic modifications of behavior. From the essentially similar impression management perspective, efforts by a person to appear helpless stem from the wish to avoid being held responsible for negative behavior. Feedback implying inner strength and control inevitably implies that the problem behavior is itself volitional—thus undermining, or sabotaging, the habitual attempt to disown personal responsibility for one's actions.

*A. E. Bergin & M. J. Lambert, The evaluation of therapeutic outcomes, in S. L. Garfield & A. E. Bergin (Eds.), *Handbook of psychotherapy and behavior change: An empirical analysis*, 2nd ed. (New York: Wiley, 1978).

The complementary theoretical positions described above relate directly to the researchers' first hypothesis: namely, that both positive and negative therapist interpretations can stimulate individuals to change. The second hypothesis, taken specifically from communication theory, is that connoting a symptom positively facilitates its eradication, whereas connoting this symptom negatively functions to maintain it. Such a paradoxical supposition hinges on the argument that symptomatic behavior is frequently evoked and sustained by well-meaning but inadequately considered endeavors by others to help the individual change. Conversely, interpretations that apparently *support* symptoms are viewed as reducing the individual's need (or even reward) for symptomatic behavior, thereby arousing the incentive to change.

To test these related hypotheses, 20 of 30 depressed "student-clients" (chosen, on the basis of scores on a depression inventory, from an initial sample of 84) were provided with two weekly 30-minute interviews. During this time they received six interpretations that connoted their depressive symptomatology either positively or negatively. The two interview conditions (which also included straightforward behavioral directives) were carefully formulated to diverge solely with respect to counselor interpretations, which conformed to a script prepared in advance. Participants in these conditions received a preliminary screening and pretest one week before their first interview and a posttest one week after their second interview (while the 10 students in the control group were given the same weekly tests but no interviews). Three weeks after the posttest—that is, one month following the second interview—*all* participants were contacted and retested. Over the course of this experiment, four different assessment instruments were employed, two of them more than once and one (the Beck Depression Inventory, 1967) at each contact to closely monitor symptom change.

Results of testing during the interview period suggested, in support of the impression management hypothesis, that both experimental conditions effectively promoted change and to a nearly identical extent. Contrariwise, students in the control group reported a "slight but constant worsening" of their depression throughout the course of the experiment. One of the study's most provocative—and potentially most illuminating—findings was that the longer-term effects of the two interview conditions were significantly different. That is, the amelioration of symptoms reported by both groups during treatment seemed to erode in the negative connotation condition but to be maintained in the positive connotation condition, thus corroborating the communication theory hypothesis. For even though in the negative connotation group depression decreased during the interview period, the subsequent reemergence of symptoms suggested that these students eventually felt compelled to reaffirm their formerly helpless posture and inability to change, despite the counselor's apparently opposite desire for them.

What is perhaps most fascinating about this result is the way it may relate to an earlier finding, that in all five scales of the experiment's relationship inventory students in the negative connotation condition rated their interviewer more favorably than did their counterparts in the positive connotation condition. As the authors comment (again citing impression management theory), although both sets of interpretations offered students an understanding of themselves counter to that which they had expected to transmit, students receiving positive interpretations may have been prevented from experiencing a relapse because these interpretations more effectively disrupted or invalidated their former behavioral strategy, thus rendering it no longer viable. Such an explanation of the "greater disruptive value" (p. 557) of the experiment's positive interpretations would serve to account for the situation that students in this treatment condition paradoxically reported less favorable reactions to their interviewers (and, indeed, the *same* interviewers were used in both experimental conditions) than those subject to negative interpretations, which actually portrayed the student's motives in a much less attractive light. Although the authors never refer to the concept, it would seem quite possible that "the greater disruptive value" they hypothesize may have been therapeutic precisely in its facilitating what in communication theory is regarded as *second-order change*—that is, in its prompting a fundamental alteration in the individual's self-concept. Such structural, or systemic, change may well have served to preclude the possibility of any simple posttreatment reversion to the old cognitions underlying their negative mood state.

Drawing on insights derived from attribution theory, the authors ponder further the circumstance that students receiving positive interpretations about their depression made symptomatic improvement, even though they interacted with counselors who, professedly, believed that their negative mood state reflected positively on them (i.e., testified to such personal characteristics as sensitivity and self-sacrifice). Using this alternate theoretical framework, the authors speculate that these students may not have been able to attribute their improvement to implicit counselor demands and therefore may have attributed their immediate change to steadfast inner qualities— which remained active after their brief counselor contact had terminated. Students in the negative interpretation condition, on the other hand, may have identified their temporary improvement as a direct reaction to the negative connotations assigned to their depression (i.e., that it signified their rejection of others, social manipulativeness, and irrational thinking). In consequence, once counselor interaction ceased—and the external motivation behind their improvement was removed—symptoms rapidly reemerged.

Pithily enumerating some of the limitations of their study, such as its extremely short treatment time, the possibly skewed nature of its treatment population, and the reliance on self-report instruments to assess change, Beck and Strong soberly leave open the matter of the experiment's clinical generalizability. Even given these reservations—and several others that might be raised if one were obligated to evaluate "definitively" their research and presentation of results—this experiment deserves acknowledgment for its general care and theoretical suggestiveness. For these reasons it has been discussed at greater length than the other empirical studies here reviewed.

The last experiment to be considered here is very closely connected to the preceding study. In fact, this experiment frequently alludes to its simultaneously published complement, and regularly compares its hypotheses and results to it. Written by Feldman, Strong, and Danser (1982), and in some ways more ambitious than the Beck and Strong study, it seeks to explore the comparative effects of consistent and inconsistent combinations of paradoxical and nonparadoxical interpretations and directives.

Dealing similarly with a moderately depressed student population, this experiment assigned its 50 final participants (out of 108 prospects) to four interview conditions (each involving two 40-minute counseling sessions) and a no-interview control condition. For all students depression was assessed over a two-month period. The interview conditions were designed to differ from one another only in relation to the interpretations and directives received: paradoxical interpretations with paradoxical directives, paradoxical interpretations with nonparadoxical directives, nonparadoxical interpretations with paradoxical directives, and nonparadoxical interpretations with nonparadoxical directives. It should be noted that interpretations, whether paradoxical or nonparadoxical, were very much the same as employed in the Beck and Strong study, as were also the instruments used to evaluate therapeutic change.

In discussing their hypotheses, the authors make the important point that Beck and Strong's experiment combined not only nonparadoxical interpretations with the nonparadoxical directive to engage in less depressive behavior but also paired paradoxical interpretations with this straightforward directive—a cognitive-behavioral juxtaposition hardly representative of paradoxical strategy as implemented in actual clinical practice. (And, indeed, a further criticism that might be leveled at *both* these studies is that the standardized and nonspecific positive interpretations offered for the students' depression do not really seem to imply that the negative mood state be maintained, so that whether they were adequately calculated to elicit a paradoxical reaction from individual participants might well be questioned.) As a kind of replicative expansion of the Beck and Strong experiment, these researchers decided to structure their study to test the interrelated hypotheses that more therapeutic change would be produced from a consistent combination of paradoxical interpretations and directives than from inconsistent combinations, which in turn would produce more beneficial change than a consistent pairing of nonparadoxical interpretations and directives. Secondarily, the experiment sought to find additional evidence for Beck and Strong's findings that (1) interventions with paradoxical elements resulted in more lasting symptom remission than nonparadoxical interventions, and (2) positive, or "paradoxical," interpretations of symptomatic behavior led subjects (in sharp contrast to those receiving negative interpretations) to attribute therapeutic change to stable internal sources—thus more effectively safeguarding their improvement.

Overall, results of this study somewhat disappointed researcher expectations. Although students in the four interview conditions experienced a greater remission of depressive symptoms than those subject only to testing (i.e., the control condition), several of the experiment's major hypotheses were not upheld. For example, the consistent paradoxical condition was not superior to the inconsistent condition pairing paradoxical interpretations and nonparadoxical directives; nor was the consistent nonparadoxical condition inferior to the inconsistent condition combining nonparadoxical interpretations and paradoxical directives. Rather, conditions including paradoxical interpretations were superior to conditions not including such interpretations, independent of the nature of the directives linked to them. The empirical grounds for viewing paradoxical interpretations as superior to nonparadoxical interpretations in effecting change goes beyond Beck and Strong's study in finding that paradoxical interpretations had greater therapeutic effects not only at follow-up but during treatment as well. The fact that the particular nature of the directives themselves made very little difference in inducing change is one of the study's more suggestive findings—and it is consistent with the two experiments on student procrastination reviewed earlier (i.e., Lopez & Wambach, 1982; Wright & Strong, 1982).

The second set of hypotheses—proposing that conditions containing some sort of paradoxical intervention would be correlated with an internal attribution of change, thus enabling students to maintain this change, whereas the consistent nonparadoxical condition would be associated with external attribution for such change and with symptom relapse—were not generally supported. The results here, however, involve so many complicating factors, variations, and exceptions that it is very difficult to know exactly what to make of the findings. At the very least, the evidence seems far more equivocal than that found in support of paradoxical interpretations in the experiment's first set of hypotheses.

In closing their discussion the authors enumerate the study's shortcomings in almost identical fashion to Beck and Strong's frank admission of experimental limitations. Yet their brief self-criticism reveals little awareness of other experimental flaws, which can be seen as somewhat compromising the investigation's final significance. Most of these deficiencies are theoretical and relate to the accurate conceptualization of therapeutic paradox. The circumstance that the reference section includes not a single theoretically oriented study on paradoxical therapeutic strategies is suggestive. In particular, the interactional dynamics of paradoxical reframings and injunctions seem only dimly appreciated by the authors. No cognizance, conceptual *or* practical, of the therapeutic double bind is demonstrated; and paradoxical interventions are explicitly stated to be therapeutic only when defied, ignoring all the literature on the effectiveness of compliance-based paradoxical strategies.

Moreover (and, as suggested at the outset, this is a problem with virtually all empirical investigations of therapeutic paradox), this experiment makes no attempt to assess whether students responded to either the paradoxical interpretations or directives as being, indeed, "paradoxical." Confidently interpreting this study's results is made even more problematic by its use of the term "inconsistent." One might well ask: "Inconsistent to *whom*?" In the experimental context, there appears to be some reason to doubt whether students reacted to the supposed inconsistency of certain cognitive-behavioral pairings as in fact inconsistent. In brief, given the study's lack of any systematic method for reliably obtaining student feedback on the different experimental manipulations, precisely what was being measured in the experiment, as well as what was responsible for the reported change, remains somewhat hazy. Consequently, the ultimate meaning and importance of the results must also be judged less than clear.

These reservations having been stated, it yet deserves to be said that the foregoing study—and the seven other clinical and quasiclinical investigations reviewed in this section—offer much more than earlier anecdotal testimony in support of systemic paradoxical strategies. Although, even considered collectively, these explorations could not be said to demonstrate conclusively the effectiveness of such strategies in eliciting and maintaining beneficial change, their results generally seem very promising. Obviously additional controlled experiments on these techniques are needed to confirm their comparative therapeutic efficacy. Given the richness and fertility of the subject, it is hoped that many such experiments will be undertaken in the near future.

PART THREE

Conclusion

CHAPTER 6

Toward a Theory of Paradox in Psychotherapy

THERAPEUTIC PARADOX AS BRINGING TOGETHER DIVERSE THEORETICAL OUTLOOKS

Repeatedly in these pages it has been suggested that the widespread use of paradoxical strategies obscures the boundaries traditionally separating the major schools of therapy. Whether explicit or implicit, almost all of the diverse therapeutic approaches contain practices that involve some sort of reframing and symptom prescription. To the surprise or confusion of a broad miscellany of patients and clients, therapists of varying theoretical viewpoints have shown themselves prepared to redefine in unprecedented ways the complaints presented to them and, however covertly, encourage their presenters to maintain or increase these dysfunctional behaviors. Whether such patients or clients are told to practice their symptom intentionally or to avoid any deliberate attempt at change, paradoxical tactics have in common their willful defiance of client expectations. And it may be precisely in this defiance that the many forms of paradoxical intervention are capable of having such a strong impact on their recipients. Over and over in the literature therapists have remarked on the value of taking clients cognitively unawares, of making them wonder, doubt, or otherwise begin to question the assumptions that have kept their problems rigidly fixed. As Selvini Palazzoli (1981), for example, has observed: "Anything predictable is therapeutically inefficient" (and correspondingly) "people are most influenced when they expect a certain message and receive instead a message at a totally different level" (p. 45).

These comments, pragmatic to the point of being almost atheoretical, suggest something of the ideational *translatability* of the many different explanations offered for therapeutic paradox. For however much the proposed rationales may diverge from one another, they all imply the same general viewpoint toward human motivation and the nature of change. At a metatheory level—on a plane above all the varying assumptions that

151

divide the major theoretical orientations—it would appear that the dominant forces which govern behavior are apprehended similarly. Indeed, what
conclusion is better warranted from the circumstance that, as is becoming
almost commonplace to note, well-seasoned therapists of different theoretical persuasions all seem in their therapy to be doing very much the same
thing? Although the considered use of the term "paradoxical" to suggest
some of the essential resemblances among discrepant theoretical approaches is relatively recent, its employment for such a synthesizing purpose
clearly seems to be increasing as practitioners more and more recognize the
value of therapeutic indirection in prompting significant change.

Mozdzierz et al. (1976), who conclude that paradox is involved in all
effective therapy, reflect that finally the only real consideration for the
therapist is not whether to employ such strategies but simply whether
their use is to be conscious. The position of these authors seems closely
related to one expressed by Evans (1980), who somewhat resignedly
admits: "Much of my resistance towards paradoxical interventions diminished some time ago when I realised that I had been practising [them]
for years" (p. 274). In the end, what we might with only mild hyperbole
refer to as the "therapeutic prevalence" of paradox is best indicated by
this volume's abundant documentation of the fact that all the major
theories of human behavior have somehow "allowed" for the practical
incorporation of symptom prescription devices. And at this point it
should be obvious that regardless of how varied the concepts used to
justify the utilization of such techniques may be, in actual practice their
implementation is fairly similar.

In *Psychotherapy East and West* (1961), Watts argues that if the key
intent of therapy is to confront clients with their neurotic or self-deceiving
assumptions so that the more they adhere to them the more they find
themselves in a double bind, it is virtually irrelevant whether the theory
behind treatment be "Freudian, Jungian, Rogerian, Existential, Interpersonal, or simply eclectic" (p. 163). For the extreme nondirectiveness of a
Carl Rogers encompasses just as much double-binding judo as the far more
directive approach of a John Rosen (whose innovative "absurdist" methods have been delineated earlier in the chapter on paradox and psychoanalysis). In a context which also centers on symptom prescription tactics,
Raskin and Klein (1976) note how experienced clinicians frequently interact in much the same way with clients—"despite the language and con-
structs they use when initiating their juniors into the fraternity." Immediately following this sober (though cynical) observation, these authors feel
compelled to conclude: "There are even relatively few niceties of theory
that clearly separate the therapies into opposing camps—*the theory may
not count for much*" (p. 554; emphasis added).

Here we need to examine the fundamental question of whether contrasting theories are, indeed, *essentially* opposed if they rely on similar procedures and techniques. Is it not possible that each theory represents little more than a separate turn of the same kaleidoscope—the kaleidoscope itself being the common origin for the various symmetrical patterns or organizations it "causes" to appear? However divergent any particular pattern may be from the ones preceding and following it, each configuration is related to the others in that it necessarily embodies the same parts and emanates from the same source. Additionally, not only is each formation an assemblage of bits or fragments which, collectively, can be perceived as a unified and coherent whole, but also each whole is itself but a fragment of the almost unlimited possibilities permitted by its inherently generative source.

Seen from this metatheoretical viewpoint, different theories of psychotherapy may be appreciated as combining the same essential elements of change—though each does so in its own uniquely limiting fashion, thereby creating an illusorily distinct identity. For however "original" each formulation of human behavior and change may seem, the basic *components* of this inferential construction remain constant and invariable. Only the radical differences in terminology and emphasis function to preserve the misleading appearance of disparity among approaches that are finally much more complementary than their individualizing vocabularies labor to suggest.

The complementary relationship of discrete, but not irreconcilable, theories of human behavior is perhaps nowhere more evident than in those discussions of therapeutic paradox whose viewpoint is best deemed eclectic. However inadvertently, these discussions—curiously heterogeneous yet coherent as well—function much less to illuminate the boundaries among the various schools of therapy than to dim or downright obfuscate them. Seeking to elucidate the use of paradoxical "joining" techniques within a psychoanalytic context, for instance, Marshall (1976) offers a learning theory explanation ordinarily confined to a strict behaviorist orientation. Furthermore, Marshall's proposed rationale is subsequent to his frank admission that the paradoxical tactics which he is characterizing within an analytic framework bear close relationship to those generally associated with a communication-systems viewpoint. Rabkin (1977), in striving comprehensively to account for the efficacy of a specific paradoxical directive used with a client, resorts to no less than *nine* separate treatment designations. These labels and phrases—from "getting into one's feelings" to "placing the patient in a therapeutic double bind" to "stimulus management" (p. 160)—inevitably betray the arbitrariness of traditional theoretical demarcations, whose actual existence may be much more apparent than real. The congruous incongruity of Rabkin's elaborately hybrid interpretation also serves to indicate the ultimate interchangeability of the potentially infinite variety of possible treatment rationales. Even more important, his speculative account serves to underscore the inadequacy of any single explanation in fully (or "definitively") explicating the richly intricate and multileveled dynamics of a paradoxical (or, for that matter, almost *any*) therapeutic intervention.

In such a context of kaleidoscopic multiplicity, the position taken by Haley in his seminal work, *Strategies of Psychotherapy* (1963), warrants serious questioning. This position, at first sight so commonsensical as to approach the axiomatic, actually begins to appear somewhat simplistic in light of the above discussion. Haley argues that the particular therapy a clinician engages in will be grounded on his assumptions about the origins of psychopathology and the nature of change. Consequently, if symptoms are viewed as a result of conditioning, the therapist will devise a treatment plan which stresses deconditioning; if symptoms are perceived as resulting from "repressed ideation," the therapist will focus on bringing the repressed ideas into awareness; and if symptoms are judged to be interpersonal power tactics, the therapist will devise interventions expressly to prevent the client from controlling the therapeutic relationship symptomatically (p. 13). Obviously, such a stance on the intimate connection between one's theoretical affiliations and the kind of therapy one practices is designed to account for some of the sharp differences separating the behavioral, analytic, and communications approach to treatment. But Haley's commonsensical reasoning ignores the circumstance that most therapists, despite their professed theoretical allegiance, tend in the immediate therapeutic situation to be eclectic, or at least to be governed by largely atheoretical here-and-now perceptions of a client's emotional and mental needs and capacities. That is, it may finally be more logical to conclude that a clinician's explanation of a treatment's effectiveness is predominatly a post hoc inference based on abiding theoretical commitments than to assume that such a treatment was linearly derived from the conceptual framework preceding it.

Moreover, the discrete theoretical realms that Haley alludes to may not be mutually exclusive, or even opposed, if they are understood as primarily representing different *levels* of conceptualizing what is essentially the same psychological (and social-psychological) phenomenon. If the various theoretical schools diverge less in substance than in emphasis or focus of attention—whether it be intrapsychic, interpersonal, or some combination of the two—then the therapy inevitably linked to the theory will also differ primarily in emphasis. Supposedly incompatible theoretical assumptions are therefore quite capable of giving rise to kindred (or, indeed, identical) therapeutic techniques—the case in point here being, of course, *paradoxical* techniques, which so plainly cover the theoretical spectrum. Nevertheless, because specific methods of intervention are hypothesized in accordance with the practitioner's theoretical persuasion, any rationale proposed for their effectiveness will invariably be based on the vocabulary the practitioner is most comfortable in using.

If all this seems rather circular, such circularity may well reflect the way most therapists operate conceptually. And such circularity may in the end indicate that the divergent interpretations offered for a single paradoxical technique may all constitute complementary bits, pieces, or levels of the same basic explanation. Here again is the notion of a metatheory functioning "practically" to unite or synthesize the apparently conflicting theories on which it is built. Correlatively, all the various theories of paradox must be deemed incomplete inasmuch as each fails to take adequately into account the multiple layers of motivation underlying human behavior. Because of this lack of social-psychological three-dimensionality, each theory is doomed to reflect only partially the complex reality it strives to clarify.

After Haley (1963) schematically joins some of the major theoretical orientations with their corresponding therapeutic methods, he considers the possibility that these approaches, despite their well-enunciated differences, have in common the cultivation of a very similar relationship between therapist and client. Finally, Haley posits, it is through this interaction—unprecedented in the client's life and prompting him toward fundamental behavioral adjustments—that beneficial change is produced. The facilitation of client awareness about his defense system, or the painstaking alteration of his past conditioning, is regarded as—if not exactly *irrelevant* to the therapeutic process—at least as secondary to it. This argument, although generally well-documented and compelling, yet seems limited to the extent that it, too, tends toward unidimensionality.

Indeed, what may restrict the explanatory value of all the major theoretical positions is their inevitable exclusiveness. Such exclusiveness typically betrays these different schools of thought into presenting simplistically (and thereby distorting or falsifying) competing theoretical viewpoints. For instance, Jacobson and Margolin (1979) question the assumption by communication theorists that symptomatic behaviors depict the way a family has chosen to relate to one another—that these behaviors actually represent an unconscious agreement (or collusion) among family members. These authors instead adopt what they consider a more "parsimonious" stance: that apparently aversive behaviors in a family really *are* aversive. To a certain degree their point is sensible and well-taken. But their own behaviorist perspective, which induces them to look upon dysfunctional behaviors literally rather than metaphorically (as do the far more symbolically minded communication theorists), at last seems unnecessarily restrictive. For there is much evidence in the clinical literature to suggest that most symptoms are not merely deplored but desired as well. Practically, to take a family at its word that it would like help in eradicating a problem is to risk seriously underestimating the ambivalence inherent in virtually every therapeutic situation.

It needs, particularly, to be stressed that Jacobson and Margolin, at the same time that they endeavor to distinguish between a communication-systems and behaviorist viewpoint, do confess that the change process frequently involves a struggle between therapist and clients because of the ambivalence many clients demonstrate toward altered behavior. And although these authors *explain* such ambivalence within an orthodox behav-iorist framework, the circumstance that they then proceed to depict (as an antidote for this resistance) a paradoxical intervention that, in itself, is indistinguishable from those advocated by strategic therapists suggests, once again, that *in the actual therapeutic situation* theory may not count for nearly as much as is conventionally assumed. Moreover, as has already been argued, the fact that two distinct theories are yet able to advocate what is basically the same symptom-encouraging technique serves to indicate a broad compatibility between them. To return to our earlier metaphor, the theories may in the end "oppose" one another little more than contrasting patterns engendered by the same kaleidoscope. Or, to adopt a seminal image from gestalt theory, whether a part of a whole is perceived as figure or ground, the overall *objective* picture remains the same. Finally, what makes psychological theories often *seem* incompat-ible, or mutually exclusive, is their conceptualizing the same essential phenomena at different levels of abstraction.

As a final comment on Jacobson and Margolin's generally incisive dis-cussion of paradox used within a behaviorist setting, it might be noted that these writers tend somewhat to simplify the position of communication theorists. This simplification reflects that of almost all advocates of a single theory, who inevitably seek to expound its superiority over rival conceptu-alizations. Such an inclination, however understandable, nonetheless has the unfortunate result of exaggerating discrepancies among the major theo-retical orientations and of making appear essential points of divergence that may in reality be far more stylistic than substantive.

TRANSCENDING THEORETICAL BOUNDARIES TO EVOLVE A "METATHEORY" OF THERAPEUTIC PARADOX

Until now this discussion has focused on practical clinical similarities among conceptually dissimilar approaches to therapy, suggesting something of the ultimate complementariness of apparently conflicting theoretical vantage points. Such a position, however, is not intended to imply, anarchistically, that different explanations for the efficacy of different *types* of paradoxical interventions are equally valid. For instance, the dynamics of a compliance-based paradoxical technique (say, directing a stutterer to try to stutter deliberately) need to be seen as diverging significantly from a defiance-based injunction (such as ordering a stubbornly disobedient teenager *not* to follow a potentially helpful recommendation). Whereas the former strategy may be appropriately conceptualized in terms of breaking the vicious cycle of anticipatory anxiety, the latter maneuver is probably best understood in terms of its generating a therapeutic double bind by capitalizing on the youth's desperate need to rebel. Additionally, certain paradoxical tactics (e.g., "joining" techniques) are best apprehended as serving principally to enable the therapist to enter into a constructive alliance with an individual or family; others as inducing recipients to behave in a way that must fatally undermine their symptom-maintaining belief system; and still others as operating specifically to impart to clients a realization of the basic controllability of their supposed involuntary behavior.

Given the likelihood that a multitude of explanations or rationales may be required to account adequately for the dynamics of the many varied applications of therapeutic paradox, *is* there any sort of "meta-explanation" or more general theory which, at a more abstract level, might serve to bind together such an unmanageably diverse assortment of interpretations? At this juncture it should be apparent that any broader exposition of the efficacy of different but related paradoxical interventions would need to cross traditional theoretical boundaries. For it would need somehow to unite techniques which—at least as delineated by their expositors—are as conceptually distinct as the works of Freud from Frankl, or Frankl from Haley.

To date, only a single brief article seeks to outline the essential commonality of the many varied applications of therapeutic paradox. This study, by Omer (1981), is entitled "Paradoxical Treatments: A Unified Concept." Standing very much alone in the literature, it warrants a short review.

Omer begins his exploratory essay by noting the obvious fact that paradoxical therapeutic techniques have developed out of diverse theoretical persuasions and that the rationales offered for them have therefore differed as widely as have the backgrounds of their proponents. Totally neglecting (and apparently unaware of) the paradoxical methods employed by both analytic and gestalt therapists, Omer regrettably confines his study to (1) the use of paradoxical intention in Frankl's logotherapy—and how such "hyperintention" and humor effectively neutralizes the anticipatory anxiety underlying the symptom; (2) the employment of paradoxical directives in the systems approach, and their explanation in terms of the therapeutic double bind; and (3) the use of massed and negative practice in behavioral treatment, and their justification according to such learning theory principles as conditioned inhibition and satiation.

While tersely summarizing the main techniques of these three clinical orientations, Omer calls attention to their explanatory limitations. That is, the rationale provided for a paradoxical tactic employed within one treatment frame cannot satisfactorily account for paradoxical strategies utilized in other approaches. Although paradoxical methods *across* theoretical persuasions are essentially similar in their encouraging patients either to continue to behave symptomatically or to avoid any efforts at improvement, the divergent rationales offered for these related techniques fail to mirror this abiding kinship. As Omer reflects at the outset of his essay: "The question at hand is whether [the different] approaches have only superficial similarities, consisting at bottom of quite different change producing agents, or whether it is better to subsume them all under one broad explanatory principle which then may serve as a bridge between the various paradigms" (p. 320).

In search of a "single common denominator" (p. 322) to account for the efficacy of therapeutic paradox, Omer proposes as an integrative concept the notion of "symptom decontextualization." This unifying idea is grounded in two closely connected arguments. First, the author contends that all paradoxical strategies deliberately modify the expression, or "form," of symptomatology—either by requesting that the patient exaggerate it, practice it at an accelerated pace, engage in it humorously, or manifest it in a different social environment. This description is generally accurate, though it should be noted that there are many instances in the literature where patients have indeed been instructed to practice the symptom or dysfunctional behavior exactly as it occurred prior to treatment. The author's second argument (or, more precisely, the second part of what is really a single two-pronged argument) is that paradoxical interventions alter not simply the form, but the *context*, of one's symptoms. The previous pattern of suppression (or attempted suppression) gives way to one of open expression. Beneficial change in therapy therefore may derive not from the prescription per se but from the symptom decontextualization that this prescription inevitably produces. Omer compares this concept to a jigsaw puzzle, in which a piece (i.e., the individual's symptom) can fit into or "complete" the whole only if the other pieces are in place. If the puzzle is dismantled or falls apart, the separate piece loses its supports and ceases to fill any purposeful function. Symptoms too, the author reasons, may be forfeited when the context that has sustained them is no longer present.

It is fairly easy to locate flaws in Omer's puzzle analogy. Nonetheless, his metaphor is useful in suggesting the inevitable interdependence or "entanglement" of symptoms—whether such intricacies be perceived intrapsychically, interpersonally, socially, or as comprising multiple relationship levels. Further, the concept of symptom decontextualization is valuable in its expansive capacity to elucidate the dynamics of therapeutic paradox as it is employed not only with individuals, but with couples, families, and groups as well. For, regardless of the specific target of a paradoxical strategy, the requisite alterations in symptom context operate to render the symptom futile and meaningless. Alienated from the whole that has (however inadvertently) nurtured it, the symptom must sooner or later die from lack of sustenance.

In illustrating the different kinds of contextual modification fostered by paradoxical techniques, Omer refers to these alterations as affective, cognitive, interpersonal, or even physical in focus. Such contextual changes are, of course, hardly to be understood as completely discrete or mutually exclusive. Indeed, the author chooses to conclude his essay by suggesting the possibility that the more widespread the dimensions of contextual modification in a paradoxical treatment, the shorter the time and the greater the likelihood that significant improvement will take place.

One might wish to object that Omer's thesis, finally, is too broad, that in the end it may be explanatory of *all* successful therapeutic methods— paradoxical and nonparadoxical alike. Such a contention would be similar to pointing out, say, that the specifically behavioral device of "cognitive restructuring" might also be viewed, globally, as accounting for what transpires in all instances of beneficial therapy, behaviorist or otherwise. In fact, it may be that "restructuring" and "decontextualizing" are descriptive of the same basic phenomena, though each construct *appears* to be separate and distinct in its concentrating on a different point, or phase, in the overall sequence of change. As these speculations may suggest, just as different types of paradoxical intervention may be effective for reasons which, fundamentally, are extremely similar, it may also be possible that paradoxical interventions facilitate change for the same underlying reasons as do nonparadoxical methods.

A second rationale, proposed by Fay (1978), for the general employment of paradoxical tactics may also be susceptible to attack because of its overly extensive applicability. Fay postulates that paradoxical interventions are effective because they "disrupt fixed habit patterns and games by nonreinforcement of the existing pattern" (p. 155). But, doubtless, it could be contended that all successful treatments in therapy are successful because, in one way or another, the dysfunctional individual or system ceases to be reinforced through the symptom. Obviously, once a symptom loses its secondarily positive aspects and becomes simply aversive, it must lose virtually all chances of survival.

In addition, it could be said that a maladaptive behavior is discontinued because, experientially, it has been discovered to be less reinforcing than some more adaptive alternative. In either case, changed behavior is not dependent on whether or not the therapeutic intervention was "paradoxical." Although there may be a certain simplicity and elegance in making use of reinforcement principles to explain the efficacy of paradoxical interventions, not only can *all* change be elucidated in such terms but explanations based on reinforcement inevitably involve a less-than-satisfying circularity. Moreover, reinforcement interpretations are so "available," so universally "serviceable," as to render them of limited use in any extensive exploration of the various parameters of therapeutic change.

Before closing this discussion, one last theoretical speculation about the efficacy of paradoxical strategies might be offered. This explanation, although it may well clarify something of the special dynamics involved in paradoxical tactics, is also vulnerable to the criticism that it characterizes the mechanics of change in nonparadoxical procedures as well. In brief, it might be asserted—very much in line with traditional analytic tenets (see, e.g., Fenichel's *The Psychoanalytic Theory of Neurosis*, 1945)—that symptoms derive from and are maintained for the principal purpose of protecting individuals from experiencing anxiety (although in many cases they are incapable of adequately fulfilling this purpose). Simple, straightforward efforts to persuade clients to relinquish symptomatic behaviors are generally doomed to failure precisely because these behaviors are emblematic of a decision that originally had substantial anxiety-reducing effects. Viewed from this perspective, almost all endeavors by the therapist early in treatment to directly influence clients to adopt healthier behaviors must be deemed misguided. For such attempts can succeed only in reawakening the original anxiety which the symptom (however unconsciously) was brought into existence to alleviate or displace. And with this anxiety freshly aroused, the client's resistance to change must be aroused also. By instead *siding with* symptoms and suggesting their legitimacy, the therapist may effectively quell the anxiety associated with symptom removal, thereby prompting the client to risk the immediate subjective discomfort of altered behavior.

Techniques that skillfully contrive to "defend" or "uphold" a client's symptom—even though such advocacy takes place in an interpersonal context mutually understood as existing to eliminate it—may enable the individual so supported to begin to view asymptomatic behavior as constituting much less of a hazard to personal adaptation and survival. The unprecedented *external support* provided by the professional endorsement of maladaptive functioning may serve, subjectively, to render the client's anxious clinging to such defensive behavior irrelevant, redundant, or both. As the symptom is implicitly redefined by the therapist's curiously accepting and even encouraging attitude toward it, the client's fear-inspired resistance toward change may well be tempered or eradicated. Whereas the symptom has typically been used as a defense against felt threats from others, this self-protective rationale for its maintenance may lose its cognitive-affective meaning as the therapist takes measures actually to prescribe it.

Given the relative effectiveness of most symptoms in warding off anxiety—at least immediately—their typical persistence should be easily understood. To offset their anxiety-ameliorating value and induce the symptomatic individual to renounce what *appears* to be their comparative advantage over nonsymptomatic alternatives, therapeutic interventions must minimize the sacrifices, deprivations, and risks associated with their abandonment. Paradoxical strategies, when carefully formulated and implemented, are ideally suited to the task of reducing client anxiety about change. In their scrupulously avoiding any active threat to the client's symptomatic—or "dysfunctionally expedient"—orientation toward reality, they forestall or preclude much of the resistance toward considering new thoughts and behaviors. By *not* requesting change, by *not* giving the client the impression that treatment will directly challenge those behaviors suspected somehow to be necessary for personal adjustment, the therapist greatly increases the possibility of the client's becoming newly willing to reevaluate the need to be symptomatic. By telling the client not to change, or at least to "go slow" about the whole matter of changing, the therapist may be seen as offering the profoundly reassuring message that any change which does take place will (1) be self-chosen, and (2) proceed at a subjectively comfortable pace.

Finally, in certain defiance-based paradoxical interventions, the therapist's strategic endorsement of the symptom may operate to redirect the client's anxiety about being divested of it to a *counteranxiety* about retaining it specifically at the therapist's behest—and thereby forfeiting a much coveted autonomy. In such cases the anxiety motive may be seen as dovetailing with the motive of psychological reactance alluded to earlier, thus compelling the client actively to resist his own former resistance to change. As Seltzer (1983) puts it: "The heightened sense of vulnerability and consequent defensiveness [of the typical clinical population] should suggest the susceptibility of such persons to interventions which direct through a calculated indirection that permits the affirmation of autonomy even in the submission to the therapist's . . . implicit goals" (p. 69). Such neutralization or redirection of reactance can be seen as effectively counteracting the basically fear-inspired resistance to change in many instances where a more straightforward approach might succeed only in solidifying this resistance.

In addition, if the therapist actually *recommends* the symptom, the oppositional client—left with little to rebel against but the symptom itself—may begin to experience this symptom as no longer able to furnish any tactical advantage over the therapist. To allay the anxiety resultant from losing this badly needed advantage, such a client may be prompted to renounce the symptom so as to "resecure" his former position in treatment. Symptomatic behavior may become extremely uncomfortable when it no longer elicits the expected feedback but, on the contrary, is subtly reframed as "controlled" externally by a therapist who openly permits or prescribes it. Obliged to look at his dysfunctional behavior in a new—and far less favorable—light, the negativistic client may be much more willing to experiment with nonsymptomatic alternatives.

Continually in this section the argument has been advanced that interpretations of therapeutic change traditionally regarded as contrasting may more accurately be viewed as complementary. Moreover, it is reasonable to assume that this change does not represent a single climactic event but a coherent *sequence* of events. If such is the case, it would seem theoretically advantageous to regard change as multidetermined as well as occurring at stages or intervals, each of which may be defined in fairly predictable terms. To combine Omer's hypothesis with Fay's—and also with that proposed immediately above—it might be postulated that paradoxical strategies operate to "decontextualize" symptoms and by so doing undermine the reinforcement cycle serving to maintain them, which in turn favorably alters the "risk quotient" attributed by the individual to nonsymptomatic behaviors.

Once again, it might be objected that virtually *all* successful therapeutic procedures function in some way to decontextualize dysfunctional behaviors, interfere with their secondary reinforcement, and assist individuals (and families) to overcome the anxiety linked to change. The only response to such an objection is that although it probably is true that the essential mechanisms of change are the same regardless of whether this change has been effected "paradoxically" or "nonparadoxically," it may also be true that the element of surprise and confusion by definition inherent in paradoxical methods may somehow enable them in particular cases either to succeed where more conventional techniques have failed or to facilitate change with greater *efficiency* than other, more "orthodox," interventions.

Still, it can hardly be overemphasized that successful paradoxical interventions do not necessarily promote a different *kind* of change—nor do they in some manner restructure the *process* of this change. Typical descriptions of, and arguments for, the use of paradoxical tactics indeed reflect justifications commonly made for nonparadoxical treatment modes. For instance, proponents of all the major schools of therapy have advanced the position that the principal determinant of dysfunctional behavior is fear, and that various types of psychopathology can be understood as an individual's attempt (however poorly realized) to gain some measure of control over this fear. Dysfunctional behaviors, consequently, are perceived as essentially *avoidant* behaviors—that is, they are perceived as depicting the individual's anxious refusal to cope with fears directly.

Such stark behavioral devices as flooding and implosion can be viewed as "stripping" certain clinical problems down to their inmost core: the raw fear that governs the individual's maladaptive (and increasingly desperate) habit of avoidance. Virtually all forms of therapy, however, can be conceptualized—and, in fact, have been conceptualized—in terms of how they deal with the patient's or client's "fear motive" and the psychologically unhealthy responses to which this motive inevitably gives rise. If paradoxical strategies can be seen as helping the individual productively to confront those fears that have constituted the foremost personal obstacle to change, so also can nonparadoxical methods be seen as expressly devised to accomplish this crucial task. Although paradoxical procedures for prompting change may be tactically divergent from more traditional change techniques, the therapeutic objective in either case remains the same. In short, effective treatment must somehow succeed in empowering individuals to overcome, or "work through," their fears—so as to put them to rest once and for all.

Such empowerment seems curiously reminiscent of Watzlawick's (1978) "anything, except *that*" notion of the central barrier to therapeutic change. In Watzlawick's own provocative words:

> It may be a useful simplification to postulate that whoever comes into therapy signals in one way or another: Anything, except *that*. By this I mean that emotional suffering creates a willingness to do *anything* for its alleviation, except one and only one thing; and this "one thing" is exactly what causes his suffering. . . . The only possible solution always lies in the direction of the greatest anxiety and, therefore, the strongest resistance. (p. 139)

If Watzlawick's "that" is related precisely to what arouses the most opposition from the patient or client, this is so because it is linked by the individual to what most threatens his emotional, mental, and physical survival. Whether the individual's fear be of rejection, failure, disapproval, or anything else perceived as hazardous, the *reaction* to this fear will invariably be characterized by some type of evasion. Thus the therapeutic task, *regardless of the clinician's particular theoretical approach*, must focus on influencing the individual to recognize the essential irrationality of his fears. Only through the development of such enlightened self-awareness may the individual finally be impelled to give up his personally disabling response of avoidance. Very few change strategies are as blatantly directive as implosion and flooding—or even as paradoxical intention, which Frankl (1967) describes simply as a procedure in which "the patient is encouraged to do, or wish to happen, the very things he fears" (p. 146). Yet virtually all methods of facilitating change can be seen as striving to induce clients to grapple anew with their fears and, by so doing, triumph over the often debilitating effects that have resulted from their habitual efforts to avoid them.

The reality-testing component essential to all varieties of therapy also suggests how paradoxical change strategies fit into a larger conceptualization of therapeutic change. That is, paradoxical tactics may differ *in form* from more conventional modes of intervention, but their goal of inducing clients to challenge experientially their ultimately painful assumptions about reality are identical. Whether or not a treatment approach employs the term or concept of "reframing," it should be obvious that across theoretical persuasions the view is held that clients must learn cognitively, affectively, and behaviorally that their perception of the world involves serious inaccuracies. And such a lesson can be profitably learned only through their willingness to test the reality which previously they hardly dared question. The "corrective emotional experience" often alluded to as fundamental in any significant behavior change may be seen as a direct outcome of the client's having successfully been encouraged to think and act in ways till then avoided. For only through actually entering the vibrant and pulsating waters of reality can an individual finally realize that they are not in fact shark-infested, as had in the past fearfully been assumed.

In the end, immersing oneself in the waves and currents of the real world functions to restore one's sense of personal determination. Although rationales for paradoxical strategies frequently stress their utility in helping clients to reestablish feelings of self-control, *all* therapies can be perceived as endeavoring to assist clients in comprehending the voluntariness—and thus controllability—of behaviors that have come to appear nonvolitional.

Just as symptom prescription techniques seek indirectly to impel clients to experience their symptoms as *belonging to* them and consequently within their capacity to change, so do all modes of therapeutic intervention strive to help individuals assert final control over dysfunctional behaviors. Self-control—quite possibly the paramount goal of all therapy—hinges on the individual's willing decision to renounce those avoidant behaviors that have necessitated treatment in the first place. And here, once again, we are reminded of the essential relatedness not only of the various schools of therapy but also of the various paradoxical and nonparadoxical methods which they promulgate.

FROM THEORETICAL SPECULATION TO EMPIRICAL EXAMINATION: THE CHALLENGE FOR RESEARCH

To be sure, it is one thing to speculate about the therapeutic utility of paradoxical strategies and quite another to devise experiments that will adequately support (or disconfirm) the many conjectures used to justify their employment. Scientifically, perhaps the primary value of theorizing is to help point the way for empirical research through generating hypotheses that can then be rigorously put to the test. For only through reliable and accurate examination and measurement can the various assumptions linked to therapeutic paradox meaningfully be explored.

Despite the need to investigate experimentally (1) the different rationales proposed for using paradoxical strategies and (2) the comparative efficacy of these interventions in bringing about beneficial change, it must be conceded that the task is sufficiently formidable to have attracted few researchers. As these pages have indicated, the richness of theoretical explanation in the literature on therapeutic paradox is unfortunately counterbalanced by a paucity of clinical outcome studies on the subject. Similarly, the promising fertility of projects suggested by this literature is more than matched by the discouraging practical difficulties in controlling for the host of variables which such undertakings would inevitably involve.

Yet the usefulness of additional research in this area should be evident. There is indeed much to study. Paradoxical interventions come in many forms and contain many variants. They can be—and have been—employed for treating a broad range of clinical problems. Moreover, they have been implemented with many different types of clients, cooperative as well as resistant, and with virtually every age group; and they have been adopted in diverse treatment facilities, inpatient as well as outpatient. Finally, not only do the large variety of paradoxical tactics call for perusal across a wide range of clients and patients, symptoms, and settings but, in each case, their efficacy requires direct comparison with other viable treatment modes.

If empirical explorations of paradoxical treatments are to attain any sort of clinical (as opposed to merely statistical) significance, they must demonstrate a clear cognizance of the many variables essential to estimating a treatment's effectiveness. Not only must the different variables be meticulously defined and measurement or assessment operations painstakingly delineated (to ensure reliability and permit replication), but every effort feasible must be made to rule out alternative explanations for the results derived (e.g., the possibility that altered behavior has in fact been caused by factors extraneous to the treatment under scrutiny). Additionally, a standardized assessment battery that meets well-defined and agreed-upon criteria needs to be used to accurately gauge both subjective and objectively observable behavioral changes. In order that the study have maximal generalizability, each variable must be controlled as much as clinically practicable. The importance of thoroughly screening clients to be subjected to treatment, so as to obtain a clearly demarcated, homogeneous sample, can hardly be overestimated. Factors pertaining to the dysfunctional behavior itself, such as its frequency, chronicity, severity, and stressfulness all must be taken into account. Closely related client variables, such as the *need* to be symptomatic (or the felt risk of trying out new behaviors) and the motivation to change, also necessitate investigation and measurement. Still other relevant experimental considerations—including therapist variables (such as the strength of professional position and influence) and variables connected to client-therapist interaction (such as the degree of rapport and certain qualitative aspects of the communication process)—need to be carefully weighed in evaluating the final meaning of obtained results.

Assuming the therapist's/researcher's awareness and sophistication about clinical-experimental design and, too, the willingness to subscribe to the arduous procedures requisite to "realizing" it in practice, there is a great deal of useful research to be undertaken in the realm of paradoxical treatment. As long as the particular therapeutic strategies are clearly specified and do not entail substantial (and undefinable) variations in administration, there is no reason that their comparative value in effecting significant behavioral change cannot productively be explored.

Clinical considerations which suggest workable hypotheses relating to the employment of paradoxical procedures include their use in (1) helping to develop a sound therapeutic alliance through conveying the message of total client support—symptoms included (cf. Rogers' "unconditional positive regard"); (2) reducing the anxiety associated by clients with change; (3) helping clients to alter the irrational belief system that perpetuates the symptom; (4) "modeling" a more adaptive perspective toward the symptom (i.e., cognitive restructuring) and, closely linked to such modeling, enabling clients to take the symptom less seriously through the therapist's deliberately humorous "reframing" of it; (5) helping clients to "decontextualize" the symptom and thereby undermine its functioning; (6) helping to elicit a therapeutic *reactance* toward the symptom (cf. intentionally creating for clients a "therapeutic double bind"); (7) helping to weaken the symptom's reinforcement value; (8) undermining the symptom specifically as a "power tactic"; and, finally, (9) helping clients to recognize the controllability (or essential voluntariness) of the symptom.

Elaborating somewhat on the hypothesized clinical functions of paradoxical procedures (and in accordance with the order given above), empirical research might seek to address the following questions:

1.   To what extent are paradoxical strategies more effective than nonparadoxical approaches in enabling the therapist to enter into a constructive alliance with clients (couples or families)—that is, by their more encompassing (or "symptom-sanctioning") support of the client or family system?

2.   Can empirical studies demonstrate any consistent superiority of paradoxical interventions over nonparadoxical ones in reducing client anxiety about changing their behavior? Can it be shown, at least with clients measured to have higher levels of anxiety (or feelings of vulnerability) than most members of a typical clinical population, that paradoxical strategies more effectively counter the resistance to consider healthier behaviors? How do paradoxical and nonparadoxical techniques compare in their influencing the subjective "risk quotient" tied to altered (i.e., nonsymptomatic) behavior, thus encouraging clients to explore alternative courses of thought and action? Do paradoxical and nonparadoxical interventions differ in their ability to reduce the fear-inspired need to act (and interact) symptomatically?

3.   What is the relative efficacy of paradoxical directives in prompting clients to question their symptom-perpetuating belief systems—versus, for instance, more direct cognitive approaches, such as rational-emotive therapy? Phenomenologically, how might paradoxical interventions be seen as "playing on" belief systems?

4.   To what extent does the therapist's modeling of a fully accepting, and even endorsing, attitude toward the symptom facilitate a perception of the symptom that is less serious and more objective or detached? How much does such modeling prompt clients to alter their self-defeating regard for the symptom? What is the particular role of "therapist humor" in all of this?

5.   To what extent can Omer's (1981) "symptom decontextualization" hypothesis for the efficacy of paradoxical strategies be empirically validated? Omer speaks of symptom decontextualization as altering the "form" or "expression" of the symptom through (a) exaggerating it, (b) accelerating it, (c) engaging in it humorously, and (d) displaying it in a different social environment. How can we isolate each of these modifications and estimate their relative role in facilitating change? How can we study these modifications in different *combinations*, so as more accurately to evaluate the effectiveness of their interaction and more reliably assess the factors leading to change?

Moreover, Omer describes symptom decontextualization as occurring on four separate levels: affective, cognitive, interpersonal, and physical. To what extent can these levels be studied separately from one another? To what extent can the relative importance of these levels be meaningfully measured? To what extent may multilevels of symptom decontextualization shorten treatment time and increase the probability of significant symptom improvement?

6.   To what extent do defiance-based paradoxical interventions succeed in eliciting a therapeutic reactance toward therapist directives?—that is, to what extent does the therapist's active support of client resistance prompt clients to renounce this resistance so as to assert themselves against the therapist and thus begin to behave nonsymptomatically? *Can* empirical examination provide evidence for the view that reactance can be redirected (or "rerouted") toward the symptom itself when clients experience pressure to maintain (or exaggerate) it? Also, to what degree does actively opposing a therapist's paradoxical prescription lead to a reduction of anxiety in resistant clients?

7.   To what extent can Fay's (1978) broad "reinforcement hypothesis" about the effectiveness of paradoxical tactics be validated or disconfirmed? How might researchers derive adequate measures to study the relationship postulated by Fay between the therapist's adoption of paradoxical strategies and the diminished reinforcement capacity of the symptom? Can the question-begging circularity inherent in the general concept of reinforcement somehow be "adjusted for" empirically? If maladaptive behaviors give way to healthier alternatives through the strength of paradoxical interventions, can these more adaptive behaviors in fact be demonstrated to be more reinforcing? And are there any measurable differences between paradoxical and nonparadoxical methods in bringing about such changes in reinforcement?

8.   To what extent are paradoxical directives differentially effective in interfering with the practical advantages that symptomatic behavior may

afford clients in social transactions? If symptoms are conceptualized specifically as behavioral strategies, to what extent does the therapist's reconceptualization and prescription of them weaken their utility in enabling clients to exert a dysfunctional interpersonal control?

9.   What is the comparative effectiveness of paradoxical techniques in enabling clients to perceive the voluntariness—and consequent controllability—of behaviors previously assumed to be involuntary? *Are* paradoxical strategies more efficient in this regard than nonparadoxical approaches (as has often been postulated in the literature)? To what extent do symptom prescription devices differentially induce clients to acknowledge *responsibility for*, and thus control over, symptomatic behavior?

Finally, beyond all these considerations relating to the many different *rationales* frequently proposed for the usefulness of paradoxical interventions, research must address the following fundamental question relating to their application: With what *population(s)* specifically and under what *circumstances* are each of the many paradoxical techniques that have been described in this volume differentially effective in promoting therapeutic change? Needless to say, this consideration—as well as the large variety of questions enumerated above—will necessitate a great multitude of research projects.

This said, certain reservations about the "testability" of the rationales proposed for paradoxical strategies—and, indeed, the ultimate testability of the strategies themselves—must be made. Given the plethora of methodological problems and complexities to this point only vaguely suggested, it may in the end be impossible to derive anything approaching conclusive evidence about the relative effectiveness of paradoxical techniques (or, for that matter, most nonparadoxical techniques as well). Irreducible intricacies related to their application may resist the sort of simplification, assessment, and control necessary to interpret confidently the final meaning of any results derived from the systematic attempt to study them.

For example, the clinician's precise degree of proficiency in implementing a paradoxical strategy, a variable that frankly defies measurement, may make all the difference in the capacity of the technique to promote (and maintain) beneficial change. In general, therapy—unless it is dealing with a relatively uncomplicated problem such as simple stage fright or some transient adjustment difficulty—is an enterprise of considerable complexity and one that demands considerable sensitivity on the part of the practitioner. It may not exactly be an "art form," as has sometimes been proposed, and many basic clinical skills (such as empathy and "active listening") can to a large degree be taught. Still, it would seem safe to say that the most successful therapists do not simply "learn their trade" exceptionally well but bring to it certain personal qualities that *cannot* be learned—just as it might be said that what it takes to play a musical instrument competently is essentially different from what it takes to become an orchestral soloist. The "extra something" that resists quantification and cannot be imparted even by a master teacher makes all the difference between a musician who can play comfortably with an orchestra and a soloist who literally plays *before* one. For the same never entirely definable reasons a paradoxical (or, one might say, virtually *any*) therapeutic strategy might be used to great advantage by one therapist and have comparatively little effect when employed by another.

To use a second analogy, seeking accurately to measure the many variables present in a therapeutic undertaking may be something like trying to study "scientifically" a neo-impressionist painting by Seurat. Composed "essentially" of thousands of tiny dots of color, such a painting must eternally frustrate any spectator endeavoring to derive a more precise understanding of the artist's work by walking immediately up to it. Such proximity might well enable the viewer to count all the tiny dots and identify all their different colors. But at the same time that the painting becomes objectively "quantifiable," the basic forms and figures of which the painting is comprised are no longer intelligible. That is, the *composition*—which is finally the "heart" of the painting and constitutes its ultimate meaning—simply disintegrates as the spectator moves closer toward it so as more accurately to appreciate its literal artistic ingredients. Obviously, in such a case it might be said that the painting was never *meant* to be viewed at such close range, its representational elements designed to be appreciated only from a distance substantially removed from that at which it was originally composed.

Returning to the complex issue of devising reliable and valid clinical outcome studies, is it not possible that even though a researcher may strive to account for and measure the many different variables relevant to a particular treatment, that which is basic to understanding its relative efficacy may remain just as elusive or unquantifiable as before? Vital clinical phenomena may simply not yield their essence to anyone seeking to apprehend them using the same experimental model as that employed by the physical sciences. Endeavoring to keep the scientific faith by establishing such experimental conditions as random assignment to groups, uniformity in administering the technique (as though in therapy a technique might actually be "administered" as, say, a doctor might prescribe a drug for a virus), homogeneous treatment populations, and nontreatment control groups, may finally represent an ideal which in the world of therapy can never be realized.

All this is not to imply nihilistically that clinical researchers should not strive for as much scientific precision in their undertakings as feasible or, indeed, that they should abandon such undertakings altogether. Nor is it meant to suggest that clinical research cannot be *practically* useful—ruling out, for instance, certain treatment modes that repeatedly have been shown to offer little chance of success. Rather, it is meant to put the whole issue of clinical research into proper scientific perspective. That is, different forms of treatment can—and, in fact, *have been*—productively compared; and if researchers are reasonably conscientious about controlling for those variables *in their power* to control, clinical outcome studies may well reveal broad patterns within a treatment mode or obvious differences between treatments, which can then serve as guideposts for the practitioner. Nevertheless, given all the ambiguities and complexities of the therapeutic enterprise, it needs to be stressed that it is most unlikely that the ultimate "truth" of any of the hypotheses enumerated above relating to paradoxical strategies can be demonstrated or disconfirmed by any experiment, or even combination of experiments. Regardless of how many relevant research variables can be operationalized or otherwise adequately accounted for, empirical results will almost invariably fall short of providing the "final evidence" that every clinical researcher naturally strives to achieve.

SYMPTOM ACCEPTANCE AND ENCOURAGEMENT: HOW THE THERAPIST GAINS CONTROL OF THE THERAPEUTIC RELATIONSHIP

Having explored, at least preliminarily, some fundamental theoretical and experimental issues pertaining to the use of therapeutic paradox, it now remains to address in greater detail a question posed earlier. In brief, if different theories of psychotherapy can be understood as postulating many of the same underlying mechanisms of change—though in ways sufficiently distinct as to mask their fundamental similarity—on what level *specifically* can we reconcile their apparent discrepancies? Given the obvious circumstance that all therapy involves the existence of at least one therapist and one client, it would appear that if various schools of treatment are recognizable (despite radical dissimilarities in language) as conveying the same essential ideas about change, then the unifying element must somehow be located in the therapeutic relationship cultivated by each of them. Moreover, as Haley (1963) contends, it may be that "the 'cause' of change resides in what all methods of therapy have in common—the therapeutic paradoxes which appear in the relationship between psychotherapist and patient" (p. 179).

Perhaps the key paradox that informs the therapeutic relationship (and thereby joins divergent theoretical orientations) is the therapist's broad acceptance of client symptomatology. In almost all schools of treatment, the therapist may be seen as "permitting" symptoms, or tolerantly "letting them be"—rather than immediately setting out to challenge them and thus increase the likelihood of arousing a therapy-defeating resistance. Whether or not therapy involves actually *encouraging* symptomatic behaviors, any treatment warrants appreciation as paradoxical to the extent that it runs counter to client expectations that the therapist will seek directly to remove presenting complaints (as, say, a surgeon would remove a tumor). Although orthodox psychoanalysis may readily be distinguished from Rogers' more contemporary "client-centered" therapy, close scrutiny of these two therapeutic modes will reveal a crucial kinship in terms of the deeply supportive *nondirective* posture characteristic of them both.

This nondirectiveness—most conspicuous in client-centered therapy and psychoanalysis but (though perhaps to a lesser degree) present in other types of treatment as well—is capable of significantly reducing client attempts to control the therapeutic relationship symptomatically (Haley, 1963). Paradoxically, because the client is encouraged to take control of the relationship by being assigned the role of initiator, he is in reality unable to do so. For as long as the client's interactive role is *defined* by the therapist, he cannot really be in charge. It is precisely because continued symptomatic behavior takes place within a context chosen and controlled by the therapist that the symptom is sabotaged and begins to lose its reinforcement. As Mandel, Weizmann, Millan, Greenhow, and Speirs (1975) suggest, extending Haley's notions about symptom encouragement to include systematic desensitization, aversion therapy, implosive therapy, and gestalt therapy: "The common denominator of all these techniques is that control of the symptomatic behavior passes to the therapist, and the symptoms are directed to occur in situations which maximize their disadvantages and may, in fact, add to the distress which such symptoms usually cause" (p. 870).

The therapeutic double bind mentioned so frequently in these pages results precisely from this circumstance that a client cannot go on exploiting his symptoms to assert control in the therapy relationship when encouraged to do so. As Haley (1963) originally conceptualized it, if the client continues to behave symptomatically, he is forced to concede that the therapist is in charge, and consequently must at some level question the utility of his symptoms. If, on the other hand, he abandons his symptomatic behavior, such relinquishment requires a similar concession inasmuch as the therapist's tacitly acknowledged goal all along has been to induce him to change. The underlying paradox is that it is through the acceptance—not rejection—of the client's dysfunctional behaviors that the groundwork is laid for change. Or, to describe the interactive situation in somewhat more picturesque terms, it might be said that the foundation for the client's self-defensive symptoms must eventually topple through the therapist's subtly undermining support of them. Such an unprecedented "helping" relationship, at least to Haley, represents "the essential interpersonal context of any therapeutic change" (p. 53).

It can hardly be overemphasized that it is through the therapist's defining as acceptable virtually *all* the behaviors offered to him by the client that a constructive control of the relationship is secured. And this control may be viewed as *the* prerequisite for effective therapy. Furthermore, the therapist only increases such regulatory power by also accepting what the client does *not* offer him. That is, if the client has decided to withhold necessary information in order to control the relationship, the therapist may seize this control simply by encouraging such withholding. And, as Erickson has persuasively indicated (Haley, 1973), this encouragement functions practically to prompt the client to divulge material previously felt to require the most zealous protection.

Given the therapist's overall stance of acceptance, client resistance generally must either lose something of its habitual tenacity or become fatally weakened by a new willingness to try out less symptomatic behaviors—born of the client's desperate need to reestablish some form of control by "one-upping" the therapist. If treatment is successful, the final outcome of the therapist's *interpersonal* control is for the client to initiate a much healthier form of *self*-control (undertaken expressly to counter the feelings of futility now tied to his former dysfunctional means of control). Through the therapist's paradoxical support of the client's behavioral status quo, the client's resistance—and his symptoms may be understood generally as the manifestation of this resistance—may be transformed from an obstacle to change to an unusually efficient *vehicle* of change.

PARADOX IN HYPNOTHERAPY: THE CONNECTING LINK?

The Utilization of Symptoms

Repeatedly in the communication-systems literature, reference is made to the ideas and practices of hypnotherapist Milton Erickson. These citations frequently intimate that Erickson's accomplishments with cases of inordinate difficulty reveal something essential about the principles of successful therapy. The many efforts made to schematize Erickson's often daring procedures—whether semantically, neurolinguistically, strategically, or otherwise—may all be viewed as serving to identify his approach in dialectical, or paradoxical, terms. Consequently, it may be worthwhile to examine a few of Erickson's basic methods by way of indicating how he (and hypnotists in general) effect change through therapeutic paradox.

Probably the core of Erickson's influential ideas on facilitating change is located in his prevalent notion that effective therapy requires the clinician fully to accept whatever the patient brings to treatment. Erickson's key concept of "utilization" has been mentioned earlier and derives from his well-known position that the cure for a patient's symptoms *already* resides within the patient, needing only to be evoked by the therapist. That is, the inner resources for therapeutic change can be found in the patient's psychosocial history, and the principal job of the therapist is to assist him in overcoming the resistance which has prevented him from getting in touch with—and implementing—these resources. In this conceptual context, Zeig (1980a), seeking to illuminate Erickson's innovative methods, has proposed that "symptom prescription is a technique that enables the patient to discover and demonstrate to himself that he has such resources, and that he can initiate the change that he requests." Elaborating on this fundamental paradoxical strategy in a way which organically connects it both to hypnosis (or at least Ericksonian hypnosis) and psychotherapy, Zeig concludes:

> Symptom prescription technique follows from the principles of hypnotic induction and psychotherapy espoused by Erickson, which stress (1) meeting the patient at his point of reference; (2) accepting and using the patient's behavior and motivation to make small therapeutic modifications; and (3) eliciting the cure/trance that was previously dormant. Symptom prescription is a way of bypassing natural resistance to change and helping the patient to use potential that he had not previously recognized. (p. 22)

The Utilization and Reframing of Resistance

In the late fifties, Erickson (1959) explicitly contrasted his willingness to accept and utilize his subject's resistance to go into a trance with the then prevalent attitude of hypnotists, which was to regard such resistance as an obstacle that had to be surmounted if a trance were to be induced. To Erickson, it was much more efficient for the therapist simply to allow or cooperate with the patient's resistance than to enter into a struggle to make him relinquish it. By such acceptance of the patient's presenting behavior, however inimical to trance induction it might appear, a hypnotic state might actually be facilitated. Throughout his distinguished career, Erickson stressed the importance of meeting the patient's psychological needs, maintaining that receptivity to these needs ultimately functioned to reduce the primary hindrances to change.

The paradoxical notion of utilizing resistance specifically to induce a trance state is very similar to the more general idea of supporting resistance to aid in therapeutic change. In fact, a hypnotic trance can be defined as a mental state of heightened suggestibility, and—seen within a therapeutic context—fostering such suggestibility is extremely important because it may relate directly to altering maladaptive behaviors. In an article called "The Use of Symptoms as an Integral Part of Hypnotherapy" (1965), Erickson discusses the necessity of accommodating the patient's obstructive and irrational conduct in order to establish a firm interpersonal groundwork for change. And this lifelong conviction that therapists had to learn to respect and constructively utilize that which initially was likely to appear hopelessly detrimental to treatment may be seen as underlying most of the techniques that have been labeled "paradoxical"—not simply in Erickson's engagingly original work but in the general psychotherapy literature as well. For almost all the various techniques of "siding with" the patient's symptoms are designed to prompt the patient to recognize their nonessential, or "disposable," nature.

To Haley (1973), the rigidly symptomatic patient and resistive hypnotic subject bear close comparison in that both types of individuals do not openly refuse to cooperate with straightforward therapeutic suggestions but merely communicate an *inability* to do so. Thus the "art" of therapy and hypnosis is, similarly, to so handle this professed incapacity as to bring about productive change. By accepting the individual's general resistance to cooperate and even encouraging it, both the hypnotist and therapist may succeed in influencing him to comply with potentially useful directives. Since resistant behavior is tactically redefined as "cooperative," the individual finds himself following instructions regardless of what he does or does not do. And once his mental set has become one of cooperation, he can be "diverted" into trying out new and less symptomatic behaviors.

The paradoxical practice of positively redefining symptoms and noncooperative conduct has already been reviewed in the chapter on the systems approach. But a few words might be added here to suggest how such benign reframing holds an essential place in modern hypnosis. Arguing that too often therapists pay only "lip service" to the idea of utilizing the patient's resistance—while in reality reacting to this negativism as indicative of the patient's ill-preparedness for treatment—Watzlawick (1978) concludes that such therapists have much to learn from hypnotherapy. For here, "the ability to utilize resistance and to reframe any setback as a sign of progress has always been considered decisive for ultimate success" (p. 145). The vast potential of such an orientation should be obvious. Certainly in a hypnotic context, to use *all* of the subject's behaviors as signalling the deepening of his trance state is to do everything possible to foster the sort of therapeutic support and alliance vital to inducing the patient to give up his resistances and consider anew the possibilities of change.

Adapting such reframing in hypnosis to common practices in gestalt therapy, Levitsky (1976) notes the value of accepting, or "staying with," the client's resistance so as to move unimpeded toward therapeutic goals. By way of illustration, one of his examples may be cited:

Patient says: "I can't concentrate; my mind wanders."
T[herapist]: "Fine, let it wander. Just tell me where it wanders."(Patient recounts the material.)
T[herapist]: "Good. Where do you wander now? Now, can you take a deep breath, relax and let your mind wander some more?" (p. 121)

Levitsky, commenting on this clinical vignette, describes it as "a classical example of paradoxical hypnotic technique at its best." For it contrives at once to impart to the patient the message that he is free to do what he wishes to do and yet what the therapist wishes him to do also. Even though the author is not inclined to conceptualize this example in terms of, say, analytic notions about negative transference or systems ideas about symptom prescription, it is clear that his general method of accommodating (and thus counteracting) resistance is essentially kindred to these other modes of therapeutic direction. Moreover, *all* of these treatment modes may be perceived as cognate to the fundamental hypnotic principle of responding to patient resistances by adapting trance induction procedures to comply with, and thereby neutralize, them.

Haley (1963), who views as a prerequisite to effective treatment the therapist's gaining control over patient resistances, perceives this control as obtained similarly in hypnosis and therapy. In both settings the patient is placed, through the covert posing of a paradox, into a double bind that nullifies the power of his resistances to exert control over the relationship. As postulated by Haley, when a hypnotic subject is strategically encouraged to express his resistance after having first been requested to cooperate, it is very difficult for him to take control of the situation. If he continues to resist, he is now complying with the hypnotist's directives, so that his oppositionalism ceases to be viable as a means of taking charge of the relationship. Given the hypnotist's unexpected—and thereby disarming—permissiveness, he cannot *not* follow instructions. Such a trance-promoting double bind is perceived as parallel to the therapist's tact of encouraging a patient to behave symptomatically within a framework expressly designed to help him relinquish his symptoms. If symptoms are in fact best seen as stratagems for achieving interpersonal control (as has been Haley's contention for over two decades now), the therapist's cordial acceptance of them precludes their use for gaining control of, and thereby sabotaging, treatment. Whether the context is one of hypnosis or psychotherapy, this professional stance of "calculated indulgence" puts the patient in a double bind that renders practically impossible his defensively rigid habit of noncooperativeness.

Directing Patients "Spontaneously" to Change Their Behavior

Hypnosis is also compared to therapy by Haley (1963, 1973) in its incongruent, or paradoxical, request that the patient change his behavior spontaneously. Paradoxical injunctions, regarded as playing a crucial role in almost all methods of trance induction, are also held to be essential in therapy in that these provocatively conflicting demands prompt concrete behavioral changes. Whether these changes take the form of trance behavior or less symptomatic behavior, their felt spontaneity indirectly paves the way for the patient to develop a more secure sense of autonomy. Haley (1973), in noting a key problem common to hypnosis and therapy—that is, how to direct a patient to behave differently but on his own initiative—describes a typical procedure used by Erickson as enjoining the patient to act in one way such that he is provoked to assert his independence, and begin to accept the voluntariness of his behavior, by acting in another (much healthier) way. In this manner, Erickson (and probably any other successful therapist) "engineers" a spontaneity designed to enable the patient to grow and, ultimately, to *outgrow* the need for external help and support. For once the patient has been induced to act spontaneously, he is able to begin tapping his own resources for handling problems whose solutions have previously eluded him.

THE ESSENCE OF THERAPY AS PARADOXICAL

The Paradoxical Nature of Symptoms

Weeks and L'Abate (1982) maintain that "most theories of psychopathology and psychotherapy have described symptoms in strictly negative terms" and "as an enemy" to therapy (p. 27). This contention, though not without a certain *literal* accuracy, fails to take into account the fact that all major schools of therapy include practices that imply a much more favorable view of symptoms. True, behavior therapy tends to look at symptoms in a less than hospitable manner. And even *paradoxical* behavioral techniques, which explicitly encourage the manifestation of symptoms, may in a sense be seen as confronting them quite as much as supporting them. Nevertheless, therapists of virtually all theoretical persuasions have found it useful to adopt a more or less neutral (if not exactly positive) stance toward symptoms. To threaten their existence (through symptom-challenging interventions) before the client has begun to resolve some of his ambivalence toward them seems intuitively to be understood as detrimental to the therapeutic process. Whether or not symptoms are actually viewed as *allies* of the therapist or as *vehicles* of change (as is the case in almost all paradoxical approaches), experienced therapists generally refrain from actively opposing them.

If paradoxical and nonparadoxical orientations to therapy appear to diverge sharply from one another as regards their outlook on symptoms, this discrepancy may merely indicate that the former perspective reveals far more *conscious* awareness than the latter of their adaptive functions— though, as Buda (1972) soberly observes, "[this] adaptation is mostly inadequately accomplished, both within the personality and in the interpersonal field" (p. 201). For even the more traditional therapies, which would seem to do little more than "tolerate" symptoms, betray in their avoiding any sort of frontal assault on them a certain deference, perhaps even grudging admiration, for the self-protective purposes they manage (however inefficiently) to serve.

In the end, defining a symptom positively may be akin to Rogers' unconditional positive regard. The symptom may be fundamentally misguided and upheld at great personal expense, yet it does have its adaptive elements and—as an intrinsic and "necessary" aspect of the individual's coping style—must be accepted if the therapist is to have maximum influence on the client. Although therapist and client may indeed agree on the advisability of reducing or removing the *need* for the symptom, the therapeutic undertaking still requires that the clinician treat symptomatic behaviors with a certain forebearance and respect.

The Paradoxical Nature of the Therapist's Role

To restate some of the above points, therapists across theoretical approaches are friendly and receptive to clients. As a prerequisite for working constructively with client problems, this professional congeniality is essential and inevitably involves accepting the client as a whole—symptomatic behavior included. That is, the therapist generally can help alleviate or eradicate symptoms only within the larger context of accepting them. The therapist's empathy, also routinely held to be a prerequisite for effective therapy, must somehow contrive to "support" the symptom at the same time that it commiserates with the client for its painful and self-defeating aspects. In a family therapy setting the therapist is often obliged to extend this curiously two-faced, or paradoxical, stance by siding with different family members, even though they may be articulating diametrically opposed viewpoints. And here the paramount importance of reframing—one of the key paradoxical stratagems employed (whether consciously or not) by every school of therapy—is perhaps most in evidence. For to win the confidence, trust, approval, or merely *attention* of various family members, antagonistic positions may require redefinition as complementary, and collusive or conspiratorial behaviors necessitate relabeling as cooperative.

The therapist's empathically accepting attitude toward client symptoms has other functions as well. Interpretations of dysfunctional behavior, for instance, are more likely to be received favorably if clients find them palatable—if not flattering, then at least sympathetic and short of judgmental. However worthy of criticism or condemnation such behavior may be, the therapist may yet need to find ways of condoning (if not exactly justifying) this conduct in order for clients to lower their defenses and begin to realize their freedom and ability to change it. Espousing a psychodynamic perspective, Schlesinger (1982) argues that the feelings of threat which govern the resistant patient require that the therapist not strive directly to educate, cajole, or admonish him but rather to "empathiz[e] with him in his difficulty with the transference figure." In supporting this benign approach, the author explains:

> Go[ing] with the resistance rather than oppos[ing] it may sound paradoxical, but it is derived from the larger view of psychotherapy as a process and the general principles to begin where the patient is, to facilitate the expression of what the patient is trying to say, to work from the surface, to deal with defenses against affects and affects before everything else, and to allow the patient to be as active as possible in the treatment. (p. 39)

In a similar vein, Mozdzierz et al. (1976), adopting a specifically Adlerian viewpoint, note: "Paradoxically, negativism is potentially one of the most powerful forces which can be used for pro-social growth. With unconditional acceptance of patients, by joining them in their negativism and utilizing this potent trait, they may make therapeutic movement" (p. 175).

The not uncommon recommendation that therapists maintain an attitude of *detached concern* toward clients—that they simultaneously remove themselves from yet intimately relate to their client's problems—suggests how an appropriate professional stance is inevitably a paradoxical one as well. The fact that this "uninvolved involvement" is usually without precedent in the interpersonal history of clients may be seen as subtly prompting them to react in a similarly unprecedented manner. The gentle and almost indiscernible provocation inherent in such a novel relationship may succeed in assisting clients to themselves reconceptualize both the risks and possibilities of change.

Haley's (1962, 1963, 1973) communications vantage point reveals another way of appreciating the paradoxes that pervade the therapeutic undertaking. Describing the peculiarities in the therapist-client relationship, Haley emphasizes the complexities, ambiguities, and apparent contradictions intrinsic to it. For instance, within a context of helpful assistance, the therapist avoids making any direct request for improved behavior. Within a framework defined as one person's aiding another to change, the so-called helper focuses on accepting the person desiring help as he *already* is—not as, presumably, he wishes to become. Although Haley's global characterization of therapy may be a bit overgeneralized, particularly with respect to certain behaviorist forms of treatment, most experienced practitioners would agree that methods which simply tell clients what to do are rarely as "practical" as more indirect modes of intervention. Paradoxically, *not* attempting directly to influence clients and *not* taking a definite stand against their symptoms is frequently more effective in getting clients to alter their maladaptive behaviors than more straightforward approaches. In short, therapeutic change may be most likely to occur when little or no pressure is exerted on the client to achieve it.

One last attempt to delineate the therapist's complex, and paradoxical, role might briefly be mentioned. This is B. Nelson's (1965) intriguing portrayal of the therapist as not only a professional "mediator" but also a "double agent." To Nelson, at the same time that the therapist must become, or *appear* to become, an ally of the client—by empathically sharing his view of himself, other people, and the world—he must contrive to induce the client to relinquish these finally self-defeating perceptions. Treatment cannot be viable without the therapist's accommodation of the client's outlook (however distorted that outlook may be). But, on the other hand, it cannot begin to be successful without the therapist's locating some vital method whereby the client may be impelled to question his false assumptions.

Although Nelson's theoretical allegiances are analytic, his basic notions about the therapist's role closely reflect those of other practitioners. It is, moreover, safe to say that most theorists sensitive to the seemingly contradictory functions of the therapist are also sensitive to the advisability of employing interventions which mirror this dual advocacy position. And, finally, all the paradoxical strategies discussed in this book may be understood as, in a sense, *deriving from* the paradoxical role of the therapist employing them.

The Paradoxical Nature of the Therapeutic Process

If a client's "cure" can be viewed as becoming disencumbered of unnecessary mental and emotional pain, the "medicine" for this cure is itself often painful to ingest. The antidote for one's inner hurt may well be *more* hurt—although the hurt comes in a somewhat different form and is administered in carefully controlled (or "homeopathically therapeutic") doses. It has become almost mundane in the psychotherapy literature to observe that for most varieties of treatment to be effective clients must work *through*, rather than *around*, the pain or problem they have brought to therapy. Across theoretical persuasions it is commonly held that if clients are to cease being incapacitated by dysfunctional behavior, they must first agree to the disagreeable and willingly confront their internal demons. This fundamental similarity among different therapeutic schools may be disguised by artificially distinct lexicons, but the notion that successful treatment involves prompting clients to face fears they have routinely avoided is a pervasive theme in virtually all methods of therapy.

By far the most direct method of arranging for clients to work through the pain underlying their self-protective symptom (which can be viewed as a sort of infected bandage covering a never adequately healed wound) are the behaviorist devices of flooding and implosion. As already detailed in Chapter 3, these procedures seek to have clients reexperience their worst fears to the point of extinction. One of the principal assumptions behind these symptom-confronting techniques is that the client's habitual avoidance of subjectively threatening situations has only served to exacerbate this threat and compel increased efforts at avoidance. This struggle to stave off anxiety thus becomes itself increasingly fraught with anxiety as the imagined threat becomes, through the client's very avoidance (or the *self-message* unwittingly communicated by such avoidance) more and more menacing. The flooding/implosion cure, designed to disrupt this ever-intensifying vicious cycle, is simply to have the client stop in his fleeing tracks and face his fear. By such a voluntary "about face," he may at last "stare down" this fear and be rid of it once and for all.

The foregoing rationale for flooding and implosion may be somewhat simplified, but it is an essentially accurate account of these extremely directive—and challenging—procedures. Moreover, although few other methods in therapy are as immediately provoking or fear-inspiring, almost all strategies of therapy strive to put clients in touch with the source(s) of their fear and their resultant resistance to change. Paradoxically, clients may vanquish their fears only by first succumbing to them. This general idea of defeating fear through surrendering to it is, it needs to be stressed, hardly contemporary. Gerz (1966), in discussing the various explanations offered to justify paradoxical intention, cites not only Oppenheim's (1911) exercises for accustoming patients to fear-evoking situations (e.g., instructing the physician to walk across an open field with an agoraphobic patient), but also Freud's arguments for such carefully modulated confrontation. In Freud's own words: "One can hardly ever master a phobia if one waits until the analysis influences him to give it up" (Gerz, 1966, p. 552). To Freud, some voluntary exposure to the anxiety-laden situation had to be undertaken by the patient if the patient were to use analysis to finally resolve this phobia. Striking a more modern—though complementary—note, Frankl (1960) contends, "logotherapeutically," that paradoxical intention (whether it involves the patient's freely facing his phobia or giving in to an obsessive-compulsive habit) "consists [of] a reversal of the patient's attitude toward his symptom, [which thus] enables him to detach himself from his neurosis" (p. 534).

Thus far the paradoxical nature of therapy has been explained primarily in terms of how client fears are handled through inviting or encouraging them. More generally, therapy can be seen as paradoxical in the discomfort, and even pain, it regularly evokes from clients seriously working on (and through) their problems. Probably no one has described the unpleasant aspects of being involved in the therapeutic process more thoroughly than Haley (1963), whose characterization of therapy as a "benevolent ordeal" has frequently been noted. To Haley, although the essential framework of therapy is one of helpfulness, within this benign framework the client must undergo (regardless of the type of treatment employed) a punishing ordeal. This ordeal results from the therapist's allowing or even directing the client to continue with unchanged behavior, while at the same time linking such continuation to an ordeal that will cease only when the behavior is abandoned. That is, the client can triumph over this ordeal (which varies with the particular method of therapy used) only by giving up the maladaptive behavior perpetuating his problems—which behavior, of course, is part and parcel of the *original* ordeal he entered therapy, however ambivalently, to have removed.

Yet another paradox noted by Haley that typically informs the therapeutic process (or, more accurately, the *relationship* on which this process hinges) might be mentioned. This paradox indirectly suggests something of the accepting/confronting posture that the therapist adopts toward the problems clients bring to treatment. In Haley's words:

> In general, a psychotherapist treats a patient as if [he] cannot help behaving as he does. He is assumed to be driven by forces outside of his control and provoked by thoughts and fantasies of which he in unaware. Whatever distress he provides himself or others, it is clearly not his fault. Yet at the same time the framework of psychotherapy is based upon the premise that the patient can help behaving as he does—that is why he is there for treatment. (p. 185)

The simplicity and elegance of this argument is hard to resist. More important, however, it serves to indicate how the very context of therapy may maximize the chances for beneficial changes in behavior. For this context enables the therapist to mix empathy, support—and perhaps "absolution" as well—with carefully timed intimations that the client may be an active participant in his and others' distress and could, if so desired, alter his behavior so as to end such needless suffering.

THE THERAPIST'S TAKING RESPONSIBILITY FOR CLIENTS' TAKING RESPONSIBILITY FOR THEIR PROBLEMS

The Therapist's "Benevolent Refusal" to Help Clients

It has already been shown how therapists of all persuasions attempt to influence clients in paradoxical or indirect ways so as either to preempt their resistance or utilize it to full therapeutic advantage. It remains to examine how this uniquely nondirective direction prompts clients to take initiative for solving their own problems. For in the end it is not the therapist but the client who must modify maladaptive behavior if the goals of therapy are to be reached. And this process of "working through" invariably depends on the development of the client's sense of autonomy, self-reliance, and willingness to accept increased responsibility for the condition and quality of his life.

The sometimes painful necessity of withholding help from a client in order for him to help himself is dramatically suggested by the gestalt-oriented Simkin (in Fagan & Shepherd, 1970), who in a therapy presentation at a professional workshop openly pondered:

> Now, as therapists, you see here a beautiful . . . dilemma, a therapeutic dilemma. Somebody plays helpless, and you want to help, and *part* of you is aware that if I were going to help, I would reinforce Mary's helplessness. *But* if I don't help, am I being a therapist? (p. 167)

Compare such question-begging to the quandary enunciated by Fanshel and Labov, who in a book entitled *Therapeutic Discourse* (New York, 1977) address what they term "the fundamental paradox of therapy" in this manner:

> The most general goal of therapy is to bring the patient to the point at which he can function independently and no longer needs help; but can a person be taught not to need help by giving him help? (p. 32)

The only conceivable way to resolve this therapeutic predicament, of course, is for therapists to take the paradoxical (yet consummately logical) position that, indeed, they *cannot* help clients, but that they may be able to help clients help themselves. It may very well be that one of the most pragmatic ways of distinguishing different schools of treatment is in how they contrive to deliver this paramount message of self-help. For transcending all theoretical boundaries is the prevailing notion that, finally, clients must learn that it is they—and they alone—who control their symptomatic behavior. It is they who must cultivate the personal resources without which no amount of external assistance can ever be adequate to resolve their problems. Only through nurturing their own inner dependency will the ultimately self-demeaning request for outside help give way to the inner strength that renders such aid unnecessary.

Psychoanalysis may be understood as "quietly emphatic" about the need for patients to struggle with their problems (or transference issues) in the predominantly passive role it assigns the therapist. Watts (1961), discussing elements of judo in the analytic interaction, describes how the analyst responds to all the patient's attempts to shift the responsibility for cure onto his shoulders by somehow accepting—or even demanding— such behavior without actually accommodating it. During the transference, for example, the analyst permits the patient to see him, dependently, as a parental figure but subtly frustrates the patient's efforts to induce him to take parental responsibility for his problems. And this gentle but nonetheless provocative stance by the analyst is designed (through its painstakingly calculated forebearance) to promote the development of self-responsibility.

The gestalt practices of Perls and his followers take a virtually identical posture in handling a patient's entreaties that the therapist assume obligation for his cure. To accept such therapeutic accountability is viewed as in fact antithetical to effective treatment. As Perls himself (1976) put it, "To bring about the transformation from external to self-support, the therapist must frustrate the patient's endeavors to get environmental support. This he cannot do if sympathy blinds him to [the patient's] manipulations" (p. 106). Similarly, client-centered, or nondirective, therapy stresses the importance of not conceding to the client's attempts to obtain ready-made answers or solutions to problems which he himself must summon up the courage to resolve. In the famous case of Gloria (whose half-hour interviews with Perls, Rogers, and Ellis in the instructional film series "Three Approaches to Psychotherapy," 1965, are well-known in the field), one brief segment of Gloria's single session with Rogers has been transcribed as follows:

> Again she asks . . . for an [authoritative] answer: "You're just going to sit there and let me stew in it and I want more." Rogers replies, "No, I don't want to let you just stew in your feelings, but on the other hand, I also feel that this is the kind of very private thing that I couldn't possibly answer for you. But I sure as anything will try to help you work toward your own answer." (Meador & Rogers, in R. J. Corsini, ed., *Current Psychotherapies*, 1973, p. 161)

Unquestionably, behavior therapists are much more directive and frequently propose concrete remedies for their clients' symptoms. But even here it is the clients who must willingly "activate" the solution—whether this be to confront their irrational fears or to train themselves to better manage certain environmental stimuli so as to overcome disabling habits. The systems approach to treatment is also comparatively directive, though it is far less direct in its actual tactics. As was suggested earlier in describing Ericksonian hypnotherapy, therapists working from a systems perspective avoid offering clients any stock cures for their problems but instead seek to elicit appropriate remedies from within the clients themselves. Clients are placed in an unprecedented situation whereby they must "spontaneously" be struck by a solution of their own—although typically such a solution is one the therapist has had in mind all along.

Here again, it may be instructive to recall Haley's (1963) ideas on how the therapist's encouragement of symptoms indirectly encourages the client to abandon them and, in the process, accept a responsibility for them previously denied. For, in the present context, Haley's frequently cited argument on the double bind as generic to all therapy may, indeed, be seen as coming full circle. The importance of the therapist's gaining control of therapy through nonconfrontationally allowing or encouraging the client to keep his symptoms has already been discussed. But it is imperative to add that the therapist *also* allows, and indirectly encourages, the client to reexert control over therapy through beginning to exert more control over *himself*—which can be done only by the client's first coming to recognize his basic responsibility for the problems that have precipitated treatment.

The Therapist's Helping Clients to Recognize the Voluntariness of Their Behavior

In a sense, accepting complete responsibility for one's problems is possible only if one comes to see one's dysfunctional behaviors as voluntary. Therapists of all persuasions share the burden of somehow communicating to clients the fact that they are the ones responsible for their distress simply because they have within them the power to alleviate it. To effectively achieve control of their behavior, clients must first be made to realize that they *can* help themselves, that because their behavior is at bottom self-willed, they are free to alter it or—if such modification is not really tenable—to *reconceive* it so that it ceases to cause them distress or constitute a serious hindrance to them.

Perhaps the cardinal assumption made by every professional involved in the practice of therapy is that there is a fundamental discrepancy between clients' deep-seated beliefs that their dysfunctional behavior is involuntary, or spontaneous, and the actual circumstance that it is volitional. For without such an assumption therapy would hardly be feasible. By the same token, however, if clients are to develop awareness of the self-controllable nature of their behavior (whether this behavior is physical, mental, or emotional), the therapist must avoid imparting the message that any changed behavior has been externally caused—that is, induced by the therapist himself (see, e.g., Haley, 1963). He must guide clients into making their own self-realizations and uncovering their own (nonsymptomatic) abilities and potential. He may mediate but he cannot directly lead. For clients must, *self*-confrontingly, discover their own path to the fuller understanding of self that will ultimately empower them to govern their life without the handicapping constraints they themselves have imposed. And, doubtless, the final paradox of therapy is that the therapist must at once offer help and refuse it, so that any "cure" achieved must be appreciated by clients as deriving from their own innate capacities as self-determining, self-controlling, human beings.

Appendixes

Appendix A

Selected Writings on the Planning and Execution of Paradoxical Strategies

INTRODUCTION

The essentially "how to" articles featured here have been included to increase both the scope and utility of this book. Until now the concentration has been on elucidating paradoxical procedures within and across theoretical orientations, on characterizing their nature and the rationales proposed for them. Given such an expository emphasis, the text has not focused on the details of how therapists actually *carry out* these strategies. It is one thing to hypothesize that a paradoxical treatment plan might be useful in working with an individual or family, and quite another to specifically determine the most appropriate strategy, present it convincingly to its recipient(s), and, despite various obstacles and objections, follow through with it so as to maximize its potential impact.

The supplementary writings chosen for this section go substantially beyond the definitions and descriptions of paradoxical strategies presented earlier. In an assortment of ways they are all devoted to delineating the particular skills required for the effective employment of these strategies. They address concretely the concerns which any practitioner, regardless of theoretical persuasion, is likely to have in deciding whether their use might be advantageous—especially in problematic cases where more conventional interventions have already missed their mark. Because essays that center on case histories often have limited suggestiveness across the whole range of possible therapeutic applications, articles excerpted here generally deal much less with case material than with principles to be kept in mind when intervening paradoxically. These highly pragmatic selections may also be viewed as designed to instruct therapists in the

189

"paradoxical care and handling" of clients. As such, though they relate directly to earlier sections, they "complete" them as well, adding a certain human dimension which, of necessity, may have been somewhat neglected to this point.

In the interest of avoiding repetition, almost all of the following selections have been edited (as indicated, except for material omitted either at the beginning or end of a selection, by ellipses). More or less standard introductory material, whether definitional, historical, or theoretical, has generally been abridged or deleted, so that each excerpt might better pinpoint certain "when" and "how" considerations of working paradoxically. Although administering paradoxical strategies is typically best done with a certain lightness, this hardly means that they can afford to be taken lightly by the therapist. Careful deliberation is necessary if they are to be employed productively; and the writings that follow are all concerned with aiding the practitioner in becoming more sophisticated about their proper clinical usage.

The discerning reader is likely to be struck by a few inconsistencies—at times outright contradictions—among these selections. Unquestionably differences of opinion do exist as to the "correct" administration of paradoxical procedures: for example, just how early (or late) in treatment they ought to be implemented. It should be noted, therefore, that no editorial effort has been made to conceal such discrepancies or, for that matter, to explicitly call attention to them. These discrepancies may in fact largely reflect individual therapist preferences (or "style") relating to client interaction and treatment planning. To convey the impression that working paradoxically must be dictated by a rigid set of rules would be to seriously misrepresent the many genuinely creative (and playful or spontaneous) aspects of a clinical approach virtually *intended* to be unorthodox. Similarly, it should be stressed that the writings reprinted here are not meant to be taken as literal prescriptions but, more loosely, as guidelines for practitioners interested in exploring new ideas and expanding their clinical resources. And—relating to the clinical focus of these writings—it needs to be realized that although a selection may address the use of a paradoxical technique within a specific context (e.g., with a couple or within a particular treatment setting), most suggestions about implementing such procedures can fairly easily be translated to other therapy situations.

Deciding which essays would best assist the therapist in developing acumen in employing paradoxical strategies has been a most challenging task. To begin with, as the more than 500-item bibliography should indicate, many possible candidates for inclusion had to be omitted. Frequently this was done with much regret, for many selections undeniably would have added something to the breadth of this undertaking. Seminal contributions to the literature, such as those by Frankl, Adler, Dunlap, Watzlawick, and Selvini Palazzoli, were particularly difficult to eliminate. It was decided, however, that not only were the works of these authors available in book form but that, in addition, the more recent studies reprinted here did in fact incorporate much of their innovative thinking—in a sense, even "advance" it by evolving a more systematic schema governing the choice and implementation of paradoxical methods.

Many other selections had to be disqualified because, though extremely rich and suggestive, they centered much more on specific case material than on more general methodological considerations. And still other writings had to be ruled ineligible because, despite their attention to concrete issues of application, they were heavily geared toward an extreme clinical population infrequently encountered by most therapists. Finally, several selections had to be rejected simply to hold this book to moderate proportions. As a way of at least suggesting to the reader which writings (to this author, at least) represent the most important contributions to the field, such writings have been highlighted in the bibliography by an asterisk immediately preceding them. It is hoped that the reader wishing to embark upon a further exploration of paradoxical therapeutic strategies will find this coding useful.

Each of the writings excerpted here should help promote a greater working knowledge of paradoxical strategies. Newton's essay is noteworthy in its representing perhaps the first attempt to methodically set forth the many conditions related to the successful employment of what the author terms "symptom scheduling." The brief selection from Haley is useful in conceptualizing, and exemplifying, a paradoxical intervention in terms of eight separate yet interdependent stages. Considering the value of paradoxical prescriptions in the context of marital therapy, Sluzki delineates with exceptional clarity different tactics that can be employed to counter a couple's maladaptive mode of interaction. Also concerned with dysfunctional interaction is Papp's terse discussion, which pinpoints some crucial considerations regarding the appropriate application of paradoxical strategies with families. Primarily for the sake of completeness, a selection from de Shazer, on prescribing an *analogue* of the symptom (a stratagem frequently associated with Erickson), has been included. This metaphorical variant of symptom prescription is surely one of the most creative and may be particularly valuable in helping conflictual families. Another Ericksonian contribution on symptom prescription, by

Zeig, represents an extensive effort to apply many of that great innovator's ideas to this fundamental paradoxical procedure. Focusing on three central *types* of paradoxical procedure—symptom redefinition, escalation, and redirection—is the selection by Fisher, Anderson, and Jones, which seeks to outline the patient characteristics applicable to each type, as well as to enumerate the various circumstances in which a paradoxical approach may, in fact, be counterindicated. Also interested in classifications governing the proper employment of paradoxical strategies are Rohrbaugh and his colleagues, whose distinction between compliance- and defiance-based interventions, and the situations appropriate to each mode, is of critical importance in using such interventions successfully. Proposing a set of guidelines for the constructive implementation of "written paradox" are Weeks and L'Abate, whose excerpt on paradoxical letters illuminates the special impact of intervening paradoxically not simply within a session but—through the power of the written word—*between* sessions as well. The final selection, by O'Connell, provides a convenient synopsis of the various rationales therapists have offered clients to persuade them to follow a paradoxical directive. Similar to the other writings excerpted here, its interest is both professional and practical. It is hoped, therefore, that this selection, combined with those preceding it, will serve as a manual for practitioners looking for additional guidance and direction in putting the age-old "wisdom" of therapeutic paradox to full clinical advantage.

SELECTIONS

JOSEPH R. NEWTON

CONSIDERATIONS FOR THE PSYCHOTHERAPEUTIC TECHNIQUE OF SYMPTOM SCHEDULING[*]

Omitting any discussion of theory or research, Newton's pioneering essay focuses squarely on the many practical considerations relevant to implementing paradoxical techniques effectively. His viewpoint may seem somewhat dated in that the device of "symptom scheduling" does not adequately account for many variations in the basic method. Moreover, reframing (with all its subtle complexities) is generally outside his purview—particularly since his

---

[*]From *Psychotherapy: Theory, Research and Practice*, 1968, 5, 95–103. (a) Reprinted with permission.

interest centers more on the use of paradoxical procedures with single clients than with couples or families. This early effort is nonetheless outstanding in its conscientious attention to detail and its clear articulation of essential questions that the clinician must confront before determining how best to approach client problems "noncommonsensically."

A specific psychotherapeutic technique has recently received appreciable attention by psychotherapists. The technique has been variously referred to as "negative practice," "therapeutic paradox," "paradoxical intention," and "reactive inhibition." While there are differences in emphasis and intent among users of the technique, the essence of it is that the clinician *encourages* the patient to *continue* in his symptomatic behavior. Put otherwise, the clinician *schedules the occurrence of the patient's symptoms so that they are exhibited by the patient under systematic and specific conditions*. In the present work the technique is referred to as "symptom scheduling." This designation has been chosen because it is indifferent to the several prevailing theoretical positions, and it refers directly to the concrete operations of the therapist as he uses the technique. The goal of the technique of symptom scheduling is that of change in the manifestation of the symptom—often change in the sense of symptom relief but also, when the symptom is importantly involved in a married couple's interlocking and complementary character traits, change in the sheer sense of disruption of enduring behavior patterns.

. . . The aim of the present work is neither to report successful treatment of a patient nor to add to existing theory; rather, the main consideration is the technique *qua* technique—to put it simply, *how* a clinician uses the technique of symptom scheduling. Toward this goal a set of principles, or guidelines, pertinent to the efficient and effective use of the technique are set forth. Also, it is hoped the principles will help answer questions that often arise when the technique is used, such as: what symptoms should be scheduled? when is the most propitious time for scheduling symptoms? what if the patient refuses to cooperate? do some schedules facilitate patient change more than others? what does a clinician do when a schedule has no effect? and of course other questions as well.

●   ●   ●

The principles, then, for using the technique of symptom scheduling are set forth below. They have been classified according to the patient's *symptom*, the therapist's *schedule*, or the *therapist*, himself. To make the presentation as clear and meaningful as possible each principle first is expressed in abstract form, an illustrative clinical example follows, and the principle is then articulated by a brief discussion.

SYMPTOM

The four principles pertinent to the symptom of the patient are: (1) expandable (2) current (3) interpersonal, and (4) stressful.

EXPANDABLE. The therapist selects for scheduling a symptom that allows, on subsequent occasions, a greater intensity or duration; symptoms that cannot readily be expanded are more difficult to change with the technique. *Clinical example*: A patient presents the syndrome of anxiety state with the main feature that of free floating anxiety. It could be unrewarding for the therapist to schedule the occurrence of anxiety since it is omnipresent and holds little promise of being expandable. The therapist might rather choose a representative situation in which the anxiety occurs, e.g., when the alarm goes off in the morning, and schedule the patient to set the alarm and feel anxious six times a day. This symptom can be expanded since the therapist can manipulate the number of times per day, the duration of the times, the occurrence of the times (e.g., when the husband is *not* home), and so forth.

A substantial number of the symptoms of patients seen in clinical practice, of course, have the quality of being expandable. It is included as a principle for the purpose of underscoring its importance. Symptoms with clear physiological limits, e.g., masturbation and sexual intercourse, and symptoms that are ubiquitous in nature, e.g., free floating anxiety, are more difficult to treat with the technique.

CURRENT. Symptoms that are current are more amenable to change with symptom scheduling than are low-grade, chronic symptoms. *Clinical example*: One patient reported a severe and debilitating rabies phobia of long duration, yet because she was not experiencing the symptom at that time a schedule seemed inadvisable. On the day a rabid dog escaped from the city pound her symptoms did, indeed, become current and symptom scheduling was followed by rapid symptom remission.

This principle recognizes that an exacerbated symptom is more likely to be changed with symptom scheduling than a chronic symptom. Benign, long-term symptoms also can be scheduled with favorable results, but the ego-syntonic properties they often acquire call for special considerations indicated by some of the other principles.

INTERPERSONAL. Those symptoms that involve and influence persons other than the patient seem more amenable to the technique than do intrapsychic symptoms. *Clinical example*: In a woman who is frigid and also must compulsively wash her hands, this guideline suggests that the clinician would focus first on the frigidity.

The distinction between interpersonal and intrapsychic symptoms is, of course, somewhat forced, and at this stage in our understanding of the phenomenology of symptoms it may depend more on the theoretical posture of the therapist than on the nature of the symptom. Nevertheless, the interpersonal principle has been very important in practice and needs to be considered each time the technique is used. Haley (1963) has forcefully put forth this principle with an elegant theoretical scheme and many instructive examples. Observation of the interpersonal principle serves to unlock the patient-therapist dyad that usually is formed in individual psychotherapy. That is, scheduling an interpersonal symptom usually requires the cooperation of the spouse (or some significant other person) and invariably has some effect on the people involved. Often what follows is a disruption of the interlocking character traits of the marital partners and the spouse's request to be seen.

STRESSFUL.   Within wide limits, the effectiveness of symptom scheduling varies directly with the patient's level of subjective distress. *Clinical example*: On innumerable occasions psychotherapy has proceeded along conventional lines, with a patient reporting both current and chronic symptoms. When, however, the patient arrived for an hour in marked distress with a symptom, then symptom scheduling was employed with beneficial results.

This principle is especially pertinent to patients with a substantial degree of hysterical traits and symptoms. Often, these patients will manifest what appears to be exceptional disturbance (e.g., a paralyzed limb or very gripping reports about life circumstances) and yet they may not *feel* distress at the time. In these cases it is especially important for the therapist to observe the stressful principle and act accordingly, for example: he may wish to schedule an interpersonal symptom so that customary ways of relating are disrupted and more stress is felt; he can wait for natural events in the environment to increase the patient's distress; or he can proceed along conventional psychotherapeutic lines to make the symptom ego-dystonic.

SCHEDULE

The ten principles relevant to the schedule devised by the therapist are: (1) expandable (2) interpersonal (3) stressful (4) rationale (5) humor (6) specific (7) within-session timing (8) changing sessions (9) office exercises, and (10) patient-associate. The first three principles, i.e., expandable, interpersonal and stressful, have direct counterparts under the symptom category and consequently have been given identical names. It is, in fact, helpful to consider these principles as "tied" across the symptom and schedule categories so that, for example, if the clinician assesses the expandable nature of the symptom he in turn examines the expandable properties of the schedule.

EXPANDABLE. It is helpful if schedules are such that they can be readily expanded by the therapist. *Clinical example*: A patient was told to have an argument with her husband every night at 8:00 for five minutes. This schedule was expandable in that the time could easily be extended from five minutes to 10 minutes, 10 minutes to 15 minutes and so on, and the schedule also could call for arguments at other times during the day.

Just as the clinician may wish to consider the expandable nature of a symptom, he also may find it profitable to devise a schedule that is expandable. Disregard of these two principles may result in the clinician scheduling a symptom that has inherent limitations—as far as further scheduling is concerned—and in his inability to increase the schedule on later occasions. It appears better for the therapist to start conservatively with a schedule that can be expanded than to begin with a schedule that asks too much of the patient or one that has narrow limitations.

INTERPERSONAL. Schedules involving persons together with the identified patient facilitate the effect of the technique of symptom scheduling. *Clinical example*: Arguments between spouses have been scheduled with very beneficial results. With an interpersonal schedule of an argument it is important to have the persons argue in their normal way, and not to have the schedule require any new or different behavior from the participants.

This interpersonal principle has been so impressive in clinical work that we have referred to it as the "power of the third party." An interesting observation is that the few times this consideration has been followed with couples who are dating instead of being married, the results have been mixed and often unproductive. In spite of the intense emotional involvement often evident with unmarried couples, the fact that they are not married appears to afford them some escape from the binding quality of the schedule.

STRESSFUL. The schedule is more effective when it stresses the patient to some extent. *Clinical example*: A patient who was panphobic and scared that in public places her heart would stop and she would be shaky, nervous, pass out, get embarrassed, and the like, was told that for six of the next seven days at 10:30 A.M. she was to have all these symptoms for five minutes. Furthermore, she was to have *more* of them, i.e., in number and intensity, than she ever had before.

This guideline is not meant to sanction sadism on the part of the therapist, and it is definitely undesirable for the therapist to appear sadistic from the viewpoint of the patient. Rather, this principle holds that the effects of the technique are increased when the patient hurts with his condition *and* is stressed by the schedule. Haley (1963) has made the most explicit use of this principle in his inclusion of an "ordeal" with the technique of symptom scheduling. As the name implies, an ordeal is an onerous task the patient is asked to do together with the symptom exercises. For the above clinical example it could have been to get up at 2:00 A.M. each day and clean the house. The present writer has discussed elsewhere the role of the ordeal in symptom scheduling (Newton, 1968b).

RATIONALE.   Some sort of rationale accompanies symptom scheduling—if the therapist does not explicitly provide one the patient will implicitly. *Clinical example*: A very simple explanation may do, such as "you said you had these crazy things happen to you. Now you are going to have to do something equally crazy to get rid of them." If the therapist, however, has a theory about symptom scheduling or some notions about the etiology of the patient's symptoms, a more complex rationale along these lines could be offered.

Patients react to symptom scheduling in any number of different ways, but often there are elements of disbelief, surprise and puzzlement. This, of course, is not unexpected since the technique *is* quite enigmatic and some sort of explanation is reassuring to a patient. Gerz (1962), Frankl (1965), and Haley (1963) each provide a rationale and these differ considerably in length and emphasis. From the present viewpoint it seems reasonable for rationales to differ from therapist to therapist, as well as for each therapist to have several rationales. Depending on the patient and the form of his cooperation, then, the therapist can use what he believes to be the most appropriate rationale.

HUMOR.   Scheduling the symptom in a humorous context sometimes is beneficial and, with certain patients, perhaps necessary. *Clinical example*: Therapist: "As you practice these peculiar exercises, try to have more of the symptoms than you ever had before. I want you to have the best case of them that ever has been recorded in medical history."

Frankl (1960) and Gerz (1962) make extensive use of humor and it is conceived by them as an integral part of the technique. In the present context, humor is considered similarly to the therapist's use of a rationale. That is, the therapist uses his clinical judgment with each patient and in one instance he may rely on humor exclusively, whereas at another time he may wish to present the technique in just as grim a fashion as the patient has presented himself. More often than not, however, there is a light quality to the relationship when the technique is used and a twinkle in the therapist's eye.

SPECIFIC.   The therapist is specific and detailed when he provides a schedule for a patient. *Clinical example*: A college student complained of "anxiety" before participating in discussions in a particular class. The anxiety was not scheduled at that time and instead the student was questioned intensively regarding the nature of his anxiety, when, where and how the class met, and so forth. Then the student was told to feel fearful, make his hands shake, voice quiver, and to lose track of his thoughts, for five minutes before each session of the class, Monday through Friday.

Two important purposes are served by this principle. First, a specific schedule tends to circumscribe the initiative of the patient as he practices the schedule. Eventually, of course, the aim of psychotherapy *is* for the patient to assume initiative and responsibility for his affairs, but when the technique of symptom scheduling is used patient initiative often results in the patient departing from the therapist's instructions and generally poor results often follow. Second, this consideration also serves in an oblique way the goal of situation analysis set forth by Von Eckartsberg (1966) and Van Zaig (1966). That is, with the therapist indicating specifically the days and times of the schedule, as well as the patient's behavior, feelings and affect, it is far easier for the therapist to inquire later regarding the patient's concrete experiencing during the scheduled situation.

WITHIN-SESSION TIMING.   The therapist explains the schedule to the patient with at least ten minutes remaining in the psychotherapy session and preferably much longer. *Clinical example*: A patient was scheduled, and then at the next session she expressed many important concerns about herself although her reaction to the schedule was not mentioned. In closing the session, the therapist casually advised staying on the schedule for another week and a flood of the patient's feelings was unleashed. This opportunity could not be pursued because the patient had another appointment a few minutes later.

This consideration may appear obvious but it is included because it can be readily overlooked in clinical practice. During any hour, the therapist cannot suggest a schedule until sufficient information has been gathered, and then the schedule often leads to protestations of inability by the patient, many minute questions and, very often, presentation of material totally unexpected by the therapist and only tangentially related to the schedule. The therapist usually will wish to leave ample time for discussion of these concerns.

CHANGING SESSIONS.   When the technique is used the therapist may wish to shorten the sessions and increase their frequency per week. *Clinical example*: After a therapist has scheduled a patient's symptoms during their regular Monday hour, he may ask the patient to come in for 20 minute sessions on the following Wednesday and Friday.

While this principle suggests a drastic revision of the classical, 50 minute hour, it is advanced because the effects of symptom scheduling are most evident immediately after the patient practices his symptoms for the first time. By having the patient return soon thereafter the therapist is able to capitalize on the change, or lack of change, in the patient.

OFFICE EXERCISES.   Particularly reluctant patients can be asked to practice the schedule in the therapist's office before trying it at home. *Clinical example*: A patient had objected to a schedule that had her try to make her heart flutter because she might "bring it on" and there was no one home to help her. The therapist then encouraged the patient to try it in his office, explaining that if one is to have a heart attack there is no better place than in the hospital.

Gerz (1962) has used this consideration often. It seems appropriate when a patient resists his schedule because of strong fears of the untoward consequences. There are some patients who even refuse the office exercises and on these occasions some form of "patient associate" may be used. Also, Skinner's method (1953) of successive approximations may be considered, whereby the therapist schedules a relatively benign part of the patient's symptom-complex and then works successively to the more feared aspects. Unfortunately, Skinner's method has not been used enough with symptom scheduling to assess its usefulness.

A PATIENT-ASSOCIATE.   When a patient cannot accept a schedule, it may be helpful to bring into the therapy hour a former patient who has had success with symptom scheduling. *Clinical example*: The research for this paper did not permit investigation of this principle. On a few occasions it has been possible to refer to the therapist's personal experience using an adaptation of the technique on himself, and this has seemed beneficial to patients.

This consideration stems mainly from Gerz (1962) in which several instances of its application are reported. In his work the principle appears to be used mainly in inpatient settings but it could hold equally as well for outpatient treatment. There is a small sample of patients treated by the present therapist who have completely rejected symptom scheduling. As indicated above, reports of the therapist's personal experience with the technique seems to have brought some patients to the point where they could try the schedule, and it is a distinct possibility that more patients might have accepted the schedule if they had met with former patients who had obtained relief with the technique.

THERAPIST

The six principles for the therapist are: (1) patience (2) understanding the symptom (3) treatment goal (4) orientation (5) relationship, and (6) follow up.

PATIENCE.   The therapist must be patient and wait for the appropriate conditions before scheduling the symptom. *Clinical example*: Part of the research on which these principles are based involved meeting symptomatic college students who also were fairly well intact. While the therapy sessions lasted over ten weeks (an hour a week), with a few of these persons the technique could never be used because the symptoms did not satisfy the principles contained herein.

Assigning "patience" to the level of a principle of symptom scheduling may appear inconsequential since it plays no small part in the psychotherapy of all clinicians. Its status as a principle, however, follows from the way in which the technique of symptom scheduling is construed in a treatment plan. This point is discussed in the conclusions below and it suffices here only to state that symptom scheduling is a specific technique of psychotherapy and not a general method—the therapist needs patience with the technique in order to use it appropriately in a larger therapeutic scheme.

UNDERSTANDING THE SYMPTOM.   The more clearly the therapist has in mind the symptom in all of its vagaries, the better able is he to use the technique of symptom scheduling. *Clinical example*: Even with monosymptomatic patients complaining of nailbiting, compulsive ear pulling, speech blocks and the like, time spent in understanding the symptom is not wasted.

Similar to some of the other considerations, emphasizing an understanding of the symptom may be stating the obvious for many clinicians. It is included because enthusiasm with a new development often results in temporarily relinquishing older methods—it has happened to us in our investigation of this technique! Firm knowledge of a patient's symptoms, however, can be very helpful in symptom scheduling. Such an understanding will permit an assessment of the extent to which the symptom is appropriate for scheduling (as listed above under Symptom) and it will aid the clinician in giving a specific schedule (as listed above under Schedule). Also, if attempts to schedule the symptom fail, the clinician is in a much better position to evaluate the failure and to plan further treatment for the patient.

TREATMENT GOAL.   While more often than not in clinical practice *the* treatment goal is a fiction and at any one moment a hierarchy of more or less temporary treatment goals exist, nevertheless when the therapist uses symptom scheduling he is commiting himself to a goal of symptom change. A *clinical example* of this principle is unnecessary.

Two points need to be made regarding this consideration. First, commitment to a symptom goal does not presuppose that the technique is directed only at symptom remission. Whereas the immediate goal may be symptom relief, a secondary goal could be to promote a patient's awareness of the interpersonal consequences of his symptom, and a tertiary goal could be to assess the transferences of the psychotherapeutic relationship. If, however, the therapist cannot be satisfied with a goal of symptom change at the time of scheduling, patients sense the therapist's ambivalence and will, in turn, respond ambivalently. Second, a curious result of the technique is that when the therapist focuses on the patient's symptoms, the patient often will defocus from the symptoms, i.e., material unrelated to the schedule or his symptoms is brought up. It is as if the patient experiences threat on some level of awareness and apparently unrelated material follows. Under certain circumstances the therapist may wish to discard the schedule and follow through with the new material, but in doing so he should recognize that the patient, with some justification, will expect not to practice schedules on subsequent occasions.

ORIENTATION. Use of the technique of symptom scheduling requires that the therapist is active, direct and even at times authoritative. *Clinical example*: When a reconstituted psychotic woman, severely incapacitated by many fears and phobias, refused the technique and questioned its value, the therapist replied, "I can think of nothing, absolutely nothing, that you could do right now to help yourself more than these exercises."

This consideration is implied from the way the technique is conceived and used but it is stated here to remove any shred of ambiguity. The quality of the therapist's activity, of course, depends largely on the particular patient and his unique blend of symptoms, defenses, and impulses. With one patient, as in the above clinical example, the therapist will find it necessary to be exhortative and dogmatic; with another perhaps all that is needed is a deft question or two by the therapist, after which the patient verbally commits himself to the schedule; and with still another patient a relaxed, almost jovial use of the technique could be in order. This does not mean that a therapist needs hours of experience with the technique before he can be appropriately active, but rather the emphasis is that the therapist should be active when the occasion requires—and sometimes active in a most unusual sense!

RELATIONSHIP. It is necessary for the therapist to have clearly in mind the strength of the psychotherapeutic relationship as the technique is used.

Clinical example: Early in the research with the technique the present writer scheduled a patient's symptoms during the first hour and the patient never returned! Clearly, the relationship had not been sufficiently considered.

The importance of this principle can hardly be exaggerated. Haley (1963, and personal communication, 1965) has particularly emphasized the therapeutic relationship and some evidence pertinent to his theory of the relationship has been reported and discussed elsewhere (Newton, 1968b). While the ways in which a therapist can assess the quality and strength of the relationship are important matters, little is known about them at the present time. However, two general observations appear to be pertinent: first, the patient should feel that the therapist understands his problems and symptoms. The technique of symptom scheduling involves considerable activity and direction by the therapist and when the patient does not feel understood, use of the technique often is followed by the patient feeling coldly and unfeelingly manipulated with poor therapeutic results. Second, the therapist's attitude is one of unconditional regard (Rogers, 1957) for the patient with his symptoms. In a general way this probably holds for most therapists most of the time. What is meant here is something a bit more specific and has been well put by Gendlin (1964)— the therapist assumes that the patient is "up against" something dislikable in himself, and the therapist's prevailing attitude is that of commitment to the patient in that which he is "up against."

Follow Up. An extensive inquiry during the psychotherapy session following symptom scheduling can be exceptionally informative and helpful. *Clinical example*: Even when patients report complete success with the schedule, complete failure with the schedule, total remission of the symptoms, or obviously avoid discussing the schedule, a follow up can be held and the results invariably are helpful.

While reactions to symptom scheduling vary every bit as much as people vary, often patients are reluctant to describe their experience with a schedule or are content to report it tersely. Several pertinent questions by the therapist (e.g., at what point did you stop the schedule? what happened at that time? how did you feel when you were doing the exercises? how did your spouse respond to the exercises? what do you make of what you are doing?) often provide information along several helpful lines. First, knowing how the patient responded behaviorally, affectively and ideationally to the schedule is a considerable help in future use of the technique. Sometimes what appears to the therapist as a minor variation in the schedule will permit the patient to use the technique much more fully. Second, the therapist often is able to perceive psychodynamics from a very different vantage point. Since the effects of the patient's psychodynamics are manifested under controlled and specific behavioral conditions, there will be much less need for abstract inferences by the therapist. Third, a careful inquiry into the results of the schedule may suggest to the therapist qualities of the relationship that heretofore he only suspected or was unaware of. And last, it is beginning to appear that the manner in which a patient responds to his schedule is some evidence for his motivation for psychotherapy in general. That is, symptom scheduling involves more motivation than the usual—merely verbal—psychotherapy in that the patient is required to commit himself forcefully to an explicit course of behavior (and sometimes a painful one at that!) It seems that a solid effort by the patient in this activity is a helpful index of his more general motivation for psychotherapy.

CONCLUSIONS AND IMPLICATIONS

There are various considerations, then, for the therapist in using the technique of symptom scheduling. The principles set forth are pertinent to the symptoms presented by the patient, the schedules formulated by the therapist, and the therapist's clinical judgment and behavior. While the principles are forwarded to facilitate the rational and effective application of symptom scheduling, they also are conceived as hypotheses to be examined further in controlled, laboratory situations.

At this point, it is appropriate to consider the technique in its larger clinical context as well as to indicate some of its implications. According to the present conception symptom scheduling is not a theory of psychotherapy (though for a dissident view see Haley, 1963) nor is it a general clinical method. Rather, it is conceived to be a specific and circumscribed technique useful when the therapist wishes to change in some way the nature of a psychiatric symptom. Similar to support of defenses, suggestion, environmental manipulation and the like, symptom scheduling is one of several techniques in the clinician's armamentarium—perhaps to be used not at all with one patient and possibly frequently with the next. A particularly interesting property of this technique, in comparison with conventional psychotherapy, is that it is far less dependent on a patient's verbal sophistication: it would be possible to use symptom scheduling with a mute patient! An intriguing possibility, then, is that the technique may be especially suited for one of the most vexing problems of clinical treatment—that of the psychotherapy of the psychologically naive, action-oriented, lower class patient (Hollingshead and Redlich, 1958).

If symptom scheduling is most effective with interpersonal symptoms and interpersonal schedules then it should be a valuable aid in couple therapy. Haley (1963) has made this point well, and here only the flexibility of the technique needs to be emphasized. For example, when one married couple was confronted with the extent to which they protected each other from awareness of their weaknesses, they both became gloomy and despondent with the woman exhibiting a subclinical depression. One co-therapist then used an adaptation of the technique, in which the symptoms were ignored but the couple was directed at specific hours over the weekend to behave *as if* the other person were *perfectly capable*. Both patients demurred, with the woman expressing "fear of what might happen." The schedule was reiterated, however, with the other co-therapist affirming the importance of the schedule. Upon the couple's return four days later they explained they "had the best weekend in months." They "felt free" and both were happy. Of especial interest to the clinician were the results of the follow up to the schedule. Each patient had misinterpreted the therapist's instructions, clearly and predictably along the lines of his own particular pathology! The therapists then had the opportunity of following through on the unique misperceptions of reality of each patient.

Often families appear to be impervious to the usual psychotherapeutic interventions. The technique of symptom scheduling, however, has features that suggest its application to this mode of treatment: the therapist must be active and directive (heightened activity by the therapist is uniformly reported in family treatment); clear, detailed and explicit instructions must be given (a hallmark of disturbed families is unsatisfactory communication); interpersonal symptoms and interpersonal schedules appear to be especially useful (most theoreticians are impressed with the interpersonal, systemic properties of disturbed families and only secondarily concerned with the intrapsychic structure of individual members); and no *new* or *different* behavior on the part of the family members is required (things new and different are anathema to members of disturbed families). Scheduling family members to practice their usual interaction patterns at regular times and under specific conditions surely will disrupt their inflexible behavior patterns, and may help them to observe and experience each other as separate entities—and separation in the sense of differentiation of family members is one of the major goals of family treatment (Boszormenyi-Nagy and Framo, 1965). Consider, for instance, the classic family with an overadequate mother who, every night after supper, rages at the ineffective father while the identified patient-child is beset by "delusions of persecution." It appears eminently possible to schedule such rages every night, and particularly the father's faint groans of protest and feebleness. We would predict that such scheduling would disrupt the rigid behavior patterns of the parents and may even make the delusions of the child somewhat less imperative. In the budding psychology of pathogenic families, adaptations and innovations in technique are worth exploring, if not indeed requiring exploration.

The technique of symptom scheduling offers a special challenge to the clinician: a challenge both to assess the principles elucidated in this paper and a challenge to adapt the technique and to use it creatively in various treatment settings. With such efforts, it can be hoped that the nature of intrapsychic and interpersonal symptoms will become clearer, and the agents that make for patient change will become more identifiable.

REFERENCES NOT INCLUDED IN BIBLIOGRAPHY

Bowen, M. (1965). Family psychotherapy with schizophrenia in the hospital and in private practice. In I. Boszormenyi-Nagy & J. L. Framo (Eds.), *Intensive family therapy*. New York: Harper & Row.

Frankl, V. E. (1966). Logotherapy and existential analysis: A review. *American Journal of Psychotherapy, 20*, 252–260.

Gendlin, E. T. (1964). A theory of personality change. In P. Worchel & D. Byrne (Eds.), *Personality change*. New York: Wiley.

Hollingshead, A. B., & Redlich, F. C. (1958). *Social class and mental illness*. New York: Wiley.

Rogers, C. R. (1957). The necessary and sufficient conditions for therapeutic personality change. *Journal of Consulting Psychology, 21*, 95–103.

Skinner, B. F. (1953). *Science and human behavior*. New York: Macmillan.

Van Zaig, J. (1966). The situation in psychotherapy. *Psychotherapy: Theory, Research and Practice, 3*, 170–172.

Von Eckartsberg, R. (1966). On situation analysis. *Psychotherapy: Theory, Research and Practice, 3*, 167–169.

JAY HALEY

GIVING DIRECTIVES*

Haley's approach to family treatment, as it includes the strategic use of paradoxical tactics, is succinctly represented in this excerpt. Here the author breaks a paradoxical intervention into eight stages, illustrating the therapist's task in each of these stages through the use of a case history. As do other selections, Haley's guidelines stress a point that can hardly be overemphasized: namely, that a paradoxical strategy involves much more than delivering to a client (or family) an antiexpectational directive. To be effective, the context for such a directive must be carefully prepared and the directive itself must be followed through systematically, with an awareness that successfully altering a troublesome behavior requires that the therapist prompt adjustments going considerably beyond any simple eradication of the presenting symptom.

*From *Problem-Solving Therapy*. San Francisco: Jossey-Bass, 1976. Reprinted with permission.

To use the paradoxical approach a therapist must develop skill and must practice. He also needs to be able to think about problems in a gamelike or playful way even though he realizes that he is dealing with grim problems and real distress. He also needs to tolerate the emotional reaction of the family toward him, since this approach forces them to deal with him in ways they have never dealt with a helper before.

The design of a therapist's directives in this approach is relatively simple. He observes how the family members deal with each other and directs them to behave in that way. How he gives the directive, how he makes it seem reasonable, and how he reacts to a change and follow-through can require more innovation than the design of the task.

STAGES OF A PARADOXICAL INTERVENTION.   To summarize the paradoxical approach, the proper stages can be illustrated with a case example. A nine-year-old boy was referred to a clinic for a problem of compulsive masturbation. He masturbated at school and at home in front of his mother and sisters. The problem was so severe that he had worn holes in the crotch of his pants, and his mother reported he had been hospitalized for blood in his urine. The problem had existed since the boy was five years old. A child therapist had worked with the problem for a year and a half with no improvement. He had tried insight into the problem, had tried some rewards and punishments, and he had met regularly with the boy's mother. He referred the case hoping that family therapy would help. The family was on welfare and the father had been dead for several years. There were three older daughters in the family, two of them living outside the home. The twenty-year-old daughter had two small children who were also in the home.

The stages of the paradoxical approach can be summarized. First, as in all directive therapy, one must establish a relationship defined as one to bring about change. This definition is usually implicit in the framework when someone asks for therapy, but it can be emphasized. Second, one must define the problem clearly. In this case the problem was defined as public masturbation. Third, one must set the goals clearly.

The goal was not to stop the boy from masturbating but from masturbating in public and without pleasure. Setting goals clearly is particularly important if one is using an effective therapeutic technique.

Fourth, one must offer a plan. It is helpful to offer a rationale to make a paradoxical directive reasonable, although one can also leave the plan implicit and merely give the directive. In this case the first step in the plan involved the mother and other family members and the second plan involved the boy. The therapist asked the mother to let him deal with the problem with the boy privately, although he also wished to see the whole family together at times. The mother agreed. In this way the therapist attached the boy to himself and made the problem an issue between two males. Later, when he saw the boy alone, he offered the rationale that his paradoxical request for an increase in the masturbation was to prevent the boy from doing it on days when he did not enjoy it.

Fifth, one must gracefully disqualify the current authority on the problem. The authority of the problem may be a spouse or a mother or some other family member. Usually someone is trying to help the person solve the problem, and that someone must be defined as not doing the right thing.

In this case, the mother had taken the boy from doctor to doctor for years to solve the problem. The therapist suggested that she would become upset when the boy improved. The mother did not like that idea. The therapist asked what she might do with herself when the boy was over the problem. She thought she could find something else to do with herself. A purpose in dealing this way with the mother is to encourage her to prove that she will not get upset when the boy improves. The only way she can prove this is to help the boy become normal and show she is not upset. Therefore she is working at home to improve the boy while the therapist is working in the office to improve him and they are working together. In the therapy the mother was, of course, seen alone to interest her in school and work so she would have more in her life than this problem son (and an even more problematic daughter).

Sixth, the therapist must give the paradoxical directive. As part of defining the problem, the therapist asked the boy to make a baseline chart on how often he masturbated. The boy came in the following week and reported the number of times. He said that he enjoyed it most on Sunday. The therapist gave the paradoxical directive that the boy do it more on Sunday when he enjoyed it and not on the other days when he enjoyed it less. He was asked to do it eight times on Sunday, twice as often, perhaps getting up early to get it done.

Seventh, the therapist should observe response and continue with encouragement of usual behavior. The therapist should not relent for rebellious improvement or if the person is upset but reemphasize the rationale and the plan. If the person improves and does less, the therapist should define that as not cooperating because the request was for more problem behavior.

In this case the boy had done his masturbating on Sunday, but he had also done it on Monday when he was not supposed to. To punish himself, he was asked to do it twelve times on the next Sunday. Masturbation was also made more of an ordeal by requiring him to undress completely, fold up his clothes, and so on.

The next week the boy came in without the baseline paper, had joined a hockey team, and was more cheerful. The therapist insisted more on the masturbation. By the fifth interview the boy had rebelled and masturbated less than required on Sunday. The therapist condemned him for not cooperating and, as punishment, required him to masturbate once each day in the livingroom in the presence of his mother and sisters. It had taken five weeks to arrange that the boy do exactly what he had been doing as a presenting problem. Now it was to be done as a punishment. (Some clinicians would have difficulty being this punishing, but given the severity of the problem, and the fact that the boy was only being asked to do what he was already doing, this therapist did not find it difficult.)

Eighth, as change continues, the therapist should avoid credit for it. Accepting credit means that relapses occur in relation to the therapist. Although a therapist might want to "share" with a client and explain what he is really doing, the risk is a relapse caused by the therapist's need for comfort. A way to avoid credit is to be puzzled by the improvement.

In this case, the therapist recessed for two weeks. The first week he required the maturbation program. The second week he left unclear what the boy was to do. This omission allowed the therapist to judge the amount of spontaneous change (rather than a methodical extinguishing of the behavior). If the boy gave up the public masturbation, the therapist would drop the issue. If he had not, the procedures would be reinstituted.

In two weeks the boy reported that he had done little or no masturbating the second week and seemed to have lost interest in it. The therapist dropped the matter and talked to the boy about going to camp (which had not been previously allowed by mother).

The therapist continued the therapy focused on the mother and daughter problem, with the boy present but not involved around the issue of his symptom. A few weeks later the masturbation was inquired about, and the mother said at times the boy provoked her by putting his hands in his pants while watching television. This action was not made an issue, and in a followup a few weeks later the problem was gone.

The mother was allowed to show that she did not get upset when the boy improved, and the boy's general manner became more mature in a matter of a few weeks. He even made some trouble with a friend at school, which he had never done before because he was a quiet boy and a good student. The therapist and mother defined this kind of trouble as normal for a boy that age. The teacher confirmed that he was changing.

It should be emphasized that in this case the paradoxical maneuver was used within a family context. The therapist dealt with the boy about other issues, such as sports and girl friends. He also dealt with the mother about other interests in her life. When the boy improved and became less obedient, the mother showed that she did not get too upset about the change. The shift to the daughter's problems allowed the mother to be less focused on the boy. All these aspects were part of the therapy and not merely of the paradoxical maneuver. There were also stages to the therapy and not merely an encouragement of the symptom and a backing off when improvement occurred. It was necessary to follow through in a systematic way.

CARLOS E. SLUZKI

MARITAL THERAPY FROM A SYSTEMS THEORY PERSPECTIVE[*]

The unorthodox prescriptions for couples included in this excerpt from Sluzki generally have in common their forcing symptomatic patterns to crack under their own strain. Here the author considers the messages embedded both in symptoms and in the therapist's prescriptions dialectically contrived to counteract them. Sluzki's approach emphasizes the homeostatic processes governing interpersonal systems, as well as the role of symptoms in preserving this basically dysfunctional equilibrium. The paradoxical prescription, viewed as strategically intruding upon and ultimately arresting maladaptive interpersonal cycles, actively contests those rules in the couple's relationship that have given rise to their problem and served to maintain it. As theoretically suggestive as is Sluzki's essay, it is yet eminently practical. His specific guidelines— concise and almost disarmingly straightforward—demystify paradoxical treatment strategies and should help the inexperienced practitioner gain increased confidence in using them.

PRESCRIPTIONS FOR THERAPEUTIC INTERVENTIONS

•   •   •

#6. If A and B concur in defining A as victim and B as victimizer, *then* find a way of reversing the roles/labels and state the reversal forcefully.

The positions of "victim" and "victimizer" are the result of a punctuation in the sequence of events, that is, of an arbitrary decision on the part of

[*]In T. J. Paolino & B. S. McCrady (Eds.), *Marriage and Marital Therapy*. New York: Brunner/Mazel, 1978. Reprinted with permission.

one or both participants about who leads and who follows. The issue of "punctuations," as well as procedural matters dealing with this prescription, will be discussed in the context of #7, which is partly a concrete application of this prescription. In the case of victim-victimizer couples, as well as in symptomatic-nonsymptomatic dyads, it is difficult for members to change *from within* the rules that govern the system. They require an outside intervention to step out of recurrent patterns.*

The following constitutes an example of such an intervention in a dyad: The present author recently saw a couple who were locked in a relationship in which the wife's nagging, complaining negativism contrasted sharply with the husband's appeasing optimism. Each of them was expressing mounting dissatisfaction and resentment, and both concurred in defining her as the victimizer and him as the victim. I praised her for having decided to take the heavy load of the villain (cf., Prescriptions #6 and #8), though to help to make him look good while she remained the "mean one" must have had some kicks for her. But, I continued, there are no kicks like the kicks of being the "good guy," and he was selfishly keeping most of the assets to himself. They looked quite surprised, but went along with the reasoning and the metaphors. I prescribed that he should respond to any statement of hers by being as pessimistic as possible—regardless of how really pessimistic he might be at that moment, without leaking to her the true nature of his feelings. I prescribed her to remain as pessimistic as before, "in order not to make the task more difficult for him" (cf., Prescription #11). To analyze these prescriptions: (1) The prescription acknowledged that he *could* be genuinely pessimistic; (2) her habitual behavior was being relabeled as a gesture of good will; (3) if they followed instructions, they would quite quickly reach a deadlock that would force her to extricate the positive side of the matter; (4) nobody—but the therapist, perhaps—would be blamed for any escalation into pessimism between them, totally eliminating any label of victim and victimizer; and (5) they were being granted a humorous way out of confrontations, used by them thereafter on occasions. In fact, both expressed a remarkable reduction of the conflicts and a general improvement in the relationship from there on, while I, correspondingly, expressed concern about their unexplainable and too dramatic change (cf., Prescriptions #9 and #12).

A word of caution. If the couple's agreement on who is the victim or victimizer strikes the therapist as very farfetched, the agreement may represent a "folie à deux" or other strong family myth, in which case it

*The protagonistic couple of Albee's "Who's Afraid of Virginia Woolf" provides a paradigm of impotence from within. (Cf. an outstanding interactional analysis of that play in Watzlawick et al., 1967.)

should either be challenged very cautiously, or an alternative track, such as working toward changing the pattern while retaining the couple's definition of it, could be chosen.

> #7. If A and B describe a sequence of events that leads to conflict or to the emergence of symptoms, *then* search for the events or steps that precede what has been described as the first step in the sequence. If you cannot specify it, nonetheless state its existence. If it has been detected, and is accepted by A and B as possible, then repeat the cycle (i.e., search for a still previous step, or at least assert its existence).

Except perhaps in the very early stages of parent-child relationships, there is no totally passive, victim-like position in interpersonal situations within small systems. All members are contributing parties to the interactional sequences, the behavior of each member being induced by and in turn inducing the other. At the most, in certain circumstances one of the actors *appears* to be the victim. However, this constitutes an "optical illusion" derived from the fact that observers—and frequently also the participants—*punctuate the sequence arbitrarily*. That is, the chicken/egg puzzle is arbitrarily solved by designating one of the participants as the initiator and the other as the reactor. But, is it that he nags because she withdraws or that she withdraws because he nags?

The punctuation of the sequence of events is the result of the arbitrary and almost unavoidable introduction of context markers in the sequence of interactions (Bateson and Jackson, 1964). Even though some behaviors may be defined as *stimuli*, some as *responses*, and some as *reinforcement* (a calibration of the stimulus in the light of the response), each communicational act can be considered "simultaneously a stimulus, a response and a reinforcement, according to how we slide our identification . . . up and down the series" (Bateson, 1963, p. 176).

Leaving aside those couples who display a conflict format centered in punctuations—"you nag, no, you withdraw" type—most couples reach agreement about punctuation of events both in their history and in their present life, and any quest for alternative punctuations may meet with considerable resistance on their part. However, persistence may uncover many family myths and other covert agreements, and may provide leads toward dramatic restructuring of the rules of the relationship.

A couple was seen in conjoint therapy after one interview with the woman triggered a stormy depression, which was accompanied by bursts of unbearable anxiety and somatic symptoms such as daily vomiting, headaches and abdominal pain. The proposition of the therapist that there was some behavior in the nonsymptomatic partner that preceded and contributed to explain the IP's symptoms was met with total incredulity by both partners. In a subsequent crisis of the symptomatology that followed a period of quiescence, the therapist was able to detect and show to both members that when the husband started to experience anxiety due to mounting responsibilities in his complex job, the wife would respond to that cue with a flair of symptoms. Immediately, the husband would become involved in taking care of her and simultaneously his anxiety would vanish, freeing him for an effective performance at work (which became quite shaky due to his anxiety once when she was on vacation and a new requirement of his job took place). As a result of this observation, the therapist expressed his worries about what would happen to the husband if her symptoms subsided (Prescription #9), suggested to her that she produce symptoms out of phase (Prescription #10) and centered his attention on the husband's anxiety, acknowledging the wife's valuable contribution whenever she reported experiencing symptoms (Prescription #8). The whole symptomatic pattern broke within three months, after five years of plaguing the couple's life, as they replaced their hidden homeostatic agreement with one that was more mutual and did not require the presence of symptoms.

#8. If A complains about a symptom, *then* find a way
of complimenting A for what A is doing for B.

This prescription, still a spinoff of #6, is also the first of a series of prescriptions centered in positive connotation, symptom prescriptions and paradoxical interventions.* It can be utilized to set in motion the notion that the therapist is going to apply a dialectic logic instead of the traditional causal one utilized up to that moment by the couple (and, in fact, by most people). There are several messages embedded in this prescription: A is defined as having control over the symptoms at a certain level; the connotation of the symptom is changed, from negative to positive, as the symptom is

---

*The reader interested in pursuing this theme beyond the limits of these short comments should consult, in the first place, the innovative work of Haley (1963, 1977), as well as Watzlawick, Weakland and Fisch (1974) and Selvini Palazzoli et al. (1975).

defined as having some positive value (it is accomplishing a useful function for the other member of the couple)—therefore, a certain shared responsibility of A and B over the symptom is implied; and the therapist will not confront the system by means of suppressing the symptom. Overall, a viewpoint characterized by the emphasis on interpersonal processes and shared responsibility is introduced.

In several examples throughout this chapter, the prescription to "compliment the symptom" appears as an introductory step for more complex paradoxical interventions, that is, for interventions which generate a bind that can only be solved by the patients' extinguishing the symptomatic behavior or breaking interactional stereotypes (cf., for instance, the case included in the comment to Prescription #6).

> #9. If symptomatic member A reports a decrease in the intensity of symptoms in the last week(s), *then* express vague worries and recommend a slight relapse, even soliciting the aid of B to achieve that relapse, and/or express worry that B may develop some symptoms.

Symptomatic patients and their mates may try to avoid change by attempting to define the symptom as something devoid of context. The interactional view allows the therapist to see otherwise: Symptoms accomplish functions for the system, and all members contribute somehow to their maintenance. But, how to proceed with this assumption without transforming the session into an arena for the confrontation of the two ideologies—the couple's and the therapist's? Beyond the sterility of a discussion about intentionality, the risk lies in appearing to be as explicitly aligned with the system's tendencies toward change. The habitual response of the members of this alignment is to hurry and stabilize the system following the patterns already familiar to them, and hence strengthen the status quo and the symptoms.

In fact, order (morphostatic properties) and change (morphogenesis) are complementary tendencies of interpersonal systems. They maintain a fine balance through complex homeostatic processes. When any living system deviates toward one of the poles, processes are activated that pull the system in the direction of the opposite tendency, thereby keeping the system within a clearly defined equilibrium between both. The triumph of the morphostatic tendencies are total rigidity and death of the system. The triumph of morphogenesis is total dissolution and, equally, death of the system. The balance between both tendencies is crucial both for stability and for change within the system.

Therefore, if the therapist wishes to favor change within a rigidified system, he/she should transit along that fine line. That can be done, in some cases, by maintaining a front defending stability while freeing the system from restrictive rules that prevent the members from working out changes. Symptoms, frequent barometers of these processes, can be useful tools in this type of paradoxical intervention, as has already been illustrated in the last example.

The prescription of symptoms—be it the very symptom that brought the couple to the consultation or any other one—is a powerful therapeutic tool that can be introduced—in general, with amazingly little resistance— through the tack followed by this prescription (and the next ones up to #13).

> #10. If A has a symptom that fluctuates within the
> day or the week, *then* instruct A to select times
> in which the symptom improves to tell B that it
> is worse.

It was mentioned above that couples with a symptomatic member tend to punctuate the sequence of events in such a manner that the symptom appears to be the (uncalled for, unintentional) *stimulus*, and that the partner's behavior is defined as the *response*. Ways to alter that punctuation were also proposed (Prescriptions #6–9). The present prescription is still another way of dealing with these issues.

Through prescribing a symptom to a symptomatic member in the presence of the mate, the therapist aims at shattering the very pattern that perpetuates the symptom. That effect occurs through two mechanisms: (a) When the patient is told "fake the symptom, and fake it well," the other member of the dyad is implicitly being told that the symptomatic behavior to which he/she may be exposed to *may* be false, therefore inhibiting "spontaneous" responses that in turn may reinforce and perpetuate the symptom; and (b) it subtly increases the consensus about the patient's control over the symptom, and decreases the chances of his/her claiming spontaneity. At the same time, it evokes its counterpart, that if the subject can *produce* a symptom through a prescription, he/she may also be able to *reduce* it. One of the key interactional attributes of symptoms, namely, the fact that they are considered spontaneous by the participants, is drastically questioned by a well-placed symptom description.

This prescription is illustrated in several examples in this chapter. To provide still another one: It corresponds to a first interview with a couple whose explicit problem was centered in her stubborn insomnia, recent loss of appetite, and fluctuating weakness and irritability which she related to her insomnia. She had four offspring from previous partners and had been living with this mate for some three years. He expressed worries about her symptoms and elegantly tolerated her condition, as well as his role as healthy partner of a sick lady. The exploration of the context or origin, as well as any function the symptom might have been serving in the system (i.e., the effects of the symptoms on his behavior, or on the behavior of any other member of the family), failed to produce any additional meaningful information.

In the course of that interview, the therapist stated that the symptoms the woman was presenting were correlates of depression without feelings of sadness. The man reacted immediately by stating, defensively, that she didn't have any reason to be sad. To defuse, the therapist proposed that maybe it had to do with old sadness (nothing to do with the present context) and prescribed that, in the course of the next week, she should behave as though she were very, very sad, especially on those days in which she was least sad, and asked him to help her in that task by letting her express her sadness without trying to counter-argue or shush her. The therapist added that they would probably find the task surprisingly difficult to comply with. She agreed that it was against the grain of her tendencies to show her sad side. The man stated, in turn, that he did not foresee any difficulty in his share, because, "After all, she may be just acting it."

In the next session, they reported that she cried as never before, and that he felt that he was helping her get rid of the pain by just being there, instead of feeling defensive about it. Two stormy sessions followed in which several current frustrations were discussed, and the crisis subsided with a drastic change in the couple's style of coping with conflict. The presenting symptoms were not even mentioned during that period, and when explored, they were reported as having vanished.

The symptom prescription seemed to accomplish the function of facilitating a break in an otherwise repetitive cycle that kept them locked, until then, in their respective roles of sick and sane.

> #11. Whenever a prescription of a behavior or of a symptom is made, the more basic the implied change, the more trivial it should be made to appear: involve both members in the prescription and admonish that, in spite of its sounding trivial, they will find it difficult to comply.

The maintenance and exacerbation of conflicts, problems or symptoms are frequently the result of the positive feedback loop created by those very behaviors of other members of the system aimed at resolving the difficulty; thus, the attempted solution becomes part of the problem (cf., Haley, 1963; Hoffman, 1971; Watzlawick et al., 1974; Wender, 1968).

The benevolent prescription by the therapist of those same behaviors which are considered symptomatic by the members of the system severely challenges the very rules that tend otherwise to perpetuate the symptoms. The illegitimate, spontaneous, parasitical behavior becomes legitimate, non-spontaneous and a useful part of the process. The complaint becomes the compliance and the disappearance of symptoms a non-compliance. The very behavior that was used previously as a marker of roles becomes now the result of a prescription by the therapist. The system is robbed of a basic rule.

The more challenging the change implied by the prescription, the less it should appear to be: Otherwise, the investment of the therapist in the specific change becomes itself a marker, and the members of the couple may tend to utilize the alternative outcomes of the prescription to reward or punish the therapist, or each other. For the same reason the expression of doubts is included: Whatever the outcome, the therapist will have made a correct prediction, which precludes any improvement or relapse made "in his behalf." Further, relapses may even be encouraged, a strategy that, as already discussed in regard to Prescription #10, conveys the notion that the symptomatic or problematic behavior is under the control of the actor, rather than an allegedly random process. Once this is established, the main interactional value of a symptom, its being there *in spite of* the participants, is lost, and, with it, the symptom itself.

The reason behind the recommendation of prescribing behaviors to both members must be quite clear by now—to further establish their joint responsibility for the problem and its solution, through further blurring the distinction between symptoms or problematic behaviors and their counterpart in each member.

A rather long example will illustrate several of these prescriptions.

It relates to the couple already introduced in the example for Prescription #7. Their conjoint treatment started with a façade of an individual therapy: a 30-year-old wife of a diplomat was brought to the office, completely crippled by a myriad of severe emotional and somatic symptoms—oppressive headaches, daily vomiting, intense anxiety and severe depression, all triggered by a move to San Francisco from their country due to his work. Her husband was engaged promptly in the treatment, and shortly afterwards therapy clearly was dealing fully with what Jackson (1965) named the "marital *quid pro quo*." In their case, the trade-off was that her symptoms allowed him to be free of anxiety—mainly around death and departures—which otherwise overwhelmed him occasionally, and his protective behavior allowed her to remain childlike while in control of most of the decisions in the relationship.

The sequence described here corresponds to a period in which they were dealing with the prospect of another move because of a change in his job responsibilities. During the session she complained of headaches and anxiety—one-tenth as intense as previously, but nonetheless there. In the course of that session, I praised her for her sacrifices on behalf of the couple, praised him for allowing her to be so useful, and proceeded to prescribe for him, almost as a game, that in the next week he should try another tack: Instead of appeasing her whenever she complained of her symptoms, he should tell her immediately his own worries or problems, competing with her to see who suffered more, regardless of the "true" intensity of his problems or worries. In turn, I instructed her to be very sensitive about her body, and to communicate to him whenever she felt anything unpleasant.

In the following session, predictably, they reported that he was quite anxious and she didn't have any symptoms, even though she felt irritable. He commented, frustrated, that she hardly gave him any chance to express his worries, that she flooded him with her problems and symptoms. I told him to tell it to her. He did. She answered that, in fact, she was fully aware of how worried he was about his future job and he replied that what really worried him was how to wrap up neatly his present responsibilities. She brushed him off: "But, dear, you don't have any problems whatsoever in the office right now; everything is under control." I commented that it seemed to me that her definition of helping, right then, was to appease, while his definition of being helped was to be listened to. He agreed. She stated, tears in her eyes, that the fact of the matter was that she also felt frustrated because he did not allow her to open up to him, a statement which startled him. He told her, astonished, that her statement went completely against his sense of how things were, and that he considered himself very sensitive in relation to her and allowed her to speak to him about anything whenever she felt anxious in order to facilitate her relief. She told him, quite tenderly, that that was true whenever she was loaded with symptoms, but it was not so for those things that truly worried her the most, that for those other things he was like a father, shushing her, minimizing her, treating her like a child.

I pointed out that what she described was also what she did with him when she minimized the issue of the office. I stressed the fact that the shushing technique probably had been useful for both of them, but both were saying it was no longer satisfying. They both agreed and concurred that they would try to defend their right to be anxious. I proposed a new twist: "When you detect anxiety in your mate, ask yourself, 'What is going on with me?' and whenever you feel yourself anxious, ask yourself, 'What is going on with my mate?'"

> #12. If the couple reports having complied with the task or prescription, *then* express surprise and predict amiably that it cannot last and that they will find it difficult or even fail next time.

The maneuver wraps up the three previous ones. Its rationale is the same as for the prediction of difficulties in the compliance of a seemingly trivial symptom prescription: to divest the symptom of any value as "reward" or "punishment" vis à vis the therapist.

This presentation can be enhanced further if the therapist also praises the couple for having achieved something that is difficult, namely, complying with a symptom prescription, a statement that further reframes the symptom as a non-spontaneous behavior while binding the couple in a positive experience of joint creation (in spite of the fact that what they have created is identical to what brought them to the consultation!)

> #13. If A (and/or B) expresses and/or attributes to the other feelings that have negative connotations in our culture—i.e., a connotation that to have those feelings is to be mad or bad or sick—*then* relabel or reframe that feeling into one of positive connotation.

To reframe or relabel consists of changing the frame of reference against which a given event is considered or judged, thus changing the meaning and value judgment of the event (without any change in the event itself).

When a patient, who seeks consultation due to vomiting that seems to be triggered by stressful events, is told, "Good, you should not stop vomiting until those things that bother you change. How wise of your body to devise such a clever way of forcing some changes in your unpleasant situation!" the complaint (vomiting), is not at all changed but the frame (from something that "just happens" to something that is purposeful) and its value, from negative (as an annoying symptom) to positive (as behavior leading to change), are both changed.

Reality depends on our beliefs. There is not one given interpretation of it that is more "correct" than the other. At the most, there are some that are more consensual than others. Therefore, different observers may in turn provide different meanings to the same given act. With the attribution of meaning comes a value judgment—the adjudication of a given value within different "scales" such as goodness-badness, sanity-madness, health-sickness. And those values, when firmly attached to members of a family system, pin them down to fixed roles, as they consolidate interactional roles within the family.

The simple act of relabeling someone's "anger" as hurt, or someone's "depression" as sadness, or someone's symptom as an act of kindness and good will, exerts a dramatic, exorcizing effect on the system.

It is important to point out here that to *relabel* a problem or a symptom does not mean to *minimize* it (an issue discussed in depth by Haley, 1976). There are specific cases in which a symptom may be underplayed—through maneuvers such as that of "inflating" a minor symptom of the nonsymptomatic member in order to achieve a symmetrical stand with both members. But, overall, to simply minimize a symptom can be not only a futile wishful thinking but even a disqualification that may endanger the therapy.

#14. If A talks "crazy" in the midst of an interaction
between you and B, *then* tell A not to interrupt
or distract and follow your interaction with B.

In one of the training videotapes produced at the Philadelphia Child Guidance Clinic in recent years, entitled "Coming Home from the Hospital," there is a sequence that illustrates this point vividly—even though it takes place in a session with a larger family. The therapist, Gary Lande, M.D., is speaking with the parents of an adolescent daughter who has been just released from a mental hospital, when the identified patient introjects into the conversation a bizarre statement about clothes and their symbolic meaning. The therapist tells her benevolently, "We don't fall for that type of thing here," and goes on with the conversation with the parents. No further crazy talk takes place in the whole session, even though the identified patient participates actively.

This prescription on "crazy talk" is an illustration of the principle that, if the symptomatic behavior is deprived of its interactional power, of its value as a message, a substantial contribution to its elimination has occurred. Through dealing with "crazy" behavior as if it were mere "misbehavior," the therapist *de facto* relabels the symptom with a nonpathological tag. At the same time, he/she will provide the other, nonsymptomatic members with a model of how the symptomatic behavior can be handled.

REFERENCES NOT INCLUDED IN BIBLIOGRAPHY

Bateson, G. (1963). Exchange of information about patterns of human behavior. In W. S. Field & W. Abbot (Eds.), *Information storage and neural control.* Springfield, IL: Charles C. Thomas.

Bateson, G., & Jackson, D. D. (1968). Some varieties of pathogenic organization. In D. M. Rioch & E. A. Weinstein (Eds.), *Disorders of communication.* Baltimore: Williams & Wilkins. Also in D. D. Jackson (Ed.), *Communication, family and marriage.* Palo Alto: Science & Behavior Books.

Hoffman, L. (1971). Deviation-amplifying processes in natural groups. In J. Haley (Ed.), *Changing families.* New York: Grune & Stratton.

Jackson, D. D. (1965). Family rules—Marital quid pro quo. *Archives of General Psychiatry, 12,* 589–594.

Wender, P. H. (1968). Vicious and virtuous circles: The role of deviation-amplifying feedback in the origin and perpetuation of behavior. *Psychiatry, 31,* 317–324.

PEGGY PAPP

PARADOXICAL STRATEGIES AND COUNTERTRANSFERENCE[*]

This pithy "question and answer" selection—which, given its systemic outlook, is somewhat confusingly titled—attempts in a few well-chosen paragraphs to delineate the proper execution of paradoxical procedures. Responding to an instructor's complaint that family therapy trainees at times use (or rather, abuse) these techniques to act out their own negative feelings toward apparently resistant families, Papp sets forth the major criteria that must be followed if therapists are to employ such methods constructively. Considerations important in deciding when to work with families paradoxically, as well as errors typical of therapists first adopting this approach, are both suggestively outlined here.

Question: The clinical practicum in family therapy which I teach in a graduate school program, is eclectically oriented, with a psychodynamic flavor. Over the last couple of years, as paradoxical techniques (e.g., prescribing the symptom) have become more popularized, I find a

[*]Reprinted with permission from *The American Journal of Family Therapy*, 7, 2, 11–12, 1979, © Brunner/Mazel, Inc.

number of our trainees gravitating toward using them. I have no objection in principle to these approaches, but I find that trainees often seem to use them when they feel cornered, locked out, frustrated or angry at families. What cues can I use to help my trainees focus on and become more aware of—so that when they use these paradoxical interventions they will do so for the family instead of against it? A related question is, when, aside from moments of the therapist's own anxiety, are paradoxical approaches not indicated?

Discussion

Quite naturally, along with the increased interest in the use of paradox in family therapy comes increased confusion, as it is a complicated technique which requires skill and practice to apply.

In the Brief Therapy Project of the Ackerman Institute for Family Therapy, we have been experimenting with paradoxical interventions over the past five years, and have developed a certain criterion for their use. This criterion is based on our evaluation of family flexibility and motivation. If motivation is high enough and resistance low enough for a family to respond to direct interventions, such as logical explanations, suggestions or tasks, there is no need to resort to a paradox. Also, there are certain crisis situations, such as violence, sudden grief, attempted suicide, incest or child abuse, in which a paradox would be inappropriate, as the therapist needs to move in quickly to provide structure and control. We reserve paradoxical interventions for interrupting long-standing, rigid, repetitious patterns of interaction which do not respond to a logical approach. A paradox can then be used as a weapon against resistance and as a way of changing the relationship between the family and the therapist. It should not be used unless the therapist understands the meaning of the symptom in the family and prescribes it in a way which *changes the functioning of the system.*

One prevalent mistaken notion is that simply prescribing the symptom is therapeutic. The symptom must be prescribed in a particular way and under particular circumstances to have any benefit. If it is scheduled, it should be scheduled at a designated time and place, with a designated member of the family. For example, in a case in which the presenting problem was persistent headaches in a nine-year-old daughter, the therapist, Olga Silverstein, defined the headaches as "worry headaches" and decided they were brought on by the child's need to help her mother worry about all the family problems, because her father refused to worry. The child's worry was spilling over into school time and interfering with her studying. She was instructed by the therapist to worry for half an hour every morning before school, so she wouldn't need to take time from her school work to do this. Her father was instructed to help her worry so she wouldn't feel alone. They were not to tell mother what they had worried about. This served the purpose of realigning the family and diffusing the relationship between mother and daughter, forming a closer relationship between father and daughter, and involving father in the family concerns without pressure from mother, to which he had become allergic. Merely prescribing the headaches without connecting them with the family system would have been of dubious value.

Another common misconception arises around the use of what we in the Brief Therapy Project refer to as a "systemic paradox." This is a paradox in which the symptom is connoted positively, defined as serving an essential function in the family system, and prescribed along with the system. Beginning therapists often prescribe the behavior of various family members without connecting them. This *connection* between the symptom and the system is crucial. For example, in a family in which the son, Billy, was failing in school, the therapist connected his failure with a subverted conflict between mother and father over father's lack of ambition and failure in business. Turning to Billy, this therapist told him that for the time being it was important for him to protect father from mother's disappointment by keeping her disappointment focused on him. Otherwise, mother might begin to nag father and he might become depressed and withdraw. Since Billy was younger and more resilient, he could take mother's disappointment better than father, and should continue to do so. The therapist thus defined the system which maintained the symptom, defined the *connection* between the two, and prescribed both. The formulation of a systemic paradox must be both accurate and, at the same time, unacceptable to the family. It was accurate to say that mother nagged Billy when she was disappointed in father, but defined and prescribed in this way it was also unacceptable to the family. The therapist had confronted them with the demands of their own emotional system.

A common error made by beginners in attempting this kind of paradoxical intervention lies in simply prescribing the symptomatic behavior of the identified patient, such as "Billy, you should continue to keep mother's disappointment focused on you." This is meaningless and confusing. Another frequent error lies in prescribing each individual family member's behavior separately, such as, "Billy, you should continue to keep mother's disappointment focused on you; mother, you should continue to nag Billy; and father, you should continue to withdraw." This lacks therapeutic impact as here again the symptom is not connected with the system in a circular definition. The power of this type of paradox lies in the reason *why* each person should continue their behavior, as the reason why contains a definition of the symptom-producing cycle. Once this cycle has been exposed, the family finds it difficult to continue it in the same way.

STEVE DE SHAZER

BRIEF FAMILY THERAPY: A METAPHORICAL TASK*

Any collection of supplementary writings on the administration of paradoxical interventions would be incomplete without one portraying how such procedures can be symbolically, or metaphorically, implemented. By now several therapists have explored ways in which certain problematic behaviors (and behavioral sequences) might be prescribed indirectly, through the use of an analogue precisely tailored to fit them. de Shazer's essay represents a particularly whimsical version of this alternate paradoxical mode, as it may be incorporated within a brief treatment model. Describing a metaphorical task expressly designed to disrupt a family's troublesome interactive pattern, the author illustrates his set of nine guidelines for successfully carrying out this especially devious strategy for systemic change. One interesting justification for such deviousness, rarely mentioned in the literature, is that it may serve—through its very playfulness—to reduce the potential pain that clients may implicitly associate with change.

The purpose of this paper is to describe an approach used at the Brief Family Therapy Center to make family therapy less painful. This particular version of the procedure cannot be used with all families, and cannot be used under all conditions. All surgery does not follow the same precise steps as an appendectomy. However, the basic format of preceding a *task* with a *compliment* to the family can provide an effective "anesthetic" with most families. (For further development of this model, see de Shazer [1982].)

Several concerns face the therapist who wants to design an effective intervention: a) how to design the intervention, and then b) how to implement that design in such a manner that the family will find it a useful clue to solving their puzzling complaint. Various therapists seem to agree that designing interventions is difficult because the plan should encompass not only the troublesome behavior of an individual (the symptom), but it should include the entire family interaction pattern which surrounds the troublesome behavior.

Palazzoli (1974) described a "family ritual," as a one time only task that seems designed to dramatically undermine the family's need for a symptom. She noted that this sort of task is uniquely tailored to a particular family system, it is difficult to invent, and it is not reusable with other families, no matter how similar the system. More recently she described a "ritual prescription" (1978) that is usable with families that have one or

---

*Reprinted from Volume 6, Number 4 of *Journal of Marital and Family Therapy*. Copyright 1980, American Association for Marriage and Family Therapy. Reprinted by permission.

more problem children. Except for minor details, this task does not vary from family to family.

Papp (1977) described "prescribing the system" which is a paradoxical intervention that instructs the family to continue doing what it is already doing, but to do so for the good of the family rather than because they cannot help it. de Shazer described several different types of interventions with families and couples (1975, 1978, 1979a), in which the troublesome behavior was prescribed, sometimes in a metaphorical manner; that is, the pattern was prescribed in a different form meant to suggest an analogy between the "original problem" and the assigned task. These therapists seem to agree that what needs to be changed is that pattern. Therefore, the task is modeled after some version of the family's troublesome pattern. It is not the complaint/symptom itself by itself, but rather the pattern which is seen as a means of producing change.

For example, a family shows a therapist how two (or more) members conflict, even though they wish to stop this conflict. A prescription of the conflictual pattern can be given as long as the task contains elements which make it *different* from the troublesome pattern. Simply, a metaphorical task must shift the involuntary and painful elements of the troublesome pattern into some activity that is voluntary, deliberate, or even playful.

Since *each family has a unique manner of attempting to cooperate* (de Shazer, 1982), any assigned task must be built on their patterns. Otherwise, the task or prescription is likely to seem meaningless to the family, and they will not perform it. If the family has first been given a *compliment*, a "yes set" (Erickson and Rossi, 1979) can develop which increases the likelihood that the family will perform the task and thus change can be promoted.

Effective tasks seem to follow certain guidelines which can help a family to change with as little pain as possible. Goffman (1974) has studied the process of changing "serious" activities into "playful" activities. These guidelines can be applied in whole or in part to help change the serious business of family complaints. Upon occasion, a task can have playful results which produce laughter. Though it can be beneficial, it is not a necessary result. The purpose of using these guidelines is to change the complaint pattern by using that pattern in a modified form and in a different context as a basis for a task.

GUIDELINES

1. The playful acts are so performed that their ordinary functions are not realized. Efforts are made to equalize the strength of the players.

2. There is an exaggeration of some normal acts.
3. The normal sequence serves as a pattern that is neither followed faithfully nor completed fully, but is subject to arbitrary starting and stopping.
4. The activities called for are repetitive.
5. Any player has the power to terminate play once begun.
6. During the play the dominance order may become mixed up or reversed.
7. The play seems independent of any external needs of the participants and continues longer than would the actual interactions it is patterned after.
8. The play is social in that it involves more than one participant and the playfulness can therefore be more easily sustained.
9. Signs are available to mark the beginning and the termination of playfulness (adapted from Goffman, 1974, pp. 41–43).

Palazzoli's ritual prescription (1978), Papp's system prescription (1977), and de Shazer's systemic symptom prescription (1978, 1979a) can be seen to follow these guidelines, changing at least some of the elements in the complaint pattern when designing a prescription. All of the tasks they describe are social in nature, involving the family in the activity. There is an exaggeration of some of the family's pattern, and the activities called for are repetitive. Through the use of these guidelines, a therapist can help a family to shift a troublesome pattern into a playful activity. This allows the family an opportunity to spontaneously develop alternate patterns in as painless a manner as possible.

In the metaphorical task a family is instructed to enact the troublesome pattern in a modified form *and* in a different context. In the case example to follow, the troublesome pattern can be simply stated: mother and daughter bicker about limits in the kitchen, which leads to father's negotiating their differences as fairly as possible. In the metaphorical version, mother and daughter are assigned a conflictual activity which leads to father's judging the winner as fairly as possible.

When performing this sort of task, families will often spontaneously rewrite the ending of the metaphor which in turn helps to further undermine the original, troublesome pattern upon which it is modeled. This type of task is more useful with families that are not too rigidly stuck in the troublesome pattern. A sense of humor is a good indicator that a metaphorical task can be useful in making change less painful. Basically, if the family can be seen as conflictual, yet can be seen as caring for each other, then a metaphorical task can be useful. If the family's pattern is more rigid, then other tasks or other interventions seem more effective (Palazzoli,1978; Papp, 1977; de Shazer, 1978, 1979a, 1980).

CASE EXAMPLE

FIRST SESSION.   Mrs. S complained about her daughter's behavior: lying, cutting school, minor shoplifting. Carolyn (13) disputed each of these "charges." This led to bickering over each detail of every charge. Mr. S would intervene when he thought the bickering was getting out of hand. For the most part Mr. S agreed with his wife that Carolyn was a problem, but he did not think the problem was as serious as Mrs. S thought. He thought Carolyn's behavior was quite typical of 13-year-old girls.

Carolyn, however, took exception to these comments claiming her father was just as old-fashioned as her mother. Mr. S just shrugged and smiled. This appeared to anger Carolyn, but she was unable to provoke her father.

They described a similar pattern which frequently took place at home. If Carolyn asked her mother for permission, and mother refused; then they would start to bicker first over that specific issue, then over any other unresolved issues. When Mr. S was home, he would attempt to restore peace by negotiating the original issue. Both Carolyn and her mother saw his efforts as fair to each of them: he seemed to alternately side with first one and then the other. But he never entirely sided against his wife. He tried to accept her position and then modify it enough to pacify Carolyn for that moment, and allow Mrs. S to save face.

The therapist asked Mr. S to temporarily take over the limit setting for Carolyn during the following two weeks. Mrs. S was asked to keep a diary of her complaints about Carolyn's behavior, and her own violations of the contract. The family worked out the mechanics of the arrangement with the therapist's help. The therapist suggested that if the contract did work, it would "cool things down," and it would give mother a much needed rest. However, he predicted that the hassles would be very difficult to stop, and suggested that they not be too surprised if the contract broke down, and they had some hassles.

(This intervention was designed to test the family's flexibility and to block the troublesome bickering-negotiating pattern. If the family is flexible enough for the task to be performed and it is at least somewhat effective, then further tasks are more likely to be performed and effective. However, this intervention is not usually sufficient to stop the complaint pattern in most families. The contract is mainly a blocking of the usual pattern and is likely to break down at any time. If the bickering-negotiating hassles can be diminished by the contract, then arbitrary starting and stopping in future tasks will be more easily accepted by the family. If the family does not perform the task, or the task is not effective in inhibiting the pattern, then future interventions need to be structured differently (de Shazer, 1982) and they might include "do not change" messages (de Shazer,

1979a) because the patterns would be seen as more rigid, and a metaphorical task would likely be ineffective at least early in the therapy.)

SECOND SESSION.   The family reported a complete lack of bickering about limits during the interval. All three felt a large amount of tension during the two weeks. They did not like trying to avoid conflict because that meant Carolyn and Mrs. S had to avoid each other. Mr. S and Carolyn experienced little difficulty in either setting or enforcing the limits. Mrs. S found her complaints about Carolyn's behavior were no different from before, and that she did not find herself violating the contract at all, although she did feel tempted on two occasions.

The therapist agreed that constant tension was almost as painful as constant bickering, but suggested that parent-child conflict was not only normal but was an essential part of family life. He predicted that continued tension could only lead to further hassles. All three agreed, and then they detailed some "near misses" during the two weeks. They thought that the contract was only slightly superior to the hassles.

Prior to assigning the planned metaphorical task, the therapist can give the family a series of compliments designed to promote their agreement to perform the assignment.

"I am impressed with the ability all of you have shown to keep a lid on the hassles. I realize that this has caused some tensions, and you all have handled it well, better than most families. I was particularly struck that you, Mr. S and Carolyn, were able to work cooperatively around setting limits, and that you, Mrs. S, did not take the opportunity to bury your head in the sand, like some parents do: you continued to keep a close eye on Carolyn during these difficult times. And, I'm impressed that you were able to not interfere with the contract."

(The therapist then continued into the second step of building a "yes set," giving the task itself. The *compliment*, and the transition before the task itself are used to increase the likelihood that the family will perform the task.)

"It seems to me that bickering is a normal result of the normal build-up of tension in the family, particularly in the mother-daughter relationship, and that hassles serve as one means to relieve those tensions. As you know from backpacking, sometimes physical exercise can revive people when they are mentally and/or emotionally tired. Now, this task might seem 'meaningless' at first glance, but it is actually similar to physically exercising when mentally tired."

(The task was written before the session, and they received copies.)

"The three of you are to go to some relatively secluded spot, away from home. (Several possibilities were mentioned.) You should make this trip in silence. Once there, Mrs. S and Carolyn, you are to have a squirt gun fight, like the old-fashioned duel. Except that you should each empty your guns rather than take just one shot. And, you should have three 'rounds' or battles each time. Mr. S, you should carry a water supply and decide as fairly as possible who wins each round. I want you to perform this exercise on three specific days at three specific times in the next two weeks. Also, the return trip is to be silent."

They readily agreed to perform the exercise, and disagreed with the therapist about the task's meaninglessness. They were quite able to see the obvious "symbolic" nature of the task as equivalent to the real hassles. (No effort had been made to conceal this likeness, but the family's recognition of the equivalence is not necessary to the success of the prescription.)

(Clearly this prescription calls for the bickering-negotiating pattern, but in a vastly different context. The purpose is to prompt some spontaneously different behaviors which can change the ending of the ordinary patterns. Each of the nine points of the guidelines can be seen to apply.)

SESSION THREE.   Only during the first scheduled squirt gun fight were they able to fully perform the task. The other two times they started a duel, they were unable to complete the task beyond the first exchange of shots because they all started to laugh. They also reported an absence of "normal bickering-negotiating" during the two weeks. Since they reported some continued tensions, the therapist assigned them the same task to be performed twice prior to the next session. Times and dates were established, and the therapist included permission to laugh as an appropriate method to release tensions.

SESSION FOUR.   Each of the subsequent attempts to perform the task resulted in laughter. After the second attempt, Carolyn asked mother for permission to stay out extra late. Mother said "no" which Carolyn accepted without complaint. Furthermore, on the way to the session they had started to bicker about Carolyn's choice of clothes, but suddenly found themselves teasing and laughing which satisfied them. Therapy was terminated by mutual agreement in spite of the therapist's expressed reluctance. He suggested that it might be too soon to have any confidence in the results. In any case, he predicted that hassles around limits were likely to occur from time to time, which he reemphasized was perfectly normal. If the hassles persisted, they were urged to call. A phone contact six months later indicated that they still had normal disagreements, but seldom bickered in the old way. Carolyn had stopped shoplifting and was once again doing well in school.

CONCLUSION

The guidelines for transforming troublesome behaviors into playful behaviors help the therapist retain his focus on the systemic interaction pattern which surrounds and helps maintain the complaint pattern. Unlike a symptom prescription which is designed around one person's behavior, a systemic symptom prescription is designed to change the system itself. The *compliment* which precedes the task is designed to make any task as painless as possible, and the metaphorical task is designed to make the change even less painful. When effective, the metaphorical task redefines the serious complaint pattern into only one of the many options a family has for dealing with each other.

Not all metaphorical tasks have the potential for prompting laughter, but when it occurs the family is better off when there is a relapse. The situation cannot be seen as "quite as serious."

Families can accept such apparently absurd tasks when it is a metaphor for the real complaint pattern, and it is carefully designed so that it fits the family's unique manner of cooperating. Any sign from the family that they are rejecting the assignment means that the therapist has not found the family's way of cooperating, and therefore he should abort the planned intervention and end the session with just a series of complimentary statements. The interval between sessions can then be used to redesign the task.

REFERENCES NOT INCLUDED IN BIBLIOGRAPHY

Erickson, M. H., & Rossi, E. (1979). *Hypnotherapy: An exploratory casebook*. New York: Irvington.

Goffman, E. (1974). *Frame analysis: An essay on the organization of experience*. New York: Harper.

Selvini Palazzoli, M., Boscolo, L., Cecchin, G., & Prata, G. (1978). A ritualized prescription in family therapy: Odd days and even days. *Journal of Marriage and Family Counseling*, *4*, 3–9.

JEFFREY K. ZEIG

SYMPTOM PRESCRIPTION TECHNIQUES: CLINICAL APPLICATIONS USING ELEMENTS OF COMMUNICATION[*]

A disciple of Erickson, Zeig addresses the therapist's employment of symptom prescription as it may provoke clients to generate their own cure. In this excerpt the author considers various elements of a symptom complex (cognitive; affective, behavioral, etc.) with specific recommendations on how each of these components may be productively prescribed. Fundamental to Zeig's thesis is the notion that symptoms are communications. Thus, analyzing a

[*]From *American Journal of Clinical Hypnosis*, 1980, *23*, 23–33. (b) Reprinted with permission.

client's symptom in terms of its communicative elements can aid the therapist in determining an appropriate treatment strategy. Also included in this excerpt are five methods for increasing the possibility that a client will be responsive to the therapist's paradoxical directive—although Zeig allows as well for those occasions where client defiance of the therapist's recommendations may itself be curative.

In a companion paper, it was pointed out that the best use of the technique of symptom prescription follows from three principles of hypnosis and psychotherapy espoused by Milton H. Erickson. The three principles are: (1) meeting the patient within his frame of reference, (2) using the patient's behavior, motivations and understandings to make small therapeutic modifications, and (3) assisting the patient to establish change through his own resources and to his own credit (Zeig, 1980a). In line with this last principle, the companion paper stressed the Ericksonian notion that the patient has the resources in his personal history to make the changes that he desires from the therapy. Therefore, it is the task of the therapist to *elicit* the cure from within the patient. Through the use of symptom prescription, the patient can discover and demonstrate to himself that he can make the changes that he requests from the therapy.

The purpose of this paper is to elaborate on the use of symptom prescription technique based on Ericksonian principles of hypnosis and therapy. Where the companion paper presented a theoretical analysis and description, the present paper provides ideas for direct clinical application.

•   •   •

PRESCRIBING ELEMENTS OF THE SYMPTOM COMPLEX

On initial examination, constructing a symptom prescription for a particular patient seems to be easy and straightforward. For example, in using symptom prescription for a case of depression, the therapist might say to the patient, "I want you to be really depressed this week."

However, the symptom prescription can be quite complex, and does not need to be a one-line, overt directive to perform the presenting complaint (cf. Zeig, 1980a). Symptoms can be broken down into constituent elements, and then the therapist can choose certain elements to prescribe.

The Elements of Communication

Communications are a complex of eight elements: *contextual, relational, symbolic, behavioral, cognitive, affective, attitudinal* and *ambiguity*.

Communications occur in a particular and unique *context*. Each communication happens only once in a particular time and place. All communications have *relational* elements. Some implied statement about the ongoing relationship between the participants is always present in any communication. (The idea that communications include maneuvers involved in defining a relationship as complementary or symmetric has been well developed by communication analysts [e.g., Haley, 1963; Watzlawick, Beavin & Jackson, 1967]. Further, the use of symptomatic behavior in the process of defining and gaining control of a relationship has been addressed by both Szasz [1961] and Haley [1963].)

All communications contain *symbolic* representations. All words and many nonverbal gestures are symbolic in that they stand for something else. One of the characteristics that separates man from other animals is his well-developed and innate responsiveness to symbolic representations.

A communication consists of a *cognitive* element (thought content), an *affective* element (feeling tone) and concomitant *behaviors*. However, there is an additional element that adds to the complexity: one has *attitudes* about any element or set of elements in the communication. These attitudes consist of a new set of behaviors, feelings and thoughts.

There is one further element to any communication. Communications are *ambiguous*. Most communications (and practically all individual words) have multiple meanings. As such, communications can happen at levels that both the sender and receiver are not aware of consciously but to which they unconsciously respond. (*Ambiguity* is similar to *attitudes* in that it can be applied to other elements. Each of the other elements can be ambiguous as, for example, by virtue of not being fully specified. Thereby there can be ambiguity connected to any of the other seven elements.)

There are many different types of ambiguity. For example, there is a genetic and historical ambiguity to which therapists learn to respond. Therapists learn that patients say things on one level but mean things on another level. Therapists are trained to help patients decipher the real meaning of their ambiguous communication.

There are other types of ambiguity. One type of ambiguity has to do with the multiple meanings of words. For example, the word "forward" has a number of different meanings. Ambiguous multiple meanings of words are not often used in symptom prescription technique (although a case using this type of ambiguity in conjunction with symptom prescription will be cited in the second section of this paper).

Indirection is the type of ambiguity that is most often used in conjunction with symptom prescription. "Indirection" refers to the class of directives that are more covert and less fully specified. The patient then "projects" personal meaning into the response (the patient also has to put energy into the response in that the patient has to figure out the meaning of the communication). Directives can be more or less covertly specified, hence there are many forms of indirection.

•   •   •

The Symptom Complex

A symptom is a communication (e.g., see Szasz, 1961). Just as a communication can be divided into a number of component elements, so can a symptom. Assessing a symptom in terms of its elements can influence the choice of treatment strategy.

Therapeutic responses or directives (such as symptom prescriptions) can be composed to emphasize, address or alter any particular symptom element or set of elements. The examples below illustrate both the direct and indirect symptom prescription, but most are of the direct, or overt, type. These examples are all geared to a presenting problem of depression. Although these examples are hypothetical, this writer has used very similar forms in his clinical practice.

COGNITIVE. "There are certain thoughts, that you might not be aware of, that are part of your depression. I would like you to be depressed this week so that you can learn something about those thoughts. Make a list of these negative thoughts and bring them in to the next session."

AFFECTIVE. "You have told me that you feel sad much of the day, but you will probably agree that there are aspects of your sadness of which you are not aware. For example, you may not realize a possible pattern to your sad feeling. Therefore I would like you to keep track of how your sadness fluctuates during the day, and I would like you to make a graph of that information for me. I think it might be helpful."

BEHAVIORAL. "When you feel depressed you act differently. And there are a lot of things that you don't realize about your behavior. Now, I don't know if you can act or not but that doesn't really matter. Psychologists know that behavior effects feelings as much as feelings effect behavior. Therefore, I want you to act depressed with your body. Sit slumped, without making much eye contact with people, etc. I want you to act depressed with your body whenever you remember my instruction to do so. Keep track of how that affects your depression."

CONTEXTUAL. "This week, I would like you to take 20-minute periods, three times each day, perhaps after meals, to go into the garage and have the luxury of being alone. Sit there and experience the longest twenty minutes of compressed depression that you can image."

RELATIONAL.   "I don't want you to do anything about your depression yet, because your depression keeps your husband from experiencing his own depression, and I think that it's easier for you to be depressed than it is for him."

ATTITUDINAL.   "The problem is not just your depression. There are other things too. For example, I don't think that you have really examined your attitudes about your depression. So, this week, I want you to note in detail your thoughts and feelings about being depressed."

SYMBOLIC.   "I want you to go out and get a medium sized rock and paint it black. Carry it around with you for five days and return here in one week."

INDIRECT.

1.   "I would prefer that you didn't do anything this week about your problem, as you understand it."
2.   "One patient that I knew decided to get into his depression for one week to see if there was anything in all of that pain that he might find useful."

Choosing Elements for Symptom Prescription

It should be clear that there are many possible prescriptions and combinations of prescriptions that can be constructed for any particular symptom. In consideration of all of the categories listed above, is there any schema for deciding the correct prescription for a specific patient? In general, I think not. However, there are some guiding principles that one can use.

A symptom prescription is best when it is geared to the individual patient. Here, the diagnostic acumen of the clinician is of critical importance. If the therapist desires the patient to carry out the prescription explicitly, the clinician would do well to create a prescription that is in accord with the communication, values, expectations, style, motivations, etc. of the patient. Further, it is quite important that the therapist expect that the patient will in fact carry out the assignment (cf. Haley, 1973).

Techniques for Maximizing Patient Responsiveness

If the therapist's goal is to have the patient carry out the directive as presented, there are things that the therapist can do to maximize this possibility. The five principal possibilities are: (1) the use of a rationale, (2) the use of indirection, (3) the presentation of opportunities for the patient to reject some, but not all the directions, (4) utilization of patient curiosity, and (5) effectuation of small behavioral modifications through analysis of the patient's description of his symptoms.

The first technique, presenting a rationale, can be used to "corner" the patient and maximize the possibility that the patient will follow the directive. The reader might notice that many of the examples of symptom prescriptions provided above contain explicit rationales for doing the assignment. For example, it was suggested that the patient continue to be depressed in order to learn something about an aspect of his symptom. An additional rationale might be to suggest that the patient continue with his symptomatic behavior to keep a record of the behavioral pattern because the therapist needs concrete data. Of course, rationale should be individualized to the values and motivations of the particular patient.

The second technique, indirection, can also be used to increase the chance that the patient will carry out the assignment. (*Indirection*, as a form of ambiguity, "cuts across" the other seven elements. Any of the other seven elements can be prescribed more or less indirectly.) In general, the degree of indirection used is directly proportional to the amount of anticipated resistance. With a patient who indicates that he will neither follow the prescription nor rebel against it (and thereby act in a more asymptomatic manner), my tendency is to use more indirection in constructing the prescription. However, indirection has other uses in constructing the prescription. I have presented indirect symptom prescriptions to learn something about the patient's motivation to change and his level of responsiveness to my directions.

The third technique is to provide the patient with the opportunity to reject a part, but not all, of the prescription. The example given above of a contextually oriented symptom prescription was structured with this idea in mind. In response to this prescription, the patient could reject any of the conditions (such as the 20-minute time period, or going to the garage) and still carry out a contextual aspect of being depressed (and thereby gain some control of the symptomatic behavior).

There are other forms for providing the patient with a chance to select and/or reject a part of the prescription. For example, the patient could be directed to make a listing of either the thoughts or feelings (but not both) that surround the symptom. Further, two alternative prescriptions could be presented, one being a worse or more difficult alternative than the other. The patient could then be directed to pick whichever assignment seemed "best" to him. This general type of assignment is useful with a patient who values making independent choices and, therefore, does not respond to explicit directives.

The fourth technique for increasing responsiveness is to utilize curiosity. The patient's curiosity about therapy can be used to build responsiveness and increase motivation to do the task. I have suggested to some patients that at a later time in the session, when I deemed the timing to be right, I would present a directive that they might find useful. This procedure seeds an idea, stimulates curiosity, and enhances motivation to accept the task.

A fifth technique that I have found useful is analysis of the patient's description of his symptoms. When a patient presents a symptomatic problem, I ask him in a general and interested way to describe the symptom in great detail. I am especially interested in how the description compares with the eight elements that comprise any communication or symptom. I note which elements are stressed and which are deleted. For example, a patient may stress the feeling aspect of the symptom and ignore or delete the relational aspect.

I use this information about which elements of the symptom complex are emphasized and which are ignored by the patient to bring about small therapeutic modifications. I will use the information about which element is over- or under-emphasized to determine which element is of central meaning and importance to the patient. Generally, I will *avoid* prescribing that central element, at least initially. Instead, I will usually pick a peripheral aspect of the symptom complex and prescribe that first. The objective is to choose an aspect of the symptom that is more easily amenable to change and thereby get the patient to realize the smallest possible meaningful change.

By having the patient begin with small behavioral modifications, symptom prescription can be put to its optimal use. As noted in the companion paper (Zeig, 1980a), symptom prescription is best used to make the patient realize that he can influence his symptom and that he has the personal resources to deal with his problem (this latter realization need not be conscious). The point of symptom prescription is *not* to trick the patient out of his symptom. Although symptom prescription can be used to promote peripetia (e.g., Frankl, 1963), the best use is to promote progressive and gradual, patient-initiated change.

Additional Ideas for Use of Symptom Prescription

It is quite possible to present a symptom prescription assignment to a patient with the goal that the patient *not* carry out the assignment, and thereby behave in a more asymptomatic manner. Further, one can use prescriptions simply to "seed" the idea that the patient *can* exert some control over his symptomatic behavior. Additionally, as alluded to previously, response to a symptomatic prescription presents the therapist with diagnostic information. Moreover, the complaint that is presented is not necessarily the symptom that should be prescribed.

In dealing with a patient suffering from a chronic pain problem, I used two different symptom prescriptions in the initial session. This patient seemed to have a covert interest in proving that no technique (psychological or pharmacological) could be effective in influencing the amount of suffering that he experienced. (The situation was further complicated by the fact that litigation relating to his illness was still pending and he was "coerced" into treatment.)

I first used symptom prescription with two therapeutic goals in mind. I was interested in diagnosing his resistance and responsiveness and in demonstrating to him that he could influence the amount of perceived suffering. After getting a detailed description of his pain, I asked him to just sit back in the chair and concentrate on the pain that he was presently experiencing and report any changes (an indirect symptom prescription). The patient reported no change.

Subsequently, I gave him the homework assignment of making written predictions of how long he would be able to work on minor jobs around the house (such as tuning the car) before he was forced to stop due to pain. I asked him to make this record for me because I needed to have some baseline data to construct a treatment program. This specious rationale was used to increase the possibility that he would carry out the assignment.

One symptomatic part of this man's problem was that he anticipated pain. The anticipation of pain caused tension and anxiety which increased his suffering. Therefore, the complaint presented (pain) was not the only symptom to prescribe.

This case also shows how symptom prescription can be used for diagnostic purposes. One goal of the prescriptions was to learn something about how the patient would respond to my directives. Thereby I would learn something about his motivations and responsiveness. As the patient did not respond to either assignment, it was mutually agreed that the therapy would be postponed until the time that the litigation was completed.

REFERENCE NOT INCLUDED IN BIBLIOGRAPHY

Szasz, T. (1961). *The myth of mental illness*. New York: Hoeber-Harper.

LAWRENCE FISHER, ANN ANDERSON,
AND JAMES E. JONES

TYPES OF PARADOXICAL INTERVENTION AND INDICATIONS/CONTRAINDICATIONS FOR USE IN CLINICAL PRACTICE*

In this selection, Fisher et al. discuss therapeutic mechanisms of change in terms of symptom redefinition, symptom escalation and crisis induction, and symptom redirection. Examining how therapists may employ such paradoxical tactics to overcome difficult treatment impasses, the authors demonstrate these methods in the context of marital and family therapy. Further, relating specific patient/family characteristics to each of these methods, they suggest some useful guidelines for determining the most appropriate intervention strategy. While acknowledging the power of such tactics to effect dramatic change, the authors also take care to point out their associated risks. As many writers before them have stressed, it is essential that therapists fully understand the systemic function of the symptom before attempting, as it were, to "mediate" it out of existence. Moreover, it is essential to realize which therapy situations may call for other than a paradoxical orientation, and why. Additional cautions and contraindications are considered in the latter part of this essay; they warrant close scrutiny.

Working in a large, inpatient-outpatient teaching hospital, we found ourselves asked to consult with therapists who had run into therapeutic impasses with their patient families or individual patients. Working as a team, we observed and participated in several therapy sessions for each referral and then made a number of recommendations as to possible courses out of the impasse, using a paradoxical frame of reference.

•   •   •

. . . it became apparent that interventions based upon the paradox were those in which the therapist rechanneled the energy the family generated in an effort to maintain the symptom by: (a) redefining it by giving the behavior another meaning; (b) escalating it by promoting a crisis or increasing the frequency of its expression; or (c) redirecting it by changing an aspect of the symptom. It also became apparent that (a) insight was not required, although it often occurred as a spontaneous result of the technique; (b) symptom removal was not the initial goal because of the desire not to challenge the family's resistance; and (c) the therapist's behavior was

---

*From *Family Process*, 1981, *20*, 25–35. Reprinted with permission.

often unexpected and could not fit into the patient's existing cognitive or emotional structure.

These three strategies—redefinition, escalation and crisis induction, and redirection—plus the above three criteria were used as a theoretical formulation and as a map for therapeutic intervention. It became clear that our paradoxical stance would be maintained if we met the three criteria and utilized some form of one of the three strategies, given a particular therapeutic impasse in a particular family.

It should be kept in mind, however, that these strategies need to be viewed within the context of family dynamics and not as external "techniques" to be rigidly applied in the presence or absence of given criteria. These strategies can be helpful in thinking through a particular therapeutic impasse but only after a thorough knowledge of the family's dynamics has been obtained. More on this in a later section of this paper.

The classification of these strategies does not preclude a degree of playfulness or humor in their initiation or application. Often an idea for a paradoxical intervention seemed to emerge from the therapist as a kind of playful or even comic maneuver. A categorization of approaches, such as the one presented above, does not preclude such modes or styles of treatment; rather in our view it guides and channels them, assuring careful consideration of the dynamic picture presented by the family.

Also, it was recognized that often more than one of the three strategies might be used at the same time and that in some ways one therapeutic intervention contained aspects of more than one approach. Hence, these were seen only as rough guidelines, a kind of broadly based check sheet to assist in thinking through and deciding upon an approach to a given clinical situation. What follows is a definition of each strategy, a description of the kinds of presenting family characteristics particularly applicable to each approach (see Table 1), and a brief clinical example.

Redefinition

Redefinition is an attempt to alter the apparent meaning or interpretation the family places on the symptomatic behavior. For example, in a simple case a child's negative provocativeness can be seen as a temper tantrum, but in a particular kind of family setting it may also serve the purpose of uniting drifting parents. When such a redefinition of the "negative" behavior is identified and made public, its repeated occurrence is often made unnecessary. In this case, the symptom is then dropped by the "helpful" child.

This technique seems most appropriate with families possessing some capacity for reflection and insight, as opposed to action-oriented families.

Table 1.   Patient Characteristics Applicable to Three Types of Paradoxical Interventions

Reframing	Escalation or Crisis Induction	Redirection
Moderate resistance	Vague style	Individual settings
Non-oppositional	Super-verbal manipulation	Presenting problem with young child
Not short term	Oppositional	
Ability to reflect	Power struggle	Specific symptoms
Non-action-oriented	Marked resistance	Repetitive symptoms
Can handle frustration & uncertainty	Need to move quickly	Educational & guidance setting
	Potential for acting out	
Little or no severe impulsive or acting-out behavior	Excessively rigid	Family can respond to direction without undue sabotage
	Blocked with no area of compromise	
No pressing external problems	Adults competitive with therapist	Non-oppositional
Rigid family structure		Overly compliant
Repeated crises—not severe		

Suitable families need to have the capacity to handle frustration for reasonable periods without acting out or without impulsive displays. Such families may present with repeated moderate family crises but without the kinds of problems requiring immediate and direct action. Often these families have relatively rigid structures, and their resistance to change is judged as moderate without the occurrence of overt, hostile, oppositional behavior. In essence, families that seem most open to reframing techniques are those that can, at the minimum, reflect upon the therapist's attempts to redefine the symptom, and whose problems permit some time for the process to occur. Also, their resistance and view of the therapist are such that power struggles between patients and therapist and other forms of oppositional behavior do not dominate the situation.

An example of the use of redefinition occurred in the G family. This family was referred by a local pediatrician and came with the chief complaint that the oldest child's seizure disorder was causing family problems. Living in the house at the time were mother, father, identified patient Paula (age 11), sister (age 9), brother (age 5), and father's mother, who had come to live with them following her husband's death. In the sessions, there was little discussion of mother's family, who lived in California. Mother was one of two children; her brother, two years older than she, was living in California near their parents. It was as if Mrs. G had been absorbed into Mr. G's family when they were married and had no further contact with her own family.

Mr. G was a successful business executive who worked long hours and traveled to some extent. Mrs. G did not work outside the home. She spent a great portion of her time involved with Paula's problem, chauffeuring the children, and carrying out many of the tasks expected of her as the wife of a successful business executive.

Paula, the identified patient, looked younger than her stated age, had short hair, and was dressed in jeans and a tee shirt. She was described by parents as having a very complex and at times medically uncontrolled seizure disorder and was also intellectually retarded. At the initial session, her sister, younger by two years, looked older than her stated age, sat with her parents, listened to the conversation, combed her hair, and in general was quite preoccupied with her appearance. Paula, on the other hand, played with her 5-year-old brother.

In the first interview the discussion centered around Paula and her grand mal seizures, which were occurring at a rate of about one or two per week and seemed in many ways correlated with the level of tension in the home. Most of the family's time was spent either in responding to the seizure itself or in seeking professional help around the problem. The family had already had a great deal of professional help around the physical problem and were now seeking help around the resultant family problem. Gradually the discussion left the children and the seizure disorder and focused on the parents, with grandmother correctly perceiving that there were conflicts between husband and wife around the management of the home in general. Grandmother's self-defined position was to side with the wife as she felt her role in the family was to keep the wife's spirits up in light of Mr. G's critical attitudes.

In this, as in all families, it was quite important to discover the homeostatic rules of the family: the rules necessary for the system to maintain its equilibrium. In this case it appeared that the women, mother and grandmother, were responsible for maintaining a "well-run house." Father was excused from this because of the demands of filling an upper management job; the expectation was that the house should be quiet and comfortable when he returned home. He was not called in until things were out of control, usually related to Paula's behavior, and then was criticized by the family for being too harsh in his interventions. One method of intervention chosen by the therapists was redefinition. In this way, the system by which the family functioned was able to be maintained, although redefined in a more positive light. Father was defined and overtly labeled the "real manager" of the house (as he was in his business) and was given the job of directing how things should be done at home, as it was evident that he had very clear ideas of how the house should be managed in order to provide him with peace and quiet. The women could still maintain their control over running the house by carrying out father's directions. Rather than devaluing father for being too harsh, he was vigorously applauded for his managerial service to the family, which took a great deal of responsibility off the women's shoulders and also kept the system functioning. "Unfortunately," this relabeling brought to light the real underlying family structure, and although father liked the control he held as manager, he was not sure he could handle the responsibility.

As with the other examples that will be presented, redefinition was only one part of the therapy with this family. There were other tasks related to increasing the closeness between the couple and tasks related to altering family responses to Paula's seizure activity. But redefinition of the problem from the family's responses to Paula's seizures to a problem of family management under the direction of an unwilling executive "expert" presented the family with a task couched in different terms from their original conception. As can be seen in this example, the redefinition was incorporated into a knowledge of the family's dynamics and explained in terms of the family's idiosyncratic language, e.g., the business manager and the family manager.

Escalation

Two broad types of symptom escalation methods have been used. The first is similar in practice to early techniques based on the learning theory principle of massed practice. For example, facial tics can be placed under voluntary control in given settings by prescribing their massed occurrence several times a day. This approach takes the response out of the realm of unconscious control.

A couple in their late fifties came for treatment because the husband was ruminating about his physical ills and was depressed. His "illness" threatened to call a halt to a long-planned trip to Florida, and his wife was both concerned and disappointed. These symptoms came during the first year of his retirement from an active, successful career in insurance. His adjustment to retirement had been difficult because of the couple's lack of friends and interests outside the family. His favorite daughter, who was currently experiencing marital problems, was extremely concerned about her father's health; she visited daily and telephoned several times each day to learn of his condition. Attempts at gaining a better understanding of the dynamics of the symptom through other methods failed, and it was difficult getting the topic of conversation away from the husband's aches and pains and his dramatic requests for a cure. After several sessions, it became clear that the symptom served the function for both husband and wife of maintaining a rather enmeshed and family-based way of life. The husband's retirement caused a removal of the major extrafamilial activity for both spouses. The symptom filled the void by channeling the family's (including daughter's) energies toward "family" matters and prevented the couple from developing new, extrafamilial contacts, which the Florida trip would certainly entail.

With all of this in mind, the husband was instructed to spend the next two days in one room dressed in pajamas and bathrobe preparing a log of his every thought and physical problem. He was also to record his blood pressure and heart rate at 15-minute intervals and to report to the "doctor" twice daily. This was to "increase" his depression so as to enable us to study it as well as to gather more data in an effort to understand his physical problems more clearly. Mother and daughter were to help in this two-day effort by not allowing him to talk with them, by leaving him isolated in the bedroom, and by setting a tray with his meals outside his door without conversation so that "he could concentrate more effectively." Although this task was difficult, all parties succeeded. The technique here was to escalate the symptom as well as to redefine an aspect of the symptom by legitimizing it for purposes of the "doctor's cure." Needless to say, the husband became "sick" of his task and went to Florida instead. Again, the prescription for change was seen within the dynamics of the family and not as an isolated technique to be used regardless of setting.

The second type of symptom escalation aims at increasing in intensity or frequency certain aspects of a clinical situation by provoking a crisis. At times the patient or family is forced to deal with the feared situation, but in all cases the crisis undermines a rigid family defense and forces a decision or some kind of action.

An illustrative family in which this technique was used included a 42-year-old successful father who was a member of a suburban school board and active in the local Catholic church, a 40-year-old mother who managed the home and worked part-time in a retail children's clothing store, and four children: a boy age 18; Betty, the identified patient, age 16; and a girl and boy, ages 14 and 11, respectively. Betty was referred because management problems both at home and at school had escalated to the point that the school threatened suspension because of skipping classes and parental attempts at discipline were failing.

Betty had become pregnant 16 months previously and had given the baby up for adoption because of parental pressure. Although from time to time Betty agreed that this decision was wise, she claimed she really had no say in the matter, and both she and her mother were having difficulty working through the loss. The other family members, however, described the family as happy and congenial except for the tension caused by Betty's flagrant violation of parental demands.

Father, a successful corporation executive, was used to having his way, although his wife frequently stood up to him precipitating a full-scale battle whenever she pushed an issue. With Betty, however, he felt threatened and was enraged at her lack of compliance, threatening her possible removal from the home if her behavior did not improve. Mother reluctantly agreed. The therapists believed that mother was covertly encouraging Betty's negative behavior because of her own unresolved and unexpressed anger at her husband regarding the decision to give the baby up for adoption. Somehow she believed father was to blame for the entire episode.

In treatment, all efforts at sidetracking, redefining, supporting, and interpreting failed, and Betty's negative behavior increased with mother's subtle encouragement. The therapists, feeling somewhat paralyzed by father's attacking style and by their reluctance to take sides, decided to provoke a crisis by permitting the negative behavior to escalate to some crucial event and then to suggest that father was right all along, that the situation was untenable, and that perhaps Betty should be removed from the home. When Betty stayed out all night with a "friend" without her parents knowing her whereabouts, the therapists decided the time was ripe and the crisis was provoked. The family was covertly shocked but overtly in agreement, and they were sent home with lists of foster placements, residential schools, etc. Needless to say, they returned a week later reporting literally hours of family discussions, a markedly reduced level of family tension, and a decision to keep the family intact. In this example, the locked battle between father and mother on the one hand and Betty and father on the other was undermined by provoking a family crisis in order to force a realignment of positions and permit options for action within the family.

These techniques seem most applicable when family resistance is extreme, some form of oppositional behavior is present, and the family has successfully walled off all areas of compromise and problem-solving. By admitting defeat or escalating to the point of crisis, the therapist gains an upper hand in short-circuiting vague complaints, circumventing paralyzing resistance, or outmaneuvering the superverbal and overly logical family. This "end-running" tactic is often successful with excessively rigid, domineering, or autocratic families in which battles for control potentially undermine successful outcome.

Of particular concern, however, is the issue of timing. Crisis induction, in particular, requires careful planning as well as a series of frustrating sessions in which every attempt is made to use other, less stressful techniques. If the technique is applied too early, it will fail because of a lack of sufficient tension built up from previous failures at change. If applied too late, the family may have left treatment or given up, or an external crisis of more serious magnitude may have developed. In general, then, this technique seems most applicable with families that are excessively rigid, resistant, and highly skilled at being vague or overly explanatory in an effort to prevent change.

Redirection

This technique is similar in some ways to symptom escalation, in that both attempt to place the symptom under voluntary control. Whereas in escalation the symptom is removed by satiation under massed display or by provoking a crisis, in redirection the circumstances under which the symptom is to occur are prescribed, although the frequency is not necessarily altered. Redirection, like the other techniques, is applicable in both individual and family treatment, provided that knowledge of the family system is integrated into the conceptualization of the symptom.

A form of redirection was helpful in working with a hospitalized 45-year-old woman of Dutch origin with numerous physical complaints bordering on somatic delusion—e.g., "I feel as if there is a hole in my esophagus through which food escapes into my insides." She had had five hospitalizations over the previous nine years, each time carrying the diagnosis of schizophrenia. Her 19-year-old son was currently being prosecuted for check forgery following a six-year history of continual scrapes with the law. Her 21-year-old daughter, a well-functioning woman who was her father's pride, had just married two months earlier. The identified patient's husband, a competent supervisor of highly skilled mechanics, was finding it increasingly difficult to ignore his wife's continuous physical complaints. In family sessions it became apparent that she began ruminating about her body whenever angry exchanges between family members threatened to break out. Her husband had longstanding resentments about the restrictions on their social lives caused by her physical problems. The wife had major unexpressed disappointments with her husband going back to, among other things, his unresponsiveness eleven years earlier when she miscarried an intensely anticipated baby. It seemed that anger between them over these disappointments threatened the only emotionally supportive relationship for each of these two middle-aged people who were isolated from their families of origin in Holland. On the inpatient unit the woman quickly established a pattern of complaining to staff about her symptoms.

Redirection was used with the intent to clear the field for the very difficult marital and life problems to be approached. On the unit, staff were instructed to listen to her talk about symptoms for only ten minutes every evening at 10:00 P.M., and she was instructed to approach staff at that time even if she felt no urge.

In the family sessions, symptom talk was deferred until the last five minutes, and the family negotiated together a time for symptom talk during her visits home. Simultaneously, the family sessions supported the very difficult work of their hearing each other's anger and disappointment. As expected, the intensity of her symptoms subsided, both in terms of amount of talk and of her subjective experience of the symptoms.

Clearly, in this case, the paradoxical maneuver was only one part of what can be seen as the difficult treatment of a severe marital problem. In addition, this particular kind of intervention required, in part, the family's willingness to comply with the therapists' directives for symptom talk both during the sessions and at home.

This technique is appropriate when resistance is low, when little oppositional behavior exists, and when the family can follow through on directives without undue sabotage.

CONTRAINDICATIONS

Paradoxical techniques, while powerful in many settings, can be equally harmful if misapplied. These techniques deal directly with other fundamental family defenses and when ineptly applied can lead to a flight from treatment or to more severe crises. In fact, we suggest that of all the therapeutic interventions we have tried in clinical or consulting settings, paradoxical interventions constitute the highest risk for subsequent noshow appointments and premature terminations. This demonstrates their power, but it also indicates the need to apply these interventions carefully, in a skillful and well-timed manner, with families, couples, and individuals with whom the risk of negative outcome is small.

There are several kinds of families with which the use of paradoxical techniques as a major therapeutic modality is ill advised. Paradoxical techniques seem least applicable in *chaotic families* (Fisher, 1977), with loose and variable structures. In such families, it is often difficult to gain hold of a concrete issue to work on, and the aim of therapy may be the establishment of some kind of internal cohesion and stability rather than on eliminating particularly troublesome behaviors. Often paradoxical ploys are used to undermine powerful family coalitions aimed at resisting change. In chaotic and poorly organized families, however, there are insufficient positive and negative collusions and alliances to begin with, making these techniques inappropriate. The use of the paradox may be appropriate at later stages of intervention when some semblance of internal structure becomes stabilized and the focus shifts to other directions.

Similarly, paradoxical maneuvers are not appropriate with *childlike families* (Fisher, 1977), in which all members, including adults, tend to function on an immature level seeking parenting from the therapist. Such systems are again too loose and lack sufficient cohesiveness and unity of purpose for a paradoxical ploy to be effective. Often such families see the intervention as another rejection from a parental figure, and their need for parenting either leads to a search for a new mother or father or to an unproductive rebellion against the therapist, thereby compounding the problem.

Some kinds of *impulsive families* (Fisher, 1977), families with members who overtly express conflict in the community or at home in a socially undesirable or potentially harmful manner, are also inappropriate for paradoxical intervention. In this case, careful consideration of such techniques as escalation needs to occur in order to prevent potential harm. For example, depressive or aggressive symptoms should not be exaggerated in families in which the risk of suicide or physical harm to self or others is a real possibility. Yet in other families in which the same style is present but the degree of symptom expression is less, these techniques may be highly appropriate to force the family into action. Again, careful clinical judgment should prevail.

Insight-oriented, structural, or other kinds of interpretive techniques may be more helpful in stimulating growth than paradoxical techniques in families that are already demonstrating solid therapeutic movement. Paradoxical ploys are also inappropriate in families seeking therapy to resolve specific developmental or situational crises in which support, information, or guidance seem more appropriate. These are families that have the resources to manage the presenting difficulty but need a setting in which to work issues through or professional support and direction in solving their own problems.

Last, these techniques seem little suited to families that accept responsibility for their own behavior, in which therapeutic interventions are accepted at face value with minimal oppositional or negative behaviors, or in which control of therapy in terms of course and direction are well agreed upon and remain an unconflicted area of interaction. In general then, paradoxical procedures are contraindicated when marked resistance, power struggles, and oppositional behavior are minimally present, when family structure is so disorganized that family solidarity is minimal, or when a potential for sharp escalation of symptoms or other severe forms of acting-out behavior with strongly negative consequences is possible.

CONCLUSIONS

Other than their use by well-known (Selvini Palazzoli, Boscolo, Cecchin, & Prata, 1980) and often charismatic figures, little has been written about the planning and implementation of paradoxical procedures in everyday clinical practice. In our view, this has led to frequent misuse of these potentially powerful procedures, which often are employed as excuses for lack of skill or insufficient diagnostic study. What is clearly needed, given this situation, is more detailed study of the kinds of clinical situations that are most open to their use as well as to potential negative effects.

In our experience, the failure of a paradoxical intervention is most usually due to a lack of understanding of the dynamics of the family. Frequently, a therapist will come up with a spur-of-the-moment ploy, an off-hand idea based upon limited data. Although even the most bizarre of ideas often have merit in their absurdity, we found it necessary to set up two primary cautions about our interventions in order to reduce the chance of failure or a more serious outcome, premature termination. First, we agreed that all paradoxical interventions should be discussed with the consulting group prior to initiation. Such a consultation insured a carefully thought-through intervention by opening the case up to group scrutiny. In addition, the group was able to assist in maintaining a paradoxical set by assuring that systems dynamics were being properly considered, and by preventing regression to more linear modes of thinking, as often happens in solo practice.

Second, paradoxical interventions require a clear understanding of the family's symptom and the role the symptom plays in the life of the family. Each family member's stake in the maintenance of the symptom needs to be understood in detail from an individual as well as from a systems perspective. As such, our team agreed upon the necessity of a complete family evaluation prior to initiation of the intervention. Such an agreement reduced the chances of impulsive and therapeutic ploys that have little chance of success, not because they spontaneously arise from the clinical situation, but because often they are not carefully thought through. We learned again and again that the effective use of a paradoxical intervention requires a thorough knowledge of the family as a dynamic system.

Unlike many other types of therapeutic interventions, the approaches under discussion here require a change of set, an ability to look at what is clinically presented with a new pair of glasses, and an ability to deal effectively with the absurd, often with humor. It is quite apparent that not every therapist is suited to this kind of work in terms of style and general personality. Of all the methods of intervention we have utilized in the course of clinical experience and training, we have found no other in which such stylistic issues play such a powerful role. For example, there are some trainees who simply cannot carry off the interventions in a meaningful and convincing manner. Their physical presence, appearance, and way of relating preclude an effective intervention and sharply reduce their ability as clinical change agents using this technique. While of concern in other modalities of therapy as well, this issue appears crucial in paradoxical work. Therefore, we have found it necessary to thoroughly think through whether or not a recommendation for the use of a paradoxical technique will be productive given the personality and style of the therapist, whether trainee or staff. There is little question that therapist variables play a powerful role in the success or failure of these techniques.

As a side note in this regard, we have found a particular lack of success in teaching paradoxical techniques to very young or inexperienced therapists. Somehow they have noticeable difficulty in carrying off the intervention, even with group consultation and support. Two reasons come to mind for our first-year trainees' singular lack of success in this area. First, as mentioned above, these techniques require a finely tuned sense of timing as well as a degree of patience. New and inexperienced therapists often need continual exposure to patients over time to develop this skill; consequently, training in paradoxical formats may be best postponed to later in their training. Second, paradoxical strategies often deal with rigid family defenses that frequently lead to therapeutic impasses and binds. We have found that novice therapists do not have the first-hand experience of wrestling with the impasse, of experiencing the paralysis of a resistive family, and of developing a gut reaction to the family's desire to entrap the change agent and render him powerless. Such experience takes time to develop, and pushing young therapists into the use of paradoxical strategies in our experience often leads to the use of "cookbook" modes of intervention without the conceptual and experiential understanding of the therapeutic wrestling match.

Our experience with paradoxical techniques has in general been positive and successful when incorporated both in broad clinical practice and in training activities in which a number of approaches were utilized, depending upon the problem at hand. Although the paradoxical bandwagon has many "avant-garde" therapists jumping aboard, our experience indicates that the techniques are effective when, like all intervention strategies, they are well thought through and appropriately applied.

REFERENCES NOT INCLUDED IN BIBLIOGRAPHY

Fisher, L. (1977). On the classification of families: A progress report. *Archives of General Psychiatry, 34,* 424-433.

Selvini Palazzoli, M., Boscolo, L., Cecchin, G., & Prata, G. (1980). Hypothesizing-circularity-neutrality: Three guidelines for the conductor of the session. *Family Process, 19,* 3–12. (Editor's Note: Contrary to the authors' assertion, this particular article does not deal with paradoxical procedures but with systemic interviewing techniques in family treatment.)

MICHAEL ROHRBAUGH, HOWARD TENNEN,
SAMUEL PRESS, AND LARRY WHITE

COMPLIANCE, DEFIANCE, AND THERAPEUTIC PARADOX: GUIDELINES FOR STRATEGIC USE OF PARADOXICAL INTERVENTIONS*

The paradoxical tactics of prescribing, restraining, and positioning are here exemplified in the context of brief, problem-oriented treatment. The most originative aspect of this piece is undoubtedly in its compliance-defiance model, which involves the therapist's choosing a paradoxical intervention— or better, "mode"—on the basis of the client's demonstrated attitude both toward his symptom and treatment. Considering the perceived freedom of the symptom to the patient, as well as the social-psychological concept of reactance potential, Rohrbaugh et al. present a fourfold categorization of therapy situations. The therapist, by correctly assessing the clinical situation confronting him, may thereby be guided not only about the general suitability of a paradoxical approach but also about which specific paradoxical intervention best fits this situation. Fundamentally a "how to" article, this selection should help practitioners develop greater assurance in determining the paradoxical strategy most likely to have a positive influence on a given client or family.

PRESCRIBING, RESTRAINING, AND POSITIONING

We began our study of paradoxical interventions by attempting to define what therapists actually *do* when they apply these tactics. We tentatively concluded that a useful classification scheme might include prescribing, restraining, and positioning operations. When using a paradoxical *prescribing* strategy, the therapist encourages or instructs someone to engage in the specific piece of behavior to be eliminated. For example, a patient may be asked to practice an obsessional thought or bring on an anxiety attack, a rebellious adolescent may be encouraged to rebel, or an overinvolved mother to be more protective of her child.

When *restraining*, the therapist discourages change and may even deny that change is possible. *Soft* restraining embodies the message: "You probably shouldn't change." For example, the therapist may tell the patient to "go slow" or worry with the patient about possible dangers of improvement. *Hard* restraining is defined by the message: "You probably *can't* change." The therapist mobilizes resistance by benevolently suggesting that change may not be feasible. Restraining strategies have been described most explicitly by Haley (1973, 1976) and by Fisch, Weakland,

---

*Reprinted, with permission, from *American Journal of Orthopsychiatry*, 1981, *51*, 454–467, Copyright 1981 by the American Orthopsychiatric Association, Inc.

Watzlawick, and the Palo Alto group (Watzlawick et al., 1967, 1974).

Paradoxical positioning is also exemplified in the work of the Palo Alto group. Here, the therapist attempts to shift a problematic "position"—usually an assertion that an individual (the identified patient or a significant other) is making about himself or his problem—by accepting and exaggerating that position. This intervention is used when the person's position is assessed to be maintained by a complementary or opposite response by others. For example, when a patient's pessimism is reinforced or maintained by an optimistic or encouraging response from significant others, the therapist may "outdo" the patient's pessimism by defining the situation as even more dismal than the patient had originally held it to be. In this sense, positioning is operationally similar to what Greenberg (1973) has called an "anti-expectation" technique.

RATIONALES FOR PARADOX:
COMPLIANCE AND DEFIANCE

The model outlined is based on the idea that there are two fundamentally different rationales for using therapeutic paradox. Some paradoxical interventions are effective because the patient attempts to comply with the therapist's directive. These are called *compliance-based* strategies. Others work because the patient rebels against the therapist's influence attempt. These will be called *defiance-based* strategies.

Compliance-based strategies follow from the premise that by attempting to comply with a paradoxical prescription to act symptomatically, the patient will change. The main principle here is that the very attempt to comply with the therapist's request interrupts or short-circuits the process that perpetuates the problem. Compliance-based paradoxical interventions of this type are most likely to work with symptoms such as obsessions, anxiety attacks, and various somatic complaints that are maintained to some extent by the patient's attempts to stave them off. By attempting to bring on such a symptom deliberately, one cannot continue in usual ways of trying to prevent it, and under these conditions the symptom often dissolves or comes more under voluntary control.

Defiance-based strategies are used with the expectation that the patient will rebel or react against a suggestion or directive. In contrast to those directives that the therapist expects patients to follow, this type of paradoxical intervention is meant to influence the patient to change by rebelling. Haley (1976), who has probably written most about what we are calling defiance-based strategies, suggested that a strategic therapist, approaching an overprotective mother of a symptomatic child, might

. . . ask for more extreme behavior than the mother has been showing. For example, she should not only hover over the child, but she should also set aside a definite time to spend a whole hour warning the child about all the dangers in life (an hour is a long time). Or the therapist should take some other aspect of her behavior and make it more extreme. If this approach is done well, the mother will react by rebelling against the therapist and hovering over the child less. She will not like to do it. (pp. 70–71)*

Positioning tactics and certain of the restraining strategies are also defiance-based. There are times, for example, when a therapist might predict that change will not be possible, or that the patient's continued efforts to change will only be futile. This "hard restraining" approach has been discussed by the Palo Alto group under the rubric of "utilizing resistance" (Watzlawick et al., 1974).

THE RELEVANCE OF REACTANCE

J. W. Brehm's social-psychological *reactance theory* offers a framework for understanding how and when to use compliance-based and defiance-based interventions. The main tenet of reactance theory is that a person will experience "psychological reactance," a desire to avoid being subject to any directive that threatens to eliminate the individual's "free behavior." Reactance arousal is conceptualized as a motivational state directed toward the restoration of threatened freedoms. Whenever a therapist offers suggestions, assigns tasks, or in other ways attempts directly to influence a client, the therapist runs the risk of threatening behavioral freedoms and arousing reactance, thus increasing the likelihood of non-compliance or rebellion (S. Brehm, 1976). Although reactance effects are usually to be avoided, the defiance-based paradoxical interventions offer a means by which the therapist can *use* reactance in the service of therapeutic change.

Two assessment parameters, each related to reactance theory, are helpful in guiding the choice of intervention: One concerns the relational stance, vis a vis the therapist, of the person (or persons) to be influenced at any given time—specifically, whether there exists a high or low potential for reactance and subsequent rebellion/defiance in response to the therapist's suggestions and directions. The second parameter concerns the

---

*This example is open to the interpretation that the effectiveness of such an intervention is based more on compliance than defiance. If the mother initially tries to do what the therapist says and later rebels, she may be reacting more against the odiousness of the task itself than against the therapist's attempt to influence her (or the accompanying threat to her behavioral freedom).

specific target behavior that is to be changed or influenced—whether or not it is defined by the person to be influenced (not necessarily the identified patient or problem bearer) as "free," or under volitional control. In general, defiance-based interventions are used when the probability of reactance is high and the target behavior is perceived as free. Compliance-based paradoxical strategies are most helpful with unfree or bound target behavior, usually symptoms maintained by attempts to stave them off, and are most readily implemented when reactance potential is low.

Our main thesis concerning compliance and defiance-based paradoxical strategies is that they should be treated as separate intervention modes. The distinction is not merely conceptual, but pragmatic: In order to enhance the power of a given intervention, it is important for the therapist to decide when paradox is being used with the expectation of compliance, and when it is being used with the expectation of defiance. With compliance-based strategies, the therapist takes steps to maximize the likelihood of compliance; with defiance-based strategies, the therapist tries to maximize rebellion. S. Brehm, (1976) suggested several ways in which a therapist can reduce reactance by avoiding threats to behavioral freedoms. But probably the most powerful way to regulate compliance and defiance is to frame interventions in a manner consistent (*or* inconsistent) with the patient's own "language" or construct system. Following Erickson's (Haley, 1973) principle of accepting and using what the patient offers (in a manner analogous to psychological judo), the assumption here is that people are most likely to accept those new ideas or prescriptions for new behavior that begin in and represent extensions or variations of their own views (Watzlawick, 1978; Watzlawick et al., 1974; Weakland et al., 1974). In terms of reactance theory, using language in this manner provides a powerful way to regulate threats to behavioral freedoms, and hence minimize reactance arousal—for example, by suggesting that a patient do such and such because to do so would be a natural extension of the patient's *own* views, not those of the therapist. By contrast, when interventions are based on a defiance rationale, the converse applies: The therapist deliberately frames the directive or suggestion in a manner incongruous with the way in which the patient would prefer to see himself. For example, the therapist might tell a patient who sees himself as "all man" that he should continue to belittle his wife because to do so would help others appreciate his sensitive, emotional side. Putting it this way would presumably make him less likely to comply.

The compliance-defiance model, as outlined to this point, says more about *how* people can be influenced than about *where* (or at what level) the therapist should attempt to intervene. Before exploring clinical applications in greater detail, we will briefly describe a broader theoretical context in which the model can be applied.

WHERE TO INTERVENE: THE PALO ALTO
BRIEF THERAPY MODEL

The Palo Alto therapy approach (Watzlawick et al., 1974; Weakland et al., 1974) is brief (usually less than ten sessions), symptom-oriented, and applicable to families as well as individuals. A basic assumption is that problems arise from the mishandling of everyday difficulties and are maintained by *current* behavior of the problem bearer and those with whom he interacts. In this framework, problems are maintained primarily by the "solutions" that people apply to them. The task of therapy is to interdict the problem-maintaining solutions, or prevent them from being applied, and, in so doing, pave the way for change.

The problem-maintaining-solution principle is relevant to intrapersonal problems, where the problem-bearer misapplies solutions, as well as to more interpersonal ones, such as occur in families, where solutions are misapplied by others. For example, insomnia is a common human difficulty, but usually becomes a problem only when one identifies it as such and develops a set of rituals and techniques for getting to sleep. Since falling asleep, by its very nature, is a spontaneous event, the solution of *trying* to go to sleep serves only to maintain the insomnia. The task of the therapist is to block this "solution," which can best be done by directing the patient to try to stay awake. At other times, trying *not* to do something is the basis of symptom maintenance. Worrying about having anxiety attacks, watching for their beginning signs, or avoiding circumstances in which attacks have occurred in the past usually has something to do with bringing them on. Here, the therapist would try to block the problem-maintaining solution of "trying not to"—which can best be done with a paradoxical prescription to try to experience the symptom.

Problems are also maintained by the well-intentioned "solutions" of significant others. Appropriate grieving, for example, may inappropriately persist because family members repeatedly offer reassurances, encourage the mourner to "cheer up," or try to convince the person that things are not as bad as they seem. Similarly, attempts to reason a suspicious or paranoid person away from mistaken beliefs may only serve to make this individual more suspicious. In therapy, interrupting such "solutions" by getting others to do *less* of the same can be an important step toward problem resolution. This can, but certainly need not, be done paradoxically.

Whether to intervene in the intrapersonal or interpersonal system depends on the nature of the problem, and, more importantly, on the therapist's assessment of what is maintaining it. Thus, for an obsessional patient who repeatedly asks for reassurance, the "problem" can be seen as maintained both by what the patient is doing—trying not to think the intrusive thought—and by what the concerned spouse or parent is doing—offering reassurance. The therapist's intervention could be targeted at either solution or both—and either or both of these interventions could be paradoxical. For the obsessive individual, the therapist might offer a compliance-based symptom prescription—or if reactance potential is high, a defiance-based paradoxical strategy such as hard restraining. For the "free" problem-maintaining behavior of the parent or spouse, the therapist might prescribe even more reassurance.

PRAGMATICS OF PARADOX: GUIDELINES FOR APPLICATION

Depending on how a problem is maintained, paradoxical strategies might be used with a variety of complaints, including depression, insomnia, obsessions, panic attacks, family fights, problems in child-rearing, sexual difficulties, marital conflicts, habit disturbances, inadequate social skills, study problems, phobias, headaches, public speaking anxiety, and even psychotic states. In many of these situations, prescribing the symptom, restraining the patient from changing, or taking his view of the problem and exaggerating it can be an efficacious approach to symptom removal. When reactance potential is high, particularly with individuals who seem oriented toward defeating helpers, paradoxical influence techniques might be considered as the first line of approach.

Paradoxical strategies seem to be least applicable in situations of crisis or extreme instability (e.g., acute decompensation or acute grief reactions). Here, patients are usually more amenable to direct influence attempts, and can best be helped by the therapist's offering structure, taking control, or in other ways stabilizing the situation (Caplan, 1964). Needless to say, defiance-based paradox would be especially inappropriate in these cases. On the other hand, there are many situations where crisis *itself* becomes part of a stable pattern—and here, paradoxical interventions can be quite helpful.

With this brief therapy model as a context, let us now return to the reactance theory parameters relevant to applying the compliance and defiance-based influence techniques. The two parameters are: 1) the reactance potential of the persons to be influenced, i.e., the probability that they will resist or defy the therapist's influence attempts at a given point in time; and 2) their perception of the "freedom" of the symptom, or of the freedom of the specific target behavior that the therapist hopes to influence.

By *reactance potential* we mean the assessed probability that the person to be influenced will resist or defy the therapist's suggestions or directives at a given point in time. Ideally, this probability would take into account the importance of the specific type of behavior (freedom) that will be threat-ened. Such specificity is often difficult in practice, however, and we com-monly think in more general terms about the patient's propensity to defy *any* attempts at influence. The "given-point-in-time" aspect of the defini-tion emphasizes that reactance potential is not a static phenomenon. The probability of reactance can and often does change through the course of therapy. S. Brehm (1976) suggested it may be greatest in the first few sessions.

For many people, the potential for reactance seems to have trait qualities (i.e., they tend to defy influence attempts consistently, both across situa-tions and across behaviors). It is more precise, however, to think of reactance potential as a person-in-situation phenomenon that changes through the course of therapy, and is greater for some types of behavior (e.g., very important ones) than others. Ultimately, assessment of reactance potential is an empirical issue: The question is whether the patient will accept and comply with the therapist's suggestions and directives—and the answer usually becomes readily apparent in the course of therapy. We often assign tasks fairly early in treatment, if for no other reason than to see if the patient will carry them out. The therapist might simply ask the patient to monitor or record some aspect of the problem during the coming week. If the patient forgets, does it haphazardly, or in some other way fails to comply, we infer that the patient may respond in a similar manner to future directives. In the course of therapy, one might also find that the patient fairly consistently takes a position that is complementary or opposed to the view being advo-cated by the therapist. The crucial dimension of reactance potential, how-ever, is usually behavioral. Whether the patient actually *does* what is pre-scribed is more important than whether the patient acknowledges that the suggestion was a good one.

Assessment of the second parameter, perceived freedom, is important because it guides the therapist's choice of target behavior and intervention modes. Although the symptom or problem itself is usually defined as bound (unfree), the therapist might work toward changing it by focusing interventions on free collateral behavior of the problem bearer, *or* on problem-maintaining free behavior of significant others. Designation of a target behavior as "free" depends simply on whether the patient perceives it as such—whether the patient defines it as something that can be done voluntarily, either now or in the future. This subjective definition makes clinical assessment of perceived freedom rather straightforward—one can simply ask the patient or, better, read his "language."

When combined, the reactance-potential and freedom-of-target-behavior parameters suggest four idealized treatment situations, as shown in Table 1. Most compliance-based paradoxical interventions fall in Quadrant 4, where

Table 1.   Assessment Parameters for Using Compliance- and
Defiance-Based Paradoxical Strategies

Reactance Potential	Perceived Freedom of "Target" Behavior	
	Free	Unfree
High	1	3
Low	2	4

the target behavior (usually the symptom itself) is unfree and the potential for defiance is low. Defiance-based paradoxical strategies are used with high reactance potential and free target behavior—the conditions defined by Quadrant 1. In Quadrant 2, paradoxical interventions are generally not necessary, although compliance-based strategies designed to undercut problems by making them into an ordeal might sometimes be used here. The most difficult treatment situations are encountered in Quadrant 3 (high reactance, unfree target behavior), where the therapist's first task is to shift the focus of intervention elsewhere.

In Quadrant 4, where compliance-based paradox is used, the therapist might prescribe that a particular symptom be brought on at certain times or for specified periods each day—in short, that it be scheduled. Or the therapist might ask for an increase in the symptom—say, at twice its usual frequency or intensity. There may be some strategic advantage to prescribing that a symptom be performed *more* rather than differently, because the former is less easily defied.

The therapist's objective in compliance-based paradoxical prescribing is to induce the patient at least to *try* to comply. As has been emphasized, this can best be done by framing the prescription in terms of the patient's own idiosyncratic language. There are, however, several general or all-purpose frames that might be used. One is an extension of the patient's desire to *control* the symptom. The patient might be told that control is a two-way street, and that learning to turn the symptom off will be greatly facilitated if he can first learn to turn it on. A second general frame is based on the idea of *prediction*. Since the distressing symptom will probably happen anyway (the patient is told), it would be helpful if he could at least have greater certainty about when the discomfort will occur. He should therefore plan to be anxious, depressed, or obsessive at convenient but specified times each day (Watzlawick, 1978). A third approach, which is especially useful with psychologically sophisticated patients, is to frame the prescription as a vehicle for increasing *understanding* of the problem. Thus, a patient conversant with the principles of Gestalt Therapy might be asked to perform the symptom in order to increase his awareness of it. Similarly, to a combative intellectual couple well versed in psychoanalytic theory, the therapist might say, "There is one thing we know for sure: The reasons you think you argue are probably not the real unconscious ones. To help us discover the real reasons, it will be necessary for you to argue even more than you do now."

Quadrant 1 defines the conditions under which defiance-based paradoxical interventions are most indicated. Here, the target behavior is perceived as free and the person to be influenced is high on the reactance-potential dimension. Defiance-based interventions can focus either on the free behavior of the problem-bearer himself, or on that of problem-maintaining others. When the focus is the problem-bearer, the therapist would only rarely direct a defiance-based intervention at the symptom or problem per se. This is because the person asking for help would only rarely define the problem itself as free—if it *were* free, therapy probably would not be necessary. Cases in which the therapist would prescribe a specific problem or symptom with the expectation of defiance are usually ones where the behavior in question is considered problematic by somebody else. A common example is instructing a rebellious teenager to be even more disobedient. To him, the behavior his parents wish to see changed is usually free: He certainly *could* take out the garbage or be home on time, but he won't.

More often, the use of defiance-based paradox with high-reactant problem-bearers focuses on free collateral behavior that in some way supports the problem or plays a role in maintaining it. The shy, anxious patient may be avoiding situations that involve meeting people and risking rejection; the depressive may be unwilling to phone for an employment interview or go to church on Sunday morning; the self-effacing accountant may be reluctant to request an appointment to speak with his boss about a pay raise. In each case, the behavior (or lack of behavior) that supports the problem would probably be defined as "free." If the likelihood of defiance is high, the therapist might actively *restrain* such patients from taking specific steps which, if taken, could lead to improvement.

With other defiant people, a therapist might *prescribe* a free collateral behavior. For example, anxiety-ridden and hypochondriacal patients often spend a great deal of time telling people about their problems. While having fears, anxieties, or bodily complaints is almost inevitably in the unfree domain, *talking* about these experiences is usually another matter. In these cases, if reactance potential is high, a prescription to do even more talking, complaining, or asking for reassurance can result in the patient's doing *less*—which can be particularly important when the act of talking about a problem regularly elicits from others a problem-maintaining response such as reassurance or avoidance. As before, the manner in which such a defiance-based prescription is framed is crucial. The man who habitually tells his wife about his panicky, anxious feeling at work, yet wants to be seen as the self-reliant head of the household, might be told to complain to his wife even more frequently (say, for an hour or more every evening) so that he can better learn to accept nurturance and support. In this manner, the patient's own idiosyncratic language is used to enhance defiance.

Probably the most dramatic of the paradoxical strategies is hard restraining. This defiance-based intervention is also targeted at the problem-bearer and consists of the therapist reversing the usual problem-maintaining stance of helping others by predicting that significant change or improvement will not be possible. In effect, the therapist benignly prescribes an attitude of resignation: He threatens the patient's freedom to believe that the problem or symptom is changeable, and in so doing, sets the stage for the patient to prove him wrong by changing.

As we have said, hard restraining is most often indicated with highly reactant patients who repeatedly seek help but fail to benefit. Sometimes, when information about previous treatment experiences is available, this help-rejecting pattern can be identified early, even before therapy actually begins. As often as not, however, hard restraining is introduced after other interventions have failed and the defiant pattern has become clear. In these cases, the therapist can reverse himself in midstream: He can suggest that the initial assessment of the situation was in error, that he had probably been overly optimistic; he can then go on to suggest that further struggles to overcome the problem will only frustrate the patient and make matters worse, and that the most reasonable goal of therapy at this point is for the patient to learn to accept and live with the problem.

Positioning maneuvers are defiance-based interventions through which the therapist preempts or outdoes the patient's problematic assertions about himself or his problem. These tactics are used when it is clear that the patient's pessimistic, utopian, or paranoid attitude is maintained by responses from others which attempt to convince him to take a more "realistic" view of his situation. For instance, it is well known that encouraging a depressed person to "cheer up" can have an effect opposite to the one intended. Therefore, the therapist might agree with and exaggerate the patient's view of the problem, and might say, "Considering your situation, I am surprised you are not more depressed than you appear to be." A common response to such an uncommon stance by the therapist is for the patient to begin speaking about the brighter side of things (Weakland et al., 1974). It should be stressed that paradoxical positioning is *only* indicated when the therapist finds himself in such a reactance-laden "game of opposites." The possibility of making things worse with certain more suggestible individuals (e.g., hysterics) highlights the importance of careful assessment.

Another common use of defiance-based strategies in Quadrant 1 is to interrupt the problem-maintaining behavior of people other than the identified problem-bearer. This paradoxical approach tends to be most effective when the spouse, parent, or friend to be influenced is bothered about the problem and "sweating" as much or more than the person defined as problem-bearer. An example is the married couple who comes to therapy at the wife's initiative, the chief complaint being the husband's passivity and withdrawal, which persist in spite of her attempts to get him to talk and be lovingly spontaneous. The therapist may ascertain that the more she encourages and demands, the more he withdraws and withholds. The "free" behavior of the wife (i.e., her encouraging), while intended to solve the problem, is in actuality perpetuating it. With some evidence that she will defy attempts to influence her (as is frequently the case in such situations), the therapist might prescribe that the wife spend at least an hour every evening continuing to encourage her husband to talk. If the husband is also prone to defiance, he might be simultaneously instructed *not* to respond, with the rationale that he needs to learn to live with the situation, or that he must help his wife learn to cope better with his silence. If either wife or husband defies the prescription, some change in the usual pattern is inevitable. A similar tack might be taken when the problems of a child are maintained by the attempted solutions of an over-protective mother. The mother who is asked to do more hovering may defy the prescription by doing less.

Perhaps the most difficult treatment situations are those in which a patient presenting with an "unfree" problem is assessed to be high on the reactance-potential dimension, as represented in Quadrant 3. Many of these situations would be amenable to compliance-based prescription (paradoxical or otherwise) were it not for the patient's high reactance potential. A case in point is the obsessive individual who has a high proportion of "unfree" behavior and is consequently resistant to influence attempts. It would be ideal if the therapist could get this type of patient to try to act out his symptoms; if he did, they would probably diminish or disappear. Unfortunately, such people are poor prospects for cooperation.

This less than optimal situation still allows the therapist several options. The first, and most difficult, is to induce compliance, i.e., shift the intervention to Quadrant 4. This shift could conceivably be achieved in several ways. The therapist might make especially adroit use of language, or deliver his intervention from a "one-down" position (Watzlawick et al., 1974), thus incorporating several of S. Brehm's suggestions regarding reactance reduction, such as not coming on too strong, not being too eager to persuade, and soft-selling a task. Another compliance-induction procedure, the "illusion of alternatives," evolves from the work of Erickson (Erickson & Rossi, 1975; Haley, 1973) and also fits well with the tenets of reactance theory. Here, the therapist might offer the patient a choice between two options (e.g., "Will you try it this month or next?"), with acceptance of either likely to initiate change. A third approach, suggested by the Palo Alto group, is the *Devil's Pact*, in which the patient promises to carry out a request before hearing it. The patient may be told that there is a plan that has a high likelihood of being helpful, but that this plan will only be offered if the patient first promises to carry it out, regardless of how difficult, inconvenient, or unreasonable it may seem (Watzlawick et al., 1974).

A second approach to an "unfree" problem behavior in a defiant patient is to sidestep the unfree symptom and aim a defiance-based intervention at a "free" collateral behavior. This would switch the situation into Quadrant 1. For instance, if the patient defines his involuntary shyness as the problem, the therapist may get him to agree that he has control over *where* he will be shy rather than over the shyness itself, and then get him to agree to be shy in a bar, a discotheque, or some other place where he will be around people.

The final therapeutic situation to be discussed occurs when a "free" behavior is the target for a patient assessed to be low in reactance potential, as illustrated in Quadrant 2 of TABLE 1. This situation best fits an implicit requirement of most prescriptive therapies: That a motivated, compliant patient presents a problem that can be translated into concrete, modifiable, free components amenable to direct therapeutic influence. For example, a compliant patient may present with an "unfree" problem, but the therapist chooses to work with the patient on "free" supporting behavior. Thus, while an obese person complains that his overeating is involuntary, he may agree with the therapist's suggestions to chew each mouthful 20 times, keep a daily weight chart, eat only in a designated place, and put the fork down between each mouthful. These are free aspects of behavior, which can be changed gradually and systematically. This treatment approach may include behavior therapy's greatest successes. Paradoxical intervention is usually not necessary.

NURTURING INCIPIENT CHANGE

Paradoxical interventions rarely resolve problems completely in one or two sessions. More often, the therapist must work toward nurturing and solidifying incipient change. Once change begins, certain therapist responses can help it along while others may nip it in the bud.

With compliance-based paradoxical prescribing, where the therapist facilitates change by interrupting problem-maintaining solutions of trying too hard or trying not to have a symptom, strong praise and encouragement following initial signs of improvement may only induce the patient to try harder again, making relapse more likely. A soft restraint, or even a neutral or pessimistic response, is usually more helpful. When the therapist greets incipient change with a caution to "go slow" or "not push things too hard," he increases the chances that gains will be solidified and further progress made. It is also important to follow through on compliance-based paradoxical prescriptions with more of the same when the strategy seems to be taking hold. If a patient returns, saying that, despite all his efforts, he was unable to bring on an anxiety attack, the therapist should urge him to try even harder. Such requests can be continued until there is evidence that the patient believes the problem has truly disappeared.

Another approach to nurturing change is to prescribe a relapse. Erickson (Haley, 1973; Haley, 1976) used this tactic with patients who improved too quickly, after only a few meetings. The patient may be requested to experience himself as he was before he came to treatment, ". . . to see if there is anything from that time that they wish to recover or salvage" (Haley, 1973, p. 4). In effect, the therapist asks the patient to doubt his sudden improvement in order to prevent him from doing so spontaneously.

When improvement occurs by virtue of someone's defying the therapist's directives and predictions, praise and encouragement are especially to be avoided. The therapist might respond to incipient change with skepticism or puzzlement, and insist that improvements are only temporary. He might even chide the patient for not trying hard enough, or for continuing to struggle to change his unchangeable symptom (as in hard restraining). If improvement continues, the therapist, above all, should be careful *not* to take credit for it. When the patient does not acknowledge change despite evidence to the contrary, the therapist would be wise to acknowledge his own failure and terminate treatment.

If all has gone according to plan, and therapy with the defiant patient approaches termination, the time is ripe for predicting that a relapse will occur in the not too distant future. Since improvement has been based to a large extent on the patient's defying the therapist's expectations, there is good reason to expect that termination will bring more of the same: In a final defiant gesture, the patient may prove the therapist wrong by not relapsing.

COMMENT

At a theoretical level, the communications-theory, double-bind explanation of therapeutic paradox is more parsimonious than the compliance-defiance framework we have outlined: It explains the same phenomena with fewer principles, without the additional burden of predicting the direction of the patient's response. The therapist who can establish a double-bind situation in which the patient changes whether he complies *or* defies is also on firm ground pragmatically. We suspect, however, that elegant therapeutic double-binds are more easily conceived than successfully implemented. Because published case studies are usually successful ones, and because detailed rationales for chosen interventions are rarely supplied, the use of paradox in clinical practice has acquired a kind of magical quality. The model presented in this paper attempts to demystify the strategic use of paradoxical techniques by offering more tangible guidelines for the practicing psychotherapist.

REFERENCE NOT INCLUDED IN BIBLIOGRAPHY

Caplan, G. (1964). *Principles of preventive psychiatry*. New York: Basic Books.

GERALD R. WEEKS AND LUCIANO L'ABATE
PARADOXICAL LETTERS[*]

The literature on therapeutic paradox includes very little on the use of written messages to facilitate behavioral change. To date, Weeks and L'Abate's set of guidelines for using therapist-composed letters to upset dysfunctional marital or family systems probably offers the most helpful advice for anyone interested in experimenting with this ancillary treatment device. The double bind created by a paradoxical letter, while not different in kind from one emerging directly from a face-to-face session, is conceived by the authors as generally more compelling because much more difficult, cognitively, to resist. Adopted as a tactic of last resort, such a letter (or letters) may finally succeed in jarring couples or families loose from the interpersonal chains so uncomfortably connecting them. This excerpt succinctly illustrates how paradoxical written messages may accomplish their "chain-loosening" task through positive reframing, prescribing the defeat, and declaring the therapist's helplessness.

In order to better understand what we call a paradoxical letter, linear letters will be described first. A linear letter is written in a straightforward, easy-to-understand style. These letters provide direct feedback to the client, much like the verbal feedback given in the form of insights,

---

[*]From *Paradoxical Psychotherapy*. New York: Brunner/Mazel, 1982. Reprinted with permission.

interpretations, or confrontations. The following letter illustrates a linear message given to a couple.

A Linear Letter

Dear _____:

I have really enjoyed these sessions with you and I am quite fond of you both. You have a good sense of humor and care a lot about how the other acts and feels. You both seem to be working on communicating effectively with each other.

I have the impression, though, that sometimes you focus on money problems to avoid confronting issues more sensitive to you both. When you blame or put each other down and fail to deal with issues directly, communication and growth of the relationship remain at a standstill. Just because one of you behaves in a hurtful way does not justify the other one's behaving in a similar way.

Although you seem to have a lot of commitment to this relationship, you tend to use your friends to escape from marital responsibilities. By making your friends more important than your marriage, your involvement with them detracts from your relationship with your partner. I think you have to decide whether you want to be married or whether you want to remain single.

Sincerely,

Paradoxical letters are more difficult to describe than linear letters. At best, only general guidelines can be offered for the construction of paradoxical letters. Over the years we have used a variety of formats and our ideas about what works best have gradually emerged.

Writing a paradoxical letter requires the expenditure of additional time and effort. Even a short letter may require an hour to compose, edit, and revise. The letter forces the therapist to consider the intervention carefully. It helps the therapist distance from the intervention in a way that is different from making interventions in a session. Moreover, the intervention must be self-contained. It must target a specific behavior to be changed and then be precisely formulated to make that change.

The letter may be constructed and given to the client(s) immediately after the session. The disadvantage of this approach is that the client must wait while the therapist prepares the letter and the therapist is pressured to compose the letter quickly. Letters composed under these conditions may not be as precise as they could be. The advantage of this approach is that the therapist can give the client(s) the letter and observe their reactions. But this also has a disadvantage. The client(s) may try to undo the bind created by the letter. In order to prevent this counter-therapeutic event from occurring, the letter should be read to the client(s) or given to them—and then the session ended immediately.

We recommend that the letters be written after the session and then mailed to the client(s) the next day. Under these conditions, the therapist has plenty of time to think through the interventions to be used.

We usually find that letters require time to be effectively formulated. The day after the session finishing touches can be made on the letter. Sometimes the delay helps the therapist gain a different perspective on the problem, resulting in the formulation of an entirely new letter. One of the consequences of using paradoxical letters is that the therapist is usually limited by the number of letters that can be developed simultaneously. Letter-writing is so time-consuming and mentally demanding that only a few cases can be treated at any particular time.

The length of the letter sent to the client is vitally important. We suggest using short letters. Normally, the letter should not exceed one page and it should contain no more than two or three points. Letters which are longer or contain too many points seem to be shotgun approaches. They suggest a confused therapist and are likely to confuse the client. The letter should be concise and precise.

A problem that is common to all letters is their readability. The client(s) must be able to understand the words. It is easy to forget that clients may lack reading skills even when their vocabularies appear adequate. The therapist should attempt to match the reading comprehension level of the client(s) to the extent possible.

The paradoxical letter may involve only one method or it may involve the combination of several methods. Our guidelines on the "how" of paradoxical intervention can be followed in conjunction with the methods presented. We have used virtually every method with clinical success in letters. As we stated earlier, there has been one combination of methods which has been particularly flexible and clinically effective—the use of positive connotation, reframing or relabeling, prescription, and restraining in the same letter.

The therapist needs to be careful not to be prescriptive in the sense of being evaluative or judgmental. Shoulds or oughts are to be avoided. Prescriptions are made in the paradoxical sense. In short, the client is placed in the bind of being told not to change that which is desired to be changed. The elegance of a paradoxical strategy is that the client discovers a solution; it is not provided for the client ready-made.

Almost all letters are perceived as cryptic, obscure, confusing, perplexing, or noncommonsensical in nature. The letter is rarely seen as direct or clear. The ambiguity of the letter helps to secure the client's involvement, since the person or system receiving the letter must work on deciphering its meaning.

We have used paradoxical letters in a variety of situations. In some cases we have used letters beginning after the first session. These were cases we felt strongly would be resistive or where we detected a great deal of resistance or reactance during the first interview. In other cases the paradoxical letters followed an initial period of assessment during which straightforward interventions failed. The use of paradoxical letters is probably best reserved as a means of last resort. If straightforward interventions fail and then verbal paradoxical interventions fail or seem to lack the impact they need, then it is definitely appropriate to use the letters.

Once the use of letters begins, it does not need to be a routine practice, although our most common pattern has been to use letters on a continuous basis for a while until significant change has occurred. It is, however, possible to use them only when an impasse is reached or when the therapist wishes to punctuate the importance of certain changes. The letters may serve all the functions mentioned earlier, plus add a shock effect to the treatment. Clients do not expect to receive written communications from therapists, except bills.

●　　　●　　　●

TECHNIQUES USED IN PARADOXICAL LETTERS

There are certain patterns and problems which appear frequently in highly dysfunctional families. These patterns or problems can be managed in a variety of ways, including the use of written paradoxes. The next few letters represent some paradoxical approaches to dealing with these common patterns. In each case a written message was given to the family.

Reframing Positively

This method may be used in families when the children are acting out to protect the parents' relationship. The parents in these families feel defeated by their children and sometimes by each other. The parents may say they support each other while each secretly feels the other is not being a good parent. The defeating pattern can be reframed in order to tie it to success, enjoyment, caring, protectiveness, closeness, intimacy, etc. The following is a typical letter, much like the ritualized prescriptions used by Selvini Palazzoli et al. (1978). The rules are:

1. Father will read this letter to other members of the family.
2. The letter will be read after dinner on Monday, Wednesday, and Friday evenings.
3. Mother will remind Father to read the letter.
4. Please do not discuss the content of this letter with anyone outside of counseling.

Dear _____ :

We [the parents] are appreciative of your protecting us because as long as you act up neither Mother nor I will need to look at ourselves and deal with our middle age. You will also help your brother to stay the way he is.

Consequently, we will understand that any time you blow up it will be to protect us and your brother. We hope, therefore, that you will continue protecting us, because we need it.

Prescribing the Defeat

After reframing a behavior, the next step is to prescribe the behavior. Since the defeat is now a positive expression, it follows that the family should assist, continue, and even escalate, i.e., increase whatever they are doing to defeat each other. To make sure that the reframing and prescription are not going to be ignored or forgotten, it is helpful to put them in writing and to ritualize them, i.e., "Read this letter after supper on alternating days, either Mondays, Wednesdays, and Fridays, or Tuesdays, Thursdays, and Saturdays," as the Milano group recommends (Selvini Palazzoli et al., 1978). This letter can be given to the child from the last example to read to his parents following these instructions:

1. To be read by son to other members of the family.
2. Please read on Mondays, Wednesdays, and Fridays after dinner.
3. Mother is to remind son to read and if she forgets, father and daughter are to remind.
4. Do not discuss contents outside of counseling.

Dear _____ :

I [the therapist] am impressed with the way in which you show how much you care about this family and especially your mother. I feel you need to be congratulated for having violent temper tantrums, because these tantrums serve as a safety valve for what your father and mother cannot do. I admire you for the way in which you show your loyalty to your mother.

If this is the way you want to protect your parents from each other and continue keeping them apart, you should continue to blow up, but do this on Monday, Wednesday, and Friday of each week. Be sure to break some inexpensive item in your home and continue these outbursts, because if you stop, they might get back together.

The prescription of the behavior usually helps the child control the behavior that is problematic. This type of letter may help the parents see their part in the problem such that they begin to change spontaneously.

Congratulating the Family

In some families there is a game of divide and conquer. There are alliances and coalitions between and among family members which make order impossible. The family is split into several factions, with each bidding for power. The following message has been used to deal with this pattern:

Dear _____:

I am impressed with the ability you have developed to defeat each other. This keeps your family together and unchanged. To succeed by defeating is hard to master, but when instructions are unclear and not negotiated, then it is easier to not follow through.

I admire you for wanting every family member to feel the power of defeat. You are assured of this power as long as instructions are given without everyone having an investment in them. One person can then use this against another, and in this way keep the family the same.

I want to congratulate the family for knowing how to be happy by defeating and by being defeated. Since this seems successful, I would encourage you to continue doing what you are doing and by no means would I encourage Mother and Dad to share authority and responsibility with each other, because this change could break up the family.

This circular letter not only gives the family a more positive description of their relationship, but promotes an evaluation of the family system. In very resistant families this is a way to begin establishing and strengthening parental boundaries.

Admission of Defeat and Helplessness

This is a favorite ploy used by the Milano group (Selvini Palazzoli et al., 1975/1978). Such an admission seems to mobilize family members into an attempt to do the opposite, that is, win. Even better, one should start therapy with the full realization (Andolfi, 1979a) that underneath the pleas for help there is a hidden agenda that pulls for defeat in each and every family. This hidden agenda is present and needs to be present from the outset of each therapy. If and when the therapist becomes aware of defeat or the possibility of defeat, the following type of message may be useful:

Dear _____:

I am aware that, because of the power of this family, I am feeling a real sense of defeat and helplessness. I do know I have power that you cannot speak to, but yours is also special. You are a special family that I cannot fight with. I don't know where I could have found a better family than you to defeat me.

This verbal message provides the family with an incentive for continuing their therapy. Not only does this admission of defeat on the therapist's part assure the family's continued participation in therapy, in order to win, but the parents also learn something about the strength of their influence when they are united.

Reinforcing the Declaration of Impotence

The strategy of declaring impotence described by Selvini Palazzoli et al. (1975/1978) and others is generally considered a one-time brief intervention. When it becomes necessary to use this strategy, the therapist may need to reinforce it and make a paradoxical prediction. Even though the clients may say they feel confident in the therapist, the therapist may want to predict that they are sure they will ultimately let the clients down. In order to reinforce the declaration of impotence and help the clients examine their reasons for not being able to change, a second message may be given to the family. The message is a general statement that could be used with practically any family:

Dear _____:

Your standards for living are so high that few individuals, including me, can really live up to them. You should be congratulated for your search for perfection (and equating perfection to goodness and imperfection to badness). In spite of all the pressures to lower your standards, we hope that you can keep them up because this world needs people like you who can uphold standards against all pressures both inside and outside the family. We doubt whether we can live up to your standards and wonder whether we will ever be able to meet them any time in the future. Keep up the good work! We will fail to meet your standards and wonder whether we really can help you.

REFERENCE NOT INCLUDED IN BIBLIOGRAPHY

Selvini Palazzoli, M., Boscolo, L., Cecchin, G., & Prata, G. (1978). A ritualized prescription in family therapy: Odd days and even days. *Journal of Marriage and Family Counseling*, *4*, 3–9.

D. SEAN O'CONNELL

SYMPTOM PRESCRIPTION IN PSYCHOTHERAPY*

This last selection represents possibly the most concise description of the various ways that clients may be psychologically prepared for a paradoxical intervention. Much has been made in this book of the many rationales clinicians have used to justify to themselves their decision to intervene paradoxically. The uniqueness of this excerpt is in its convenient summary of several of the rationales practitioners have used to justify to their clients prescriptions that, at least initially, would seem antithetical to therapeutic goals. Although, contrary to most of the writings reprinted here, O'Connell's focus is on individual rather than systemic treatment, most of his guidelines may yet be adapted for use with couples and families. It should also be noted that O'Connell's eleven rationales are hardly meant to be exhaustive. They are best appreciated as a starting point, or impetus, for the therapist's own creativity in devising rationales most consonant with the client's (s') problem, situation, and world view.

CLINICAL APPLICATIONS

Theoretical comprehension of symptom prescriptions (as well as other paradoxical interventions) is one thing; applying this understanding in clinical practice is quite another. The successful utilization of paradox in the counseling suite requires acumen and creativity, developed from accumulated experience. This being so, strict procedural rules for the delineation and presentation of interventions, as well as codifications of specific interventions for specific symptoms, cannot be laid down. No published work on symptom prescription, moreover, attempts to do so; each case is approached idiographically. Nonetheless, a few general guidelines governing the use of symptom prescription can be formulated.

Stockbrokers, lawyers, salespersons, news announcers, and schoolteachers must all possess a constellation of personality virtues and qualities in order to achieve the results dictated by their roles. The case is the

*From *Psychotherapy: Theory, Research and Practice*, 1983, *20*, 12–20. Reprinted with permission.

same with psychotherapists, but to a greater extent. Without having the basic facilitating qualities of warmth, positive regard, affective accuracy, sincerity, and effective communication, a therapist is not likely to achieve lasting therapeutic results, no matter what technique is used. Paradoxical prescription is no exception.

More specifically related to the symptom-prescriptive approach is the generalization that the directive to exaggerate and rehearse the symptom must, as far as possible, be accompanied by a *rationale* for doing so. This clinical guideline appears to be commensurate with the experiences of Palazzoli and Erickson, who usually give an explanation for their prescriptions. The following rationales have proven highly effective for getting a patient or client to follow therapeutic directives. *Naturally, the employment of any particular one of these rationales is dependent on the type of symptom presented and the patient's attitude toward it. Some are clearly inappropriate in some contexts.*

1. *Attempt Solutions.*   You have tried a number of common-sense solutions. You have tried hard to follow the well-meant advice of friends, associates, and family. But you still have your problem, so common sense hasn't worked. It seems to be time to try something which is *not* sensical, something quite different, perhaps drastically different. You did not develop your problem using common sense so you probably can't solve it using common sense either. So let us agree to try something like "reverse psychology," which goes against the logical and common-sense approaches you have already tried, but failed with.

2. *Develop Insight.*   You seem to need more understanding and insight into your problem. But you don't get this insight by fighting the problem or trying to avoid it. You are right in wanting to know more about the dynamics and *causes* of this problem. Right now it just seems to take you over, something comes over you, and you don't know what it is. So to get this understanding you need, I suggest you perform some experiments, and force yourself to have this problem and have it at a specific time and place, a number of times. When you do this, preferably when there are no other distractions, pay particular and minute attention to what you are doing to make the problem emerge. Monitor all your feelings, thoughts, sensations, and behavior when you make the problem worse.

3. *Collect Information.*   You are obviously quite unfamiliar with many of the facts relevant to your problem. I suggest you become more familiar with it and get more information about it, so we can know more precisely what it is we are dealing with. I suggest you give yourself the chance to bring your problem into clearer focus before we decide on a

solution. You can do this by rehearsing it more often, consciously and deliberately, at particular times and in certain places.

4. *Change Strategies.* You seem to need to develop new ways of *responding* to your problem. Therefore it is imperative that you actually force yourself to bring it on so you can discover and practice new ways of controlling it, because if you are not experiencing it you can't solve it (e.g., In order to overcome your temptation you must *have* the temptation).

5. *Assess Seriousness.* As your therapist, I need to know how serious your problem is. In fact, I need to know if things can get any worse for you. I need to examine the severity of your problem, and the only way I can do this is for you to bring the problem on as intensely as you can. So in order to help me, I am asking you to try to make this problem worse.

6. *Run the Course.* Sometimes problems must go through a predictable sequence before they naturally disappear. They have to run their course, like many other things in life. And in running their course, problems usually get worse before they get better. I'm suggesting that you seriously work at making your problem worse, that you deliberately intensify it. By doing this you will speed up the sequences your problem must go through, and you will consequently get through it more quickly.

7. *Have Fun.* You are taking your problem extremely seriously. That may be the biggest part of it, in fact. Many people find that problems go away when they regard whatever it is that bothers them with amusement. They begin to see something odd, something funny, something even absurd about their problem. Then they are cured of it. I'd like to see you get the joke. You can do this by *not* working seriously on your problem, but by allowing yourself to keep it until the humor in it dawns on you.

8. *Go Slowly.* Everyone goes through a time of transition which is important to them. Sometimes these transitions are so new that hurrying through them is dangerous and reckless. For the time being, I suggest that you process your changes slowly, and that you change slowly. For now, just let your problem be. Let it stay. Keep it, and simply notice any changes as they easily occur.

9. *Take Charge.* Some of the important things you have said about your problem clearly indicate that you feel helpless about it. In effect, you are a victim of your symptom, quite impotent in the face of it. It takes you over. I suggest you take *it* over, put yourself in charge of it and learn how to control it, instead of letting it control you. You can do this by planning to have it at certain times and in certain places. Elevate and intensify your symptom at will. Make it happen for the purpose of learning to take charge of it.

10. *Be Yourself.* Your symptom sets you apart from other people. It makes you special and unique. You can stand out in a crowd with it. Other ordinary people can be intrigued by it, enchanted by it, and you can hold

their attention with it, just like a stutterer holds attention when s/he stutters. I think your symptom will turn out to be one of your greatest assets, so I recommend you do not try to lose it. Instead, try to remain yourself by preserving it with practice and by letting it be appreciated. In effect, you do not have a problem.

11. *Explore the Irrational.* Most people's problems, like yours, arise in an irrational way, in an unconscious part of their mind. So I don't think it would do you much good to try getting over your problem by being rational about it, by thinking about it, by reasoning about it, by talking intellectually about it, or even by *doing* something reasonable about it. You didn't think your way into it, so you probably can't think yourself out of it. In fact, you need to do something very irrational in order to get over it. One of the most irrational things you can do is make your problem worse or have it more often, *on purpose*.

In addition to the points already made concerning therapist regard and rationales for intervention, two other general guidelines recommend themselves for symptom prescription. The first has to do with timing, the second with symptom context.

First, symptoms are ideally prescribed in the initial session. This has the merit of giving the patient something to do immediately, thus defining therapy as a problem-solving process which doesn't waste time. Patients also feel they have been given something definite, which most of them desire. Moreover, it puts the therapist in charge, defining him or her as the expert he or she is supposed to be.

Second, if the symptom implicates other people—which is usually the case—then the intervention must implicate them also. That is, whatever is prescribed must fit the *context* in which the symptoms occur. For example, a woman who presents herself for therapy as being drained, nervous, and at the end of her wits due to her husband's gambling should be given an intervention which directly implicates the spouse. In this case, she may be asked to encourage him to gamble by joining him whenever it is possible for her, or by giving him poker chips as a "present" when he least desires them. This not only changes her frame of reference from fear and worry to encouragement but will predictably alter her spouse's gambling patterns.

The use of symptom prescription in psychotherapy is grounded in a very definite philosophical framework and theory of human nature. The framework stipulates, first, that human beings are free and ultimately responsible for what they do, including what they do in therapy. From this it follows, second, that the job of the therapist is to make the observations and provide the interventions which will give patients or clients a context for solving their problems on their own. Consonant with this is a third point, namely, that solving psychological problems is the only appropriate purpose for therapy. Its concern is to bring about relief by inducing the sufferer to *change*. Whether the change is "intrapsychic" or "behavioral" does not matter; in any case the disjunctivity of "inner" and "outer" is specious. The purpose for psychotherapy, stated in this fashion, exposes its own paradoxical nature. Like many other procedures, its ultimate aim is its own demise.

Appendix B

A Checklist of Symptoms and Problems Treated Paradoxically

To increase the usefulness of this book's substantial bibliography of over 500 items, the following checklist attempts to relate as many of these items to specific symptoms, problems, and dysfunctional relationships as feasibly possible. With a few exceptions, it has not been considered practical to include under specific headings writings that contain several undeveloped case descriptions or vignettes—each touching upon a different disorder. The emphasis here is rather on particular clinical problems as they have received more or less sustained attention in the treatment literature on therapeutic paradox.

It will be noticed that some headings are intentionally broad (e.g., "Childhood Problems" and "Marital Conflict"). Such headings have been included (1) to direct readers to important contributions to specific clinical populations, and (2) to provide a handy reference guide to studies which address a variety of problems within a specific population. However, no blanket category for "Family Problems" has been provided, for it would contain so many entries as to be virtually useless. The alternative course taken here has been to list under the appropriate symptom (e.g., anorexia, delinquency, or enuresis) those investigations focusing on a family's entering treatment to get help expressly with a symptomatic child or teenager. But it has not been considered viable to attempt a listing of all of the large bulk of studies that deal with dysfunctional families generally.

As a kind of global qualification of this checklist, it might be mentioned that therapists using paradoxical strategies do *not*, typically, place that much stress or value on traditional diagnostic categories—choosing instead to focus on the transactional or communicational pattern which underlies the problem or symptom. In fact, many systems thinkers eschew the whole notion of "identified patient," much preferring to conceptualize cases in terms of symptomatic *families*: that is, as single ill-functioning units requiring treatment which concentrates on altering maladaptive behavioral sequences among family members.

Still, the writings referenced here—though cited generally in accordance with conventional symptomatic categories—focus much more on symptoms as coping mechanisms than as psychological "afflictions." Most frequently, symptoms are viewed not as something one *has* but as characterizing that which one *does*. Because of such operational assumptions, this literature usually implies that it is the motive behind the symptom that must constitute the fundamental consideration in treatment planning. Consequently, depending on the similarities or differences in the perceived motive, two different symptoms might warrant essentially the same intervention strategy, whereas one and the same symptom might call for a number of relatively different paradoxical tactics. To be maximally useful, the literature on therapeutic paradox needs, therefore, to be inspected at least as much for the intra- and interpersonal dynamics it addresses as for the specific symptom it immediately involves. Finally, the desire in assembling this checklist to emphasize the underlying causes of a behavior rather than simply its overt manifestation has led to a fairly generous use of cross references—for example, directing the reader interested in the symptom of anorexia to consider also the listings under "Aggression and Acting-Out."

It is hoped that this extensive checklist (along with the reference list which concludes virtually every study cited below) will enable the reader to explore—to whatever degree desired—how paradoxical strategies have been effectively employed to deal with a whole host of dysfunctional behaviors. One last explanatory note: Where two dates immediately follow an author's name, the second date refers to the year in which the article cited was reprinted in book form.

ACADEMIC/CAREER PROBLEMS
(*see* Procrastination; Vocational
Problems; "Writer's Block")

ACROPHOBIA (*see also* Phobias)
Pendleton & Higgins (1983)

ACTING-OUT BEHAVIORS (*see*
Aggression and . . .)

ADDICTIVE BEHAVIORS (*see*
Alcoholism; Substance Abuse)

ADOLESCENT PROBLEMS (*see also*
Childhood Problems, and under
specific problems—e.g.,
Aggression, Anorexia, etc.)
Amanat (1979)
Evans (1980)

ADOLESCENT PROBLEMS—*Cont.*
Fisch et al. (1982)
Framrose (1982a)
Frey (1984)
Haley (1973)
Hoffman (1981)
Kraus (1980)
Mandel et al. (1975)
Marshall (1972, 1982)
Marshall (1976, 1982)
Mazza (1984)
Strean (1961)
Watzlawick et al. (1974)
Will (1983)
Williams & Weeks (1984)

AGGRESSION AND ACTING-OUT
    (*see also* Adolescent Problems;
    Delinquency; School Problems)
    de Shazer (1975)
    de Shazer (1980)
    Jenkins (1980)
    Krumboltz & Krumboltz (1972)
    Madanes (1980b, 1981)
    Madanes (1984)
    Mandel et al. (1975)
    Marshall (1976, 1982)
    Papp (1977)
    Strean (1959, 1970)
    Strean (1961, 1970)
    Strean (1964)
    Strean (1968)
    Whitaker (1975)

AGING AND THE AGED,
    PROBLEMS OF
    Haley (1973)
    Herr & Weakland (1979)
    Hyer (1983)

AGORAPHOBIA (*see also* Phobias)
    Ascher (1981b)
    Chambless & Goldstein (1980)
    Efran & Caputo (1984)
    Foa, Jameson, Turner, & Payne
        (1980)
    Goldstein (1978)
    Mavissakalian, Michelson,
        Greenwald, & Kornblith
        (1983)
    Michelson & Ascher (1984)
    Watzlawick et al. (1974)

ALCOHOLISM (*see also* Substance
    Abuse)
    Boulanger, Laguesse-Leluron, &
        Jadot (1980)
    Daggett, Kempner, & Costello
        (1982)
    Haley (1973)
    Held & Heller (1982)
    Madanes (1981)
    Marlatt (1978)
    Shore (1981)

ALCOHOLISM—*Cont.*
    Zeig (1980a)

ANGER (*see* Aggression and
    Acting-Out)

ANOREXIA NERVOSA (*see also*
    Aggression and Acting-Out)
    Albertini (1979)
    Andolfi (1979b)
    Andolfi, Angelo, Menghi, &
        Nicolo-Corigliano (1983)
    Buddeberg & Buddeberg (1979)
    Elkaim (1982)
    Hart (1983)
    Hoffman (1981)
    Hsu & Lieberman (1982)
    Madanes (1984)
    Mirkin (1983)
    Oberfield (1981)
    Rosen, L. W. (1980)
    Schwartz (1982)
    Selvini Palazzoli et al. (1974)
    Selvini Palazzoli et al. (1978)
    Wynne (1980)

ANTISOCIAL BEHAVIOR (*see*
    Aggression; Delinquency)

ANXIETY (*see also* Phobias, and
    under specific phobias)
    Barlow & Wolfe (1981)
    Fay (1978)
    Fisch et al. (1982)
    Heide & Borkovec (1984)
    Lamb (1980)
    Last et al. (1983)

ASTHMA (*see also* Psychosomatic
    Symptoms)
    Weinstein (1983)

BINGE EATING (*see also* Bulimia)
    Loro & Orleans (1981)

BLUSHING (*see* Erythrophobia)

BORDERLINE PERSONALITY
    DISORDER
    Coleman (1956)
    Coleman & Nelson (1957)
    Nelson, M. C. (1962)

BORDERLINE PERSONALITY
    DISORDER—*Cont.*
    Scanlon (1980)
BULIMIA (*see also* Anorexia)
    Madanes (1981)
    Moley (1983)
    Wynne (1980)
CHEMICAL ABUSE (*see* Alcoholism;
    Substance Abuse)
CHILDHOOD PROBLEMS (*see also*
    Adolescent Problems, and under
    specific . . . problems—e.g.,
    Enuresis, Temper Tantrums, etc.)
    Fay (1978)
    Fisch et al. (1982)
    Haley (1973)
    Hare-Mustin (1976)
    Jessee & L'Abate (1980)
    Jessee et al. (1982)
    Kagan (1980)
    Krumboltz & Krumboltz (1972)
    Madanes (1980b, 1981)
    Madanes (1984)
    Marshall (1972, 1982)
    Marshall (1976, 1982)
COMPULSIVE BEHAVIORS (*see*
    Habits; Obsessive-Compulsive
    Disorders; and under
    specific . . . behaviors—e.g.,
    Gambling, Masturbation, etc.)
COUPLES CONFLICT (*see* Marital
    Conflict)
DELINQUENCY (*see also* Adolescent
    Problems; Aggression; Childhood
    Problems)
    Aichhorn (1965)
    Chase, Shea, & Dougherty (1984)
    Fay (1978)
    Framrose (1982b)
    Kolko & Milan (1983)
    Marshall (1974)
    Watzlawick et al. (1974)
DEPERSONALIZATION NEUROSIS
    Blue (1979)

DEPRESSION
    Beck & Strong (1982)
    Cade & Southgate (1979)
    Coyne (1984)
    Fay (1978)
    Feldman, Strong, & Danser (1982)
    Fisch et al. (1982)
    Haley (1973)
    Hoebel (1977)
    L'Abate (in press)
    Madanes (1981)
    Madanes (1984)
    Watzlawick & Coyne (1980)
    Watzlawick et al. (1974)
    Weeks & L'Abate (1982)
DRIVING PHOBIA (*see also* Phobias)
    Ascher (1980)
DRUG ABUSE (*see* Alcoholism;
    Substance Abuse)
EATING DISORDERS (*see* under
    specific . . . disorders)
ENCOPRESIS
    Bornstein, Sturm, Retzlaff, Kirby, &
        Chong (1981)
    de Shazer (1975)
    Selvini Palazzoli et al. (1974)
ENURESIS
    Erickson (1954)
    Erickson & Rossi (1975)
    Madanes (1980b, 1981)
    Protinsky & Dillard (1983)
ERYTHROPHOBIA (*see also*
    Phobias)
    Boeringa (1983)
    Lamontagne (1978)
    Timms (1980)
FEARS, PATHOLOGICAL (*see*
    Anxiety; Phobias; and under
    specific phobias)
FIRESETTING (*see also* Aggression;
    Childhood Problems)
    Krumboltz & Krumboltz (1972)
    Madanes (1980b, 1981)
    Madanes (1984)

GAMBLING, COMPULSIVE
Victor & Krug (1967)

HABITS, MALADAPTIVE (*see also*
under specific habits—e.g.,
Thumbsucking)
Azrin, Nunn, & Frantz (1980a)
Carroll, Sloop, Mutter, & Prince
(1978)
Dunlap (1930)
Dunlap (1932)
Dunlap (1942)
Dunlap (1946)
Fay (1978)
Marlatt & Gordon (1980)

HEADACHES (*see also* Psychosomatic
Symptoms)
Madanes (1980b, 1981)

HEADBANGING (*see also* Habits)
Mogel & Schiff (1967)
Wooden (1974)

HYSTERICAL SYMPTOMS
Haley (1973)
Madanes (1981)
Oberfield (1981)
Viaro (1980)

IDENTITY CRISIS
Fish (1973)

INSOMNIA
Ascher & Efran (1978)
Ascher & Turner (1979)
Ascher & Turner (1980)
Borkovec & Boudewyns (1976)
Dattilio (1984)
Fogle & Dyal (1983)
Lacks et al. (1983)
Relinger & Bornstein (1979)
Relinger et al. (1978)
Riveros (1984)
Turner & Ascher (1979)
Turner & Ascher (1982)
Turner & DiTomasso (1980)
Warner (1977)

JEALOUSY, PATHOLOGICAL
Fay (1978)
Im, Wilner, & Breit (1983)

JEALOUSY—*Cont.*
Teismann (1979)

MARITAL CONFLICT (*see also*
Jealousy; Sexual Problems)
de Shazer (1978)
Fay (1978)
Haley (1963)
Haley (1973)
Hoffman (1981)
Jacobson & Margolin (1979)
Keller & Elliot (1982)
Madanes (1980a)
Madanes (1981)
Papp (1976)
Papp (1980b)
Protinsky & Quinn (1981)
Rabkin (1980)
Sluzki (1978)
Todd (1984)
Watzlawick et al. (1974)
Zeig (1980b)

MASTURBATION, COMPULSIVE
(*see also* Habits)
Haley (1976)
Madanes (1984)

NARCISSISM, PATHOLOGICAL (*see
also* Borderline Personality
Disorder; Psychosis;
Schizophrenia)
Spotnitz & Nagelberg (1960)
Spotnitz, Nagelberg, & Feldman
(1956)
Strean (1968)

NEGATIVISM (*see* Aggression)

NIGHTMARES AND NIGHT
TERRORS
Madanes (1980b, 1981)
Madanes (1984)

OBESITY
Haley (1963)
Haley (1973)
Loro & Orleans (1981)

OBSESSIVE THOUGHTS (*see also*
Obsessive-Compulsive Disorders)
Kellerman (1981)

OBSESSIVE THOUGHTS—*Cont.*
  Milan & Kolko (1982)
  Rachman (1976)
  Roy & Lamontagne (1976)
  Sahakian (1969)
  Solyom et al. (1972)
  Wolpe & Ascher (1976)
OBSESSIVE-COMPULSIVE
    DISORDERS (*see also* Obsessive
    Thoughts)
  Frankl (1955)
  Frankl (1960, 1967b)
  Frankl (1967a)
  Frankl (1975, 1978)
  Gerz (1962)
  Gerz (1966)
  Grossman (1964)
  Haynes (1978)
  Marks (1975)
  Meyer (1966)
  O'Conner (1983)
  Rachman & Hodgson (1980)
  Wolff (1977)
PAIN MANAGEMENT
  Erickson (1958)
  Erickson (1965)
  Rybstein-Blinchik (1979)
PARANOIA (*see also* Psychosis;
    Schizophrenia)
  Adler (1956)
  Fay (1978)
  Fraser (1983)
  Jackson (1963)
  Sherman (1961)
  Zeig (1980a)
PHOBIAS (*see also* under specific
    phobias)
  Ascher (1980)
  Boulougouris, Marks, & Marset
    (1971)
  Crowe, Marks, & Agras (1972)
  D'Zurilla, Wilson, & Nelson
    (1973)
  Fay (1978)
  Frankl (1955)
  Frankl (1960, 1967b)

PHOBIAS—*Cont.*
  Frankl (1967a)
  Frankl (1975, 1978)
  Gerz (1962)
  Gerz (1966)
  Johnston et al. (1976)
  Malleson (1959)
  Marks (1975)
  Marshall, Gauthier, & Gordon
    (1979)
  Rachman (1969)
  Shipley (1979)
  Stampfl & Levis (1973)
PROCRASTINATION
  Lopez & Wambach (1982)
  Watzlawick et al. (1974)
  Wright & Strong (1982)
PSYCHOPHYSIOLOGICAL
    SYMPTOMS (*see* Psychosomatic
    Symptoms, and under
    specific . . . symptoms)
PSYCHOSIS AND PSYCHOTIC
    BEHAVIOR (*see also* Paranoia;
    Schizophrenia)
  Ayllon (1963)
  Ayllon & Michael (1959)
  Bergman (1980)
  Bergman (1982)
  Erickson (1965)
  Jackson & Watzlawick (1963)
  Lindner (1955)
  Rosen, J. H. (1953)
  Rosen, J. H. (1962)
PSYCHOSOMATIC SYMPTOMS
    (*see also* under specific . . .
    symptoms—e.g., Asthma)
  Ascher (1979)
  Bornstein et al. (1981)
  Erickson (1954)
  Erickson (1965)
  Fisher, Anderson, & Jones (1981)
  Gentry (1973)
  Held & Heller (1982)
  Sluzki (1978)
  White (1979)
  Zeig (1980b)

REBELLIOUSNESS (*see* Adolescent Problems; Aggression; Childhood Problems; Delinquency; School Problems)

RETARDATION, problems related to
Bergman (1980)
Carroll et al. (1978)

SCHIZOPHRENIA (*see also* Paranoia; Psychosis)
Andolfi et al. (1980)
Close (1970)
Cottraux & Cury (1976)
Davis (1965)
Haley (1963)
Jackson & Yalom (1964)
McFarlane (1983)
Selvini Palazzoli et al. (1978)
Spotnitz (1969)
Spotnitz et al. (1956)
Walker & McLeod 1982)

SCHOOL PROBLEMS (*see also* Adolescent Problems; Aggression; Childhood Problems; "Writer's Block")
Andrey, Burille, Martinez, & Rey (1978)
Bergman (1983)
Bowman & Goldberg (1983)
Hess (1980)
Kesten (1955)
Krumboltz & Krumboltz (1972)
L'Abate, Baggett, & Anderson (1984)
Macaruso (1979)
Papp (1980a)
Strean (1959, 1970)
Watzlawick et al. (1974)
Williams & Weeks (1984)

SEIZURES, PSYCHOGENIC (*see also* Psychosomatic Symptoms)
Madanes (1980b, 1981)
Madanes (1984)

SELF-DENIGRATION (cf. negative self-statements)
Cade & Southgate (1979)
Fay (1978)

SELF-DESTRUCTIVE BEHAVIORS (*see also* Suicidal Thoughts)
Andolfi (1979b)
Fay (1978)

SEXUAL PROBLEMS AND DYSFUNCTIONS
Fay (1978)
Frankl (1960, 1967b)
Frankl (1967a)
Frankl (1975, 1978)
Gentry (1978)
Haley (1973)
Shelton & Levy (1981)
Stekel (1920)
Vandereycken (1982)
Watzlawick et al. (1974)
Weeks & L'Abate (1982)

SLEEP DISTURBANCES (*see* Insomnia)

SMOKING (*see* Habits)

SNAKE PHOBIA (*see also* Phobias)
Sargent (1983)

STUTTERING AND STAMMERING (*see also* Anxiety; Phobias)
Dunlap (1946)
Nystul & Muszynska (1976)

SUBSTANCE ABUSE AND ADDICTION (*see also* Alcoholism; Delinquency)
Framrose (1982b)
Morelli (1978)
Reilly (1984)

SUICIDAL THOUGHTS, THREATS, AND ATTEMPTS (*see also* Aggression; Depression)
Fay (1978)
Haley (1973)
Madanes (1984)
Whitaker (1975)

TEMPER TANTRUMS (*see also* Aggression)
Hare-Mustin (1975)
Madanes (1981)
Zarske (1982)

THUMBSUCKING (*see also* Habits)
Haley (1973)
Yoder (1983)
TICS, PSYCHOGENIC
Clark (1966)
Dunlap (1946)
Hersen & Eisler (1973)
Jones (1960)
Lazarus (1964)
Rafi (1962)
Walton (1964)
Yates (1958)
TRUANCY (*see* School Problems)
URINARY RETENTION (*see also*
Psychosomatic Symptoms)
Ascher (1979)
VIOLENCE (*see* Aggression;
Delinquency)
VOCATIONAL PROBLEMS AND
REHABILITATION
Cottone (1981)

VOCATIONAL PROBLEMS—*Cont.*
Daggett (1978)
Daggett et al. (1982)
Fay (1978)
Lopez (1983)
VOMITING PHOBIA
O'Conner (1983)
Ritow (1979)
VOMITING AND STOMACH
ACHES (*see also* Anorexia;
Bulimia)
de Shazer (1979a)
Madanes (1980b, 1981)
Madanes (1984)
Musliner (1980)
Sander (1974)
WORK PROBLEMS (*see* Vocational
Problems)
"WRITER'S BLOCK" (*see also*
Procrastination)
Henning (1981)

A Comprehensive Bibliography on Paradoxical Therapeutic Strategies

This extensive bibliography contains more than 500 items. By way of highlighting some of the most seminal or suggestive writings on this increasingly unwieldy subject, an asterisk (*) has been appended to them. In many cases the editorial decision "to asterisk or not to asterisk" has been most difficult, so that these indicators are best viewed simply as initial recommendations for further study. Obviously, a good many unasterisked items may be of great potential interest to individual readers; an uncoded entry, therefore, hardly warrants being seen as having only minor significance. It should also be noted that in several instances an article by an author later reappears (though perhaps in somewhat altered form) in a book by that author, making a certain amount of repetition unavoidable.

Although the attempt was to make this listing as complete as possible, perfunctory or undeveloped references to paradoxical procedures have intentionally been omitted—as have most writings only peripherally related to such methods. A number of works cited in the text have not been included here because they were not, in themselves, seen as sufficiently germane to the subject of therapeutic paradox. Moreover, the listing of studies on paradoxical behavioral techniques is purposefully selective, since to enumerate all these studies (e.g., the plethora of papers on flooding and implosion) would be greatly to increase the bulk of this compilation *without* at the same time adding substantially to its overall usefulness. Extensive reference lists to facilitate further reading in behavioral paradoxical tactics are available elsewhere (e.g., Boudewyns & Shipley, 1983), although it should be emphasized that such procedures are almost never discussed in this literature as paradoxical.

Finally, despite the considerable care taken in assembling this bibliography, the author has little doubt that a few substantive references have probably escaped his attention. It can, however, safely be asserted that the many, many pages of sources which follow should satisfy all but the most insatiable reader on this rich and ever-expanding area of psychotherapy.

Adams, H. (1977). Toward a dialectical approach to counseling. *Journal of Humanistic Psychology, 17,* 57–67.

*Adler, A. (1956). *The individual psychology of Alfred Adler* (H. L. Ansbacher & R. R. Ansbacher, Eds. & Trans.). New York: Harper & Row.

Aichhorn, A. (1965). *Wayward youth.* New York: Viking. (Original work published 1925)

Albertini, R. (1979). Use of paradoxical injunction with a hospitalized adolescent. *Hospital and Community Psychiatry, 30,* 163–164.

Amanat, E. (1979). Paradoxical treatment of adolescent resistance. *Adolescence, 14,* 851–862.

Anderson, C. M., & Stewart, S. (1983). *Mastering resistance: A practical guide to family therapy.* New York: Guilford.

Anderson, S. A., & Russell, C. S. (1982). Utilizing process and content in designing paradoxical interventions. *American Journal of Family Therapy, 10,* 48–60.

Andolfi, M. (1974). Paradox in psychotherapy. *American Journal of Psychoanalysis, 34,* 221–228.

Andolfi, M. (1979a). *Family therapy: An interactional approach* (H. R. Cassin, Trans.). New York: Plenum.

Andolfi, M. (1979b). Redefinition in family therapy. *American Journal of Family Therapy, 7,* 5–15.

*Andolfi, M. (1980). Prescribing the family's own dysfunctional rules as a therapeutic strategy. *Journal of Marital and Family Therapy, 6,* 29–36. (Reprinted in F. W. Kaslow (Ed.), *The international book of family therapy.* New York: Brunner/Mazel, 1982.)

Andolfi, M., Angelo, C., Menghi, P., & Nicolo-Corigliano, A. M. (1983). *Behind the family mask: Therapeutic change in rigid family systems* (C. L. Chodorkoff, Trans.). New York: Brunner/Mazel.

Andolfi, M., & Menghi, P. (1976). [The prescription in family therapy, I.] *Archivio di Psicologia, Neurologia e Psichiatria, 37,* 434–456.

Andolfi, M., & Menghi, P. (1977). [The prescription in family therapy: Therapeutic paradox, II.] *Archivio di Psicologia, Neurologia e Psichiatria, 38,* 57–76.

*Andolfi, M., Menghi, P., Nicolo, A. M., & Saccu, C. (1980). Interaction in rigid systems: A model of intervention in families with a schizophrenic member. In M. Andolfi & I. Zwerling (Eds.), *Dimensions of family therapy.* New York: Guilford.

Audrey, B., Burille, P., Martinez, J. P., & Rey, Y. (1978). [Treatment of a case of school maladjustment by brief family therapy.] *Enfance* (2-3), 143–164.

Antebi, E. (1981). The paradoxical nature of family art therapy. *Pratt Institute Creative Arts Therapy Review, 2,* 37–45.

Aponte, H. J., & Van Deusen, J. M. (1981). Structural family therapy. In A. S. Gurman & D. P. Kniskern (Eds.), *Handbook of family therapy.* New York: Brunner/Mazel.

Ascher, L. M. (1979). Paradoxical intention in the treatment of urinary retention. *Behaviour Research and Therapy, 17,* 267–270.

*Ascher, L. M. (1980). Paradoxical intention. In A. Goldstein & E. B. Foa (Eds.), *Handbook of behavioral interventions: A clinical guide.* New York: Wiley.

Ascher, L. M. (1981a). Application of paradoxical intention by other schools of therapy. *International Forum for Logotherapy, 4,* 52–55.

Ascher, L. M. (1981b). Employing paradoxical intention in the treatment of agoraphobia. *Behaviour Research and Therapy, 19,* 533–542.

Ascher, L. M., & DiTomasso, R. A. (in press). Paradoxical intention in behavior therapy: A review of the experimental literature. In R. M. Turner & L. M. Ascher (Eds.), *Behavior therapy.* Springer, Berlin.

Ascher, L. M., & Efran, J. S. (1978). Use of paradoxical intention in a behavioral program for sleep onset insomnia. *Journal of Consulting and Clinical Psychology, 46,* 547–550.

Ascher, L. M., & Turner, R. M. (1979). Paradoxical intention and insomnia: An experimental investigation. *Behaviour Research and Therapy, 17,* 408–411.

Ascher, L. M., & Turner, R. M. (1980). A comparison of two methods for the administration of paradoxical intention. *Behaviour Research and Therapy, 18,* 121–126.

*Ayllon, T. (1963). Intensive treatment of psychotic behavior by stimulus satiation and food reinforcement. *Behaviour Research and Therapy, 1,* 53–62.

Ayllon, T., & Michael, J. (1959). The psychiatric nurse as a behavioral engineer. *Journal of the Experimental Analysis of Behavior, 2,* 323–334. (Includes use of stimulus satiation.)

Azrin, N. H., Nunn, R. G., & Frantz, S. E. (1980a). Habit reversal vs. negative practice treatment of nailbiting. *Behaviour Research and Therapy, 18,* 281–285.

Azrin, N. H., Nunn, R. G., & Frantz, S. E. (1980b). Habit reversal vs. negative practice treatment of nervous tics. *Behavior Therapy, 11,* 169–178.

Bandler, R., & Grinder, J. (1975). *The structure of magic, I: A book about language and therapy.* Palo Alto: Science & Behavior Books.

Bandler, R., & Grinder, J. (1979). *Frogs into princes: Neuro linguistic programming.* Moab, UT: Real People Press.

Baptiste, D. A. (1983). Family therapy with reconstituted families: A crisis-induction approach. *American Journal of Family Therapy, 11,* 5–15.

Barcai, A. (1967). The therapeutic utilization of defense mechanisms: Rapid improvement in in-patients. *Psychotherapy: Theory, Research and Practice, 4,* 155–158.

Barker, P. (1981). *Basic family therapy.* Baltimore: University Park Press.

Barlow, D. H., & Wolfe, B. E. (1981). Behavioral approaches to anxiety disorders: A report on the NIMH-SUNY Albany research conference. *Journal of Consulting and Clinical Psychology, 49,* 448–455.

Barrack, R. A. (1978). A survey and critique of paradoxical intention (and symptom prescription). Unpublished doctoral dissertation, Rutgers University.

Barrows, S. E. (1982). Interview with Mara Selvini Palazzoli and Giuliana Prata. *American Journal of Family Therapy, 10,* 60–69.

Bateson, G., Jackson, D. D., Haley, J., & Weakland, J. H. (1956). Toward a theory of schizophrenia. *Behavioral Science, 1,* 251–264.

Bateson, G., Jackson, D. D., Haley, J., & Weakland, J. H. (1963). A note on the double bind—1962. *Family Process, 2,* 154–161.

Baum, M. (1971). Flooding or response prevention or detainment or forced reality-testing: A note on nomenclature. *Psychological Reports, 28,* 558.

Beck, J. T., & Strong, S. R. (1982). Stimulating therapeutic change with interpretations: A comparison of positive and negative connotation. *Journal of Counseling Psychology, 29,* 551–559.

Becvar, R. J. (1978). Paradoxical double binds in human-relations training. *Counselor Education and Supervision, 18,* 36–44.

*Beisser, A. (1970). The paradoxical theory of change. In J. Fagan & I. L. Shepherd (Eds.), *Gestalt therapy now: Theory, techniques, applications.* Palo Alto: Science & Behavior Books.

Bennett, M. I., & Bennett, M. B. (1984). The uses of hopelessness. *American Journal of Psychiatry, 141,* 559–562. (Discusses utility of interventions that may arouse hopelessness in clients—cf. reframing.)

Bentovim, A., Barnes, G. G., & Cooklin, A. (Eds.). (1982). *Family therapy: Complementary frameworks of theory and practice* (2 Vols.). New York: Grune & Stratton.

Berger, M., & Roussillon, R. (1979). [Paradoxical therapies and symptom prescription.] *Evolution Psychiatrique, 44,* 495–524.

*Bergman, J. S. (1980). The use of paradox in a community home for the chronically disturbed and retarded. *Family Process, 19,* 65–71.

*Bergman, J. S. (1982). Paradoxical interventions with people who insist on acting crazy. *American Journal of Psychotherapy, 36,* 214–222.

Bergman, J. S. (1983). Prescribing family criticism as a paradoxical intervention. *Family Process, 22,* 517–522.

Bernstein, A. (1984). A session with Jack: A demonstration of mirroring by ego-syntonic joining. In E. M. Stern (Ed.), *Psychotherapy and the abrasive patient.* New York: Haworth.

Bertalanffy, L. Von (1968). *General systems theory.* New York: Braziller.

Birchler, G. R. (1981). Paradox and behavioral marital therapy. *American Journal of Family Therapy, 9,* 92–94.

Blue, F. R. (1979). Use of directive therapy in the treatment of depersonalization neurosis. *Psychological Reports, 45,* 904–906.

Bodin, A. M. (1981). The interactional view: Family therapy approaches of the Mental Research Institute. In A. S. Gurman & D. P. Kniskern (Eds.), *Handbook of family therapy.* New York: Brunner/Mazel.

Boeringa, J. A. (1983). Blushing: A modified behavioral intervention using paradoxical intention. *Psychotherapy: Theory, Research and Practice, 20,* 441–444.

*Bogdan, J. L. (1982). Paradoxical communication as interpersonal influence. *Family Process, 21,* 443–452.

Boghosian, J. (1983). The biblical basis for strategic approaches in pastoral counseling. *Journal of Psychology and Theology, 11,* 99–107.

Borkovec, T. D. (1972). Effects of expectancy on the outcome of systematic desensitization and implosive treatments for analogue anxiety. *Behavior Therapy, 3,* 29–40.

Borkovec, T. D., & Boudewyns, P. A. (1976). Treatment of insomnia with stimulus-control and progressive relaxation procedures. In J. D. Krumboltz & C. E. Thoresen (Eds.), *Counseling methods.* New York: Holt. (Includes brief case history on paradoxical intention.)

Bornstein, P. H., Sturm, C. A., Retzlaff, P. D., Kirby, K. L., & Chong, H. (1981). Paradoxical instruction in the treatment of encopresis and chronic constipation: An experimental analysis. *Journal of Behavior Therapy and Experimental Psychiatry, 12,* 167–170.

Boudewyns, P. A. (1975). Implosive therapy and desensitization therapy with inpatients: A five-year followup. *Journal of Abnormal Psychology, 84,* 159–160.

*Boudewyns, P. A., & Shipley, R. H. (1983). *Flooding and implosive therapy: Direct therapeutic exposure in clinical practice.* New York: Plenum.

Boudewyns, P. A., & Wilson, A. E. (1972). Implosive therapy and desensitization therapy using free association in treatment of inpatients. *Journal of Abnormal Psychology, 79,* 259–268.

Boulanger, M., Laguesse-Leluron, J., & Jadot, M. (1980). [Reframing: A type of paradoxical intervention with alcoholics.] *Acta Psychiatrica Belgica, 80,* 227–235.

Boulougouris, J. C., & Marks, I. M. (1969). Implosion (flooding): A new treatment for phobias. *British Medical Journal, 2,* 721–723.

Boulougouris, J. C., Marks, I. M., & Marset, P. (1971). Superiority of flooding (implosion) to desensitisation for reducing pathological fear. *Behaviour Research and Therapy, 9,* 7–16.

Bowman, P., & Goldberg, M. (1983). "Reframing": A tool for the school psychologist. *Psychology in the Schools, 20,* 210–214.

Brehm, S. S. (1976). *The application of social psychology to clinical practice.* Washington, DC: Hemisphere.

Brehm, S. S., & Brehm, J. W. (1981). *Psychological reactance: A theory of freedom and control.* New York: Academic Press.

Breit, M., Im, W., & Wilner, R. S. (1983). Strategic approaches with resistant families. *American Journal of Family Therapy, 11,* 51–58.

Bross, A., & Gove, P. (1983). Paradox: A common element in individual and family psychotherapy. In A. Bross (Ed.), *Family therapy: Principles of strategic practice.* New York: Guilford.

Buda, B. (1972). Utilization of resistance and paradox communication in short-term psychotherapy. *Psychotherapy and Psychosomatics, 20,* 200–211.

Buddeberg, B., & Buddeberg, C. (1979). [Family therapy of anorexia nervosa.] *Praxis der Kinderpsychologie und Kinderpsychiatrie, 28,* 37–43.

Buss, A. (1976). Development of dialectics and development of humanistic psychology. *Human Development, 19,* 248–260.

Cade, B. W. (1979a). An interactional view of problem maintenance: The Davies family. *Journal of Adolescence, 2,* 51–63.

Cade, B. W. (1979b). The use of paradox in therapy. In S. Walrond-Skinner (Ed.), *Family and marital psychotherapy: A critical approach.* London: Routledge & Kegan Paul.

*Cade, B. W. (1980a). Resolving therapeutic deadlocks using a contrived team conflict. *International Journal of Family Therapy, 2,* 253–262.

Cade, B. W. (1980b). Strategic therapy. *Journal of Family Therapy, 2,* 89–99.

Cade, B. W. (1982). The potency of impotence. *Australian Journal of Family Therapy, 4,* 23–26.

*Cade, B. W. (1984). Paradoxical techniques in therapy. *Journal of Child Psychology and Psychiatry and Allied Disciplines, 25,* 509–516.

Cade, B. W., & Southgate, P. (1979). Honesty is the best policy. *Journal of Family Therapy, 1,* 23–31. (Relates to "deliberate use of pessimism.")

Carpenter, J., Treacher, A., Jenkins, H., O'Reilly, P. (1983). "Oh no! Not the Smiths again!": An exploration of how to identify and overcome stuckness in family therapy. Part II: Stuckness in the therapeutic and supervisory systems. *Journal of Family Therapy, 5,* 81–96.

Carroll, S. W., Sloop, E. W., Mutter, S., & Prince, P. L. (1978). The elimination of chronic clothes ripping in retarded people through a combination of procedures. *Mental Retardation, 16,* 246–249. (Includes use of stimulus satiation.)

Chambless, D. L., & Goldstein, A. (1980). The treatment of agoraphobia. In A. Goldstein & E. B. Foa (Eds.), *Handbook of behavioral interventions: A clinical guide.* New York: Wiley. (Includes brief section relating to paradoxical intention.)

Chase, J. L., Shea, S. J., & Dougherty, F. I. (1984). The use of paradoxical interventions within a prison psychiatric facility. *Psychotherapy, 21,* 278–281.

Chubb, H. (1982). Strategic brief therapy in a clinic setting. *Psychotherapy: Theory, Research and Practice, 19,* 160–165.

Clark, D. F. (1966). Behavior therapy of Gilles de la Tourette's syndrome. *British Journal of Psychiatry, 112,* 375–381. (On massed practice.)

Close, H. T. (1970). Gross exaggeration with a schizophrenic patient. In J. Fagan & I. L. Shepherd (Eds.), *Gestalt therapy now.* Palo Alto: Science & Behavior Books.

Cohn, R. C. (1970). Therapy in groups: Psychoanalytic, experiential, and Gestalt. In J. Fagan & I. L. Shepherd (Eds.), *Gestalt therapy now.* Palo Alto: Science & Behavior Books.

Coleman, M. L. (1956). Externalization of the toxic introject: A treatment technique for borderline cases. *Psychoanalytic Review, 43,* 235–242.

*Coleman, M. L., & Nelson, B. (1957). Paradigmatic psychotherapy in borderline treatment. *Psychoanalysis, 5,* 28–44.

Conoley, C. W., & Beard, M. (1984). The effects of a paradoxical intervention on therapeutic relationship measures. *Psychotherapy, 21,* 273–277.

Constantine, J. A., Fish, L. S., & Piercy, F. P. (1984). A systemic procedure for teaching positive connotation. *Journal of Marital and Family Therapy, 10,* 313–315.

Corsini, R. J. (1982). The relapse technique in counseling and psychotherapy. *Individual psychology: Journal of Adlerian Theory, Research and Practice, 38,* 380–385.

Cottone, R. R. (1981). Ethical issues related to use of paradoxical techniques in work adjustment. *Vocational Evaluation and Work Adjustment Bulletin, 14,* 167–170.

Cottraux, J., & Cury, N. (1976). [Treatment of a chronic catatonic schizophrenic by token economy: Play and paradox in behavior therapy.] *Perspectives Psychiatriques, 58,* 285–290.

Coyne, J. C. (1984). Strategic therapy with depressed married persons: Initial agenda, themes and interventions. *Journal of Marital and Family Therapy, 10,* 53–62. (Includes many "positive reframing" suggestions.)

*Coyne, J. C., & Biglan, A. (1984). Paradoxical techniques in strategic family therapy: A behavioral analysis. *Journal of Behavior Therapy and Experimental Psychiatry, 15,* 221–227.

Crowe, M., Marks, I., & Agràs, W. (1972). Time-limited desensitisation, implosion and shaping for phobic patients: A crossover study. *Behaviour Research and Therapy, 10,* 319–328.

Daggett, S. R. (1978). Rapid problem resolution: An "uncommon-sense" approach to rehabilitation. *Journal of Applied Rehabilitation Counseling, 9,* 13–16.

Daggett, S., Kempner, K., & Costello, J. (1982). The effectiveness of rapid problem resolution with rehabilitation failures. *Rehabilitation Counseling Bulletin, 25,* 259–267.

Dattilio, F. M. (1984). Sleep disturbances and behavior therapy. *Personnel and Guidance Journal, 62,* 373. (On paradoxical intention.)

*Davis, H. L. (1965). Short-term psychoanalytic therapy with hospitalized schizophrenics. *Psychoanalysis and the Psychoanalytic Review, 52,* 421–448.

Deatherage, G. (1979). The clinical use of "mindfulness" meditation techniques in short-term psychotherapy. In J. Welwood (Ed.), *The meeting of the ways: Explorations in East/West psychology.* New York: Schocken.

Dell, P. F. (1981a). Paradox redux. *Journal of Marital and Family Therapy, 7,* 127–134.

Dell, P. F. (1981b). Some irreverent thoughts on paradox [and] More thoughts on paradox [rejoinder by Dell to comments by Jessee & L'Abate, Selvini Palazzoli, & Watzlawick]. *Family Process, 20,* 37–42; 47–51.

Dell, P. F. (1982). Family theory and the epistemology of Humberto Maturano. In F. W. Kaslow (Ed.), *The international book of family therapy.* New York: Brunner/Mazel.

Deschenes, P., & Shepperson, V. L. (1983). The ethics of paradox. *Journal of Psychology and Theology, 11,* 92–98.

de Shazer, S. (1974). On getting unstuck: Some change-initiating tactics for getting the family moving. *Family Therapy, 1,* 19–26.

de Shazer, S. (1975). Brief therapy: Two's company. *Family Process, 14,* 79–93.

*de Shazer, S. (1978). Brief therapy with couples. *International Journal of Family Counseling, 6,* 17–30.

*de Shazer, S. (1979a). Brief therapy with families. *American Journal of Family Therapy, 7,* 83–95.

de Shazer, S. (1979b). The confusion technique. *American Journal of Family Therapy, 7,* 23–30.

de Shazer, S. (1979c). On transforming symptoms: An approach to an Erickson procedure. *American Journal of Clinical Hypnosis, 22,* 17–28.

*de Shazer, S. (1980). Brief family therapy: A metaphorical task. *Journal of Marital and Family Therapy, 6,* 471–476. (Reprinted in Appendix A.)

de Shazer, S. (1982). *Patterns of brief family therapy: An ecosystemic approach.* New York: Guilford.

Dimond, R. E. (1980). The wisdom of paradox: A new perspective on contralogical methods of problem formulation and resolution. *Psychology, 17,* 29–41.

Dolliver, R. (1972). The place of opposites in psychotherapy. *Journal of Contemporary Psychotherapy, 5,* 49–54.

Dowd, E. T., & Swoboda, J. S. (1984). Paradoxical interventions in behavior therapy. *Journal of Behavior Therapy and Experimental Psychiatry, 15,* 229–234.

Drye, R. C. (1974). Stroking the rebellious child as an aspect of managing resistance. *Transactional Analysis Journal, 4,* 23–26.

Dubin, W. (1980). Treating alienation in the family. In L. R. Wolberg & M. L. Aronson (Eds.), *Group and family therapy, 1980.* New York: Brunner/Mazel.

Dubois, P. (1908). *Psychic treatment of nervous disorders.* New York: Funk & Wagnalls.

Dunlap, K. (1928). A revision of the fundamental law of habit formation. *Science, 67,* 360–362.

Dunlap, K. (1930). Repetition in the breaking of habits. *Science Monthly, 30,* 66–70.

Dunlap, K. (1932). *Habits: Their making and unmaking.* New York: Liveright.

Dunlap, K. (1942). The technique of negative practice. *American Journal of Psychology, 55,* 270–273.

*Dunlap, K. (1946). *Personal adjustment.* New York: McGraw-Hill.

D'Zurilla, T. J., Wilson, G. T., & Nelson, R. (1973). A preliminary study of the effectiveness of graduated prolonged exposure in the treatment of irrational fear. *Behavior Therapy, 4,* 672–685. (Involves use of flooding/implosion.)

Efran, J. S., & Caputo, G. C. (1984). Paradox in psychotherapy: A cybernetic perspective. *Journal of Behavior Therapy and Experimental Psychiatry, 15,* 235–240.

Elkaim, M. (1982). [Anorexia nervosa: Individual and family therapy approaches—A systems approach to several cases of anorexia nervosa.] *Feuillets Psychiatriques de Liège, 15,* 252–265.

*Erickson, M. H. (1954a). A clinical note on indirect hypnotic therapy. *Journal of Clinical and Experimental Hypnosis, 2,* 171–174. (Reprinted under the title "Indirect Hypnotic Therapy of a Bedwetting Couple," in J. Haley, ed., *Advanced techniques of hypnosis and therapy: Selected papers of Milton H. Erickson, M.D.* New York: Grune & Stratton, 1967; and in J. Haley, ed., *Changing families.* New York: Grune & Stratton, 1971.)

*Erickson, M. H. (1954b). Special techniques in brief hypnotherapy. *Journal of Clinical and Experimental Hypnosis, 2,* 109–129. (Reprinted in J. Haley, ed., *Advanced techniques of hypnosis and therapy,* 1967.)

Erickson, M. H. (1958). Naturalistic techniques of hypnosis. *American Journal of Clinical Hypnosis, 1,* 3–8. (Reprinted in J. Haley, ed., *Advanced techniques of hypnosis and therapy,* 1967.)

Erickson, M. H. (1959). Further clinical techniques of hypnosis: Utilization techniques. *American Journal of Clinical Hypnosis, 2,* 3–21. (Reprinted in J. Haley, ed., *Advanced techniques of hypnosis and therapy,* 1967.)

Erickson, M. H. (1965). The use of symptoms as an integral part of hypnotherapy. *American Journal of Clinical Hypnosis, 8,* 57–65. (Reprinted in J. Haley, ed., *Advanced techniques of hypnosis and therapy,* 1967.)

*Erickson, M. H., & Rossi, E. L. (1975). Varieties of double bind. *American Journal of Clinical Hypnosis, 17,* 143–157.

Erickson, M. H., Rossi, E. L., & Rossi, S. I. (1976). *Hypnotic realities: The induction of clinical hypnosis and forms of indirect suggestion.* New York: Irvington.

*Evans, J. (1980). Ambivalence and how to turn it to your advantage: Adolescence and paradoxical intervention. *Journal of Adolescence, 3,* 273–284.

Fabry, J. B. (1968). *The pursuit of meaning: Logotherapy applied to life.* Boston: Beacon.

Fabry, J. (1982). Some practical hints about paradoxical intention. *International Forum for Logotherapy, 5,* 25–30.

Fabry, J., Bulka, R., & Sahakian, W. (Eds.). (1979). *Logotherapy in action.* New York: Aronson.

*Fagan, J., Shepherd, I. L. (Eds.). (1970). *Gestalt therapy now: Therapy, techniques, applications.* New York: Science & Behavior Books.

*Farrelly, F., & Brandsma, J. (1974). *Provocative therapy.* San Francisco: Shields.

*Fay, A. (1976). Clinical notes on paradoxical therapy. *Psychotherapy: Theory, Research and Practice, 13,* 118–122. (Reprinted in A. A. Lazarus, ed., *Multimodal behavior therapy.* New York: Springer, 1976.)

*Fay, A. (1978). *Making things better by making them worse.* New York: Hawthorn.

Feldman, D. A., Strong, S. R., & Danser, D. B. (1982). A comparison of paradoxical and nonparadoxical interpretations and directives. *Journal of Counseling Psychology, 29,* 572–579.

Feldman, L. (1976). Strategies and techniques of family therapy. *American Journal of Psychotherapy, 30,* 14–28.

Fellner, C. (1976). The use of teaching stories in conjoint family therapy. *Family Process, 15,* 427–431.

*Fisch, R., Weakland, J. H., & Segal, L. (1982). *The tactics of change: Doing therapy briefly.* San Francisco: Jossey-Bass.

Fish, J. M. (1973). Dissolution of a fused identity in one therapeutic session: A case study. *Journal of Consulting and Clinical Psychology, 41,* 462–465.

*Fisher, L., Anderson, A., & Jones, J. E. (1981). Types of paradoxical intervention and indications/contraindications for use in clinical practice. *Family Process, 20,* 25–35. (Reprinted in Appendix A.)

Fitzgerald, J. L. (1980). Self-transcendence: An instrument for interpreting paradoxical intention and dereflection. *Dissertation Abstracts International, 40* (10-B), 4999–5000.

Foa, E. B., Jameson, J. S., Turner, R. M., & Payne, L. L. (1980). Massed vs. spaced exposure sessions in the treatment of agoraphobia. *Behaviour Research and Therapy, 18,* 333–338.

*Fogle, D. O. (1978). Learned helplessness and learned restlessness. *Psychotherapy: Theory, Research and Practice, 15,* 39–47.

Fogle, D. O., & Dyal, J. A. (1983). Paradoxical giving up and the reduction of sleep performance anxiety in chronic insomniacs. *Psychotherapy: Theory, Research and Practice, 20,* 21–30.

Foucault, M. (1973). *Madness and civilization: A history of insanity in the Age of Reason.* New York: Random House-Vintage.

Four walls treatment. (1972, October 2). *Time*, p. 101. (On "Morita Therapy.")

Framrose, R. (1982a). Adolescent enmeshment: A case for brief strategic therapy. *Journal of Adolescence, 5,* 149–157. (Involves symptom prescription.)

Framrose, R. (1982b). From structure to strategy with the families of solvent abusers. *Journal of Family Therapy, 4,* 43–59.

Frankl, V. E. (1955). *The doctor and the soul: From psychotherapy to logotherapy.* New York: Knopf.

*Frankl, V. E. (1960). Paradoxical intention: A logotherapeutic technique. *American Journal of Psychotherapy, 14,* 520–535. (Reprinted in V. E. Frankl, *Psychotherapy and existentialism,* 1967b.)

Frankl, V. E. (1963). *Man's search for meaning* (rev. ed.). New York: Washington Square.

Frankl, V. E. (1967a). Logotherapy. *Israel Annals of Psychiatry and Related Disciplines, 5,* 142–155.

Frankl, V. E. (1967b). *Psychotherapy and existentialism: Selected papers on logotherapy.* New York: Washington Square. (Includes reprinting of Frankl's, 1960, and Gerz's, 1962, articles.)

Frankl, V. E. (1969). *The will to meaning: Foundations and applications of logotherapy.* New York: World.

*Frankl, V. E. (1975). Paradoxical intention and dereflection. *Psychotherapy: Theory, Research and Practice, 12,* 226–237.

Frankl, V. E. (1978). *The unheard cry for meaning: Psychotherapy and humanism.* New York: Simon & Schuster. (Chapter on paradoxical intention and dereflection essentially minor revision of Frankl's 1975 essay.)

Fraser, J. S. (1983). Paranoia: Interactional views on evolution and intervention. *Journal of Marital and Family Therapy, 9,* 383–391.

Fraser, J. S. (1984). Paradox and orthodox: Folie à deux? *Journal of Marital and Family Therapy, 10,* 361–372.

Freud, A. (1946). *Psychoanalytic treatment of children.* London: Imago. (Original work published 1928)

Freud, S. (1958). *The standard edition of the complete psychological works of Sigmund Freud* (Vols. 1, 12, 17). London: Hogarth.

Frey, J., III (1984). A family/systems approach to illness-maintaining behaviors in chronically ill adolescents. *Family Process, 23,* 251–260.

Gelder, M. G., Bancroft, J. H. J., Gath, D. H., Johnston, D. W., Mathews, A. M., & Shaw, P. M. (1973). Specific and non-specific factors in behavior therapy. *British Journal of Psychiatry, 123,* 445–462. (Empirical study of flooding and systematic desensitization.)

Gentry, D. L. (1973). Directive therapy techniques in the treatment of migraine headaches: A case study. *Psychotherapy: Theory, Research and Practice, 10,* 308–311.

Gentry, D. L. (1978). The treatment of premature ejaculation through brief therapy. *Psychotherapy: Theory, Research and Practice, 15,* 32–34.

Gerz, H. O. (1962). The treatment of the phobic and the obsessive-compulsive patient using paradoxical intention. *Journal of Neuropsychiatry, 3,* 375–387. (Reprinted in V. E. Frankl, *Psychotherapy and existentialism,* 1967b.)

Gerz, H. O. (1966). Experience with the logotherapeutic technique of paradoxical intention in the treatment of phobic and obsessive-compulsive patients. *American Journal of Psychiatry, 123,* 548–553.

*Gerz, H. O. (1979). Paradoxical intention. In J. Fabry, R. Bulka, & W. Sahakian (Eds.), *Logotherapy in action.* New York: Aronson.

Goding, G. (1979). Change and paradox in family therapy. *Australian Journal of Family Therapy, 1,* 9–15.

Goldberg, C. (1977). *Therapeutic partnership—Ethical concerns in psychotherapy.* New York: Springer.

*Goldberg, C. (1980). The utilization and limitations of paradoxical intervention in group psychotherapy. *International Journal of Group Psychotherapy, 30,* 287–297.

Goldsmith, S. (1983). Strategic psychotherapy in psychiatric consultations. *American Journal of Psychotherapy, 37,* 279–284.

Goldstein, A. J. (1978). Case conference: The treatment of a case of agoraphobia by a multifaceted treatment program. *Journal of Behavior Therapy and Experimental Psychiatry, 9,* 45–51. (Includes use of paradoxical intention.)

Gottlieb, B. S., & McNamara, J. R. (1979). Comparison of response exaggeration techniques. *Journal of Clinical Psychology, 35,* 776–778.

Greenberg, G. S. (1977). The family interactional perspective: A study and examination of the work of Don D. Jackson. *Family Process, 16,* 385–412.

Greenberg, G. S. (1980). Problem-focused brief family psychotherapy. In L. R. Wolberg & M. L. Aronson (Eds.), *Group and family therapy, 1980.* New York: Brunner/Mazel.

*Greenberg, R. P. (1973). Anti-expectation techniques in psychotherapy: The power of negative thinking. *Psychotherapy: Theory, Research and Practice, 10,* 145–148.

Greenberg, R. P. (1980). Anti-expectation psychotherapy techniques. In R. Herink (Ed.), *The psychotherapy handbook.* New York: New American Library.

Greenberg, R. P., & Pies, R. (1983). Is paradoxical intention risk-free? A review and case report. *Journal of Clinical Psychiatry, 44* (2), 66–69.

Greenwald, H. (1967). Play therapy for children over twenty-one. *Psychotherapy: Theory, Research and Practice, 4,* 44–46.

Greenwald, H. (1973). *Decision therapy.* New York: Wyden.

Grossman, D. (1964). Ego-activating approaches to psychotherapy. *Psychoanalytic Review, 51,* 401–424. (Includes use of paradigmatic techniques.)

Grunebaum, H., & Chasin, R. (1978). Relabeling and reframing reconsidered: The beneficial effects of a pathological label. *Family Process, 17,* 449–456.

Gurman, A. S. (1981). Integrative marital therapy: Toward the development of an interpersonal approach. In S. H. Budman (Ed.), *Forms of brief therapy.* New York: Guilford.

Gurman, A. S. (1982). Using paradox in psychodynamic marital therapy. *American Journal of Family Therapy, 10,* 72–74.

Guthrie, E. R. (1935). *The psychology of learning.* New York: Harper. (Relates to theoretical explanation of negative practice.)

Haley, J. (1958). An interactional explanation of hypnosis. *American Journal of Clinical Hypnosis, 1,* 41–57. (Reprinted in D. D. Jackson, ed., *Therapy, communication, and change.* Palo Alto: Science & Behavior Books, 1968.)

Haley, J. (1962). Whither family therapy? *Family Process, 1,* 69–100.

*Haley, J. (1963). *Strategies of psychotherapy.* New York: Grune & Stratton. (Chapter 6, "Marriage Therapy," has also appeared in *Archives of General Psychiatry,* 1963, *8,* 213–234; and in H. Greenwald, ed., *Active psychotherapy.* New York: Atherton, 1967.)

*Haley, J. (Ed.). (1967). *Advanced techniques of hypnosis and therapy: Selected papers of Milton H. Erickson, M.D.* New York: Grune & Stratton.

*Haley, J. (1973). *Uncommon therapy: The psychiatric techniques of Milton H. Erickson, M.D.* New York: Norton.

*Haley, J. (1976). *Problem-solving therapy: New strategies for effective family therapy.* New York: Harper & Row. (Excerpted in Appendix A.)

Haley, J. (1980). *Leaving home: The therapy of disturbed young people.* New York: McGraw-Hill.

Haley, J. (1984). *Ordeal therapy: Unusual ways to change behavior.* San Francisco: Jossey-Bass.

Hand, I., & Lamontagne, Y. (1974). [Paradoxical intention and behavioral techniques in short-term psychotherapy.] *Canadian Psychiatric Association Journal, 19,* 501–507.

Hanks, W. L. (1983). "There's something about that name." *International Forum for Logotherapy, 6,* 31–33. (On paradoxical intention.)

Hannum, J. W. (1980). Some cotherapy techniques with families. *Family Process, 19,* 161–168.

Hansen, J. C., & L'Abate, L. (1982). *Approaches to family therapy.* New York: Macmillan.

Hare-Mustin, R. T. (1975). Treatment of temper tantrums by paradoxical intervention. *Family Process, 14,* 481–486.

*Hare-Mustin, R. T. (1976). Paradoxical tasks in family therapy: Who can resist? *Psychotherapy: Theory, Research and Practice, 13,* 128–130.

Hart, O. van der (1983). *Rituals in psychotherapy: Transition and continuity.* (A. Pleit-Kuiper, Trans.). New York: Irvington. (Original work published 1978)

Hartman, W. J. (1968). Discussion [of J. R. Newton's Considerations for the psychotherapeutic technique of symptom scheduling]. *Psychotherapy: Theory, Research and Practice, 5,* 194–195.

Havens, L. (1968). Paradoxical intention. *Psychiatric and Social Science Review, 2,* 16–19.

Haynes, R. (1978). Treatment of an obsessive-compulsive checker. *Behaviour Research and Therapy, 16,* 136–137. (Uses procedure referred to as "satiation training," though it is described in terms of paradoxical intention.)

Heide, F. J., & Borkovec, T. D. (1984). Relaxation-induced anxiety: Mechanisms and theoretical implications. *Behaviour Research and Therapy, 22,* 1–12.

Held, B. S. (1984). Toward a strategic eclecticism: A proposal. *Psychotherapy, 21,* 232–241.

*Held, B. S., & Heller, L. (1982). Symptom prescription as metaphor: A systemic approach to the psychosomatic-alcoholic family. *Family Therapy, 9,* 133–145.

Helson, H. (1964). *Adaptation level theory.* New York: Harper.

Hennig, L. H. (1981). Paradox as a treatment for writer's block. *Personnel and Guidance Journal, 60,* 112–113.

*Herr, J. J., & Weakland, J. H. (1979). *Counseling elders and their families: Practical techniques for applied gerontology.* New York: Springer.

Hersen, M., & Eisler, R. M. (1973). Behavioral approaches to the study and treatment of psychogenic tics. *Genetic Psychology Monographs, 87,* 289–312. (Includes section on massed practice.)

Hess, T. (1980). [Paradoxical interventions in systemic family therapy.] *Familiendynamik, 5,* 57–72.

Hodgson, R., & Rachman, S. (1970). An experimental study of the implosion technique. *Behaviour Research and Therapy, 8,* 21–28.

Hoebel, F. C. (1977). Coronary artery disease and family interaction: A study of risk factor modification. In P. Watzlawick & J. H. Weakland (Eds.), *The interactional view.* New York: Norton. (Involves paradoxical strategy used to treat depressive reaction following major surgery.)

Hoffman, L. (1976). Breaking the homeostatic cycle. In P. Guerin (Ed.), *Family therapy.* New York: Gardner.

Hoffman, L. (1980). The family life cycle and discontinuous change. In E. A. Carter & M. McGoldrick (Eds.), *The family life cycle: A framework for family therapy.* New York: Gardner.

*Hoffman, L. (1981). *Foundations of family therapy: A conceptual framework for systems change.* New York: Basic Books.

*Hogan, R. A. (1968). The implosive technique. *Behaviour Research and Therapy, 6,* 423–431.

Hsu, L. K. G., & Lieberman, S. (1982). Paradoxical intention in the treatment of chronic anorexia nervosa. *American Journal of Psychiatry, 139,* 650–653.

Huber, J. (1968). *Through an Eastern window.* New York: Bantam Books.

Hull, C. L. (1943). *Principles of behavior.* New York: Appleton.

Hyer, L. A. (1983). Case history: Paradoxical letters in family therapy. *Clinical Gerontologist, 2,* 58–61.

Im, W., Wilner, R. S., & Breit, M. (1983). Jealousy: Interventions in couples therapy. *Family Process, 22,* 211–219.

*Jackson, D. D. (1963). A suggestion for the technical handling of paranoid patients. *Psychiatry, 26,* 306–307.

Jackson, D. D., & Watzlawick, P. (1963). The acute psychosis as a manifestation of growth experience. *Psychiatric Reports, 16,* 83–94. (Also in D. D. Jackson, ed., *Therapy, communication, and change.* Palo Alto: Science & Behavior Books, 1968.)

Jackson, D. D., & Yalom, I. (1964). Family homeostasis and patient change. In J. Masserman (Ed.), *Current psychiatric therapies* (Vol. 4). New York: Grune & Stratton.

*Jacob, R. G., & Moore, D. J. (1984). Paradoxical interventions in behavioral medicine. *Journal of Behavior Therapy and Experimental Psychiatry, 15,* 205–213.

Jacobs, M. (1972). An holistic approach to behavior therapy. In A. A. Lazarus (Ed.), *Clinical behavior therapy.* New York: Brunner/Mazel. (Includes use of paradoxical intention.)

*Jacobson, N. S., & Margolin, G. (1979). *Marital therapy: Strategies based on social learning and behavior exchange principles.* New York: Brunner/Mazel.

Jenkins, H. (1980). Paradox: A pivotal point in therapy. *Journal of Family Therapy, 2,* 339–356.

Jenkins, J., Hildebrand, J., & Lask, B. (1982). Failure: An exploration and survival kit. *Journal of Family Therapy, 4,* 307–320.

*Jessee, E. H., Jurkovic, G. J., Wilkie, J., & Chiglinsky, M. (1982). Positive reframing with children: Conceptual and clinical considerations. *American Journal of Orthopsychiatry, 52,* 314–322.

*Jessee, E., & L'Abate, L. (1980). The use of paradox with children in an inpatient treatment setting. *Family Process, 19,* 59–64.

Jessee, E., & L'Abate, L. (1981). Comments [on P. F. Dell's Some irreverent thoughts on paradox]. *Family Process, 20,* 42–44.

Johnson, J., Weeks, G. R., & L'Abate, L. (1979). Forced holding: A technique for treating parentified children. *Family Therapy, 6,* 123–133.

Johnston, D. W., Lancashire, M., Mathews, A. M., Munby, M., Shaw, P. M., & Gelder, M. G. (1976). Imaginal flooding and exposure to real phobic situations: Changes during treatment. *British Journal of Psychiatry, 129,* 372–377.

Jones, H. (1960). Continuation of Yates' treatment of a tiquer. In H. J. Eysenck (Ed.), *Behavior therapy and the neuroses.* Oxford: Pergamon. (On massed practice.)

Kaczanowski, G. (1967). Logotherapy—A new psychotherapeutic tool. *Psychosomatics, 8,* 158–161.

Kagan, R. M. (1980). Using redefinition and paradox with children in placement who provoke rejection. *Child Welfare, 59,* 551–559.

Kandel, H. J. (1978). Paradoxical intention: An empirical investigation. *Dissertation Abstracts International, 39* (1-B), 384–385.

*Keith, D. V., & Whitaker, C. A. (1978). Struggling with the impotence impasse: Absurdity and acting-in. *Journal of Marriage and Family Counseling, 4,* 69–77.

Keith, D. V., & Whitaker, C. A. (1981). Play therapy: A paradigm for work with families. *Journal of Marital and Family Therapy, 7,* 243–254.

Keller, J. F., & Elliot, S. S. (1982). Reframing in marital therapy: From deficit to self-sacrifice as focus. *Family Therapy, 9,* 119–126.

Kellerman, J. (1981). Hypnosis as an adjunct to thought-stopping and covert reinforcement in the treatment of homicidal obsessions in a twelve-year-old boy. *International Journal of Clinical and Experimental Hypnosis, 29,* 128–135. (Includes peripheral use of paradoxical intention.)

*Kesten, J. (1950). Learning for spite. *Psychoanalysis, 4,* 63–67. (Reprinted in H. S. Strean, ed., *New approaches to child guidance,* 1970.)

Kolko, D. J., & Milan, M. A. (1983). Reframing and paradoxical instruction to overcome "resistance" in the treatment of delinquent youths: A multiple baseline analysis. *Journal of Consulting and Clinical Psychology, 51,* 655–660.

Kondo, A. (1975). Morita therapy: Its sociohistorical context. In S. Arieti & G. Chrzanowski (Eds.), *New dimensions in psychiatry: A world view.* New York: Wiley.

Kopp, S. B. (1976). *If you meet the Buddha on the road, kill him! The pilgrimage of psychotherapy patients.* Toronto: Bantam Books.

Kopp, S. B. (1978). Tantric therapy. *Journal of Contemporary Psychotherapy, 9,* 131–134.

Kora, T., & Sato, K. (1958). Morita therapy: A psychotherapy in the way of Zen. *Psychologia, 1,* 219–225.

Kovacs, A. L. (1982). Survival in the 1980s: On the theory and practice of brief psychotherapy. *Psychotherapy: Theory, Research and Practice, 19,* 142–159. (Includes strategic use of reframing and symptom prescription.)

Kraus, L. M. (1980). Therapeutic strategies with adolescents. *Social Casework, 61,* 313–316.

Krisch, K. (1981). [Paradoxical intention, de-reflexion and the logotherapeutic theory of the neurosis: A critical survey.] *Psychotherapie Psychosomatik Medizinische Psychologie, 31,* 162–165.

Krumboltz, J. D., & Krumboltz, H. B. (1972). *Changing children's behavior.* Englewood Cliffs, NJ: Prentice-Hall. (Includes chapter on "the satiation principle.")

Kutzin, A. (1980). Paradoxical experiential therapy: A description of the technique and rationale of a nonbehavioral therapy for an unselected patient population. *Journal of Contemporary Psychotherapy, 11,* 131–153.

L'Abate, L. (1976). *Understanding and helping the individual in the family.* New York: Grune & Stratton.

L'Abate, L. (1977). *Enrichment: Structured interventions with couples, families, and groups.* Washington, DC: University Press of America.

L'Abate, L. (in press). The paradoxical treatment of (marital) depression. *International Journal of Family Therapy.*

L'Abate, L., Baggett, M. S., & Anderson, J. S. (1984). Linear and circular interventions with families of children with school related problems. *Family Therapy Collections, 9,* 13–27.

L'Abate, L., & Farr, L. (1981). Coping with defeating patterns in family therapy. *Family Therapy, 8,* 91–103.

L'Abate, L., & L'Abate, B. L. (1979). The paradoxes of intimacy. *Family Therapy, 6,* 175–184.

L'Abate, L., & Weeks, G. (1978). A bibliography of paradoxical methods in psychotherapy of family systems. *Family Process, 17,* 95–98.

Lacks, P., Bertelson, A. D., Gans, L., & Kunkel, J. (1983). The effectiveness of three behavioral treatments for different degrees of sleep onset insomnia. *Behavior Therapy, 14,* 593–605. (Includes use of paradoxical intention.)

Lamb, C. S. (1980). The use of paradoxical intention: Self-management through laughter. *Personnel and Guidance Journal, 59,* 217–219.

Lamontagne, Y. (1978). Single case study: Treatment of erythrophobia by paradoxical intention. *Journal of Nervous and Mental Disease, 166,* 304–306.

Lange, A., & Hart, O. van der (1983). *Directive family therapy* (M. A. Shadeff & J. Quysner, Trans.). New York: Brunner/Mazel.

Lankton, S. R., & Lankton, C. H. (1983). *The answer within: A clinical framework of Ericksonian hypnotherapy.* New York: Brunner/Mazel.

Lantz, J. E. (1978). *Family and marital therapy: A transactional approach.* New York: Appleton.

Lapinsohn, L. I. (1971). Relationship of the logotherapeutic concepts of anticipatory anxiety and paradoxical intention to the neurophysiological theory of induction. *Behavioral neuropsychiatry, 3,* 12–14; 24.

Last, C. G., Barlow, D. H., & O'Brien, G. T. (1983). Comparison of two cognitive strategies in treatment of a patient with generalized anxiety disorder. *Psychological Reports, 53,* 19–26. (Compares coping self-statements with paradoxical intention.)

Latner, J. (1974). *The Gestalt therapy book.* New York: Bantam Books.

Lazarus, A. A. (1964). Objective psychotherapy in the treatment of dysphemia. In H. J. Eysenck (Ed.), *Experiments in behavior therapy.* Oxford: Pergamon. (Involves successful use of negative practice in treating tics.)

Lazarus, A. (1971a). *Behavior therapy and beyond.* New York: McGraw-Hill. (Includes technique called "blow up," which is essentially identical to paradoxical intention.)

Lazarus, A. (1971b). New techniques for behavioral change. *Rational Living, 6,* 2–7. (Also on blow-up technique.)

Lehembre, J. (1964). [The paradoxical intention method of psychotherapy.] *Acta Neurologica et Psychiatrica Belgica, 64,* 725–735.

*Lehner, G. F. J. (1954). Negative practice as a psychotherapeutic technique. *Journal of General Psychology, 51,* 69–82.

Leitenberg, H. (1976). Behavioral approaches to treatment of neuroses. In H. Leitenberg (Ed.), *Handbook of behavior modification and behavior therapy.* Englewood Cliffs, NJ: Prentice-Hall. (Includes discussion of flooding/implosion.)

Levant, R. F. (1984). *Family therapy: A comprehensive overview.* Englewood Cliffs, NJ: Prentice-Hall.

Levis, D. J., & Hare, N. (1977). A review of the theoretical rationale and empirical support for the extinction approach of implosive (flooding) therapy. In M. Herson, R. M. Eisler, & P. M. Miller (Eds.), *Progress in behavior modification* (Vol. 4). New York: Academic Press.

Levitsky, A. (1976). Combining hypnosis with Gestalt therapy. In E. W. L. Smith (Ed.), *The growing edge of Gestalt therapy.* New York: Brunner/Mazel.

*Levitsky, A., & Perls, F. S. (1970). The rules and games of Gestalt therapy. In J. Fagan & I. L. Shepherd (Eds.), *Gestalt therapy now.* Palo Alto: Science & Behavior Books.

*Lindner, R. (1955). *The fifty-minute hour: A collection of true psychoanalytic tales.* New York: Rinehart.

Lopez, F. G. (1983). A paradoxical approach to vocational indecision. *Personnel and Guidance Journal, 61,* 410–412.

Lopez, F. G., & Wambach, C. A. (1982). Effects of paradoxical and self-control directives in counseling. *Journal of Counseling Psychology, 29,* 115–124.

Loro, A. D., & Orleans, C. S. (1981). Binge eating in obesity: Preliminary findings and guidelines for behavioral analysis and treatment. *Addictive Behaviors, 6,* 155–166. (Involves "programmed binge-ing.")

Love, S., & Mayer, H. (1959). Going along with defenses in resistive families. *Journal of Social Casework, 40,* 69–73. (Reprinted in H. S. Strean, ed., *New approaches to child guidance,* 1970.)

Lukas, E. (1982). The "birthmarks" of paradoxical intention. *International Forum for Logotherapy, 5,* 20–24.

Macaruso, M. C. (1979). Treating emotionally disturbed children. In J. Fabry, R. Bulka, & W. Sahakian (Eds.), *Logotherapy in action.* New York: Aronson.

Madanes, C. (1980a). Marital therapy when a symptom is presented by a spouse. *International Journal of Family Therapy, 2,* 120–136.

*Madanes, C. (1980b). Protection, paradox and pretending. *Family Process, 19,* 73–85.

*Madanes, C. (1981). *Strategic family therapy.* San Francisco: Jossey-Bass.

*Madanes, C. (1984). *Behind the one-way mirror: Advances in the practice of strategic therapy.* San Francisco: Jossey-Bass.

Madanes, C., & Haley, J. (1977). Dimensions of family therapy. *Journal of Nervous and Mental Disease, 165,* 88–98.

Malleson, N. (1959). Panic and phobia. *Lance, 1,* 225–227. (Involves use of flooding.)

Mandel, H. P., & Cooper, I. J. (1980). Paradoxical intention and hypnosis and brief psychotherapy: A case report. *Ontario Psychologist, 12,* 6–12.

*Mandel, H. P., Weizmann, F., Millan, B., Greenhow, J., & Speirs, D. (1975). Reaching emotionally disturbed children: "Judo" principles in remedial education. *American Journal of Orthopsychiatry, 45,* 867–874.

Marks, I. M. (1972). Paradoxical intention. In W. S. Agras (Ed.), *Behavior modification: Principles and clinical applications.* Boston: Little, Brown.

Marks, I. M. (1975). Behavioral treatments of phobic and obsessive-compulsive disorders: A critical appraisal. In M. Hersen, R. M. Eisler, & P. M. Miller (Eds.), *Progress in behavior modification* (Vol. 1). New York: Academic Press. (Discusses flooding/implosion procedures.)

Marks, I. M. (1978). Exposure treatments: Clinical applications. In W. S. Agras (Ed.), *Behavior modification* (2nd ed.). Boston: Little, Brown.

Marlatt, G. A. (1978). Craving for alcohol, loss of control, and relapse: A cognitive-behavioral analysis. In P. E. Nathan, G. A. Marlatt, & T. Loberg (Eds.), *Alcoholism: New directions in behavioral research and treatment.* New York:

Plenum. (Discusses use of carefully supervised "programmed relapse" in treatment of alcoholics.)

Marlatt, G. A., & Gordon, J. R. (1980). Determinants of relapse: Implications for the maintenance of behavior change. In P. O. Davidson & S. M. Davidson (Eds.), *Behavioral medicine: Changing health lifestyles.* New York: Brunner/Mazel.

Marshall, R. J. (1972). The treatment of resistances in the psychotherapy of children and adolescents. *Psychotherapy: Theory, Research and Practice, 9,* 143–148.

Marshall, R. J. (1974). Meeting the resistances of delinquents. *Psychoanalytic Review, 61,* 295–304.

*Marshall, R. J. (1976). "Joining techniques" in the treatment of resistant children and adolescents. *American Journal of Psychotherapy, 30,* 73–84.

*Marshall, R. J. (1982). *Resistant interactions: Child, family and psychotherapist.* New York: Human Sciences Press. (Chapters 3 & 4 based on 1976 and 1972 articles respectively.)

Marshall, W. L., Gauthier, J., & Gordon, A. (1979). The current status of flooding therapy. In M. Hersen, R. M. Eisler, & P. M. Miller (Eds.), *Progress in behavior modification* (Vol. 7). New York: Academic Press.

Massey, R. (1983). Passivity, paradox, and change in family systems. *Transactional Analysis Journal, 13,* 33–41.

Mavissakalian, M., Michelson, L, Greenwald, D., Kornblith, S., & Greenwald, M. (1983). Cognitive-behavioral treatment of agoraphobia: Paradoxical intention vs self-statement training. *Behaviour Research and Therapy, 21,* 75–86.

Mazza, J. (1984). Symptom utilization in strategic therapy. *Family Process, 23,* 487–500.

McFarlane, W. R. (Ed.). (1983). *Family therapy in schizophrenia.* New York: Guilford.

McGeoch, J. A., & Irion, A. L. (1952). *The psychology of human learning.* New York: Longmans Green.

Meador, B. D., & Rogers, C. R. (1973). Client-centered therapy. In R. Corsini (Ed.), *Current psychotherapies.* Itasca, IL: Peacock.

Metsch, H. (1983). [On paradoxical instructions.] *Partnerberatung, 20,* 68–72.

Meyer, V. (1966). Modification of expectations in cases with obsessional rituals. *Behaviour Research and Therapy, 4,* 273–280. (Involves procedure kindred to paradoxical intention.)

Michelson, L., & Ascher, L. M. (1984). Paradoxical intention in the treatment of agoraphobia and other anxiety disorders. *Journal of Behavior Therapy and Experimental Psychiatry, 15,* 215–220.

Milan, M. A., & Kolko, D. J. (1982). Paradoxical intention in the treatment of obsessional flatulence ruminations. *Journal of Behavior Therapy and Experimental Psychiatry, 13,* 167–172.

Minuchin, S., & Fishman, H. (1981). *Family therapy techniques.* Cambridge, MA: Harvard University Press.

Mirkin, M. P. (1983). The Peter Pan syndrome: Inpatient treatment of adolescent anorexia nervosa. *International Journal of Family Therapy, 5,* 179–189.

Mogel, S., & Schiff, W. (1967). "Extinction" of a head-bumping symptom of eight years duration in two minutes. *Behaviour Research and Therapy, 5,* 131–132. (On massed practice.)

Moley, V. A. (1983). Interactional treatment of eating disorders. *Journal of Strategic and Systemic Therapies, 2,* 10–28.

Morelli, G. (1978). Paradoxical intention: A case study of an effective method of treating alcoholism and drug abuse. *Psychology, 15,* 57–59.

Morganstern, K. P. (1973). Implosive therapy and flooding procedures: A critical review. *Psychological Bulletin, 79,* 318–334.

Morganstern, K. P. (1974). Issues in implosive therapy: Reply to Levis. *Psychological Bulletin, 81,* 380–382.

*Mozdzierz, G. J., Macchitelli, F. J., & Lisiecki, J. (1976). The paradox in psychotherapy: An Adlerian perspective. *Journal of Individual Psychology, 32,* 169–184.

Muller-Hegemann, D. (1963). Methodological approaches in psychotherapy. *American Journal of Psychotherapy, 17,* 554–568. (Includes brief section on paradoxical intention.)

*Musliner, P. (1980). Strategic therapy with families and children. *Journal of the American Academy of Child Psychiatry, 19,* 101–117.

Mylar, J. L., & Clement, P. W. (1972). Prediction and comparison of outcome in systematic desensitization and implosion. *Behaviour Research and Therapy, 10,* 235–246.

Nelson, B. (1965). The psychoanalyst as mediator and double agent. *Psychoanalytic Review, 52,* 45–60.

*Nelson, M. Coleman. (1962). Effect of paradigmatic techniques on the psychic economy of borderline patients. *Psychiatry, 25,* 119–134.

Nelson, M. Coleman. (1979). Comment. *Voices, 15,* 76–77.

*Nelson, M. Coleman, Nelson, B., Sherman, M. H., & Strean, H. S. (Eds.). (1968). *Roles and paradigms in psychotherapy.* New York: Grune & Stratton.

*Newton, J. R. (1968a). Considerations for the psychotherapeutic technique of symptom scheduling. *Psychotherapy: Theory, Research and Practice, 5,* 95–103. (Reprinted in Appendix A.)

Newton, J. R. (1968b). Therapeutic paradoxes, paradoxical intentions, and negative practice. *American Journal of Psychotherapy, 22,* 68–81.

Nichols, M. P. (1984). *Family therapy: Concepts and methods.* New York: Gardner.

Noonan, J. R. (1969). A note on an Eastern counterpart of Frankl's paradoxical intention. *Psychologia: An International Journal of Psychology in the Orient, 2,* 147–149.

Nystul, M. S., & Muszynska, E. (1976). Adlerian treatment of a classical case of stuttering. *Journal of Individual Psychology, 32,* 194–202.

Oberfield, R. A. (1981). Family therapy with adolescents: Treatment of a teenage girl with *globus hystericus* and weight loss. *Journal of the American Academy of Child Psychiatry, 20,* 822–833.

*O'Connell, D. S. (1983). Symptom prescription in psychotherapy. *Psychotherapy: Theory, Research and Practice, 20,* 12–20. (Excerpted in Appendix A.)

O'Connor, J. J. (1983). Why can't I get hives: Brief strategic therapy with an obsessional child. *Family Process, 22,* 201–209.

Olds, D. D. (1981). Stagnation in psychotherapy and the development of active technique. *Psychiatry, 44,* 133–140. (Eclectic approach includes use of paradoxical strategies.)

*Omer, H. (1981). Paradoxical treatments: A unified concept. *Psychotherapy: Theory, Research and Practice, 18,* 320–324.

Oppenheim, H. (1911). *The textbook of nervous disorders for physicians and students* (5th ed.). New York: Stechert.

*Ormont, L. (1974). The treatment of pre-Oedipal resistances in the group setting. *Psychoanalytic Review, 61,* 429–441.

Ott, B. D., Levine, B. A., & Ascher, L. M. (1983). Manipulating the explicit demand of paradoxical intention instructions. *Behavioural Psychotherapy, 11,* 25–35.

Papp, P. (1976). Brief therapy with couples groups. In P. J. Guerin (Ed.), *Family therapy: Theory and practice.* New York: Gardner.

*Papp, P. (1977). The family who had all the answers. In P. Papp (Ed.), *Family therapy: Full length case studies.* New York: Gardner.

*Papp, P. (1979). Paradoxical strategies and countertransference. *American Journal of Family Therapy, 7,* 11–12. (Reprinted in A. S. Gurman, ed., *Questions and answers in the practice of family therapy.* New York: Brunner/Mazel, 1981. Also reprinted in Appendix A.)

*Papp, P. (1980a). The Greek chorus and other techniques of paradoxical therapy. *Family Process, 19,* 45–57. (Reprinted in S. Minuchin & H. Fishman, *Family therapy techniques.* Cambridge, MA: Harvard University Press, 1981.)

Papp, P. (1980b). The use of fantasy in a couples' group. In M. Andolfi & I. Zwerling (Eds.), *Dimensions of family therapy.* New York: Guilford.

*Papp, P. (1983). *The process of change.* New York: Guilford. (Includes "revised version" of Papp's 1980a article.)

Patterson, C. H. (1980a). *Theories of counseling and psychotherapy* (3rd ed.). New York: Harper & Row. (Includes section on paradoxical intention and dereflection.)

Pelletier, K. R., & Garfield, C. (1976). *Consciousness East and West.* New York: Harper. (Includes discussion of Morita therapy.)

Pendleton, M. G., & Higgins, R. L. (1983). A comparison of negative practice and systematic desensitization in the treatment of acrophobia. *Journal of Behavior Therapy and Experimental Psychiatry, 14,* 317–323.

Perls, F. S. (1971). *Gestalt therapy verbatim.* New York: Bantam Books.

*Perls, F. S. (1976). *The Gestalt approach and Eye witness to therapy.* New York: Bantam Books.

Perls, F., Hefferline, R., & Goodman, P. (1951). *Gestalt therapy: Excitement and growth in the human personality.* New York: Julian.

Peterson, L., & Melcher, R. (1981). To change, be yourself: An illustration of paradox in Gestalt therapy. *Personnel and Guidance Journal, 60,* 101–103.

Pollard, J. W. (1979). Symptom prescription: The paradoxical interaction of extrinsic on intrinsic motivation. *Dissertation Abstracts International, 40* (2-B), 899.

Polster, E., & Polster, M. (1973). *Gestalt therapy integrated: Contours of theory and practice.* New York: Brunner/Mazel.

Protinsky, H., & Dillard, C. (1983). Enuresis: A family therapy model. *Psychotherapy: Theory, Research and Practice, 20,* 81–89.

Protinsky, H., & Quinn, W. (1981). Paradoxical marital therapy with symptom triangulation. *Family Therapy, 8,* 135–140.

Protinsky, H., Quinn, W., & Elliott, S. (1982). Paradoxical prescriptions in family therapy: From child to marital focus. *Journal of Marital and Family Therapy, 8,* 51–55.

Puig, A. (1983). Relabeling or restructuring as a supportive therapeutic intervention in problems of academic stress. *Journal of College Student Personnel, 24,* 273–274.

Rabkin, R. (1976). A critique of the clinical use of the double bind. In C. Sluzki & D. C. Ransom (Eds.), *Double bind.* New York: Grune & Stratton.

Rabkin, R. (1977). *Strategic psychotherapy: Brief and symptomatic treatment.* New York: Basic Books.

Rabkin, R. (1980). The midgame in strategic therapy. *International Journal of Family Therapy, 2,* 159–168.

Rachman, S. (1969). Treatment by prolonged exposure to high intensity stimulation. *Behaviour Research and Therapy, 7,* 295–302. (On flooding/implosion.)

Rachman, S. (1976). The modification of obsessions: A new formulation. *Behaviour Research and Therapy, 14,* 437–443. (Combines response prevention with satiation training.)

Rachman, S., & Hodgson, R. (1980). Obsessions and compulsions. Englewood Cliffs, NJ: Prentice-Hall. (Includes discussion of flooding/implosion.)

Rafi, A. A. (1962). Learning theory and the treatment of tics. *Journal of Psychosomatic Research, 6,* 71–76. (Involves successful use of negative practice.)

*Raskin, D. E., & Klein, Z. E. (1976). Losing a symptom through keeping it: A review of paradoxical treatment techniques and rationale. *Archives of General Psychiatry, 33,* 548–555.

Reilly, D. M. (1984). Family therapy with adolescent drug abusers and their families: Defying gravity and achieving escape velocity. *Journal of Drug Issues, 14,* 381–391.

Relinger, H., & Bornstein, P. H. (1979). Treatment of sleep onset insomnia by paradoxical instruction: A multiple baseline design. *Behavior Modification, 3,* 203–222.

Relinger, H., Bornstein, P. H., & Mungas, D. M. (1978). Treatment of insomnia by paradoxical intention: A time-series analysis. *Behavior Therapy, 9,* 955–959.

Riebel, L. K. (1981). The concept of paradox as a construct in psychotherapy. *Dissertation Abstracts International, 42,* 3831-B. (University Microfilms, No. 8205203)

*Riebel, L. (1984a). A homeopathic model of psychotherapy. *Journal of Humanistic Psychotherapy, 24,* 9–48.

*Riebel, L. (1984b). Paradoxical intention strategies: A review of rationales. *Psychotherapy, 21,* 260–272.

*Rimm, D., & Masters, J. (1979). *Behavior therapy: Techniques and empirical findings* (2nd ed.). New York: Academic Press. (Includes sections on negative practice, stimulus satiation, implosion, and flooding/response prevention.)

Ritow, J. K. (1979). Brief treatment of a vomiting phobia. *American Journal of Clinical Hypnosis, 21,* 293–296.

Riveros de Carbone, J. (1984). Maurice and Mr. Sleep. *International Forum for Logotherapy, 7,* 55–56. (Use of paradoxical intention to cure young boy's insomnia.)

Robin Skynner, A. C. (1981). An open-systems, group-analytic approach to family therapy. In A. S. Gurman & D. P. Kniskern (Eds.), *Handbook of family therapy.* New York: Brunner/Mazel.

Rohrbaugh, M., Tennen, H., & Eron, J. (1982). Paradoxical interventions. In J. H. Masserman (Ed.), *Current psychiatric therapies* (Vol. 21). New York: Grune & Stratton.

*Rohrbaugh, M., Tennen, H., Press, S., & White, L. (1981). Compliance, defiance, and therapeutic paradox: Guidelines for strategic use of paradoxical interventions. *American Journal of Orthopsychiatry, 51,* 454–467. (Reprinted in Appendix A.)

*Rosen, J. H. (1953). *Direct analysis: Selected papers.* New York: Grune & Stratton.

Rosen, J. H. (1962). *Direct psychoanalytic psychotherapy.* New York: Grune & Stratton.

Rosen, L. W. (1980). Modification of secretive or ritualized eating behavior in anorexia nervosa. *Journal of Behavior Therapy and Experimental Psychiatry, 11,* 101–104. (Involves prescription of "idiosyncratic feeding patterns.")

*Rosenbaum, R. L. (1982). Paradox as epistemological jump. *Family Process, 21,* 85–90.

Roy, I., & Lamontagne, Y. (1976). [Behavior therapy techniques in the treatment of ruminations: A review.] *Vie Medicale Au Canada Française, 5,* 958–963. (Includes brief sections on flooding/implosion and paradoxical intention.)

Rybstein-Blinchik, E. (1979). Effects of different cognitive strategies in pain management. *Journal of Behavioral Medicine, 2,* 93–101. (Involves successful reduction of pain through "reframing" it.)

Sahakian, W. S. (1969). A social learning theory of obsessional neurosis. *Israel Annals of Psychiatry and Related Disciplines, 7,* 70–75. (Includes brief mention of paradoxical intention.)

Sander, F. (1974). Freud's "A case of successful treatment by hypnotism (1892–1893)": An uncommon therapy? *Family Process, 4,* 461–468.

Saposnek, D. T. (1980). Aikido: A model for brief strategic therapy. *Family Process, 19,* 227–238.

Sargent, G. (1983). Treatment of snake phobia: Combining paradoxical intention with behavior modification. *International Forum for Logotherapy, 6,* 28–30.

Saslow, G. (1971). Expanding staff repertoires of treatment behavior. In G. Abroms & N. Greenfield (Eds.), *The new hospital psychiatry.* New York: Academic Press.

Sato, K. (1958). Psychotherapeutic implications of Zen. *Psychologia, 1,* 213–218.

Scanlon, P. L. (1980). A Gestalt approach to insight-oriented treatment. *Social Casework, 61,* 407–415.

Schaefer, C. E., Briesmeister, J. M., & Fitton, M. E. (1984). *Family therapy techniques for problem behaviors of children and teenagers.* San Francisco: Jossey-Bass.

Schlesinger, H. J. (1982). Resistance as process. In P. L. Wachtel (Ed.), *Resistance: Psychodynamic and behavioral approaches.* New York: Plenum.

Schutz, E. A. (1983). Therapeutic challenge model. *Journal of Strategic and Systemic Therapies, 2,* 1–14. (Presents paradigm that explicitly challenges clients through use of paradoxical tactics.)

*Schwartz, R. C. (1982). Parental reversals: A framework for conceptualizing and implementing a class of paradoxical interventions. *Journal of Marital and Family Therapy, 8,* 41–50.

Schwartzman, J. (1982). Symptoms and rituals: Paradoxical modes and social organizations. *Ethos, 10,* 3–25.

Searight, H. R., & Openlander, P. (1984). Systemic therapy: A new brief intervention model. *Personnel and Guidance Journal, 62,* 387–391.

Seltzer, L. F. (1983). Influencing the "shape" of resistance: An experimental exploration of psychological reactance and paradoxical directives. *Basic and Applied Social Psychology, 4,* 47–71.

Seltzer, L. F. (1984). The role of paradox in Gestalt theory and technique. *Gestalt Journal, 7,* 31–42.

Selvini Palazzoli, M. (1981). Comments [on P. F. Dell's Some irreverent thoughts on paradox]. *Family Process, 20,* 44–45.

Selvini Palazzoli, M., Boscolo, L., Cecchin, G. F., & Prata, G. (1974). The treatment of children though brief therapy of their parents. *Family Process, 13,* 429–442.

*Selvini Palazzoli, M., Boscolo, L., Cecchin, G., & Prata, G. (1978). *Paradox and counterparadox: A new model in the therapy of the family in schizophrenic transaction* (E. V. Burt, Trans.). New York: Aronson. (Original work published 1975.)

Shelton, J. L., & Levy, R. L. (1981). *Behavioral assignments and treatment compliance: A handbook of clinical strategies.* Champaign, IL: Research Press.

Shepperson, V. L. (1981). Paradox, parables, and change: One approach to Christian hypnotherapy. *Journal of Psychology and Theology, 9,* 3–11.

*Sherman, M. H. (1961). Siding with the resistance in paradigmatic psychotherapy. *Psychoanalysis and the Psychoanalytic Review, 48,* 43–59.

Sherman, M. H. (1968). Siding with the resistance versus interpretation: Role implications. In M. C. Nelson, B. Nelson, M. H. Sherman, & H. S. Strean (Eds.), *Roles and paradigms in psychotherapy.* New York: Grune & Stratton, 1968.

Sherry, G. S., & Levine, B. A. (1980). An examination of procedural variables in flooding therapy. *Behavior Therapy, 11,* 148–155.

*Shipley, R. H. (1979). Implosive therapy: The technique. *Psychotherapy: Theory, Research and Practice, 16,* 140–147.

Shipley, R. H., & Boudewyns, P. A. (1980). Flooding and implosive therapy: Are they harmful? *Behavior Therapy, 11,* 503–508.

*Shore, J. J. (1981). Use of paradox in the treatment of alcoholism. *Health and Social Work, 6,* 11–20.

*Sluzki, C. (1978). Marital therapy from a systems theory perspective. In T. J. Paolino & B. S. McCrady (Eds.), *Marriage and marital therapy: Psychoanalytic, behavioral, and systems theory perspectives.* New York: Brunner/Mazel. (Excerpted in Appendix A.)

Sluzki, C. E., & Ransom, D. C. (Eds.). (1976). *Double bind: The foundation of the communicational approach to the family.* New York: Grune & Stratton.

Smith, E. W. L. (1976). The roots of Gestalt therapy. In E. W. L. Smith (Ed.), *The growing edge of Gestalt therapy.* New York: Brunner/Mazel.

Smith, M. R. (1981). Paradoxical process in counseling theories: A search for a meta-theory. *Dissertation Abstracts International, 41* (7–A), 2945.

Smith, R. D. (1970). A comparison of therapeutic methods to eliminate fear. Unpublished doctoral dissertation, Georgia State University, Atlanta.

Smith, R. D., Dickson, A. L., & Sheppard, L. (1973). Review of flooding procedures (implosion) in animals and man. *Perceptual and Motor Skills, 37,* 351–374.

Solyom, L., Garza-Perez, J., Ledwidge, B. L., & Solyom, C. (1972). Paradoxical intention in the treatment of obsessive thoughts: A pilot study. *Comprehensive Psychiatry, 13,* 291–297.

*Soper, P. H., & L'Abate, L. (1977). Paradox as a therapeutic technique: A review. *International Journal of Family Counseling, 5,* 10–21. (Also in *Advances in Family Psychiatry*, 1980, *2,* 369–384.)

*Spotnitz, H. (1969). *Modern psychoanalysis of the schizophrenic patient.* New York: Grune & Stratton.

Spotnitz, H., & Nagelberg, L. (1960). A preanalytic technique for resolving the narcissistic defense. *Psychiatry, 23,* 193–197.

*Spotnitz, H., Nagelberg, L., & Feldman, Y. (1956). Ego reinforcement in the schizophrenic child. *American Journal of Orthopsychiatry, 26,* 146–164.

Stampfl, T. G., & Levis, D. J. (1967). Essentials of implosive therapy: A learning-theory-based psychodynamic behavioral therapy. *Journal of Abnormal Psychology, 72,* 496–503.

Stampfl, T. G., & Levis, D. J. (1968). Implosive therapy—A behavioral therapy? *Behaviour Research and Therapy, 6,* 31–36.

*Stampfl, T. G., & Levis, D. J. (1973). *Implosive therapy: Theory and technique.* Morristown, NJ: General Learning Press.

Stanton, M. D. (1981a). Marital therapy from a structural/strategic viewpoint. In G. P. Sholevar (Ed.), *The handbook of marriage and marital therapy.* Jamaica, NY: Spectrum.

Stanton, M. D. (1981b). Strategic approaches to family therapy. In A. S. Gurman & D. P. Kniskern (Eds.), *Handbook of family therapy.* New York: Brunner/Mazel.

*Stanton, M. D. (1984). Fusion, compression, diversion, and the workings of paradox: A theory of therapeutic/systemic change. *Family Process, 23,* 135–167.

Stekel, W. (1920). *Die Impotenz des Mannes.* Vienna: Urban & Schwarzenberg.

Sternbach, O., & Nagelberg, L. (1957). On the patient-therapist relationship in some "untreatable cases." *Psychoanalysis, 5,* 63–70. (Reprinted in H. S. Strean, ed., *New approaches to child guidance.* 1970.)

Stevens, J. O. (1973). *Awareness: Exploring, experimenting, experiencing.* New York: Bantam Books.

Stevens, J. O. (Ed.). (1977). *Gestalt is.* New York: Bantam Books.

Strauss, J. S., Bowers, M., Downey, T. W., Fleck, S., Jackson, S., & Levine, I. (1980). *The psychotherapy of schizophrenia.* New York: Plenum.

*Strean, H. S. (1959). The use of the patient as consultant. *Psychoanalysis and the Psychoanalytic Review, 46,* 34–41. (Reprinted in H. S. Strean, ed., *New approaches to child guidance,* 1970.)

Strean, H. S. (1960). Treating parents of emotionally disturbed children through role playing. *Psychoanalysis and the Psychoanalytic Review, 47,* 67–75.

Strean, H. S. (1961). Difficulties met in the treatment of adolescents. *Psychoanalysis and the Psychoanalytic Review, 48,* 69–80. (Reprinted in H. S. Strean, ed., *New approaches to child guidance,* 1970.)

*Strean, H. S. (1964). The contribution of paradigmatic psychotherapy to psychoanalysis. *Psychoanalytic Review, 51,* 365–381.

*Strean, H. S. (1968). Paradigmatic interventions in seemingly difficult therapeutic situations. In M. C. Nelson, B. Nelson, M. H. Sherman, & H. S. Strean (Eds.), *Roles and paradigms in psychotherapy.* New York: Grune & Stratton. 1968.

Strean, H. S. (Ed.). (1970). *New approaches to child guidance.* Metuchen, NJ: Scarecrow Press.

Strong, S. S. (1984). Experimental studies in explicitly paradoxical interventions: Results and implications. *Journal of Behavior Therapy and Experimental Psychiatry, 15,* 189–194.

Suzuki, D. T., Fromm, E., & DeMartino, R. (1970). *Zen Buddhism and Psychoanalysis.* New York: Harper-Colophon.

*Teismann, M. W. (1979). Jealousy: Systematic, problem-solving therapy with couples. *Family Process, 18,* 151–160.

*Tennen, H., Press, S., Rohrbaugh, M., & White, L. (1981). Reactance theory and therapeutic paradox: A compliance-defiance model. *Psychotherapy: Theory, Research and Practice, 18,* 14–22.

Timms, M. W. H. (1980). Treatment of chronic blushing by paradoxical intention. *Behavioural Psychotherapy, 8,* 59–61.

Todd, T. C. (1981). Paradoxical prescriptions: Applications of consistent paradox using a strategic team. *Journal of Strategic and Systemic Therapies, 1,* 28–44.

Todd, T. C. (1984). Strategic approaches to marital stuckness. *Journal of Marital and Family Therapy, 10,* 373–379.

Todd, T. C., & LaForte, J. (in press). *Paradoxical prescriptions: Practical guidelines for the use of prescriptions in strategic therapy.* New York: Guilford.

Tomm, K. (1984). One perspective on the Milan systemic approach. Part II: Description of session format, interviewing style and interventions. *Journal of Marital and Family Therapy, 10,* 253–271.

Troemel-Ploetz, S. (1980). "I'd come to you for therapy": Interpretation, redefinition and paradox in Rogerian therapy. *Psychotherapy: Theory, Research and Practice, 17,* 246–257.

Troemel-Ploetz, S., & Franck, D. (1977). "I'm dead.": A linguistic analysis of paradoxical techniques in psychotherapy. *Journal of Pragmatics, 1,* 121–142.

Turner, R. M., & Ascher, L. M. (1979). Controlled comparison of progressive relaxation, stimulus control, and paradoxical intention therapies for insomnia. *Journal of Consulting and Clinical Psychology, 47,* 500–508.

Turner, R. M., & Ascher, L. M. (1982). Therapist factor in the treatment of insomnia. *Behaviour Research and Therapy, 20,* 33–40.

Turner, R. M., & DiTomasso, R. A. (1980). The behavioral treatment of insomnia: A review and methodological analysis of the evidence. *International Journal of Mental Health, 9,* 129–148.

Ullmann, L. P., & Krasner, L. (1969). *A psychological approach to abnormal behavior.* Englewood Cliffs, NJ: Prentice-Hall.

Vandereycken, W. (1982). Paradoxical strategies in a blocked sex therapy. *American Journal of Psychotherapy, 36,* 103–108.

Viaro, M. (1980). Case report: Smuggling family therapy through. *Family Process, 19,* 35–44. (Involves circumventing, essentially through reframing, an agency or client's (s') resistance to family treatment.)

Victor, R. G., & Krug, C. M. (1967). Paradoxical intention in the treatment of compulsive gambling. *American Journal of Psychotherapy, 21,* 808–814.

Wachtel, P. L. (Ed.). (1982). *Resistance: Psychodynamic and behavioral approaches.* New York: Plenum.

Wagner, V., Weeks, G., & L'Abate, L. (1980). Enrichment and written messages with couples. *American Journal of Family Therapy, 8,* 36–44.

Walker, J. I., & McLeod, G. (1982). Group therapy with schizophrenics. *Social Work, 27,* 364–367.

Walton, D. (1964). Massed practice and simultaneous reduction in drive level— Further evidence of the efficacy of this approach to the treatment of tics. In H. J. Eysenck (Ed.), *Experiments in behavior therapy.* Oxford: Pergamon.

Warner, M. D. (1977). Stimulus control procedures and a paradoxical intention instruction in the treatment of sleep onset insomnia. *Dissertation Abstracts International, 37* (10–B), 5385.

*Wathney, S. (1982). Paradoxical interventions in transactional analysis and Gestalt therapy. *Transactional Analysis Journal, 12,* 185–189.

*Wathney, S., & Baldridge, B. (1980). Strategic interventions with involuntary patients. *Hospital and Community Psychiatry, 31,* 696–701.

Watts, A. W. (1961). *Psychotherapy East and West.* New York: Pantheon.

*Watzlawick, P. (1978). *The language of change: Elements of therapeutic interaction.* New York: Basic Books.

Watzlawick, P. (1981). Comments [on P. F. Dell's Some irreverent thoughts on paradox]. *Family Process, 20,* 45–47.

*Watzlawick, P., Beavin, J. H., & Jackson, D. D. (1967). *Pragmatics of human communication.* New York: Norton.

Watzlawick, P., & Coyne, J. C. (1980). Depression following stroke: Brief, problem-focused family treatment. *Family Process, 19,* 13–18.

Watzlawick, P., & Weakland, J. (Eds.). (1977). *The interactional view: Studies at the Mental Research Institute, 1965–1974.* New York: Norton.

*Watzlawick, P., Weakland, J. H., & Fisch, R. (1974). *Change: Principles of problem formation and problem resolution.* New York: Norton.

Weakland, J. H., Fisch, R., Watzlawick, P., & Bodin, A. M. (1974). Brief therapy: Focused problem resolution. *Family Process, 13,* 141–168. (Reprinted in P. Watzlawick & J. H. Weakland, eds., *The interactional view,* 1977.)

Weeks, G. R. (1977). Toward a dialectical approach to intervention. *Human Development, 20,* 277–292.

*Weeks, G. R. (Ed.). (1985). *Promoting change through paradoxical therapy.* Homewood, IL: Dow Jones-Irwin. (This very recent collection of essays on therapeutic paradox, not yet seen at time present book went into production, includes selections by C. Watson; B. W. Cade; K. G. Deissler; V. E. Frankl; L. L'Abate; S. R. Lankton & C. H. Lankton; H. Tennen, J. B. Eron, and M. Rohrbaugh; L. M. Ascher, M. R. Bowers, & D. E. Schotte; S. de Shazer & E. Nunnally; and M. J. Bopp.)

*Weeks, G. R., & L'Abate, L. (1979). A compilation of paradoxical methods. *American Journal of Family Therapy, 7,* 61–76.

*Weeks, G. R., & L'Abate, L. (1982). *Paradoxical Psychotherapy: Theory and practice with individuals, couples, and families.* New York: Brunner/Mazel. (Excerpted in Appendix A.)

Weeks, G. R., & Wright, L. (1979). Dialectics of the family life cycle. *American Journal of Family Therapy, 7,* 85–91.

Weeks, G., Wright, L., & Sloan, S. Z. (1979). More joy of paradox. *Voices, 15,* 74–76.

Weiner, M. F. (1982). *The psychotherapeutic impasse.* New York: Free Press.

Weinstein, A. (1983). The use of paradox in a medical setting. In P. Papp, *The process of change.* New York: Guilford.

Welwood, J. (Ed.). (1979). *The meeting of the ways: Explorations in East/West psychology.* New York: Schocken.

West, J. D., & Zarski, J. J. (1983a). The counselor's use of the paradoxical procedure in family therapy. *Personnel and Guidance Journal, 62,* 34–37.

West, J. D., & Zarski, J. J. (1983b). Paradoxical interventions used during systemic family therapy: Considerations for practitioners. *Family Therapy, 10,* 125–134.

*Whitaker, C. A. (1975). Psychotherapy of the absurd: With a special emphasis on the psychotherapy of aggression. *Family Process, 14,* 1–16.

White, J. (1979). Using a form of paradox as a strategy in therapy. *Journal of Psychiatric Nursing and Mental Health Services, 17,* 24–26.

White, M. (1979). Structural and strategic approaches to psychosomatic families. *Family Process, 18,* 303–314.

White, M. (1980). Systemic task setting in family therapy. *Australian Journal of Family Therapy, 1,* 171–182.

Will, D. (1983). Some techniques for working with resistant families of adolescents. *Journal of Adolescence, 6,* 13–26.

*Williams, J. M., & Weeks, G. R. (1984). Use of paradoxical techniques in a school setting. *American Journal of Family Therapy, 12,* 47–57.

Wilson, G. L., & Bornstein, P. H. (1984). Paradoxical procedures and single-case methodology: Review and recommendations. *Journal of Behavior Therapy and Experimental Psychiatry, 15,* 195–203.

Wilson, G. T., & Davison, G. C. (1971). Processes of fear reduction in systematic desensitization. *Psychological Bulletin, 76,* 1–14. (Involves use of flooding procedures.)

Wilson, G. T., & Franks, C. M. (Eds.). (1982). *Contemporary behavior therapy: Conceptual and empirical foundations.* New York: Guilford.

Wolberg, L. R., & Aronson, M. L. (1980). *Group and family therapy, 1980.* New York: Brunner/Mazel.

Wolff, R. (1977). Systematic desensitization and negative practice to alter the after-effects of a rape attempt. *Journal of Behavior Therapy and Experimental Psychiatry, 8,* 423–425. (Relates to treatment of posttraumatic compulsions.)

Wolpe, J., & Ascher, L. M. (1976). Outflanking "resistance" in a severe obsessional neurosis. In H. J. Eysenck (Ed.), *Case studies in behaviour therapy.* Boston: Routledge & Kegan Paul. (Includes successful use of flooding.)

Wooden, H. (1974). The use of negative practice to eliminate nocturnal headbanging. *Journal of Behaviour Therapy and Experimental Psychiatry, 5,* 81–82.

Wright, R. M., & Strong, S. R. (1982). Stimulating therapeutic change with directives: An exploratory study. *Journal of Counseling Psychology, 29,* 199–202.

*Wynne, L. C. (1980). Paradoxical interventions: Leverage for therapeutic change in individual and family systems. In J. S. Strauss, M. Bowers, T. W. Downey, S. Fleck, S. Jackson, & I. Levine (Eds.), *The psychotherapy of schizophrenia.* New York: Plenum, 1980.

Yamamoto, I. (1958). A comparison of Japanese Morita therapy with Frankl's existential analysis and logotherapy. In W. Bitter (Ed.), *Western therapy and Eastern wisdom.* Stuttgart: Klett.

Yates, A. J. (1958). The application of learning theory to the treatment of tics. *Journal of Abnormal and Social Psychology, 56,* 175–182. (On massed practice.)

Yoder, J. D. (1983). A child, paradoxical intention, and consciousness. *International Forum for Logotherapy, 6,* 19–21.

Zarske, J. A. (1982). The treatment of temper tantrums in a cerebral palsied child: A paradoxical intervention. *School Psychology Review, 11,* 324–328.

*Zeig, J. K. (1980a). Symptom prescription and Ericksonian principles of hypnosis and psychotherapy. *American Journal of Clinical Hypnosis, 23,* 16–22.

*Zeig, J. K. (1980b). Symptom prescription techniques: Clinical applications using elements of communication. *American Journal of Clinical Hypnosis, 23,* 23–33. (Reprinted in Appendix A.)

Zinker, J. (1978). *Creative process in Gestalt therapy.* New York: Random House-Vintage.

Author Index

Adler, A., 17, 19, 27–30, 191
Aichhorn, A., 33–34
Albee, E., 210n
Anderson, A., 30, 192, 237–248
Anderson, S. A., 110
Andolfi, M., 106, 107, 121, 267–268
Aponte, H. J., 119
Ascher, L. M., 55, 57, 58, 62, 63n, 64, 65–69
Ayllon, T., 50, 51

Bandler, R., 91
Bandura, A., 42
Barlow, D. H., 55, 63n
Barrack, R. A., 17
Barrows, S. E., 104, 111–112
Bateson, G., 16, 18, 89, 99, 211, 220
Baum, M., 51
Beavin, J. H., 5, 89–90, 231
Beck, A. T., 42
Beck, J. T., 138, 142–146, 147, 148
Becvar, R. J., 81
Beisser, A., 75, 78
Benoit, H., 11
Bergin, A. E., 143
Bergman, J. S., 108
Bertalanffy, L., Von, 89
Birchler, G. R., 45
Bodin, A. M., 94–96
Bornstein, P. H., 63n, 65
Boscolo, L., 18, 97, 229, 246, 248, 269
Boszormenyi-Nagy, I., 204, 205
Boudewyns, P. A., 54–55
Bowen, M., 205

Brandsma, J., 21, 119
Brehm, J. W., 115, 251
Brehm, S. S., 115, 251, 252, 255, 259–260
Buda, B., 17, 178
Bulka, R., 59

Caplan, G., 254, 262
Carroll, S. W., 50
Cecchin, G. F., 18, 97, 229, 246, 248, 269
Chasin, R., 106
Chiglinsky, M., 108
Close, H. T., 74
Cohn, R. C., 81
Coleman, M. L., 17, 33, 34–35, 36, 38–39. See also Nelson, M. C.

Danser, D. B., 146–148
Davis, H. L., 34, 36, 40–41
Davison, G. C., 53–54
Deatherage, G., 11
Dell, P. F., 5, 7, 110
de Shazer, S., 107, 120, 128–129, 191, 223–229
Dickson, A. L., 54
DiTomasso, R. A., 67
Dublin, J. E., 72
Dubois, P., 17
Dunlap, K., 17, 43, 46–48, 49, 191
Dyal, J. A., 71
D'Zurilla, T. J., 54

Efran, J. S., 65–66
Eisler, R. M., 48
Elliot, S. S., 107

313

Ellis, A., 42, 185
Epictetus, 108
Erickson, M. H., 18-19, 92-93, 95, 99-
  101, 118, 126, 128, 130-131, 173-
  175, 177, 185, 191, 224, 229, 230,
  252, 260, 261, 270
Evans, J., 35, 152
Eysenck, H. J., 42

Fabry, J., 59
Fagan, J., 83
Fanshel, D., 184
Farrelly, F., 21, 119
Fay, A., 4-5, 39, 159, 162, 168
Feldman, D. A., 146-148
Feldman, Y., 35
Fenichel, O., 160
Fisch, R., 13, 85, 94, 103, 212n,
  249
Fish, J. M., 113, 115
Fisher, L., 30, 192, 237-248
Fishman, H., 120
Fogle, D. O., 70-71
Foucault, M., 15-16
Framo, J. L., 204, 205
Frankl, V. E., 8, 13, 17, 19, 43, 55-61,
  69, 70, 95, 130, 136, 157, 164, 182,
  191, 197, 205, 235
Freud, A., 34
Freud, S., 9, 19, 25-27, 28, 33, 34, 51,
  60, 72, 157, 182
Fromm, E., 11
Fry, W., 89

Garza-Perez, J., 61, 63-64
Gauthier, J., 54
Gendlin, E. T., 202
Gerz, H. O., 58, 59, 60, 61, 63, 64, 182,
  197, 199
Goffman, E., 224, 225, 229
Goldberg, C., 10, 11
Goldfried, M. R., 104
Goldstein, A. J., 61-62
Goodman, P., 79
Gordon, A., 54
Greaves, G. B., 74, 77
Greenberg, G. S., 95
Greenberg, R. P., 20, 250
Greenhow, J., 172
Grinder, J., 91

Grunebaum, H., 106
Guthrie, E. R., 47

Haley, J., 8, 18-19, 87, 89, 94, 95, 98,
  99, 101, 102, 106, 112, 118-119, 126,
  128, 129, 130-131, 136, 154, 155, 157,
  171, 172-173, 175, 176-177, 180, 182-
  183, 185, 186, 191, 194, 197, 202, 203,
  205-209, 212n, 216, 219, 231, 233,
  249, 250-251, 260, 261
Hare, N., 54
Hare-Mustin, R. T., 91
Hart, O., van der, 122
Hefferline, R., 79
Helson, H., 54
Herr, J. J., 113-114
Hersen, M., 48
Hodgson, R., 54
Hoffman, L., 116-117, 216, 220
Hogan, R. A., 51
Hollingshead, A. B., 203, 205
Horney, K., 11
Hsu, L. K. G., 130, 136-137
Huber, J., 6
Hull, C., 49, 50

Irion, A. L., 47-48

Jackson, D. D., 5, 18, 89-90, 94, 211,
  216, 220, 231
Jacobs, M., 61-62
Jacobson, N. S., 8, 45-46, 99, 116, 155-
  156
Jessee, E. H., 7, 108
Johnson, V. E., 70
Jones, H., 50
Jones, J. E., 30, 192, 237-248
Jung, C. G., 9, 11
Jurkovic, G. J., 108

Kaczanowski, G., 59
Keith, D. V., 21
Keller, J. F., 107
Kesten, J., 35, 40
Klein, Z. E., 27, 48, 49, 52, 152
Kolko, D. J., 63n
Kondo, A., 13
Kopp, S. B., 11, 13-14, 81
Krasner, L., 49
Krug, C. M., 61

L'Abate, L., 3, 7, 9, 93, 102n, 108–109, 115, 123, 124, 125, 133–135, 177–178, 192, 262–269
Labov, W., 184
Lacks, P., 63n
Lamb, C. S., 61
Lambert, M. J., 143n
Lamontagne, Y., 61
Lantz, J. E., 115
Last, C. G., 63n
Latner, J., 75
Lazarus, A. A., 50, 61
Ledwidge, B. L., 61, 63–64
Lehner, G. F. J., 43, 47
Leitenberg, H., 54
Levis, D. J., 51, 53, 54
Levitsky, A., 74, 75, 80, 176
Lieberman, S., 130, 136–137
Lindner, R., 31–33, 39
Lisiecki, J., 9, 28
Lopez, F. G., 140–141, 147

Macaruso, M. C., 61
Macchitelli, F. J., 9, 28
McGeoch, J. A., 47–48
Madanes, C., 87
Malleson, N., 53
Mandel, H. P., 14, 172
Margolin, G., 8, 45–46, 99, 116, 155–156
Marks, I. M., 54
Marshall, R. J., 17, 35, 37, 38, 153
Marshall, W. L., 54
Masters, J., 44, 48, 50, 53, 54
Masters, W. H., 70
Mavissakalian, M., 63n
Meador, B. D., 185
Milan, M. A., 63n
Millan, B., 172
Miller, N., 38
Minuchin, S., 120
Morganstern, K. P., 54
Morita, S., 12, 13
Mozdzierz, G. J., 9, 12, 28, 29, 152, 179
Mungas, D. M., 65
Musliner, P., 26, 94, 102
Muszynska, E., 61–62

Nagelberg, L., 35, 39
Nelson, B., 17, 27–28, 33, 34–35, 180

Nelson, M. C., 35, 36, 37. *See also* Coleman, M. L.
Nelson, R., 54
Newton, J. R., 4, 7, 191, 192–205
Noonan, J. R., 13
Nystul, M. S., 61–62

O'Brien, G. T., 63n
O'Connell, D. S., 192, 269–273
Omer, H., 157–159, 162, 168
Oppenheim, H., 17, 182
Ormont, L., 33, 34

Palazzoli, M., *see* Selvini Palazzoli, M.
Papp, P., 107, 121, 124, 191, 220–223, 224, 225
Perls, F. S., 72, 75, 76, 79–81, 87, 184–185
Polster, E., 82
Polster, M., 82
Prata, G., 18, 97, 229, 246, 248, 269
Press, S., 8, 104–105, 249–262
Proust, M., 78

Rabkin, R., 48, 60–61, 153–154
Rachman, S., 54
Rafi, A. A., 50
Raskin, D. E., 27, 48, 49, 52, 152
Redlich, F. C., 203, 205
Relinger, H., 63n, 65
Rimm, D., 44, 48, 50, 53, 54
Riskin, J., 94
Rogers, C., 74, 152, 166–167, 172, 178, 185, 202, 205
Rohrbaugh, M., 8, 104–105, 124, 192, 249–262
Rosen, J. H., 16, 17, 30–31, 32, 33, 95, 126, 152
Rossi, E. L., 19, 92–93, 224, 229, 260
Rossi, S. I., 19
Russell, C. S., 110

Sahakian, W., 59, 61
Sander, F., 25
Saposnek, D. T., 15
Saslow, G., 61–62
Satir, V., 94
Sato, K., 12–13
Scanlon, P. L., 74, 75
Schlesinger, H. J., 179

Segal, L., 85
Seltzer, L. F., 115, 161–162
Selvini Palazzoli, M., 18, 97, 104, 109–
    110, 111–112, 120–122, 123, 127–
    128, 151, 191, 212n, 223, 225, 229,
    246, 248, 266, 267, 268, 269, 270
Shepherd, I. L., 83
Sheppard, L., 54
Sherman, M. H., 17, 39–40
Shipley, R. H., 54–55
Shore, J. J., 10
Simkin, J. S., 183
Skinner, B. F., 42, 199, 205
Sluzki, C., 84, 85, 89, 94, 120, 126, 191,
    209–220
Smith, E. W. L., 76–77
Smith, R. D., 54
Solyom, C., 61, 63–64
Solyom, L., 61, 63–64
Speirs, D., 172
Spotnitz, H., 18, 35, 36
Stampfl, T. G., 51, 53
Stanton, M. D., 4, 85, 88, 91, 99, 116,
    126
Stekel, W., 17
Sternbach, O., 39
Stevens, J. O., 78–79
Strean, H. S., 17, 18, 34, 35, 39
Strong, S. R., 138, 141–148
Suzuki, D. T., 11
Szasz, T., 231, 232, 236

Tennen, H., 8, 104–105, 249–262
Turner, R. M., 66–69

Ullmann, L. P., 49

Van Deusen, J. M., 119

Van Zeig, J., 198
Victor, R. G., 61
Von Eckartsberg, R., 198

Wagner, V., 133–135
Walton, D., 50
Wambach, C. A., 140–141, 147
Watts, A. W., 12, 152, 184
Watzlawick, P., 5, 6, 13, 14, 18, 89–90, 91–
    92, 93, 94, 96, 97, 105–106, 108, 113,
    124, 126, 130–131, 136, 163–164, 175–
    176, 191, 210n, 212n, 216, 231, 249,
    251, 252, 256, 259–260
Weakland, J. H., 13, 18, 85, 89, 96, 113–
    114, 124, 126, 132–133, 212n, 249,
    252, 258
Weeks, G. R., 3, 9, 77, 93, 102n, 108–
    109, 110, 115, 123, 124, 125, 133–
    135, 177–178, 192, 262–269
Weizmann, F., 172
Welwood, J., 11, 12
Wender, P. H., 216, 220
Whitaker, C., 20–21
White, L., 8, 104–105, 249–262
Wilkie, J., 108
Wilson, G. T., 53–54
Wolfe, B. E., 55
Wolpe, J., 42
Wright, L., 93
Wright, R. M., 141–142, 147
Wynne, L., 27

Yates, A. J., 48, 50

Zarske, J. A., 135–136
Zeig, J. K., 118, 174, 191–192, 229–
    236
Zinker, J., 82

Subject Index

Acrophobia, 275

"Acting in," 21

Adolescent problems, 226–228, 275

Aggression and acting out, 226–228, 242–243, 265–267, 276

Aging and aged, problems of, 276

Agoraphobia, 27, 276

Aikido, 15

Alcoholism, 276

Anorexia, 106, 136–137, 276

Anticipatory anxiety, *see* Paradoxical intention, and anticipatory anxiety

"Anti-expectation techniques," 20, 250

Anxiety, 160, 194, 212, 216–218, 250, 276
  and avoidance behavior, 51–55, 56, 57, 74, 79–80, 81, 131, 163–164, 253. *See also* Gestalt therapy; Paradoxical intention, and anticipatory anxiety
  about change, 115, 124, 127, 161, 162, 163, 181–182
  and therapeutic goals, 162–164, 181–182
  see also Phobias

Asthma, 276

Attribution theory, 113, 145, 147

Aversion therapy, 172

Avoidance behavior, *see* Anxiety, and avoidance behavior

Awareness (Stevens), 78–79

Bateson Project, 18, 19, 89, 98

Behavior therapy, 20, 42–71, 178
  and gestalt therapy, compared to, 73–74

and paradoxical techniques:
  nature of, 43–45
  research on, 48, 50–51, 54–55, 61–69
  and systems approach, compared to, 86–87, 88, 95–96, 155–156
  see also Implosion; "Instructed helplessness"; Massed practice; Negative practice; Paradoxical intention; Stimulus satiation

Behavior Therapy: Techniques and Empirical Findings (Rimm and Masters), 44

"Benevolent ordeal" of therapy (Haley), 112, 182, 196–197

Binge eating, 276

"Blow-up," 61

Borderline personality disorder, 34–35, 276–277

Brief Family Therapy Center (Milwaukee, WI), 223

Brief Therapy Project (of Ackerman Institute for Family Therapy), 221, 222

Buddhism: Tantric, Tibetan, and Zen, 5–6, 11–12, 74, 77. *See also* Paradox, and Eastern thought

Bulimia, 277

Change:
  first-order, 93–94, 96
  second-order, 93–94, 96, 102, 145
  see also Anxiety, about change

Change (Watzlawick et al.), 96

Childhood problems, 277

Client-centered therapy, 74, 172, 185

Cognitive restructuring, 61–62, 159, 167

Communication, elements of, 230–232

317

Communication-systems theory, *see*
    Systems (strategic) approach
Compliance-based paradoxical strategies,
    see Paradoxical strategies, compli-
    ance-based
Conditioned (or reactive) inhibition, 44–
    45, 53, 158, 193
"Confusion technique," 128–129
Converging Themes in Psychotherapy
    (Goldfried, ed.), 104
Countertransference, 220–221
Couples conflict, *see* Marital conflict
Crisis induction, 237, 238, 242–244

Defiance-based paradoxical strategies, *see*
    Paradoxical strategies, defiance-
    based
Delinquency, 33, 277
Depersonalization neurosis, 277
"Depreciation tendency" (Adler), 27–30
Depression, 96, 212, 215, 216, 232–233,
    241–242, 258, 277
    research on, 142–148
Dereflection, 57, 70
"Devil's Pact," 260
Dialectics:
    and therapy, 8–10, 75–76, 103, 212
    and truth, 11
Direct Analysis (Rosen), 17, 30–31
Directive therapy, *see* Strategic therapy
Doctor and the Soul, The (Frankl), 17
Double bind:
    pathogenic, 18, 89–90, 92, 93, 96
    therapeutic, 18, 90–93, 96, 111, 113,
        114, 119, 125, 126, 129, 131–132,
        157–158, 167, 168, 172–173, 175,
        176–177, 185, 213. *See also*
        Symptom prescription
Driving phobia, 277

Eastern thought and paradox, 10–15
Encopresis, 277
Enuresis, 277
Erythrophobia (blushing), 57–58, 62, 277
Extinction, 44, 53, 54, 61

Families:
    chaotic, 245
    childlike, 245–246
    conflict in, 107, 114, 204

homeostasis in, 88, 89, 91, 94, 97, 107–
    108, 109–110, 115, 116, 120–121,
    128, 212, 213–214, 240–241
impulsive, 246
myths in, 122, 210–211
positive feedback loops in, 216
rituals for, 121–122, 223–224, 225,
    227–229
rules in, 89, 93, 94, 120–121, 127–128,
    216
Fear, *see* Anxiety; Phobias
Fifty-Minute Hour, The (Lindner), 31–32
Firesetting, 277
Flooding, *see* Implosion
Flooding and Implosive Therapy (Boude-
    wyns and Shipley), 54–55

Gambling, compulsive, 272, 278
*Gestalt Approach and Eyewitness to
    Therapy, The* (Perls), 87
Gestalt therapy, 20, 75–83, 172, 176,
    183, 184, 257
    and accentuating submerged elements of
        self, 82
    and accepting, or "staying with,"
        symptom, 73–74, 79–82
    behaviorist approach, compared to, 73–
        74
    and dialectical theory of change, 75–76
    and Eastern thought, 74, 76–77
    and identifying with dissociated parts of
        self, 78–79
    psychodynamic approach, compared to,
        72–73
    research on, 83
    systems approach, compared to, 87–88
    and "withdrawal into fertile void," 80–
        81
"Go slow" directives, 124, 161, 261, 271.
    See also Restraining change
Grieving, 253. *See also* Depression

Habits, maladaptive, 17, 46–48, 278
Habituation, 44–45, 61
Headaches, 278
Headbanging, 278
Helplessness, therapist's declaration of,
    126–128, 267–268
Homeostasis, *see* Families, homeostasis
    in

Hypnotherapy (Ericksonian), 95, 100, 173–177
  utilizing resistance in, 174–177
  utilizing symptoms in, 173–174
Hypochondriasis, 257–258
Hysterical symptoms, 195, 278

Identity crisis, 278
If You Meet the Buddha on the Road, Kill Him! (Kopp), 11
"Illusion of alternatives" (Erickson), 260
Implosion, 44, 51–55, 61–62, 70, 73–74, 79, 163, 164, 172, 181
  distinguished from flooding, 51–52, 55
Impression management, 143, 144, 145
Insomnia, 62, 65–69, 253, 278
"Instructed helplessness," 69–71

Jealousy, pathological, 278
Judo, 14, 184

Learned helplessness, 69–70
"Learned restlessness," 69–71
Letters, paradoxical, *see* Paradoxical written messages

Madness and Civilization (Foucault), 15–16
Man's Search for Meaning (Frankl), 17
Marital conflict, 125, 196, 209–220, 278
Massed practice, 43–44, 48–50, 51, 57, 158, 241. *See also* Negative practice
Masturbation, compulsive, 206–209, 278
Mental Research Institute, 18, 94–97, 98
  Brief Therapy Center of, 96, 124, 132, 253
Metaphorical tasks, 223–229
Milan Family Therapy Group, 97–98, 266, 267
Modeling, 60, 61–62, 167
Morita therapy, 12–13. *See also* Paradox, and Eastern thought

Narcissism, pathological, 278
"Naturalistic" techniques (Erickson), 19
Negative practice, 17, 44, 46–48, 49, 51, 55, 57, 70, 158, 193. *See also* Massed practice
Negative psychology, 7
Nightmares and night terrors, 278

Obesity, 278
Obsessive-compulsive disorders, 54, 57–58, 63, 279
Obsessive thoughts, 63–64, 250, 253–254, 259, 278–279

Pain management, 236, 279
Palo Alto Group, 18, 249, 251, 260
Paradigmatic psychotherapy, 16, 17–18, 33–40
  in child therapy, 34–36, 37, 40
  classical analysis, compared to, 33–34
  indications for, 34–36
  "joining" techniques in, 33–40
  theoretical basis of, 37–40
Paradox:
  communicational theory of, 8, 18
  definition of, 5–10
    dialectical, 8–9
    interactional, 7–8
    relativistic, 6–7
  and Eastern thought, 10–15
  in psychotherapy, 171–186
  and therapeutic relationship, 171–177, 178, 183–186
  and Western thought, 10
Paradox and Counterparadox (Selvini Palazzoli et al.), 18, 97
Paradoxical family rituals, 121–122
Paradoxical injunction, *see* Symptom prescription
Paradoxical instruction (Milan group), 98, 116. *See also* Symptom prescription
Paradoxical intention, 8, 13, 17, 46, 55–69, 70, 95, 130, 164, 182, 193
  and anticipatory anxiety, 13, 17, 57–60, 68, 131, 157, 158, 236
  as behaviorist technique, 19, 43
  and "counterwill," 60
  definition of, 55, 56, 164
  and dereflection, 57, 70
  humor and detachment in, 17, 59, 60, 157, 182, 197
  and logotherapy, 56
  modeling in, 60, 167
  research on, 61–69
  and stimulus management, 60–61
  vs. symptom prescription, 131–132
  see also Symptom scheduling
Paradoxical interpretation, *see* Reframing

Paradoxical positioning, 104–105, 249–
250, 251, 258–259. *See also* Reframing
Paradoxical posthypnotic suggestion, 25–
26
Paradoxical prediction, 29–30, 268.
See also Relapse, predicting
Paradoxical Psychotherapy (Weeks and
L'Abate), 9, 102n, 134
Paradoxical strategies:
and anxiety about change, alleviating, 38,
115, 126, 160–161, 162, 167, 168,
223, 229
applicability, widespread, of, 4–5, 165,
203–204, 254
in behavior therapy, 20, 42–71, 178
compliance-based, 105, 141, 142, 157,
250, 251–252, 254, 255–257, 259–
261
compliments, use of, in, 223, 224, 227,
229
and "compression," 116
cooperating, client's manner of, and, 224,
229
and countertransference, 220–221
defiance-based, 105, 124, 141, 142, 157,
161, 168, 250, 251–252, 254, 256,
257–259, 260, 261
definition of, 7–8. *See also* Paradox,
definition of
as diagnostic device, 122, 234, 236
and Eastern thought, 10–15
for enmeshed relationships, 120, 241–
242, 250–251
ethics of, *see* Paradoxical strategies, and
countertransference
in gestalt therapy, 75–83, 176, 257
history of, in West, 15–19
humor and playfulness in, 17, 59, 60, 157,
197, 223–225, 227–229, 238
for information-withholding clients, 129,
173
as "joining" techniques, 16, 31, 110, 114,
121, 153, 157, 160–161, 179, 180.
See also Paradigmatic psychotherapy,
"joining" techniques in
metaphorical tasks in, 223–229
names and phrases for, 20–21
planning and execution of, 139, 189–
273

client responsiveness, maximizing,
233–235
following up, 202, 207–208, 260–
261
indications/counterindications, 138,
139, 221, 239, 243–244, 245–246,
254
popularity, increasing, of, 3
positive feedback in, 115, 143. *See also*
Reframing
in psychodynamic therapy, 25–41
rationales given to clients for, 197, 232–
233, 234, 256–257, 269–272
and reactance, psychological, 115, 141–
142, 161–162, 167, 168, 251–252,
254–260. *See also* Paradoxical
strategies, defiance-based
reactions to, by clients, 10, 112, 122, 123,
127, 128, 129, 139, 148, 151, 162,
197, 264–265
and reinforcement principles, 159–160,
162, 167, 168
and research:
challenge for, 165–171
criteria for, 166–167
empirical, on, 40–41, 48, 50–51, 54–
55, 61–69, 83, 129–148
inherent limitations of, 169–171
workable hypotheses for, 166–169
resistance—countering, neutralizing, or
utilizing, in, 14, 21, 25–30, 98, 114–
116, 119, 120–121, 124, 125, 126–
128, 161–162, 173, 174–177, 179,
221, 251. *See also* Paradoxical
strategies, defiance-based
responsibility and self-control, as fostered
by, 56, 59–60, 108, 111, 113, 114,
118, 119, 121, 125, 126, 131, 143,
157, 164, 167, 169, 173, 185, 216,
235
self-initiated change, as induced by, 107,
110, 128, 129, 161, 177, 230, 235,
264, 272
symptoms:
decontextualization of, through, 158–
159, 162, 167, 168
therapist's gaining control of, through,
19, 99, 108, 112–113, 118–119, 125,
127–128, 162, 172–173, 176–177,
185

value of, as undermined by, 107, 108,
112-113, 117, 119, 122, 126, 131,
143, 157, 158-159, 162, 167, 168-
169, 172-173, 182
variety of, as treated by, 4-5
in systems approach, 3, 4, 20, 84-148
theoretical boundaries as transcended by,
3-4, 19, 103-104, 151-156
theoretical confusion surrounding, 5
and therapeutic alliance, as facilitated by,
110, 119, 157, 166, 167, 178-179
toward theory of, 151-186
see also Double bind, therapeutic; specific
paradoxical strategies
Paradoxical tasks, see Symptom prescription
Paradoxical techniques, see Paradoxical
strategies
"Paradoxical Treatments: A Unified
Concept" (Omer), 157-159
Paradoxical written messages, 122-123,
262-268
research on, 133-135
Paranoia, 39, 253, 279
Performance anxiety, 62, 64, 68. See also
Paradoxical intention, and anticipatory
anxiety
Pessimism, 210
Phobias, 17, 26-27, 51-55, 57, 58, 63, 73-
74, 181, 182, 194, 196, 198, 279.
See also Anxiety; Paradoxical inten-
tion, and anticipatory anxiety
Positive connotation, 97-98, 109-110,
212-213, 222, 264. See also Re-
framing
Positive/negative interpretation, 142-145.
See also Reframing
Prescribing symptom, see Symptom
prescription
Procrastination, 140-142, 279
Progressive relaxation, 65-67, 69
"Provocative therapy" (Farrelly and
Brandsma), 21
Psychic Treatment of Nervous Disorders
(Dubois), 17
Psychoanalysis, 20, 25-33, 172, 257
and Eastern thought, 11
and gestalt therapy, 72
and research on paradoxical strategies,
40-41
vs. systems approach, 84-86, 88, 95, 96,

97, 101
and transference, 27, 34, 85, 176, 184
see also Paradigmatic psychotherapy
Psychoanalytic Theory of Neurosis, The
(Fenichel), 160
Psychosis, 31-33, 50, 279
"re-enacting aspect of" (Rosen), 17, 30-
31, 95, 126
Psychosomatic symptoms, 212, 216, 221-
222, 241-242, 250, 279
"Psychotherapy of the absurd" (Whitaker),
20-21
Psychotherapy East and West (Watts), 152

Reactance, psychological, see Paradoxical
strategies, and reactance, psychological
Redefinition, see Reframing
"Reductio ad absurdum" (Rosen), 31, 95
Reframing (Relabeling or Redefinition),
19, 101, 103, 104-109, 110-111,
120, 121, 126, 137, 140-141, 142-
145, 151, 164, 175-176, 179, 218-
219, 237, 238-241, 264, 265
to alter dysfunctional relationships, 94,
96, 107, 108
definition of, 105-106
as "interpretation," 85, 106
to overcome client resistance, 14, 19, 68,
161
and positive connotation, 109
research on, 129-130, 133-135, 136-
139, 142-148
see also Paradoxical strategies, re-
sistance−countering, neutralizing,
or utilizing; Positive connotation
Relabeling, see Reframing
Relapse:
predicting, 125, 126, 261
prescribing, 125-126, 213, 216, 261
Research, on paradoxical strategies, see
Paradoxical strategies, and research
Resistance to change, see Anxiety, and
avoidance behavior; Hypnotherapy,
utilizing resistance in; Paradigmatic
psychotherapy, "joining" techniques
in; Paradoxical strategies, defiance-
based; Paradoxical strategies, resist-
ance−countering, neutralizing, or
utilizing, in

Restraining change, 104, 105, 123-125, 264. *See also* "Confusion technique;" Paradoxical strategies, resistance—countering, neutralizing, or utilizing, in; Symptom prescription
Retardation, problems related to, 280
Reverse psychology, 7, 270

Schizophrenia, 219-220, 244-245, 280
  double-bind theory of, 18, 74, 89-90
School problems, 222, 242-243, 280
Seizures, psychogenic, 239-241, 280
Self-control directives, 58, 140
Self-denigration, 280
Self-destructive behaviors, 280
Sensate focus, 70
Sexual problems and dysfunctions, 17, 58, 62, 69, 280
Shyness, 260
Sleep disturbances, *see* Insomnia
Smoking, problematic, 50
Snake phobia, 52, 54, 280
Stimulus control, 61-62, 66-67, 69
Stimulus satiation, 44, 50-51, 61-62, 158
Strategic Psychotherapy (Rabkin), 60
Strategic therapy, 103-129
  and Aikido, 15
  theoretical basis of, 101-103
  see also Symptom prescription; Systems (strategic) approach
Strategies of Psychotherapy (Haley), 8, 154
Stuttering and stammering, 43, 69, 280
Substance abuse, 280
Suicidal thoughts, threats, and attempts, 280
Symbols of Transformation (Jung), 9
"Symptom amelioration" (Erickson), 100
"Symptom decontextualization" (Omer), 158-159, 162, 167, 168
Symptom escalation (and crisis induction), 237, 238, 241-244. *See also* Symptom exaggeration
Symptom exaggeration, 111, 118, 119-120. *See also* Symptom escalation (and crisis induction)
"Symptom faking," 214-215, 217
Symptom modification, 111, 118-119, 158
Symptom prescription, 17, 18, 90-92, 94, 103, 104, 105, 107, 110-117, 151, 264, 266-267

definition of, 111
extensions and variants of, 117-129
vs. paradoxical intention, 131-132
rationales for, 19, 96-97, 99, 111-117, 174
research on, 129-133, 135-136, 138-142, 146-148
see also Paradoxical strategies
Symptom redirection, 237, 238, 244-245
Symptoms:
  as communications, 98, 99, 231, 232
  component elements of, 232-233
  intentionality of, 113, 186, 213-214, 219
  paradoxical nature of, 177-178
  positive function of, 99-101, 103, 126, 160
  role of, in systems, 98-99, 102-103, 124, 221-222, 247
  see also Paradoxical strategies, symptoms
Symptom scheduling, 4, 192-205
  schedules, guidelines for, 195-199
  symptoms, guidelines for, 194-195
  therapist, guidelines for, 200-203
  see also Paradoxical intention; Symptom prescription
"Symptom substitution" (Erickson), 100
"Symptom transformation" (Erickson), 100
Systematic desensitization, 52, 54, 61-62, 64, 65-66, 73, 172
System prescription, 111, 120-121, 224, 225, 228
Systems (strategic) approach, 20, 84-148
  vs. behaviorist approach, 86-87, 88, 95-96, 155-156
  and Erickson, 99-101
  and Freud, 25-26, 27
  vs. gestalt approach, 87-88
  vs. psychodynamic approach, 85-86, 88, 95, 96, 97, 101
  research on:
    academic counseling experiments, 138-148
    clinical and quasiclinical studies, 132-137

Tactics of Change, The (Fisch, Weakland, and Segal), 85, 86

"Tantric therapy," 13-14
Temper tantrums, 135-136, 238, 266-
    267, 280
Textbook of Nervous Disorders (Oppen-
    heim), 17
"Theatrical representation," cure by, 16
Theories of psychotherapy, essential kinship
    among, 152-156
Theory and therapy, relationship between,
    154-155
Therapeutic double bind, *see* Double bind,
    therapeutic
Therapeutic paradox, *see* Paradoxical
    strategies; Symptom prescription
Therapist, paradoxical role of, 178-181,
    182-186
Thumbsucking, 281
Tics, psychogenic, 241, 281

Urinary retention, psychogenic, 62, 64, 281
"Utilization" techniques (Erickson), 19,
    100

"Victim/Victimizer" relationships, 209-211
Vocational problems and rehabilitation, 281
Vomiting phobia, 281
Vomiting and stomach aches, 281

Wayward Youth (Aichhorn), 33
"Who's Afraid of Virginia Woolf," 210n
"Writer's Block," 281

Yoga, 13-14

Zen Buddhism, 5-6, 11-12, 74, 77. *See also*
    Paradox, and Eastern thought
Zeno's Achilles paradox, 6